Praise for So

Sam Lesner was a legend for his 60 ye... ...ism. It was said of him that "with Sam at his typewriter, one did not need a photo." But like millions of others his life was interrupted by the Second World War. And with his reporter's eye and his storyteller's skill he wrote home, every day if he could. But there was a running conflict for the journalist: Tell it like it is from basic training to the hospital work at the Battle of the Bulge in Europe, but don't upset the family. Here is that real life American story through Sam's remarkable letters, hidden away in a storage bin for 70 years.

Bruce Sagan
Chicago journalist for 67 years
Publisher of the *Hyde Park Herald*, Chicago

I lived in England throughout the war, experiencing the results of Dunkirk, the Battle of Britain, the Night Blitz, flying bombs, and V2 rockets. It was obvious at the time that we could not have stayed in the war, let alone been on the winning side, without the intervention of the U.S.A. Therefore, I owe a great debt to American soldiers like Sam Lesner. They were such generous men.

I am pleased to recommend Somewhere in Europe *to any student of the Second World War. Wartime armies are like pyramids. A great deal is written and remembered by those at the top, but little is recollected by those at the base. Yet their stories are often fascinating and worthy of reading. And for all Jewish men who served in the Allied armies there was an extra reason for them to fight. That was the knowledge of the Holocaust and what perverted Nazism intended for all Jews. Sam Lesner was an exemplar of a Jewish man's response to the call of duty.*

Dr. John Ray
Professor of History, Kent, U.K.
Author of *The Illustrated History of WWII* (London: Weidenfeld and Nicolson, 2003)
and more than thirty books

It was really wonderful to get immersed in Sam Lesner's voice and viewpoint. As an older man in the military and an accomplished writer, his letters are often eloquent. I particularly appreciated his reflections on the prisoners who were assigned to him. The authors have done a superb job in editing the letters and bringing in additional reflections so that younger generations will be able to understand and appreciate Sam Lesner's point of view.

Deborah Dash Moore
Frederick G. L. Huetwell Professor of History &
Judaic Studies, University of Michigan
Author of *GI Jews: How World War II Changed a Generation*
(Cambridge, MA: Harvard University Press, 2005)

Somewhere in Europe

Somewhere in Europe

The World War II Letters of Sam Lesner

Edited by

Roberta Lesner Bernstein

and

Judy Lesner Holstein

SOMEWHERE IN EUROPE:
The World War II Letters of Sam Lesner

Copyright © 2018 Roberta Lesner Bernstein and Judy Lesner Holstein

ISBN-13: 978-1985578364
ISBN-10: 1985578360

Library of Congress Control Number: 2018936880

*Dedicated to the memory
of our loving and talented father
and to his legacy that lives on
through his grandchildren and
great grandchildren.*

Contents

Preface	ix
Acknowledgments	xv
Biography of Sam Lesner	xix
People Frequently Mentioned in the Letters	xxiii
Glossary	xxv
1. You're in the Army Now	1
2. Basic Training: Phase 1	26
3. Basic Training: Phase 2—Clerk Training	48
4. Post Basic: The Wait for Deployment	61
5. Post Basic: Deployment to England	74
6. France: Killing Time	86
7. Belgium: Building the Barracks	121
8. Belgium: Medical Clinic	156
9. A New Year	180
10. Belgium: Dental Clinic	205
11. Peace in Europe	256
12. Camp Twenty Grand: Waiting to Go Home	298
Epilogue	310
Bibliography	322
Index	323

Preface

What is this thing that has come over me? After all these months of despair, of loneliness, I have found myself. This is the thing I needed to see, the suffering and pain of others, to realize that my lot is not a bad one. I'm still too excited about this new avenue of thought and experience that has been opened up for me to give you an accurate picture. But I do know that someday I will be able to say to myself, "Little man, you've been through some busy days. But you've done a good job." May God grant that all these boys will live to return to their homes. 12/6/44

Sam Lesner, the author of the letters contained in this volume, was a journalist with the *Chicago Daily News*, where he started in 1928 at the age of 19. He was drafted into the Army in December 1943 at age 34 and, after basic training in North Carolina and waiting for deployment in New Jersey, spent a year in the European Theater of Operation (ETO), culminating in the end of the war in August 1945. Throughout his army service in World War II, his letters home frequently mentioned his desire to save the letters and use them later as the basis for a book of memoirs of his war experience. Following are excerpts:

2/5/44-en route – Every one of the twenty-eight men who came up from [Fort] Sheridan [Illinois] has been telling every man in earshot about the guy from the Daily News. Darling, there's a great story here and I'm going to write it as soon as I'm oriented a little more.

2/16/44 – Before I forget, yes I got all your letters and I'm going to bundle them and return them because I want you to keep every piece of correspondence between us.

2/24/44 – There is much humor in the "bull-shitting" that takes place every minute, and God willing, I'll have much to write about some day.

4/16/44 – Why didn't you tell me touch typing is such fun? Now I can write my book, or get ready to write it.

7/10/44 – Writing is my life. Because it doesn't come easy, each word sinks deep into my consciousness. I suffer acutely when mistakes are made in the process of transcribing what I have written.

> 8/7/44 – Someday I'll be able to tell the story and time will blend the thousand and one details into a tale of romance and adventure.

After Lesner returned home in September 1945, the box of saved letters got shoved, unbeknownst to his wife and daughters, into a storage bin in his house, as he plunged happily back into the life of husband and father, movie and night life critic of the *Chicago Daily News*, music teacher and performer, swimmer and avid gardener. He did tell stories from time to time about his war experiences and in later decades gave interviews to his grandsons about his life and war experiences for various school projects. But he never wrote the book.

The letters remained hidden away and apparently forgotten until they were found in recent years, neatly bound, in chronological order, in a box in Roberta's basement. She had been looking for Sam's box of movie star pictures, requested by her niece, Debbie Holstein, who had just started a job in Hollywood as a production assistant in the movie industry and wanted to decorate her apartment with Grandpa's pictures of himself with various movie stars.

Opening this box was the start of an adventure of reconnection for us, Roberta Lesner Bernstein and Judy Lesner Holstein, with our late parents as we plunged right away into devouring Sam's war letters, along with an incomplete collection of our mother Esther's letters also contained in the box. Right away, we transcribed the letters and gave copies to children, grandchildren, and cousins for a holiday present. Excited by what they read, they said that we should put the letters into a book.

Like us, they too were overwhelmed by the beauty and clarity of the war story, the firsthand, eyewitness account of the life of a Jewish soldier proudly serving in the U.S. Army in Europe to defend America and its European allies against the horrors of Nazism despite enduring separation from his wife and newborn baby.

Throughout Sam's letters, he frequently tells poignant stories of experiences of being a Jewish soldier.

This was an important aspect of World War II service for thousands of Jewish soldiers. In her book *G.I. Jews: How World War II Changed a Generation* (Cambridge, MA: Belknap Press of Harvard University Press, 2004), Deborah Dash Moore stated that "American Jews were coming to fight both an American and a Jewish battle against Nazism" (p. 93). Sam expressed this idea on numerous occasions. Moore commented further: "Jewish identity could not easily be ignored or repressed in Europe. Although Jewish GIs had left their country as Americans, crossing the Atlantic into the shadow of the Third Reich involved specifically Jewish issues that would complicate further their quest for fellowship" (p. 92).

In bringing Sam's story to light, we have learned that we are tapping into a current phenomenon of remembering and retelling the stories of countless GIs who served in World War II. In organizing this book, we encountered other

Preface

books that were the result of other families' finding hidden boxes of letters in attics, basements, and other places decades after the war and their decision to bring the letters to light in a book for public consumption, often at the urging of soldiers' children and grandchildren who found the story in the letters fascinating and compelling.

For example, Dr. George Sharpe, the father of Roberta's friend Jeanette Sharpe Kreiser, served as a battalion surgeon in the South Pacific and wrote letters daily to his wife and baby daughter (the same age as Roberta), then stowed them away upon his return home. Decades later, after Jeanette and her baby-boom siblings were grown, Dr. Sharpe retrieved his letters himself and showed them to his grandchildren, who were fascinated and urged him to publish them: George Sharpe, MD, *Brothers beyond Blood: A Battalion Surgeon in the South Pacific* (Woodway, TX: Eakin Press, 1989). In the acknowledgments, Dr. Sharpe writes:

> I found the letters in a cardboard carton forty years after the war ended. My wife, Alison, had saved all of our correspondence; I had sent back her letters as a record of our daughter's development. When I discovered the letters, I was deeply moved. As most other veterans had done, I had wrapped war memories in a pseudo-comfortable blanket of repression, thinking that I had forgotten all about the war. I was reluctant to discuss my experiences, even though vivid flashbacks of scenes would periodically cross my conscious memory. Over the years, I have found myself mourning for my comrades who died. But I was not prepared for the emotional experience that befell me when I started to reread the letters after so many years.
>
> One Sunday afternoon, on impulse, I started to read a few of the letters to my grandchildren Joshua Kreiser, age fourteen, and his sister, Debbie, age eleven. Their response encouraged me to have the letters reproduced for the family in more legible fashion. . . . Jeanette, Martha Reva, and Robert, our children, and their spouses were enthusiastic about receiving copies of the letters, but also indicated that a wider audience would benefit.
>
> . . . Finally, in 1986, I learned by accident that my unit was having a reunion in Garrison, North Dakota, and that the 6th Infantry Division was meeting in Omaha, Nebraska, the following week. I decided to attend the meetings and brought some of my letters with me. The response that I met with when I read the letters was very gratifying. Some of the spouses were very interested in their husbands' experiences, which were similar to mine, of course. Many had not heard very much about the war if they were married afterwards. I then finally resolved to write this book in the belief that others may have shared my experiences and that their families and survivors might better understand the past experience of our generation. (pp. xi–xii)

Joseph Hollander was another Jewish soldier, a refugee from Poland who managed to escape to New York after the Nazis invaded Poland in 1939. He got legal immigration papers by joining the American Army, which sent him back to Europe for his wartime service. He saved his war letters home to his wife, along with letters he received from his family who were still stuck in the horrors of Nazi-occupied Poland. He had hidden the letters in the attic of his house and never talked about them. It was only after his death in 1986 that his son Richard discovered them in a briefcase while cleaning out his parents' home. Seeing swastikas stamped on the letters from Poland, Richard felt he couldn't deal with such weighty matters at the time and closed the briefcase and took it home, where it remained untouched until 2004, when he began to study the contents of the letters, learning for the first time about his father's war experiences and the family he lost in the Holocaust. Then, with the help of his son Craig, a historian, Richard compiled the letters into a book: *Every Day Lasts a Year: A Jewish Family's Letters from Poland*, edited by Christopher Browning, Richard S. Hollander, and Nechama Tec (New York: Cambridge University Press, 2007). In the preface, Richard Hollander writes:

> I didn't volunteer to explore my father's past; it was thrust on me. In a dark attic, I literally stumbled on a briefcase containing the letters and numerous personal documents that comprise this book. . . . I don't know why he never pursued the same task [publishing his letters himself]—maybe leaving the letters and attendant documents behind was intentional. . . . From the instant I saw the briefcase in the attic . . . and looked at the letters so neatly organized and stacked in chronological order, I knew this was the path my father wanted me to travel. In retrospective moments, I realize that there is virtually no higher task or calling than to complete a mission that one's parent was unable to achieve in life. And, if reaching that objective creates a legacy for one's parent it is both humbling and gratifying. (pp. xxvii, xxviii, xxxii)

In 1998, NBC journalist Tom Brokaw published his scholarly work *The Greatest Generation* (New York: Random House, 1998) following his visit in 1994 to the Normandy beaches to prepare a documentary for NBC TV on the fiftieth anniversary of D-Day. He said of that experience:

> I was well prepared with research on the planning of the invasion—the numbers of men, ships, airplanes and other weapons involved; the tactical and strategic errors of the Germans; and the names of the Normandy villages that in the midst of the battle provided critical support to the invaders. What I was not prepared for was how this experience would affect me emotionally. . . . I underwent a life-changing experience. As I walked the beaches with the American veterans who had landed there and now returned for this anniversary, men in their sixties and seventies, and listened to their stories in the cafes and inns, I was deeply moved and profoundly grateful for all they had done. I realized that they had been all around me as I was growing up and that I had failed to appreciate what they been through and what they had accomplished. These

men and women came of age in the Great Depression, when economic despair hovered over the land like a plague. . . . When Pearl Harbor made it irrefutably clear that America was not a fortress, this generation was summoned to the parade ground and told to train for war. . . .

. . . They answered the call to help save the world from the two most powerful and ruthless military machines ever assembled, instruments of conquests in the hands of fascist maniacs.

. . . They faced great odds and a late start, but they did not protest. . . .

. . . When the war was over, the men and women who had been involved, in uniform and in civilian capacities, joined in joyous and short-lived celebrations, and then immediately began the task of rebuilding their lives and the world they wanted. They were mature beyond their years, tempered by what they had been through, disciplined by their military training and sacrifices. They married in record numbers, and gave birth to another distinctive generation, the Baby Boomers. They stayed true to their values of personal responsibility, duty, honor and faith. (pp. xxv–xxvii)

Brokaw later adds, "That's another legacy of the World War II generation, the strong commitment to family values and community" (p. 34).

It is no coincidence that Dr. George Sharpe, Joseph Hollander, Sam Lesner, and countless others shoved their letters into storage, out of sight and out of mind. As Tom Brokaw discovered, this was the common behavior for the returning GIs: "Although they were transformed by their experiences and quietly proud of what they had done, their stories did not come easily. They didn't volunteer them" (*Greatest Generation*, p. xxix). He added: "They were proud of what they accomplished but they rarely discussed their experiences, even with each other. They became once again ordinary people, the kind of men and women who always have been the foundation of the American way of life" (p. 15).

And so, just as our father wrote to our mother so many years ago of his *intentions* to publish his letters, we, his daughters, are now honored to try to carry out his wishes as a testimonial to a remarkable man, soldier, and writer.

This book is more than just a loving tribute by daughters to a father. In America and abroad, the continuing interest in World War II spans the topics of military strategy, policy, principles of freedom, and many more themes that are relevant today. Sam's letters shine a light on the inner, personal world of a 35-year-old soldier far from home, missing his wife, longing to know his newborn daughter as she grew from a few months of age to two years old. He served among the sixteen million American troops whose sacrifice changed their lives and our world from then until the present moment. Sam's letters from the war tell a universal story of love, fear, courage, service, philosophy, hope, and gratitude.

To Daddy, with love, Roberta and Judy

Acknowledgments

Just as the letters were discovered in an unexpected time and place, many serendipitous occurrences during the process of editing this book brought us the help and advice of wise and wonderful people to whom we are deeply grateful and whom we wish to thank publicly here.

In summer 2004 during a mini-college reunion, Roberta told her friends that she was excited about her recent discovery of the box of her dad's World War II letters. Her friend Jeanette Sharpe Kreiser replied that her father, Dr. George Sharpe, had compiled his World War II letters to his wife into a book about his service as a battalion surgeon in the South Pacific. Jeanette sent Roberta a copy, which she devoured, amazed at the many similarities with her own father's letters. Later, Roberta had the pleasure of telling this to Dr. Sharpe in person along with asking him advice about developing and publishing such a book. We thank both Jeanette and her now late father for their encouragement and guidance by example.

Regarding our father's frequent reflections on being a Jewish soldier fighting the Nazis, we were excited to read the 2004 publication of *G.I. Jews: How World War II Changed a Generation* (Cambridge, MA: Belknap Press of Harvard University Press), by Deborah Dash Moore, the Frederick G. L. Huetwell Professor of History at the University of Michigan in 2004.

We learned the historical details behind some of the uniquely Jewish experiences Sam encountered, such as the Army's authorization to hold High Holiday services for all Jewish servicemen in Europe in September 1944, which Sam describes as a personally meaningful experience. We are grateful for the permission to cite portions of Dr. Moore's informative work.

One day in mid-2016, as we were excitedly finishing the editing and seeing the book take shape, Rabbi Edward C. Bernstein, Sam's eldest grandchild, called and said,"I recently came across the box of those tapes of the interviews I did with Grandpa in high school and I've digitized them and am emailing them to you. Maybe they'll help with editing the letters for the book?" Stunned, but excited, we discovered that about four hours of the recorded interviews were devoted to the "War Years." We wasted no time in listening to the tapes and transcribing what turned out to be a treasure trove of complementary material. In the interviews, Sam related many of the same stories that are in the letters but with detailed information that had to be omitted from the letters due to censorship of restricted information. Extracts from these interviews have been inserted into the text of the book adjacent to the letters dealing with the same topics. We thank Eddie for his loving devotion to his grandfather in his lifetime by recording this oral history; for his strong organizational skills, which kept this material safe and ready to be retrieved; and for his efforts to resurrect these memories and make them available to us.

Rabbi Bernstein also told us that in order to better understand our father's experiences, we should read Tom Brokaw's book *The Greatest Generation* (New York: Random House, 1998). He was right. The book, whose title became the widely used descriptor of the whole of the American World War II experience, is so insightful and deeply moving. It underscores everything our father wrote and showed us that he was not alone but was deeply part of the Greatest Generation. We are awed by Brokaw's scholarly and deeply moving work and grateful to him for writing it and allowing us to reference it.

In January 2017, we heard about a talk at the Illinois Holocause Museum in Skokie, Illinois by Richard Hollander, author of *Every Day Lasts a Year: A Jewish Family's Letters from Poland*, edited by Christopher Browning, Richard S. Hollander, and Nechama Tec (New York: Cambridge University Press, 2007).

Attending the January 26 talk, Roberta was stunned by the similarities of her experiences to those of Richard Hollander.

Just as our work was enhanced by the contributions of our son/nephew Edward Bernstein, it was Richard Hollander's son Craig, who holds a Ph.D. in history from Johns Hopkins University, who did the scholarly research on the letters as part of his undergraduate thesis in the history department at Columbia University—again, a grandson seeing the importance of preserving a grandfather's written legacy. We thank Dr. Craig Hollander for underlining for us the value and importance of a grandchild's dedication to preserving a grandparent's legacy.

In the preface to his book, Richard Hollander writes, "I realize that there is virtually no higher task or calling than to complete a mission that one's parent was unable to achieve in life. And if reaching that objective creates a legacy for one's parent, it is both humbling and gratifying."

In reading these words, and in further personal discussions with Mr. Hollander, we received the go-ahead signal we craved, the approval that what we are doing in this book is right and necessary. We thank Richard Hollander for showing us the way and encouraging us.

There is a plethora of information, gathered painstakenly and with love by so many people who share the mission of preserving and telling the personal stories of World War II. While working on Sam's letters of September 1944 dealing with his unit's encampment in Carentan, France, we searched the Internet for information about Carentan. To our great joy, we discovered a blog by Erwin Jacobs, Senior Project Leader E-mental health, Trimbos-Instituut, Soest,

Acknowledgments

Netherlands. In this blog, he describes and provides pictures of Carentan following the D-Day invasion of World War II and the present-day town. Intrigued, we contacted him for permission to use his research and archival and personal present-day photos. We are deeply grateful to Erwin Jacobs for his kind sharing of this relevant information which so enhances our story.

Sam mentioned the name of his final camp before boarding the vessel that brought him home. It was called "Camp Twenty Grand." He explained that all the camps were named for cigarette brands. Intrigued by this, we researched and found a marvelous website that described the cigarette camps: SKYLIGHTERS—the website of the 225th AAA Searchlight Battalion, Larry M. Belmont, webmaster. In granting permission for us to use all of the relevant material from this fascinating website, Mr. Belmont wrote, "I am glad you found the site useful. Thanks to your father for his service. I am hard pressed to imagine a finer 'love letter' to him from his daughters than publishing his letters to your mom during the War. Good luck and best regards."

Larry Belmont and his associates who share vast information about the Cigarette Camps are among the people who made our quest and research exciting and fruitful. Our deepest gratitutde, Larry.

In doing library research for background material about D-Day and the Battle of the Bulge, we found a marvelous book, *The Illustrated History of WWII*, by John Ray (London: Weidenfeld and Nicolson, 2003). In response to our request to Dr. Ray to use text and maps from this book, he granted permission and said:

> I am now an old man, aged 88. This means that I lived in Southern England throughout the war, experiencing the results of Dunkirk, the Battle of Britain, the Night Blitz, flying bombs and V-02 rockets. I have always studied and taught history. It was obvious at the time that we could not have stayed in the war, let alone been on the winning side, without the intervention of the U.S.A. Therefore, I owe a great debt to American soldiers like your father. They were such generous men. The task that you have set yourselves sounds daunting, but the results will be most satisfying and I look forward to reading the finished work. Now, more power to your pen!

We told Dr. Ray in our permission request that his was the best of the books that we read on the subject. We are therefore extremely grateful for his permission, and moreover, we are touched by his personal reaction to our goals in publishing our father's letters, and his sweet encouragement of our task.

Sam used Yiddish liberally in his letters. When we needed translation, we turned to our dear friend and Yiddish maven Bryna Cytrynbaum. We thank her for her quick and knowledgeable responses.

Roberta's husband, Charles B. Bernstein, provided valuable help in retrieving archival documents, especially the front pages of the *Chicago Daily News* with headlines about the liberation of Paris. We thank him for the generous contribution of his time, research skills, and knowledge.

Judy's husband, Dr. Robert L. Holstein, a veteran of the U.S. Air Force Medical Corps, provided firsthand experience and knowledge about military terminology practices (including medical and dental) and historical information about World War II. In addition, he was our IT guy, who rescued us on many occasions when we encountered computer difficulties.

Sam's grandchildren (in order of birth)—Edward C. Bernstein, Aaron J. Holstein, Deborah L. Holstein, Louis C. (Aryeh) Bernstein, and Henry J. Bernstein—gave enthusiastic support for the book project about their beloved grandfather. After reading the complete letters, they urged us to create a book of the pertinent parts to share with the world, for which we thank them with love. Additional thanks goes to Debbie who inadvertently kick-started the whole project by asking to see the box of Grandpa's movie star photos. It was in the search for that box that we also uncovered the previously unknown box of letters.

And thus, we set out to publish Sam's letters. Along the way, we had the great fortune of discovering Paul Kobelski and Maurya Horgan of the HK Scriptorium of Denver, Colorado, whose graphic arts and editing expertise transformed our manuscript into this book. Our heartfelt thanks to Paul and Maurya.

Biography of Sam Lesner

Samuel J. Lesner was born the third of four children of Jacob and Syma Lesner (sometimes written Lessner) on February 16, 1909, behind his parents' little store at 1823 W. North Avenue in Chicago, Illinois. His parents had emigrated from Russia a few years before. As Sam told the story,

> My father was a musician in the Russian army. At the outbreak of the Russo-Japanese War [2/8/1904] he still had 2 years to serve. He was already married; they came from the same town [Starodub, Russia]. My mother said she took him civilian clothes and a fake passport—it was a real passport but for another man who had a disease and sold it. On a Sunday, she went to see him in the barracks. He put on the suit and took the passport and left, and she took off. Pa managed to get to London. There was an underground. He never told us much. He apparently stayed about a year. Ma came directly to Chicago and set up the store [about 1905]. Then Pa came [about 1906]. Dave, who was two years older [than Sam], was born in 1907, Mayme in 1908.

In 1912, Sam's brother Roy was born, and shortly thereafter, with the help of Syma's relatives who had come earlier and gotten established in business, Sam's parents leased a little store, with living quarters in the back, from a relative at 5207 N. Milwaukee Avenue (at Foster), in Jefferson Park. The language of the home was Yiddish, and "at night Father would read Yiddish stories to us published in the Yiddish newspapers; some of the best authors." By age 7, Sam was fluent enough and mature enough to be charged with the task of escorting his maternal grandmother, who had come to live with them, to frequent trips across town to the Yiddish theater productions at Glickman's Palace Theatre. Though the family was poor, "from the age of 8 I was aware of theater, dancing, ballet, opera. I liked to draw and paint and even decorate the house. I would tie ribbons on furniture to make things looks fancier." Sam's musical education began in grammar school: "In every classroom the musical staff was displayed with the Latin do-re-mi-fa-sol-la-ti-do for the notes. We learned to read notes early in school." He also had piano lessons and was appointed the official hallway pianist, playing the "Grand March."

While Sam's parents "thought for the early years it was better and safer for [the children] in the countryside, they were concerned about [them] getting a proper education," and so they looked for and found a store to rent back in the city in the area of Western and Logan Blvd., the Logan Square neighborhood. Sam finished eighth grade at the Brentano Elementary School at Western and Diversey (2723 N. Fairfield). For high school, he traveled to Albany Park to attend Hibbard High School at 3244 W. Ainslie. "At that time, Hibbard High School was part high school and part grade school. The top floor was the high school; the lower two floors were the elementary school. There was no high school in the area so they took part of this elementary school and made a high school out of it."

At Hibbard, he was vice president of his class, the judge of the Student Council, and, above all a columnist on the school paper, which he loved. Upon graduation in 1926 at age 16½, Sam began to work full-time at a National Tea Co. store, where he had worked part-time in high school, and "made good money and helped support the family." At age 18, he took a job at Kunse Department Store, hoping to work his way up the ladder. But after only six months the store went out of business.

Meanwhile, Sam had been studying voice at the Chicago Conservatory of Music with ambitions of becoming an opera singer. When he mentioned to his teacher, Enrico Sevillo, that he might have to stop his lessons because he had lost his job, Mr. Sevillo arranged with his friend Henry Justin Smith, the editor of the *Chicago Daily News*, for Sam to have a job in the newspaper's library, which began April 9, 1928. Starting in 1931, in addition to his work in the library, the paper occasionally sent him to review concerts.

In the late 1930s, though the Yiddish Theatre was enormously successful and popular in New York and other American cities with large Jewish populations, the American press mainly ignored it. However, in May 1940, when the celebrated actor Maurice Schwartz brought to Chicago his great company's production of "Der T'hilim Yid" ("Salvation") by Sholom Asch, booked into the Civic Opera House, the Chicago press had to take notice, and the *Daily News* sent Sam, the only person on the staff who was fluent in Yiddish, to review the show, and named him the paper's Yiddish drama critic.

In 1941, he was moved from the library to full time in the editorial department as a night club reviewer and assistant reviewer in radio and drama. In 1942, he was named Night Life Editor, the post he occupied when he was drafted at the end of 1943.

Upon returning from the war in September 1945, the *Daily News* offered him the position of movie critic. Sam also continued as night life critic.

In the late 1940s and early 1950s Sam also served as television critic for the *Daily News* and had a radio show broadcast from the Tip Top Tap, the penthouse of the Allerton Hotel on Michigan Avenue. In addition, he was a great devotee of madrigal music and taught hundreds of recorder students in classes at the Central YMCA.

Biography of Sam Lesner

In February 1966, he received the coveted Critic's Award for 1965 of the Directors Guild of America for Outstanding Motion Picture Criticism.

When the *Chicago Daily News* closed on March 9, 1978, Sam was forced into a reluctant retirement after forty-nine years and eleven months with the newspaper. Anxious to get back in action, he fashioned a new career, starting in March 1980, in the advertising department of the *Hyde Park Herald*, a weekly paper on Chicago's Southeast side, and soon he was writing a full-page column called "Hyde Parkers All." To introduce him to his readers, a staff writer wrote an article about Sam's career with the headline: "50 years on the job—he asks for more." (See epilogue for complete article.) In his column, dated February 15, 1984, the day before with his 75th birthday, he reflects on his personal life, offering bits from birth, career, and army days. (See epilogue for Sam's mini bio in his own words.)

On the day that he died peacefully in his sleep, December 19, 1990, he had turned in that morning what became his last column, which was printed a few days after his funeral.

People Frequently Mentioned in the Letters

1. Sam's family
Jacob and Syma Lesner, parents
David Lesner, older brother, serving in the Army during the war
Roy Lesner, younger brother, serving in the Army during the war
Mayme Lesner Salkind, older sister, living in Evanston, Ilinois, with her husband and two sons, Sandy and Peter
Dr. Albert Jenkins, first cousin, serving in the Army during the war

2. Esther's family
Dr. Louis (a dentist) and Hattie (Maga) Malkin, parents
Ruth Malkin Probstein, sister, living in New York, married to Herbert, mother of Joanne and Jack

3. Journalism colleagues in Chicago
Col. Frank Knox, U.S. Navy, publisher of *Chicago Daily News*
C. J. Bulliet, Sam's editor at *Chicago Daily News*
Lloyd Lewis, joined the *Chicago Daily News* in 1930 as drama critic, becoming subsequently sports editor, managing editor, and a popular columnist
Pence James, columnist, *Chicago Daily News*
Emil Garber, public relations manager of the Aragon-Trianon Ballroom in Chicago

4. Army buddies
Jack Garber, editor of camp paper in basic training camp, brother of Emil Garber, a publicist in Chicago
Manny Levin, from the South Side of Chicago
Leonard Goldhammer from Cleveland, Ohio. He was discharged from the Army as a Private First Class in November 1945. After the war he worked in Cleveland as the first director of community relations for the Cleveland Jewish Federation. Later, after moving to Los Angeles, he served as executive director of University Synagogue and assistant director of

community relations of the Jewish Federation of Greater Los Angeles, retiring in 1977. He died in Los Angeles in 1987.

Max Neiburg, a podiatrist, from Philadelphia, stationed in the 130th General Hospital. The hospital was pushed back three times by the Germans, and Neiburg was evacuated with the other Jews of the hospital because his officers were certain that if the hospital was taken, Jewish soldiers would be killed. Max felt honored to have served during the war, including the Battle of the Bulge.

5. Celebrity friends
Sophie Tucker, actress and night club performer
Dr. Will and Ariel Durant, authors of the multivolume *Story of Civilization* (Simon and Schuster).

6. French and Belgian war survivors who befriended Sam
Madame Bland and her son Jean Pierre
The Chanania family and their relatives in Chicago, the Channons
Mr., Mrs, and Mlle de Wein
Edith Seifert
Isadore and Leo Milner

Glossary

APO	Army Post Office
CBI	China-Burma-India Theater
C.O.	Commanding Officer
C.Q.	Charge of Quarters
D.S.	Dental Service
E.M.	Enlisted men
ETO	European Theater of Operation
K.P.	Kitchen Police or Kitchen Patrol
O.D.	Olive drabs
PFC	Private First Class
P.X.	Post Exchange
Q.M.	Quartermaster
S.P.U.	Stability Police Unit
T.O.	Technical Order
T.S.	Tough shit
USO	United Service Organizations

CHAPTER ONE

You're in the Army Now

PART 1
CHARLESTON: THE COUNTRY CLUB

[From Oral History interview with grandson, Edward C. Bernstein, in 1986]

ENTERS ARMY—Sam Lesner, cafe editor of The Chicago Daily News, inducted into the armed services Jan. 12, reports for active duty at Fort Sheridan Feb. 2. Mr. Lesner will write his final Cafe Table Topics column in tomorrow's edition of The Daily News.
[Seymour photo.]

SL: *I was drafted at the end of 1943 with an induction date of January 1944 and was in the service [at Fort Sheridan] by February 1944. We went to Charleston, South Carolina, for a short time and then moved (though the Army didn't give a reason) to Swannanoa, North Carolina, near Asheville, where we stayed for basic until June, when we were permitted to go home for a short time.*

I was never classified as to what I was supposed to be doing in the Army. When I was drafted, I filled out all the necessary papers and I had a pocketful of recommendations from various well-known journalists, editors, publishers and so on that I was a very good journalist and that I ought to be in the Special Services department. There was just a general agreement that that's probably where I would go. I had one recommendation from Colonel Frank Knox, who was then the publisher of the Chicago Daily News, but he was also appointed by President Roosevelt (although Knox was a Republican) as Secretary of the Navy, and, as my boss, Colonel Knox wrote this beautiful letter of recommendation to the War Department. I assumed that all this would work in my favor, but I forgot that there's nothing lower than a Basic in the U.S. Army. When you're a Basic you're nothing. The Army manuals say that twenty-eight Basics—meaning totally untrained draftees—must be attached to any new unit going overseas, especially in the hospital corps. So I happened to be one of the Basics that was drawn from this pool of Fifth Army Headquarters; they picked twenty-eight, some from Chicago, some from Michigan, some from Indiana, and we were just thrown together and shipped out.

EB: -*Were you proud fighting for America?*
SL: *Oh yes. How could you be otherwise? When I was at the* Daily News, *still working in the library cataloging newspapers and reading the terrible, heart-rending accounts of what they were doing to Jews in Germany, making lampshades out of their skins, I was filled with anguish. I felt this was the least I could do. I never resented being drafted. I felt it was my role to do whatever I could. I knew I was not combat material because I was too old, but I felt that I could do some good, and I think I did.*

Wednesday, February 2, 1944, 5:05 p.m. (Fort Sheridan, Illinois)
Darling:

So far it hasn't been too bad. I hope you got home safely and that you and my little "Love Lettuce" are OK. There is a young smart aleck of a jerk who is in charge of this barracks, but it's only temporary. I ate lunch with relish. I guess you can get into it fast. The men are oldish, quiet and nice. The army should realize that such men merit just a little more kindliness, but I guess we all have to learn to be tough. This cannot be mailed until tomorrow (Thursday) but I can't wait to write you my first love letter because I do love you. Please be brave regardless of what comes. I shall know more Thursday when I am classified. I guess I'm not very bright since I answered only about seventy of the IQ questions, but I feel certain I scored high on them. I'll do everything I can to justify your faith in me. At any rate, it'll be a period in which to store up impressions for my future writings.

We just returned from supper and it was good. My buddy is a swell guy and is looking out for me. One minute we're low and the next we're laughing. Some poor guys here have a lump in their stomachs and can't eat, but I'm OK. All my love to you, Darling, and kiss "Love Lettuce" for me. Love to the folks. Call my Ma. "Honey" – Sam

Thursday, February 3, 1944, 6:50 a.m.
Darling:

I just returned from breakfast. The first night was slightly awful as to bed and sleeping partners, and almost unbearable as to absence of sweet wife and Angel "Love Lettuce." I could feel you thinking of me. Gosh, when this is over I'll put my arms around you and "Love Lettuce" and never take them away. If I ever say that I want a vacation without you, hit me over the head. I know now that that's a fantastic idea. The day will undoubtedly be a lulu—shots and things! Pray, Darling, that I can get a weekend pass. I'll go see the chaplain. Love, "Honey" Sam

Saturday, February 5, 1944 – En route
Darling:

I started this letter on the train, a most extraordinary train, too, but I gave up because of the vibration, general noise, excitement, etc. What an experience. It took thirty some hours to get here, the Starks General Hospital in Charleston, South Carolina, but it was great fun all the way. More about the trip and train later. Now I'm trying to get this off as we just got our permanent address: Private Samuel J. Lesner, #36786054, 130th General Hospital, in c/o Starks General Hospital, Charleston, South Carolina, Bks. 8.

So far this is a great big country club. Very friendly men, all just promoted to corporals, sergeants, etc., so they're all very happy. Believe it or not, the man who just started the camp paper is Jack Garber, Emil Garber's brother. Emil, you know, is the Aragon-Trianon publicist who has been so appreciative of all that I did for him. I hope this camp paper idea will turn out OK, but in the meantime, the chaplain has discovered my musical inclinations and the interviewing major this morning fairly bloated with joy that they have a real musician in the outfit. I told them at [Fort] Sheridan that I play the accordion. That was nervy of me, but now I'm classified as such and they insist here that I send for the instrument at once. In a day or two, when I see just how the wind blows, I'll tell you to send it on to me. It's up in the bedroom closet. I'll also want you to go through my music books and send me the accordion book and others.

I bluffed my way through it once at Camp Nawakwa and I'm sure that with a week or two of practice I'll be an expert. I also want my small recorder and all the recorder music which is in the radio cabinet. Frankly, Angel, this is just a great big wonderful country club as far as we can see. The camaraderie between officers and enlisted men is extraordinary. I'm not kidding myself, however. We'll get basic training and plenty of it, but the top men around here don't know quite what to make of a bunch of raw recruits. They haven't had any here in two years. These men here are all classified as specialists and have taken the basic training course five and six times for something better to do. Your "daddy" is attached to the Medical Corps, rated the second-highest in the Army for intelligence.

I didn't have to blow my own horn. Every one of the twenty-eight men who came up from [Fort] Sheridan [Illinois] has been telling every man in earshot about the guy from the *Daily News*. Darling, there's a great story here and I'm going to write it as soon as I'm oriented a little more. I think the *News* will carry it, but if not, I have other plans.

I hope you got the telegram. Angel, love, it may be a long time until I see you and my little Darling, but God has been good. This is the best deal any man could ask for. The town of Charleston is hopeless, and I can't let you come to it, but maybe we can work out something else. All my love, My Darling. I'll write tomorrow. Sam

P.S. Kiss my little prune-face Angel!

February 7, 1944 – Western Union Telegram Arrived safely Stark General Hospital Charleston. So far well and happy. Letter following.
Love, Sam

February 8, 1944, 9:25 a.m. – Bks 8
Darling:

We've just come off of the parade ground. The rain put a temporary halt to "right front, left face, about face etc. I'll have to write these letters to you at intervals during the day, adding bits as I go along, so if it doesn't make sense, just blame Uncle Sam. The food is wonderful. We have only 338 men here. More are expected, but the total will never exceed 500, apparently, and that number can be handled easily at this place. Mess hall is very large and they don't give you the bum's rush like at a certain place I've been to recently. Our barracks is spacious and of course the air here is wonderful. I'm feeling the dampness in my feet today but I'm trying to forget it. It's possibly partly due to the GI shoes which are pretty stiff yet. Most of the boys are taking it well and Gregory turned out to be a real pal. He keeps checking to see that I'm buttoned up. It's hell here if you're caught without blouse, coat or anything unbuttoned.

[*Editors' Note: Letters that follow include lists of necessary Army supplies that must be sent from home, since the Army requires, but does not supply, them.*]

I need many small things but I'll acquire them gradually, but honey, take half a dozen wire hangers immediately and send them to me as fast as you can get them here. Everything must be hung up, and not a hanger in the place. Please do this at once. It's very important, since barracks inspection comes the end of the week. They'll probably overlook the first time, since it isn't our fault.

– Interruption – 10:30 a.m. The big boy just walked into barracks to give us the once over.

– Interruption – We're going to make beds.

– Interruption– We just returned from a wonderful lunch consisting of excellent vegetable soup, hamburger steak, baked potato, stewed tomatoes, corn, celery and carrot sticks, cake and coffee. Don't send me any food now. There's plenty here and anyhow I don't need too much sweet stuff. I do want that jar of cream. I won't be considered a sissy. These are largely medical men and that's my classification too. Don't worry about overseas. Some of these men have been here for several years. They're highly trained and may be sent across, but one rule that stands is that this type of hospital unit stays fifty miles behind the lines. The way the program works here, we can forget such matters for a long time to come. What we should remember is that this is unbelievable good luck for me, considering what other basic training stations do. Every man here has congratulated us on our good fortune in coming here.

Dolly, I don't know whether we'll be quarantined when the shots start, but if so and you don't hear from me, don't worry. I'll tell you everything in subsequent letters.

I think you had better send the accordion and the accordion book. Please look for the book carefully. I don't know just where it is but you'll find it. The boys are having radios and things sent out but I don't want anything like that. The chaplain, no doubt, will see that I have a practice place. Darling, write me all about the baby. I'm so lonely for the little prune-face. At least I can talk to you on the phone. I tried yesterday but there was a four-hour wait, which of course is impossible for a soldier who is generally confined to the post. They're taking us to a dance tomorrow at the USO center. Can you read my scrawling? I ain't used to writing letters. Please write soon, with all the news. All my love to you, the baby, the folks, Sam

February 8, 1944, 12:40 p.m. – At ease
My little "Love Lettuce":

Your Daddy is feeling fine and enjoying himself except that he misses you terribly. Be a good little girl, grow up strong and beautiful, and your Daddy will be very proud. Eat up all the spinach and don't make your mama nervous. She has so much to do now to keep things going. Smile your pretty grin all the time and everybody will love you, as if they could help it. Give Maga [Esther's mother] a kiss for me and when the other grandma sees you, give her one, too. Also the grandpas. All my love to my darling baby. Daddy

February 8, 1944, 5:45 p.m.
Honey:

There is so much to write about, and I don't write down things, so I'm always forgetting. Darling, get me a can of saddle soap. It's a cleaner for leather. Also, see if you can get a certain polish that's used for military buttons. I understand that Field's [Marshall Field and Co., a famous Chicago department store for over 150 years] carries all the supplies for the Army. I hate to worry you about these things but I need them and our own post store is very inadequate. In Charleston they rob you blind and we have been asked not to go there. The Navy has taken over the town and the Army boys stay clear of them. One more thing: I have a swell pair of military shoes with high tops in the bottom of my wardrobe. Please dig them out and send them to me. They are most necessary since I can wear them at times instead of the regular GI shoes which kill me. Don't forget, Darling. The shoes are in the wardrobe and are very muddy, but they're fine shoes. I believe I paid $10 for them. My regular shoes are coming in handy here and in a few months you can get me another pair from that Roosevelt Road store. I'll send you one of my old ones for a sample of size and style. Good night for now, Sweetheart. I'll write to your mother later. We're going to a movie. All my love. Gosh I love you, "Honey"

February 9, 1944, 8:24 a.m.
Darling:
    Here we sit, just waiting for orders. Yesterday was a most pleasant day. Informal lecture on military conduct practically all day. A little drill and then supper and a movie which turned out to be an awful waste of time.
    Honey, I need some plain white handkerchiefs, a couple of good absorbent bath towels and a couple of face towels. Also a couple bars of face soap. The Army does not furnish soap and only two bath towels, one of which was stolen at [Fort] Sheridan. Please don't send anything fancy. Maybe you can get some seconds at a sale. Just so they're white. The small bars of Swan or Ivory would be good and my dad will supply those. Just a few at a time, please, Honey, as I don't want to load down. If possible, your ma might see if she can find a regulation suit of fatigues. I believe that the government turns down some with flaws and they are disposed of to department stores and such. If you see anything like this, size 36 regular two-piece suit. They're olive drab in color. I'm afraid it's going to cost us money to keep me in the Army, but that's the way it is and everybody else is in the same fix. I wrote you about my officer shoes. In my clothes bundle which I sent home from Sheridan was included a nice pair of sweat socks. I want them too as well as the T-shirt which is in the bundle. Honey, somewhere in my stuff there must be another one of those white T-shirts. A T-shirt is an undershirt with short sleeves. If you can find them, I'd like to have them. It helps to keep the underwear clean. At the moment, I can't think of anything else. But if you can get another full-size picture of yourself, I'd love to have it. We're allowed to put them up and I want yours over the bunk. Get an ordinary leatherette frame for it with that glasstex instead of glass. Oh yes, also a needle and some neutral looking thread. That's all, Darling.
    – Interruption – Just returned from tetanus shot and blood type. We're at ease at the moment, Darling, so I'll close this with my love. Sergeant just walked in and issued a hell of an order: eleven regulations to be learned in two hours. So no more letters for today. Sam. Kiss my Love Lettuce

February 10, 1944, 1:45 p.m.
Honey:

This has to be a short fast one. We got all our field equipment today and have been practicing with it. My gosh, what a business to remember the million and one do's and don'ts. You have no idea, Darling, what this war business entails. I can't write to anyone else until some organization of mind and matter takes place with me, so if anyone complains about not hearing from me, please tell them I'll catch up eventually. Also stress that everyone writing to me includes his return address. Please send the accordion. If anything should happen that we should be moved, I'll see that someone here returns it home safely. They are all wonderful men and very patient with such a bunch of rookies as they have on hand. Gosh, we are awful. If it wasn't such serious business, you could die laughing at some of the things that are said and done. Abbott and Costello have nothing on this bunch. More later. Goodbye, Darling. Kiss my little angel. Remember, Honey, if anything happens of an emergency nature, contact the local Red Cross at once and I'll be on my way. Otherwise a delay is inevitable. As ever, "Honey"

February 12, 1944, 8:50 a.m.
Sweet Angel:

We're waiting for that dread inspection which is coming in a few moments. I meant to start this letter last night but I was so busy shining shoes and various other chores that lights went out before I even made my bed, so I fell in as is and had a horrible night, largely induced by a shot which I got earlier in the day. The darn thing induced fever and something like an awful hangover. I feel much better now and hope to find time to write you a long letter today (Saturday) or tomorrow after choir. Sweet Angel, I miss you very much, far more than I dare put into words. And I've resolved that when this is over we'll go on a vacation, but it won't be the "rugged life" type of vacation. After this I'll be happy to leave the exercise to the Boy Scouts. Oh, my back! It feels like it's broken. Undoubtedly, I'll benefit by this, but it's no picnic and anyone who chooses it for a career is plain nuts. The rain has stopped at last.

– Interruption – Resumed at 1:00 p.m. We are remaining in barracks while the rest of this post is passing inspection. Next week we'll face that ordeal. It means sparkling like a new penny.

– Interruption –

I just returned from two hours of maddening drill. Sweetheart, if you haven't sent the hangers, please do so immediately. The Army doesn't stand for excuses. They tell you to get hangers and you get them—and fast. Angel, in my letters I asked for several things. Check the letters again and see if you sent what I asked for. Eventually, I'll have the necessary things and won't have to bother you. The Post Exchange here is mostly inadequate and all the men are confronted with the same problem. I have read your sweet letters over and over. They are my one great stabilizer. Without them I would go to pieces. Angel, if I sound a bit low, don't worry. This period of adjustment is just as bad for everyone. I am enormously pleased to know that our friends haven't forsaken us. Darling, tell Hans [editor of *Music News*, a weekly publication to which Sam contributed a column: "In Lighter Vein"] to send me several copies of the last article I wrote for him. For the life of me, I can't recall one word of it. I should have a copy here, anyhow. Also put a couple away for my permanent file. I'll close now because I suspect we'll go out on the double in a few moments. Kiss my sweet Love Lettuce. Get a picture of her for me.

With all my love, "H"

February 13, 1944
Sweet Angel:

This is Sunday morning—8:25 a.m. to be exact. I feel wonderful, honest, Honey. What a surprise. I guess the Army really knows what's what. After yesterday's torture on the parade ground I thought my screaming muscles and broken back would never be normal again, but happy day, this morning I'm fit as a fiddle. I'm glad I didn't give in to temptation and go on sick call yesterday, which I could have done. Yesterday afternoon's added drill seemed to snap me out of the doldrums. Of course, there's more coming, but if I snap out of it as easily as this time, I'll be OK. Come to think of it, the darn tetanus shot is what really knocked us on our ears. Angel, this will be a short one. I must shave and dress soon to go to chapel. We saw an excellent movie last night, *Miracle of Morgan's Creek*. Sweetheart, if it isn't too much work for you, a simple slipover sweater in khaki would be appreciated. I take about a 38 these days.

The barracks is coming alive with a bang. I got up early and got an excellent breakfast. This is optional on Sunday which belongs to us completely. Until later, Sweetheart, Adios. My love to the whole gang. Get me the addresses of all the people I'm supposed to write to. Angel, sometime when you're sending along a package, throw in the little old dictionary that's in the desk. I don't want the good ones, just that little one to keep up on my vocabulary because in this man's Army everything is expressed with one word, a certain obscene four-letter word that amuses you only when your Honey uses it. I wish I could record some of this conversation around here; it's unbelievable. That four-letter word and an equally expressive phrase, "tough shit," are the extent of the vocabulary used around here. I ask you, do I need a dictionary? Kiss my Love Lettuce (Oh to see her smile!)

Love, "Honey"

February 13, 1944 2:20 p.m.
Sweet Angel:

In civilian life a man's only refuge of complete privacy is the bathroom, and in the Army his only refuge is a block of writing paper. So, reveling in such privacy as is granted me, I indulge over and over to say that I love you. At the moment, all the boys are writing and bitching about how slow the mail is. That's the reason why you're not getting my letters at regular intervals. Since Monday I have written you every day and two or three times of day. I hope all my letters are getting through. I don't think any censorship is in effect for the United States, but one never knows about these things. At any rate I have no complaints except the one legitimate one of wanting to see you and my little Angel.

The day broke clear, cold and beautiful and chapel service this morning was comforting. As I read the Lord's Prayer I felt the warmth of your love. It's strange what happens to a man when he has to leave behind him the ones he loves the best. We have returned from a brief walk about the grounds of the Post. They are not as attractive as they can be yet, but in time they will be very lovely. The hospital has sprung up since the outbreak of war and the trees which were replanted since clearing the ground are still pathetic saplings. A few virgin timbers at the riverbank are very nice and sturdy looking.

Honey, I can't tell you much about what is going to happen. All I know is that I'm classified as a medical soldier which means being thoroughly prepared for everything short of combat. Since medical soldiers are not armed, they are not expected to do any fighting. But that's all so far in the future that I'd beg you to dismiss it from your mind. With God's will—and He has been good to us—we'll be spared that ordeal. Our formal education as "medics" and our basic training starts tomorrow morning in earnest and woe unto the guy who doesn't take it as serious business. I got your letter of the 9th only today (Sunday), so you see the mail is slow both ways. I know it's futile for me to say "don't worry" if you don't hear from me every day because I carry on something awful when I don't hear from you, but eventually we'll work out some system of sending and receiving at regular intervals.

I hope you like my Valentine. It's the best I could do in the way of artwork, but the sentiment attached is carved in the most "precious metal." I have written to Mayme [Sam's sister] and my folks, to Mr. Bulliet [Sam's editor at the *Chicago Daily News*], and still have a half-dozen to go, so, Angel, good-bye for today. This is the second letter to you today. Kiss my little Angel and don't forget I want pictures of both of you. Maybe one of you together. Oh boy, would that be nice!

"Daddy"

Extra: Darling, please don't worry about my birthday. I'll need things from time to time and I'd rather you save the money for those occasions. Maybe your ma can find a mezuzah or a "Magen David," a Star of David, on Maxwell Street.

I'd like to have one and a chain to go with it since no medallions can be worn on the same chain that holds the dog tags. But don't make any extra trips for it.

Monday, February 14, 1944, 5:00 p.m.
My Angel:
[*Editors' note: Sam has asked Esther to write his next expected article for* Music News]

    A compliment for you: Your article for *Music News* is excellent and I'll look forward to seeing it in print. If Hans was as enterprising as I thought, he would have put your name on it so you could write it as a sort of personal experience in going through your husband's scrapbooks. Honey, I suggest you do the next one, too, along that line. Write it like a letter to me, reminiscing at will about the things we've seen in Chicago's nightclubs. I would be very proud if you would do it that way. You might intersperse it with bits of gossip, news items, etc. It would be a most interesting way of doing it, because, sweetheart, if this is to be a long war, I'm afraid you'll have to shoulder this responsibility and keep alive this contract for me. Dolly, did you get the $15 Hans owed me? Be sure to collect. Also, did you get my clothes from [Fort] Sheridan, and for gosh sakes, did you get your allotment check? Please answer all these questions in your next letter.

    Honey, thanks for the hangers and cream. I need three or four more strong hangers. I know you think I'm nuts, but Angel, every shirt, every trouser, every GI piece of wearing apparel has to be on a hanger in a regular order, hung over the bunk. It's the "bunk" all right, but that's the rule here and who am I to argue?

    You should see it pour. I ducked supper to stay in barracks and write this and now the boys are dribbling back and making a hell of a racket with their moronic gibberish. Darling, mail call in every barracks throughout the world is a brief drama of suffocating poignancy. The man who doesn't get a letter suddenly feels lost and confused. I'll never forget the lesson I learned here about waiting for that letter.

    Honey, what can I tell you about myself for what will happen? Your guess is as good as mine why I'm in the Medical Corps. It's considered an honor to be in this branch but we have no idea when we'll start being "honored." At the moment, we're an awful raw bunch of rookies who don't know a right face from a left in some cases. A "General Hospital," it is said, has considerable permanence of location, and if the war is concluded this year, we'll undoubtedly get no further than Stark General. Beyond that, Honey, we're in the hands of God. I can't lie to you or mislead you. A furlough is impossible for the next three months and possibly longer, depending on the turn of events for the Allies. This is a receiving station for casualties from the Italy/Africa area as I understand it, and before I'm through with my training I shall have the privilege of seeing "man's inhumanity to man." I have talked to some of the boys at the hospital recreation hall, and no matter what we're asked to do, it will be nothing compared to what they have done. Angel, don't be depressed, however. I am making my own breaks in my own way and in my own time. In the Army, it is a generally accepted axiom that being at the right place at the right time is what gives a man the real breaks. Honey, I think I'm in the right place, and when the right time comes, I'll be ready. That's why, Angel, when I ask you to send certain things, let everything else go and do it at once. Honey, the post office at 46th Street should be sufficient. It isn't necessary to go downtown. Cookie, I'm not complaining. I just want you to act quickly when I need you.

Familiarize yourself with all my music I have around and sort of keep it together. Already I'm being discussed here as a famous columnist and singer and while these are gross exaggerations, I'll have to live up to my reputation at any moment. You see, this post is really just beginning to be organized since it's a consolidation of two hospital units which joined forces only last December. The hospital proper is well established, but the military phase is still in organization, although most of the personnel are fully trained. We rookies have set the program askew, but that condition will prevail until the full complement of 500 men has been established. Currently we number 345, and many in twos and threes come dribbling in from various parts of the country. Those who know say this'll be a fine spot when it really gets going, and personally, I have found this prediction already effective. The food is good, the men intelligent and patient. That's all I can tell you because that's all I know. Eventually I'll draw my own more definite conclusions and shall write you in detail.

About furlough, well, Angel, at this point it would seem more advisable to meet in New York when the time comes rather than attempt that awful Chicago trip, unless I can get at least ten days. It is fourteen hours from here to New York and thirty-six to Chicago. If I could get three or four days off after basic training, which should be about twelve weeks, we'll meet in New York and have a holiday. If I get more time, naturally, it will be our own fireside. You must be brave, Sweetheart, and keep yourself occupied, because I'll need every ounce of your strength to help me through. I am haunted by the thought that our Angel won't know her Daddy, but I'll make it up to both of you when this is over.

Sweetheart, I promised myself not to write you any more such serious letters because I know they hurt you terribly, but you must understand that henceforth you'll both be just as real and near to me even if I fill my letters with barracks trivia. Angel, I find myself thinking of you both during class and that sort of thing can be destructive to my morale and ability to absorb what we have to learn in a hurry. I'll phone you at regular intervals and write every day, but, Sweet Angel, help me to take hold of my emotions which run riot at the nearest thought of you. I'm planning to fill my letters with observations that I can use later. This will be a good stabilizer for me. For the moment, Dear, that's all.

All my love to you and our little elocutionist. Daddy

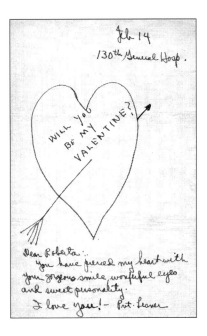

Feb 14 (1944) – 130th General Hospital
WILL YOU BE MY VALENTINE?
Dear Roberta:
   You have pierced my heart with your gorgeous smile, wonderful eyes and sweet personality.
   I love you! Pvt. Lesner

Feb 14 (1944) – 130th General Hospital
   Sweetheart: My heart is broken that I can't kiss you this Valentine's Day. Am I still your best valentine? You are mine!
   With love, Pvt. Lesner

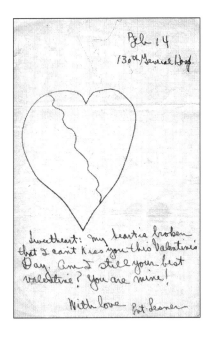

February 15, 1944, 6:30 p.m.
Sweet Angel:

You failed me today—no letter! But it's been such a beautiful day that I can stand it, knowing that tomorrow I'll have news from you. The *Daily News* has started to arrive and I know how bad the weather is in Chicago. We exercised and played soccer stripped to the waist, that's how nice it was, but yesterday made up for it. My gosh, what a dismal downpour. New rookies keep arriving daily so our formal education has been postponed until next week. Sweetheart, if you can find my Palmer's Skin Success ointment, send it to me, or else get a can. It's $.25. I have a cold blister that seems to be very touchy and Palmer's has always been wonderful for it. You see, daily shaving irritates the sore spot and it won't heal naturally. Please don't go worrying about this. It's merely one of my typical cold sores, aggravated by my general nervousness the first few days. Don't forget *Music News* for me and keep up the good job. You were wonderful.

Love, "Honey"

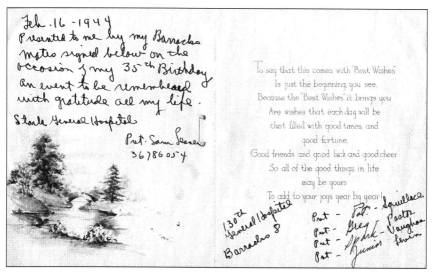

Presented to me by my Barracks mates signed below on the occasion of my 35th Birthday, an event to be remembered with gratitude all my life.
Stark General Hospital
Pvt. Sam Lesner
36786054

February 16, 1944, 7:00 p.m.
Sweet Angel:

Turning 35 without my Cookie and my Love Lettuce was an event that echoed the loneliness in my heart, but the day was very eventful and I almost forgot all about birthdays until after evening chow when four of my buddies presented me with two boxes of this nice stationery. I thought it was a joke at first, but the guys even got a beautiful birthday card for the present. I'm sending the inscribed card home to you. Please put it away. I'll treasure it as a memento of this experience. Before I forget, yes I got all your letters and I'm going to bundle them and return them because I want you to keep every piece of correspondence between us. Every one of your letters gives me added life in the news that our darling Love Lettuce is thriving so beautifully. What a treasure she is and to think that we were worried about parenthood. Sweetheart, we'll have half a dozen if this damn war doesn't make us both senile. Be patient, Angel, until Passover. Maybe they'll be gracious enough to grant me a furlough. I'll speak to the chaplain at the proper time. If it's to be a very short one, we'll meet in New York. About the income tax, see Mr. Whitehall at the *News*, but make it clear to him about our reduced income as of October 1943 etc. He has all the facts about the last filing and should have no difficulty in arriving at a proper estimate. Angel, it's really too much for me, so do the best you can.

– Interruption –

Resumed February 17, 1944, 7:15 a.m. Angel I had hopes of finishing this yesterday, mailing it and then phoning you. Well, I did none of these things. When we returned from a five-mile hike yesterday afternoon, after a morning of dentist, backbreaking calisthenics, and other duties, I collapsed in a heap to rest my feet. Incidentally, on the hike we practiced air raid diving. That is, when the signal sounds we, who are marching single file alongside both sides of the road, dive headlong into the woods, and if you land in a swamp, it's just "tough shit," as they say in the Army. I'll admit it was exciting and very real with great planes roaring overhead all the time. When I get toughened up in body a little more, I'll enjoy that sort of thing. It's dramatic as hell. During one alarm, I looked up to see that I had foolishly chosen a tree about one inch in diameter to hide behind. Some protection! I feel a little less like a rusty tin soldier this morning but my hips and legs are still screaming.

About yesterday, there was the cleaners to go to and a few other chores and then choir rehearsal at 7:30. I had intended returning at 8:30 to phone you, but alas, Capt. Jenning, who is the organist, decided I ought to give a vocal recital for his sole benefit. I sang everything he put up, including some perfectly awful compositions of his own. But I think I made a decided hit and shall soon sing a solo at the USO Center. Honey, look for my music and send me all those song cycle books that I have and some of the sheet music. If you can, catalog all of it and send me a list and I'll indicate what I need. Also, the accordion and the recorder and recorder music. My goodness, I'll come out of this Army a singer yet. Incidentally, it isn't a bad idea if they ever decide to stage another Army show. Talent is drawn from everywhere for these things. Sweetheart, that's all for now. Forgive me for not phoning. I got into barracks just ahead of lights out. All my love to you and our brown-eyed Love Lettuce. Daddy

P.S. Don't write airmail. It's a waste of money. Your last airmail took three days!

February 18, 1944 – After lunch pause

Sweetheart, there will be time for only a short one now. I didn't write yesterday because after talking to you (for which I gave up supper) I had to hurry to the cleaners and then to the movies in order to make the first show. After that I couldn't raise an arm and when I hit the bed, I went out like a light. That's a new experience for me—asleep before my head hits the pillow. But I like it. It leaves me little time to worry about things. See, Honey, I'm getting smug already. That's the Army for you. I'm kidding, of course. I'd crawl home to you and my precious child if I could leave here. Honey, moving to the new place means being 400 miles nearer home and just a four- or five-hour ride from Cincinnati, which gives me an idea. I've been hearing so much about "Cincy" since I married you [Esther's mother came from Cincinnati] that I'll bet we meet there soon. Honey, it's important that basic training is uninterrupted, but if they are right here, I'll get to see you Pesach, even if for only a day. What a wonderful time to meet one's bride again. I'll live for that moment. We got another shot today and the arm is getting sore so I'll close on this page.

Your package received in good order and am proud as punch. I got my name into the camp paper [copy below] already and just now a sergeant in our barracks said, "Who's Sam Lesner?" The boys all spoke up and pointed me out. Getting mentioned as a Basic is not bad! Here's the new address. Pass it on. Private Samuel J. Lesner number 36786054, 130th General Hospital c/o Moore General Hospital, Swannanoa, North Carolina. Love, "Honey"

February 19, 1944, 5:30 p.m.
Sweetheart:

Saturday evening without you is painful, but it would have been unbearable if I hadn't received two beautiful letters from you today at second mail call. The first call got me down when nothing showed up, but later, after being awakened from the afternoon nap—and in the Army, too, mind you!—I was handed four letters: two from you, one from my folks, and one from Emil Garber. The midday nap calls for explanation. We were turned loose after 1 p.m., after having received certain instructions about our move to Moore General Hospital from our handsome, soft-spoken commanding officer, Lt. Col. Lesher, and a much more inarticulate set of instructions from our detachment commander, Lt. Wysocki, who

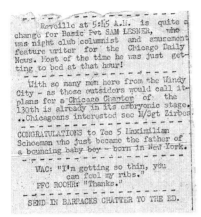

"Reveille at 5:45 A.M, is quite a change for Basic Pvt. SAM LESNER, who was night club columnist and amusement feature writer for the Chicago Daily News. Most of the time he was just getting to bed at that hour!"

describes himself as "hell on wheels." He's that, all right, but he also can turn on the charm which eradicates instantly all the bitter thoughts germinated during the day.

It is cold and very wet today, so when we were put "at ease," I headed for my bed which is not uncomfortable, or maybe I'm getting tough. The personal inspection which I mentioned in an earlier letter did not materialize this afternoon, but I cursed it pro and con since I passed up the lunch to get ready for this microscopic examination, only to hear too late that it was called off. The mess hall was closed before I could make out just what was what, so fortified with a green apple which I filched from mess yesterday, a chocolate bar, and a fistful of cookies supplied by Private Manny Levin, my barracks neighbor, I muddled through the afternoon. Consequently, I gulped supper and now I'm paying the price of indiscretion with a slight heartburn. A Coke, however, will fix that up.

Honey, you seemed disturbed when I mentioned "emergencies" and Red Cross. You don't understand. What I meant is that if ever you want to contact me immediately, the Red Cross, alone, can do it without delay. That's what I meant, and I don't want to be spared if something should go wrong. I pray God that we'll all come out of this unscathed, but there's no denying that the emotional drain on all of us is terrific and with it can come complications. Enough of this unpleasant subject.

I am slowly beginning to recall some of the moments since I entered the Army which have left a profound impression on me. Through the nightmare of processing at Fort Sheridan I carried away the first profound emotion I have experienced as a soldier. It happened, I believe, the second night we were there. Of course, the first night shall always remain in my mind as incredible. The huge barracks, dozens of scared men trying to keep cheerful, a perfect bastard of a barracks leader who introduced us to the Army's most colorful expletive, "Tough Shit" (T.S.) and a little tired guy with his face buried in his pillow, hugging a writing case with a little snapshot of a baby in it. That guy hadn't yet received the picture of his wife and he was having a very tough time trying to keep his gut down. But the next night, fortified by two good pals, this soldier learned what it was all about, and why it was necessary to separate men from those they love. Suddenly a shot was fired, and against a sky painted lavishly by a setting sun, a flag began to descend from its proud pinnacle where it had flown all day. Without any instruction or preparation, we three soldiers froze at attention the instant the shot was heard and stood proudly—with a hand salute—as the flag was furled in. Honey, the point is, as a civilian you do this sort of thing because it's tradition or something, but as a soldier you do it with your heart. I know we weren't acting; we simply had made the transition without realizing it. I experienced the same thrill when we boarded the wonderful, new troop train which brought us to Stark. That train was exclusively built for us, Uncle Sam's soldiers.

The five-mile hike this week also had its emotional impact. I went out reluctantly because my feet ached badly. But when I caught a glimpse of our standard—130th "Fighting" General Hospital—floating at the head of the long double column stretched out for a quarter of a mile, I was glad that I didn't go on sick call, which is merely a convenient way of avoiding a harder part of becoming a soldier. Later, we sat resting in the woods, like regular troops, drinking out of our own canteens, resting our heads on our helmets and generally carrying on as though this was not a brand-new experience in our lives. On the return trip we practiced the air raids which I described to you. No matter how pooped you are, and bitter about the whole thing, when that whistle blows, you dive for the nearest shelter and suddenly hear your heart pounding with excitement until the all-clear sounds. Picture us, Angel, in helmets and leggings, also wearing pistol belt from which are suspended canteen and emergency kit. Later we shall carry full field packs on our backs, and a gas mask too. When we leave this Post Tuesday morning, we shall carry similar equipment, only more of it.

I anticipate the moment of departure as a high point in my Army career, since ceremony is so much a part of Army life. Undoubtedly, the 130th standards and flags with help will be flying proudly. This Post has no drum and bugle corps for some strange reason, but I wish they did have. My God, if I could drum this outfit out of camp, I'd burst with pride. The Medical Corps, however, doesn't go in for this phase of military pomp, although military courtesy is drummed at us all day and every day. I don't feel self-conscious anymore about saluting, although when and when not to do so is still a puzzle to me. I've made some boners, but not nearly as bad as some of these guys here. No rookie wants to be marked as such, but the darned salute is a dead giveaway.

We have not been issued insignia as yet, but I do declare that in my O.D.'s [olive drabs] and Garrison hat I make a very handsome soldier, so the guys tell me. I admit I like the uniform and am extremely proud of it. I was lucky in one respect. At Sheridan they decided I was a model rookie and everything issued me fits very well. But you should see what some of the guys got. A guy called Jumbo, for instance, doesn't seem to fit into his issue with any degree of comfort, and he's a vain guy, although a treasure when it comes to friendliness and general good fellowship. He's dressing at this very moment to step out. He's a willing ox and is generally liked by the "noncoms." Across from me lives Charlie Crowe, a full-blooded Chippewa. He's quiet and cooperative. He comes from the Bad River Indian Reservation, which is only a stone's throw from Flambeau, where we spent a rugged vacation, remember.

Manny Levin, from 13th and Independence [in Chicago] is very funny and fearless. His choice of descriptive pronouns, of course, is fabulous. He has a girl who writes him countless letters and occasionally encloses a dollar or two. When there's no money forthcoming in his daily mail, Manny carries on something awful. He has a real love and respect for his sweetheart. He's an only child. Peace has descended upon Barracks 8.

I don't know what the housing arrangement will be at Moore, but if I get housed with them, I'll go mad. I like my own bunch and we are hoping we can stay together. Truly, this new bunch is made up of butchers, bakers, candlestick makers, cabbies, foundry workers, etc. I don't get the pitch, but the Army is a great leveler. Apparently, the Medical Corps has need for all these types or they wouldn't be here. More about Barracks 8 and its motley crew later. In the meantime, be of good cheer and I'll try to do likewise. Surely someday these muscles of mine will have stretched far enough to take anything they can dish out. But if I should fail, well 35 [Sam turned 35 three days earlier] is the answer. Yes, sweetheart, I think the round belly is melting away, but don't be too optimistic when starting on the sweater. I'm going to try and get myself weighed when I can find a scale. As yet there is no time for reading, so please don't do anything about books. If you find an occasional article is interesting you can send it on. When classes start next week, we'll have little time to catch a free breath, let alone read. I haven't yet learned to "shave, shower and shit" in five minutes as I heard it so aptly described in the latrine this evening. The latrine, incidentally, is a wonderful place to hear the damnedest things. No wonder the Army is constantly fighting latrine rumors.

Over and over again I read your comments on Love Lettuce and each time I choked down the tears of pride and joy. Keep well, My Love, and guard our treasure and our home. With all my love, "Daddy"

The new address is: Private Samuel J. Lesner, # 36786054, 130th General Hospital, c/o Moore General Hospital, Swannanoa, North Carolina

You're in the Army Now

February 20, 1944 – After midday chow

Honey, I just returned from seeing *Madame Curie* at the Post Theater. What a great picture. Truly a masterpiece, and Greer Garson is divine as Curie. I can't focus on anyone but you these days. You fill my every thought and frequently I find myself doing a left face when the sergeant says right. That must stop, of course, or I'll land in the guardhouse which isn't a bad idea. Picking up little bits of paper would leave my mind completely free to think of you. How much more I would have enjoyed *Curie* with you. Remind me, Honey, to take you to the movies sometime! [Editors' note: *After the war, as the Movie Critic of the Chicago Daily News, he took Esther to the movies thousands of times over the next thirty-eight years.*] Sweetheart, if I miss a day in writing, don't worry. We'll probably be pushed hither and yon without end for the next couple of days.

I promise you I'll find out about a furlough as soon as it's possible, and where we can meet. I still think Cincinnati would be ideal since it's exactly equal distance from Asheville and Chicago. Since you have so many friends there, I'm sure it would be a pleasant meeting place, although I don't intend to share you with anyone. The point is it would give me almost an extra day with you instead of riding the rails. However, if time permits, it's home for me. Until I write from Moore General, I am as ever your Cookie. Darling, don't thank me for writing; it makes me feel like a demi-god. I'm only your husband, albeit a loving one.

Part 2
The Move to Swannanoa

February 22, 1944
Darling:

I had intended writing you on the train but it was impossible since we were pretty crowded into a perfectly impossible relic of 1890. The South surely is still fighting the Civil War. Well, we made it safely—eleven hours for a trip of 310 miles, so you can imagine how we chugged along. But it was worth it. Honey, this site is something you see in a movie. That camp and hospital are spread beautifully in a valley that is circled by the most elegant mountains, the Smokies. We probably won't think they're beautiful when we start marching up and down them, but while the joy lasts, it's most satisfying. It's raining like hell at the moment and we're very happy to stay in barracks. Soon enough some S.O.B of a sergeant will come looking for a detail. The freight car carrying most of our field equipment is still standing on the siding. I got stuck with the job of loading it at Charleston, and if I get caught again I'll blow my top. But come to think of it, it's easier for me than the drilling and marching which are "tough shit" for my feet. I'm going to demand an x-ray examination of my feet which have taken the drill with extremely bad grace. I don't mean to alarm you, Honey, but if I can prove that I'm legitimately claiming an arthritic condition, I might be spared some of the torture.

A guy just offered the information that we are 485 miles from Cincinnati which is an overnight ride from here. I pray to God that I can soon get a three-day pass but we would have to meet in Cincinnati. Later this summer you can take a week and come to Asheville and then you can see this beautiful camp.

Honey, I'm writing this with a dozen guys arguing stupidly about nothing so I'll make my requests and close. I need the Palmer's Skin Success. For some reason, I decided to blossom out. I guess it's the nervousness and change of living combined, but I'll get over it OK. Now, I also need immediately at least two small face towels (white) and two items from the dime store: a shaving stick, any kind, but it must be in a plastic or cardboard container, and a small can of tooth powder, any good brand. The reason for these items is fantastic, but it's a command and must be obeyed. Also, these small items, when packed into a field pack, make it somewhat lighter, so you can see there is a reason for everything. Don't forget, Honey, face towels, a shaving stick and small tooth powder container. Hold off on the accordion and music until further notice. Candy, Darling, isn't necessary, since chocolate is available here and I don't want to eat too many sweets, especially during basic training, as they cut down energy for some reason. On long hikes we are warned about consuming too many sweets preceding it. Furthermore, by the time you see me, I want to be the Adonis you married, and believe me, Honey, I'll be a Killer Diller.

The income tax is a shock but I guess it's no use crying about it. If it's the only "big sacrifice" we make, we'll have reason to thank God. I wish it were possible for you to stay home and keep things going, but if you can help our income appreciatively, without draining your energy, I'll agree that working might be advisable. Darling, when this is over, your working days will be over for good, I promise you, if my small brain can sustain us in the style I want you to live. We do not want riches, Honey, only comfort and security.

Until tomorrow, Honey, good night. I'm afraid we have a tough day ahead. I hope this will go out in the morning. Darling, I shall send back one of your letters with each of mine. Keep them safely for me in chronological order. I treasure them, but fear to keep them with me. Inspecting officers are not given to sentiment and might order me to get rid of them. My love to your parents and call mine, Honey, and give them my love. Kiss Love Lettuce. Say hello to all our dear friends. Note new address on envelope.

Your "Boopsie"

February 23, 1944, 9:15 p.m.
Sweet Angel:

This is to be a short one as a penalty for not having heard from you today. I was desolate when second mail call produced only two dated issues of the

Daily News in which, strangely, I have only a slight interest. The day was rather inactive for me as I spent time at the dentist, got a shot and finally caught up with my group at a lecture movie which was diverting. The afternoon was devoted to the damnedest drill, but after that I was permitted to sit quietly in the sun while the other GI jerks knocked themselves out playing ball.

Honey, I haven't written you much about the place and people in it because I have no fixed impressions, but eventually I'll get around to it. We just got in a batch of hillbillies who still smoke Bull Durham and stink like the first word. My goodness, what are they doing in the high falutin' Medical Corps? I give up! I'm enclosing the caduceus and the strap pin from my wristwatch which I broke. See, Honey, if you can buy me a new one in a watchmaker shop. You can slip it into an envelope with a piece of tape as per example.

Some guys here get seven, eight, nine letters every mail call, honest. Young Manny Levin who sleeps next to me gets a mail bag full every day, and when I don't even get one little note, my heart sinks. I think, Honey, if you set a regular time every day to write, letters will come with greater regularity. The new address, I repeat, is: Private Samuel J. Lesner, 36786054, 130th General Hospital, c/o Moore General Hospital, Swannanoa, North Carolina. Note, it's North Carolina now and 400 miles nearer to home. Oh boy.

All my love to you, Angel, the baby, your loyal and good parents, and all our friends.

February 24, 1944, 11:30 a.m.
Sweetheart:

A few minutes to spare and how best to use them but to write to you a letter. Well, Darling, I can no longer resent the parody on my name. I am now officially "Sam, Sam, the lavatory man." I was one of a group assigned to latrine detail this morning, and after lunch we face the "pleasant" prospect of returning to the job, but fortunately a less smelly one.

— Interruption —I just had a mail call. I got a *Daily News* but no letter from you, so I await with pounding heart the second call. About the latrine: we washed and scrubbed and polished it as if it were the president's own, and I will say that after a few minutes of dainty dipping, I set to and had a fairly enjoyable splashing time. This afternoon we shine the brass fittings on the toilet bowls. It's a sight to see us sitting backwards on the toilet seats, shining hell out of the fittings. Sergeant (Doctor) Katz, my good friend, came in and expressed his shock and disgust at my plight. But then he did It, too, once. Such is the Army and thus the "humiliation" of man goes on endlessly. We strive to lift society to a level of decency and behold, we're suddenly thrown back centuries. It's not that the government can't afford equipment with which to do this menial work intelligently. It's designed, deliberately, to knock the sensitiveness out of one and all, because we must be ready for the final degradation, the killing, that alone determines who is right.

Sweetheart, pray for me that I might be a good, obedient soldier, but also pray that this doesn't leave a permanent and horribly coarse rhinoceros skin on me. Your sweet sensitivity to me in all my feelings and thoughts has thrilled and excited me, although I only occasionally let you see it. I am not missing the humor in this strange experience, but I simply haven't achieved perspective enough to crystallize it into active words. There is much humor in the "bullshitting" that takes place every minute, and God willing, I'll have much to write about some day.

– Interruption –Lunch—excellent. I feel much better and war and its ramifications seem very remote at the moment. At 1 p.m. we fall out for a formation, reason unknown. The prospect for the weekend is pleasant. The Jewish Welfare Board of Asheville is holding a welcoming party for the Jewish men in the 130th. If I can get a pass, I'll go with swell Jack Garber and a newfound friend, Meyer Berkowitz of the Bronx, New York, a fine intelligent boy who has gone out of the way to be pleasant to me. He was just made a sergeant. There is no Jewish activity on the post, and the few men of our faith here feel it's best if we do not make any open moves to organize. Thus, we will take advantage of Asheville and its generous Jewish citizenry.

Sweetheart, I want to rest a moment so I'll close this one, the second one today. Don't be alarmed, Honey, the mail arrangement here is appallingly bad at the moment but there is promise of improvement. Call my folks and tell them I'm writing them a long letter. Honest, Honey, I'm haunted by my failure to fulfill my obligations to them, but each moment brings new complications here and I'm doing the best I can. My love forever and ever, and I do mean you!

X for Love Lettuce. Daddy

February 24, 1944, 1:40 p.m.
Darling:

Forgive me. I passed you up yesterday and unless I do this in ten minutes, I might have to pass you up again today. I'm tortured by the thought, so accept what little I can get down. A perfect S.O.B. of a corporal is screaming his damn head off. Fortunately, I've been finally assigned to an end bed and they can't see me very easily. Yesterday was horrible. We fell in., fell out, fell in, counted off, signed payroll, but no pay yet, unloaded those G.D. freight trains again and finally collapsed at 9 p.m. after trying desperately to write a column for the camp paper. I got a good lead but that's all. Well, they'll just have to accept my writing at my convenience. My God, I thought the day would never end.

This is a magnificent layout, as to the scenery, but actually it's already overcrowded, and another 100 men are coming in. Well, the standing in line for shit, shave and shower will be never ending after they arrive. I'm not gloomy, Angel, despite this letter. I'm just overwhelmingly lonely for you and Love Lettuce. I hope that in a day or two this outfit will settle down and we'll at least be told where we can mail a letter. As it is, one has to go several blocks to accomplish this, where formerly, we had a mail room directly across from our barracks. They don't seem to give a damn that back home family and friends are uneasy and unhappy. That bastard Hitler! What a mess he made of our lives. Surely a horrible death must come to him soon.

Angel, our new barracks are comfortable and I really believe I'll feel much better in this drier climate. Honey, you should get a whiff of the mountain air that sweeps over our valley. Gosh it's luscious. My spelling and vocabulary have gone to hell, so until I can give more thought to these letters, I'll send you my great love. Tell Love Lettuce Daddy is getting strong and handsome. In a moment, the S.O.B. will scream so good-bye.

Daddy

February 25, 1944
Darling:

The utmost confusion reigns here. My God, being a soldier is complicated business. I hope you have received my telegram explaining the situation. For three days, no one seemed to know where to deposit a letter and I carried yours in my pocket, swallowing tears of despair. The noncoms were of no use. Now, finally, they have decided where a box can be placed. In the meantime, I have located the post office which is a frightful distance from our barracks, considering that everything must be done on the run, stealing time from this or that. Honey, I can't assure you of regular mail for the present. We have our behinds chased mercilessly all day. Sunday I'll write you a long letter describing in detail just what goes here. Then you'll understand better why most soldiers experience despair when it comes to keeping the family informed regularly. I steal every moment to write to you, but I never seem to accomplish much.

Today I got the baby's pictures. Honey, how can I tell you what went on inside of me. Believe me, after getting the envelope and taking an excited look, I walked into and completely through the wrong barracks without realizing it. I have them all lined up along my bed. The first chance I get, I'll get a frame and group several together. Am I supposed to send some back, or are they all for me? Oh, I thank God for such a blessing. She is far more adorable then I dared to hope. It doesn't seem possible. After all, it's only a month since I've seen her. Darling, have lots of prints made and pass them around. Please, Darling, see that my mother gets some too. It will help so much to keep the "waters calm." I also got the most magnificent box of candy from Sophie Tucker [famous nightclub performer]. What a thoughtful person she is. My only regret is that you didn't keep it. It's much too fancy for me and my bunkmates. I'll write and thank her. Your mother's candy also arrived, for which I am most grateful. But, Angel,

I don't need so much candy. Please, Sweetheart, every time you have the impulse to buy me some candy, buy it for yourself and enjoy it. That will give me pleasure.

I need several things: shorts, size 32, a couple of undershirts, and some GI socks, size 10½. If you wish you can send me these items. Don't forget the Palmer's. I've discovered I've got blanket itch. The wool blankets aren't very clean, I guess, and other guys have it too. Don't worry, it's nothing. Our actual basic hasn't started yet because of confusion here. Well I don't mind except they don't quite know what to do with us and spend a lot of time getting the program jazzed up.

Before I forget, my first column for the camp paper will appear in a day or two. I'll send it to you. I hope it will do much to "establish" me here. The Colonel [Lesher] is dead set on having our own paper, and I've gently hinted that I wouldn't mind devoting all my time to the paper. Anything can happen in this nut house. Tomorrow, Darling, I go on guard duty, so my

Good night, My Love, Daddy

Saturday, February 26, 1944 – A pause after chow
Sweetheart:

Just a few lines to keep the letters flowing. Noon chow was very good after a morning of mopping and general taking of horse manure from various stripe wearers. I've often laughed at the description of what goes on in the Army, but always took it with a grain of salt. Well, believe me, Honey, it's all true. You pile it here, pile it there, and then move the same stuff all around again. They don't allow you to assume the responsibility of moving a bench one inch on your own intelligence. Oh well, things get done their way, so the net result is the same. I haven't yet told you how beautifully I can make a bed, with hospital folds on sheets and blankets. So far, I've passed inspections successfully on this score. When I get home, I'll show you how it's done, and then we'll tear the damn thing to hell and use the bed for what it's intended. Who gives a good goddamn whether the second sheet is hospital fold or not?

I had your precious letter today just before lunch and walked to mess on clouds as billowy as those that drape themselves over the mountaintops here. Darling, you should see it. This morning the clouds, heavy with rain, settled low over the valley and through the breaks you could see the mountaintops seemingly floating in space. It's an awesome, heart-filling sight. If man could only accept the gorgeous beauty of nature and shape his life accordingly, these terrible separations and mass murders would not be possible. I know it will beat the hell out of my legs, but I'm impatient to tackle these wonderful hills. I guess a good deal of our physical conditioning will take place in the hills. Your love and faith will help me up the steep incline.

My Love Lettuce smiles at me constantly. I have three of the best snaps arranged over my bed and if Colonel Lesher doesn't unbend when he passes my bed, then I give up. Humanity is lost. But I should worry; the world is bright for me as long as I can look at those pictures every morning. Honey, I hate to be selfish, but the baby at present takes after her paternal grandmother. Next time you see my mother laugh, take a good look, then look at the pictures and since I take after my mother, it's safe to say that Love Lettuce is her daddy's image. It is safe to say that you won't object to this too much, since your sweet letters indicate that you think Roberta's daddy is a bit of all right.

– Interruption – Resumed at 6:15

We were called out for formation, then laundry, mail etc., a quick shower for tonight's guard duty, supper, report to guard quarters and now a quick close to this letter. I'll be on guard from 8 to 10, 2 to 4. The stars will be out in all their glory tonight. The sun is just setting gorgeously. I'll be thinking of you, Honey. I got your letter and Mother's. I am pleased and flattered at everyone's attention to you. More tomorrow.

Good night, Darling. Daddy

CHAPTER TWO

Basic Training: Phase 1

February 28, 1944 – At ease
Darling:
 I went out Sunday and, with some other Jewish soldiers, spent the day in Asheville. The Jewish families of Asheville, all rather well-to-do, I gather, support a Jewish Center in conjunction with the USO. It's housed in a beautiful structure, formerly a beautiful private home, and it is a warm, friendly place for Jewish soldiers to spend a free Saturday or Sunday. Since I had guard duty Saturday, I went in the following day and enjoyed the day very much. Honey, the center is badly in need of some dance records. I want to do something. If it's possible, Angel, gather up some of the popular stuff we have, and for which we have no particular use, and send them to me. It would be a swell gesture and undoubtedly put me in right with these nice people.
 I don't know how we're expected to accomplish all that we're supposed to do all in the same moment the command is given. Everything here is done in double time, but I'm gradually adjusting myself to the tempo. This morning, for instance, I found that I had dressed for reveille, attempted a bowel movement, washed, got breakfast, mopped the area of my bed and made the bed, with the damn hospital fold and all, by 7 a.m. That gave me a tense moment or two to just sit waiting for the "fall out!" This Saturday guard duty, which I mentioned over the phone, was a real workout, performed in a driving rain. I guess I have a pretty good temper after all. My job was to stop all cars coming into the Post and just my mazel [luck], into the Post came hundreds of cars or so it seemed. There was an affair for officers and their ladies, and I must say, some of them are inconsiderate, egotistical pups, while others are charming and cooperative. One or two tried to drive by the sentinel's post, but, by golly, I halted them and made them answer my questions, as instructed. I probably made an ass of myself, since in the driving rain and general bad visibility, I saluted everybody, but that's the way you learn. In the first few moments on duty I "caught" the detachment commander, and the commanding officer, Col. Lesher, so it's a good thing I had a ready and snappy salute. My post, however, from 2 to 4 a.m. wasn't bad. I could remain in the sentry's box most of the time warming my behind at a nice warm fire, and gazing out at my buddies slogging their weary

way over their posts and getting wet to the skin. So my luck held, and I think I acquitted myself with some degree of efficiency.

Angel, I must answer some of the letters tonight since I have a brief break. Our basic training started in earnest today and some of the lectures were very interesting. I think there will be a little more emphasis on brain and less on brawn from now on, although the morning calisthenics has to be faced daily with all the stoicism one can muster. We got a new exercise today that must've been invented by the devil. All in all, though, I'm gradually coming out of the daily ordeal less breathless and throbbing with each succeeding day. When I get out, I'm going over to the U. of Chicago and shake [President] Dr. Robert Maynard Hutchins' hand. Hutchins once made the classic remark: "When I feel the urge to exercise, I go to bed."

As you will see by the enclosed paper, I have contributed to the camp paper, but unless they make it at least a small part of my daily routine, I can't plan to contribute regularly. I'm supposed to write one tonight but I'm so tired I ache and want only to finish this and one or two other short letters and go to bed. They know who I am and what I can do. That's enough. If they need me, it's up to them to use my talents instead of my muscle. Frankly, I don't want to miss any of the basic training and the medical training that will be given us. It will have its value in the general knowledge to be gained from such a program. The post is not yet fully organized and many new possibilities and opportunities may present themselves in the process. I'm very popular with the boys and the column has given me a certain advantage, but there are enough goons around here to make it advisable to proceed cautiously.

The most important question, I know, in your mind is "when will we meet?" If our basic goes well they might see the light and give basic a three-day pass. In that case, you could come here and stay in Asheville. The Jewish people I met have offered to cooperate in this matter. They are most cordial. You see, we are the only military personnel in this area and the boys haven't yet turned the citizenry sour on the army. At any rate, the Jewish boys will always be treated nicely here, from what I have been able to observe briefly. The question still remains unanswered: "when can we meet?" Well, here's an example of what happened this week. One of the men here suddenly was visited by his wife who came to Asheville, but the poor bloke got only a Saturday pass and saw her for only a few hours. As much as I long to see you, Honey, I don't want anything as unsatisfactory as that. Wait a few more weeks and let's see what happens. You haven't told me of the circumstances which led up to your decision to go back to work and for whom but I assume it's for Florasynth. If that's the case, I'm sure Mr. Lakritz [Esther's previous boss] will let you take advantage of a three-day pass when the time comes. You can even fly if necessary, to save time. At any rate, I promise to make careful inquiry this week and if it looks at all hopeful, I'll telephone so as to give you the advantage.

Honey, we must face it bravely. This may be a long separation but we're not alone in this. The basic period will pass quickly for us if we both concentrate on the furlough which lies ahead. There is no favoritism here. What one gets, all get, and when passes and furloughs start being handed around, I'll get mine too. There is so much to overcome in order to gain any benefit from the experience that any brooding and imagined discrimination will make it almost unbearable. So, Honey, have faith and believe in the Almighty's power to make our future together a long and happy one. We waited a long time, and to be robbed of a year together now seems unjust, but if it ends with this year, we can count ourselves lucky.

Goodnight, Angel. Daddy

Extra special bushels of kisses for my Love Lettuce XXXXX

February 29, 1944

Angel:

This 29th day of February, an odd day that gets kicked around by the calendar makers, got some measure of revenge by turning out to be a bitch, climatically as well as eventfully. Coming in on a driving rain it has blustered all morning and now in mid-afternoon it has shown little improvement. We are at ease at the moment, dribbling back from the dispensary where we were "shot" again, and what a jolt I got out of my tetanus. I'm still seeing stars from it. We thought we would avoid calisthenics this morning, but we were wrong. We got that too. The morning, however, brought its compensations in a fascinating lecture on first aid, the types of wounds, their characteristics, and the best methods of treatment. Already I know there are two types of wounds, atraumatic, and traumatic. The first is usually produced by planned surgery; the second, by mechanical violence. Bleeding and hemorrhage and methods of stoppage were also presented, and to my surprise, the questions afterward were lively and intelligent. I'm sure I'm going to like this phase of study. I seem to get such a lift out of these classes. Major Mering, who lectures us, is a splendid man and a brilliant lecturer. He's a surgeon, of course, and I'm sure we're going to learn a great deal from him.

– Interruption – Resumed the following day. That's how damned rushed we've been.

Angel: Having just heard a horrible lecture on military guard by the detachment commander who gave us "Pacific" orders, meaning "specific," and told us to go about "identifying" people during the hours for "challenging," we are now bending our ears to an equally awful treatise on the care of clothing and equipment. The lecturer, Lt. Curtwright, however, is a charming gentleman who is stuck with a dull subject.

The wind is threatening to take this wooden shack away any moment. Darling, hurry with that sweater. The bad weather seems to have set in. — To be resumed in barracks —

Honey, I guess I'm just a little overtired and lonely, but when you see how unfair this draft business is, you begin to wonder why every man who calls himself that isn't in here pitching and bitching along with some of these unfortunate creatures. You might not believe that, but one guy here has only one eye. The other day, in the excitement of "falling out" when the sergeant screamed, the poor guy didn't have time to put in his glass eye and so went through the morning with one eye. He's not the exception. There are some awful specimens here, all preparing to do their share. I know that sounds like sour grapes, but today, somehow, I just can't help it. As I told you, the basic training is full steam ahead, and endless drilling and falling in and out has left me limp. Last night, torn by the desire to write to you, I had to forgo that daily refresher, to write another column for the camp paper. Now that I've been caught up in that sort of thing again, I can't let go, despite what I said in the letter preceding this one. There is still a ray of hope and I cling to the hope that something will come of it, although I know that soon I'll have to make a choice of the kind of hospital work I want to do. Let me make it clear. People keep asking me what I'm doing in a hospital. The answer is: nothing. I won't see the inside of the hospital until I learn all the basic military "musts." After that, upon being put through another interview, our potentialities as hospital assistants are determined in various ways. Obviously, the truck drivers, bakers, gasoline station attendants, etc., who are here will find their level in the Medical Corps in similar work. Ambulances have to be serviced and driven, men have to be fed, cooks and bakers have to prepare the food. You see, the Medical Corps isn't composed only of doctors and assistants. We are the service force for the medical unit, and since, by Geneva Agreement, medical soldiers carry no arms and do no fighting, our efforts are directed in behalf of those men who go into combat. We will see at firsthand many of the evacuated wounded when we start working in the hospital, but even now we see many of the less serious cases at the Post Exchange. It's not a pleasant sight, Angel, believe me. It makes you angry and anxious to get in and help.

Well, by now I must have completely spoiled the little pleasure you may have garnered from the generosity and attentiveness of our friends, but I guess most soldiers feel as I do. We talk big, but to see us standing around town looking like a bunch of whipped dogs isn't conducive to pleasure. I'm sorry, Honey. I'll stop now with the deep purple. Your letter and the pictures of Love Lettuce alone sustain me in my deep longing for both of you. Goodnight, Angel. Daddy

March 1, 1944

We had a written exam today and I know I would have done better if I had found time to do a little before-bedtime studying. I can't afford to let this happen again. Honey, don't be offended. Uncle Sam has been very generous. The first month's allotment, apparently, has been allowed us as an added bonus. I enclose $20, for which I have no other use. I had intended getting a bond for the baby, but perhaps it might be better to use it for her immediate needs, such as diaper service etc.

Enough about money. Here's a little something to laugh about. This being Saturday night, a lot of the boys were preparing to go to town, but it seems the corporal forgot to turn in the list of names for passes. Consequently, the passes weren't issued, so we had a party right in our barracks. Ruth's [Esther's sister] box of goodies, far more than I can possibly conceal in my small locker, arrived this afternoon. The box contained some perishables, which were already threatening to decompose, so I set them all out on a table, another guy stuck up a sign: "USO party, help yourself," and we all "fressed" [Yiddish for "stuffed oneself"]. Of course, I've kept for my own consumption most of the delicacies contained in the box, and I sent Ruth a telegram thanking her.

The most beautiful thing I have seen in a long time was "Retreat" yesterday (Friday). While we rookies did not participate, we all dressed and stood on a knoll overlooking the parade ground. The national anthem brought us to attention and a smart salute, and to me, tear-dimmed eyes and a whispered prayer for you and our darling. How I wished you could stand alongside me and witness the simple, yet profound respect paid to the flag and all it stands for. Along with the men, the Nurses Corps paraded too. They are brave women who are prepared to face anything. You should see them march! They are all women with a purpose, the dirty jobs notwithstanding. Honey, this must end somewhere, so good night, My Love.

Daddy

March 4, 1944, 7:40 p.m. – Western Union Telegram
Honey: Package and letters cheered me enormously. My love to you and Roberta.
Daddy

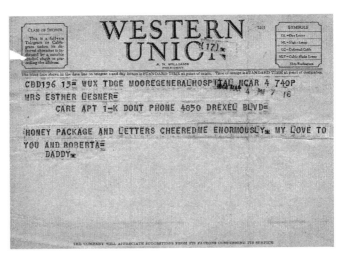

Basic Training: Phase 1

March 6, 1944

I got a perfectly beautiful bunny for Love Lettuce, but maybe I'll keep it until we meet on the 18th. Well, Cookie, I'm excited about your coming here though I'm bitter that I can see you for only a short time. Your plan to get here on a Saturday morning is wise, but unless I get some terrific break, I won't be able to get to Asheville before 6 or 6:30 p.m. on Saturday. Maybe some arrangement can be made for you to come to the post late Saturday afternoon, so that you can see it, since there will be no time on Sunday for such sightseeing. I hope to God I don't get guard duty on that weekend, but I'll ascertain that well in advance so there will be no slip up. I'll inquire about a hotel and make arrangements. A telegram that you are coming is imperative and can save me a good deal of trouble, so be sure to send it Thursday of the week you are coming. Oh, dear God, don't let anything spoil our plan. I suggest the Asheville Biltmore Hotel. It isn't bad. I'll inquire about this.

It has rained here all day and as a result we suffered through one lecture after another, ending the day on a happy note of murder in double time. We got our first lesson in the effectiveness of killing by judo, a form of Ju Jitsu. We will learn all about this in subsequent lectures and demonstrations. You see, the medical soldier carries no weapon, but there are other ways of overcoming your opponent, including eye gouging, neck breaking, foot smashing, testicle crushing and sundry other methods of maiming.

Goodnight, Cookie, I'm going to retire to my innerspring-less mattress early tonight.

A kiss for My Love, Daddy

March 7, 1944
Honey:

No letter from you today and my heart is filled with apprehension lest something is wrong. I am holding on tightly because I know a letter will come tomorrow, but it's a very terrible feeling that comes over one when the second mail call produces nothing.

Today was pleasant both as to program and weather, although we seem to have run into a cold spell. The classes are becoming increasingly interesting, but the amount of notes we take, to memorize, keep mounting and I'm going to have to work out an after duty schedule for myself so that I can get in at least an hour of studying. I wish I could convey to you just how full the day is for a rookie. It must be difficult for a civilian to understand how one doesn't even have a few minutes free sometime during the day when we're not shining shoes, fixing beds, sweeping, mopping, buttoning buttons, washing windows, coaling up stoves, spending precious moments in the chow line, laundry line, pay line, cleaning line, or standing in formations. Come to think of it, this is my "T.S." day. No letters and I didn't get my laundry bundle back and am left high and dry as far as my warm underpants go. Believe it or not, I've been wearing those nice warm woolies the Army issued, but even two pair are not sufficient if the laundry takes over a week to return the second pair.

I keep looking at the baby's pictures and each time I discover some new wonder in her angelic face. The expressions seem to change and she's always smiling at me. How I'd like to hold her. Dear God, make it soon.

A couple of jerks messed up the barracks this afternoon and tonight we had a bad hour, being restricted until everything was in top order again. But I guess the guys took the warning and will watch themselves or we'll all be "gigged" and possibly lose our passes temporarily. But these guys are too keen to get out and they'll watch their steps. We passed a fairly good personal inspection last Saturday and the commanding officer, just like in the movies, found the one item in the entire barracks that we didn't dust carefully, and that was the fire extinguisher. My buddy, Lucky Knox, who sleeps opposite me, turned red as the C.O. reached over his head to touch the extinguisher, and I, standing at rigid attention, facing Lucky, was fit to be tied watching the byplay from the corner of my eye. You see, when inspection is under way, you look straight ahead without seeing anything, and woe unto the guy who is caught following the C.O. with his eyes. The result is that immediately after he leaves, the guys all get together and find out what happened. It's a strange experience, being there, yet not seeing or hearing anything. Lucky, by the way, got "gigged" for talking in ranks when he should have been at attention, and the poor guy has special detail from 6 to 8 p.m. every night for a week. He just left to report to headquarters, since he's also restricted and has to report every hour until bed check which comes in 11 p.m. On his next hourly visit to headquarters he'll mail this for me. Lucky is a bright fellow who will be a big help in keeping me straight on Sulfathiozole, Sulfadiozine, etc., since he came out of a laboratory that specialized in sulfa drugs. I wrote a little story about him for the camp paper and he was so pleased and amazed at my ability to put words together, since he seems to have difficulty in writing to his girl in "high class" English, and he keeps asking me about words.

Honey, I'll need a few things which you can bring. I'll write you again about them and you can gather them without any trouble. More tomorrow, Angel. My faith in you is unshakable, Angel. My love to the folks. I called my dad last Saturday. He was very pleased.

Adieu. Daddy

March 8, 1944

Believe it or not, we had a real snowstorm this morning. The lovely South! Bah. You see, Honey, I'm not accumulating stuff just because I think I need it. This damn weather is unpredictable, and I've done some first-class freezing this week. We spent the day in the classroom and so were exposed only for a few minutes, although I was hoping to get out for some exercise, and get warmed up. We saw many movies—training films—and had a second class in judo, which I described to you. It's horrible in its intent, but I guess in such a world of violence it's well to know how to gouge out the other guy's eye before he gets yours. The classes in first aid, however, continue to be wholly absorbing. What a great man is Major Mering who lectures us on this subject.

Did you get the souvenir handkerchief, and did the money arrive safely? Let me know. I got a letter from Ruth. She's a genuine friend and I'll always remember her generosity in sending me the huge box of goodies. We're having a great time with it, eating in barracks whenever we're too tired to dress for supper. Yes, dear, that's another pleasant task a soldier has to occupy him between "dismissed" and the chow call. Getting completely changed into O.D.s after a day of tramping and hurrying isn't to anyone's liking around here, but no dress, no chow. So sometimes we eat our own chow and love it.

Honey, I have to make out my laundry list before lights out, so good night. My love, my heart, my soul to you and our daughter. Love to the folks. I'll answer your daddy's nice letter this week and give him my special love. "Cookie"

March 9, 1944
Honey:
All's well. I had a very pleasant day learning about such interesting things as mustard gas, chloropicrin, Lewisite, chlorine, and taking a wee sample sniff of each. Judo becomes more cruel and I shall decline the honor of becoming an expert if I can, but the medic's lectures are engrossing. You'll have to listen to me when I return because I'll be practically a doctor. Practically everything we learn is useful in civilian life. How to stem the flow of blood, treat a burn, etc., are indeed useful lessons. I shall make arrangements for us in town this weekend and shall send you a night letter with explicit instructions about the same. I hope it warms up here, or I'll have to loan you some GI long-ees. That's all for tonight, My Love.

A juicy kiss for Love Lettuce. Daddy

March 10, 1944
Darling:
No letter from you today so I feel a little lost, but tomorrow no doubt will bring two letters, or one at least. That's the way I've been getting them recently. The post office plays games with our mail. I am going to town Sunday and make a reservation for us at the Asheville Biltmore Hotel, and unless you hear from me to the contrary, you will proceed there from the station and occupy the room that will be in your name. Honey, I think we have an extra copy of our marriage license in the desk portfolio. Bring it along as we might need it. Some of the hotels take this precaution, the boys tell me, which is a good thing. It sounds

silly, I know, but with soldiers all over the place, I guess the businessmen want to protect themselves. I'll wire you as I promised, and don't you forget to send me a wire. Make it Wednesday, because Thursday we must turn in the names of those wishing weekend passes.

I'm sorry I can't leave camp before 5 p.m. according to a strict rule here, but I'll try my powers of persuasion on the noncoms as soon as I get your telegram. I might be able to whittle it down to 1 p.m. However, I want you to go to the Hotel, get some rest, and I'll come as quickly as I can. The camp is a half hour ride by bus from Asheville. If it's possible, you might be able to take a bus about 3 p.m. and come to the camp so you can see it. In that case you will go to the Red Cross building to which you will be directed by the M. P. at the gate, and the Red Cross will send for me, since I don't think you'll be permitted near our area. With a little fast talking on your part, you can possibly get me out before 5 p.m. It has been done. The Red Cross will do anything. My plea to the sergeant will be that I have some important business to turn over to you, relative to my "contract" with *Music News*, and must have a little extra time to give you full instruction on how to proceed with the series of articles I'm "contracted" to write for the magazine. I shall tell him that you are undertaking the job. That ought to hold water, I guess. Well, we'll have a glorious Sunday together. I just hope the weather is right.

Today it warmed up considerably and it looks like it will hold for a while. If it isn't too much, I'd like you to bring my accordion with you. You don't know how much I miss some form of music, of which there is absolutely none here. I could have great fun with the accordion and really learn to play it. Bring the instruction book with it. I also want: one pair pajama bottoms, two top pieces, slippers—size 7, wooden clogs for the shower room. I've changed my mind about the bathrobe. It's much too bulky and I'd have a hell of a time finding room for it. The pajamas will be just as good. Send some metal polish and an old toothbrush for cleaning buttons and some of my underwear that isn't yet reduced to a dust cloth. That's all, I guess. Oh yes, a small scissors would be appreciated.

The important thing to remember is for you to go to the Hotel and rest. I'll try and phone you there at lunchtime and tell you what's what. So don't get excited and nervous. The Red Cross in Asheville will answer any questions if you are uncertain about anything. The buses to Moore General Hospital run at frequent intervals and are boarded at the main bus terminal. At any rate, you can always call Moore General Hospital, ask for the Detachment Headquarters of the 130th General Hospital, and explain who you are. I'm sure all will go right and I'll try to phone the Hotel. If that doesn't work, I'll arrive as soon after 5:00 as it's possible. I'll keep the baby's doll until you get here. I want you to take it home to her. It's the cutest thing I've ever seen and I can just see her gurgling at it. Golly, if I could hug her, I'd be a new person.

Basic Training: Phase 1

We learned today that no three-day passes are possible until basic is over. I'll tell you in detail about it next Saturday.

Love to all. Your Daddy

March 12, 1944
Darling:

I'm sneaking this while an impossible lecture is under way. Here are final instructions. Go to the Asheville Biltmore Hotel, where I made a reservation in my name. Be sure you go to the Asheville Biltmore, as there is a hotel also known as the Asheville. Ours is the Biltmore! When you register notify the operator of your presence so I can call you. These Southern operators react slowly. Honey, we're going to a formal dance Saturday night so bring your pretty blouse and long black skirt if possible. The weather is nice so I can't advise what else you'll need, but your fur coat isn't necessary.

Get me a pair of garters, any kind. If the accordion is too bulky, send it by express. I think that will be better. Don't forget metal polish and a small wire brush if you can find one. Buttons have to sparkle for next inspection. I'm very hungry and very bored with the lecture. Goodbye, My Love, until Saturday. Love to Love Lettuce, Daddy

March 15, 1944—Telegram to Sam from Esther:
ARRIVING ASHEVILLE 9:40 AM MARCH 18ᵀᴴ CAROLINA SPECIAL LOVE ESTHER

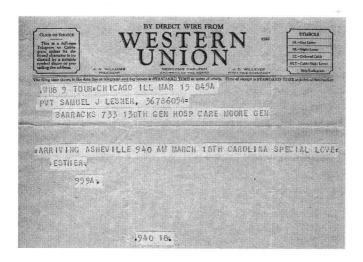

March 21, 1944—In class
Sweet Angel:

    I couldn't get off a letter to you yesterday as I had hoped because I found myself confronted with the task of writing a column, and Hitler should want to live as much as I wanted to write a column, and this war would be practically all over and I could come home to my Angel and Cherub. However, I have received so much fine comment on the column that I couldn't let [Jack] Garber down. After a terrible day of utter loneliness for you, lights out was a welcome release and I was asleep by 10 p.m. It has turned cold again and your love embraces me in the stitches of the sweater and I'm very snug. There is very little that is new at this time, Angel. The classes proceed with varying degrees of interest or boredom, and the endless marching continues.

    At the moment, I dread the thought of your giving up the apartment, but I can't go on without seeing you and the baby, so I guess we have no choice. If I remain here, you will come live here for a while. I wouldn't say anything to Carl, the janitor, or the renting agent at this time, since you are free to leave the apartment whenever you deem it necessary. There is always the possibility that I can get home for a few days after basic and I want to spend them with you in our own home. At any rate, the next three or four weeks will settle the whole problem for us. Be brave, Angel. I love you more than I can say. The lecturer just said we have a quiz on gases tomorrow, a subject on which I am not very well versed, so I'm in for a study period tonight. Goodbye, Angel

March 22, 1944—At ease
Sweet Angel:

    Having just finished supper, after a grueling six-mile hike, I can think of no greater delight than to write you, albeit briefly. It seems my army life has as many complications as the worst days of my civilian activities. I guess I'm what is known as a joiner. I get involved in so many things. In less than an hour I have to be at choir practice and then rush back and cram for a tough exam on chemical warfare tomorrow. We also face a four-hour hike tomorrow night—7 to 11 p.m. Last night I wanted very much to augment my classroom note with a more intelligent letter but I received a memo from Major Mering to be present at a band rehearsal. One doesn't ignore such memos as they are in the nature of an order. Besides, it won't hurt to stay on the right side with the major. Angel, don't forget to send the binoculars, and the still missing accordion is becoming a bit of strategy on my part. I'm afraid I talked myself right into that one, and now I must bluff my way through, so you see I had better produce an accordion pretty soon. As I told you, I'm to be the orchestra leader or something, and won't be expected to play too much. Just stand up and sing a chorus or two, just like a real glamour boy. At present, however, our big problem is to get the sax, trumpet and cornet to play in harmony, which seems to be a major undertaking at the moment.

Darling, I'm convinced that I must do anything to get classified finally as "Special Service." I can't see myself being a bedpan commando, a stretcher bearer, or a canker sore mechanic. I'm sure Special Service will grow increasingly more important in the Medical Corps as we plunge into the bloody mess of making human beings again of the shredded combatants.

Enough now, Angel. I have two more short letters to get off in the next half-hour. My love, My Love, I miss you. Say hello to all and sundry kith and kin. Sweetheart, I want the small recorder very, very much. It will be ideal for my orchestra.

GI Daddy

March 23, 1944
Sweet Angel:

Your nice long letter just received and while I agree to all that you plan to do, I'm terrified lest you build your hopes too high and then meet disappointment. As I told you, no one here knows the right answer, and those that possibly might guess it aren't saying anything. In other words, whether our basic is for six or sixteen weeks no one seems to know. We are in our fourth week now, and if they carry out their plan, we will be interviewed about the middle of April. The findings then no doubt will determine what's to happen to most of us. Some will possibly be sent to other hospitals for their specialist training, and still others will stay here. That uncertainty is awful to live through. I have no special desires in the field of hospital work and still have no idea what to ask for. There is no special service as such in the organization of a General Hospital, so there is the possibility that I might go to a Name General Hospital which would be the greatest break in the world since it would mean permanent location in this country. However, I suspect that the men here want me as something of an organizer in matters musical. However, I must also take some specialized training in emergency medical treatment, which I can get at this hospital, I suppose. You see, I'm going around and around and coming out nowhere. Angel, I'm merely trying to prepare you for a possible disappointment. I am going to town Saturday and will call the lady who spoke to us; also Mrs. Weiss who offered to help.

Once you are free, and if I can find a suitable place, you can come for whatever time is allotted to us. I'm still completely in the dark about the status of family men as regards passes, after the six weeks, since, technically, we are Basics until we finish the specialist training too. That's the main crimp in our plans. Darling, please note this point. So far we have heard only rumors on the point, and nothing official. That's why I have urged you to be not too hasty in breaking up [the apartment] since it will mean living with your mother for possibly two months or more. If I can see you only on weekends, it would be better for you to stay put until this can be remedied. I know you'll be terribly disappointed at reading this, but until I know exactly what's what, I beg you to be patient. None of the boys have been successful in obtaining more than a weekend pass, and if they do get out during the week, they get only a Saturday or Sunday pass. You will need help with the baby as she grows older, and if I'm not with you in the evenings to help, I don't think you will be very happy with such an arrangement. Yet I wouldn't have you come without the baby.

The April moving is OK, Honey, if you think you can stand the possible "wait" until we can be together on something like a family basis. I agree that saving money is wise in such a time. God willing, we'll find an apartment as lovely as the one we are leaving when the time comes. I've taken such great pride in our home and possessions, that taking it apart threatens to leave a wound that only you and Love Lettuce can heal. Darling, this will leave you as uncertain as before, but take the course you have decided upon and be brave. I am sure we will soon solve our problem. We are leaving on a night hike in a few minutes so I close with all my love. Tomorrow, My Angel, I'll write again.

Daddy

March 24, 1944 - Telegram to Sam from Esther:
HAVE PULLMAN TICKET FOR MARCH 31ST ARRIVING ASHEVILLE WITH ROBERTA 9:40 APRIL 1ST CALL ME SATURDAY NIGHT REGARDING SAME EXPLANATORY LETTER ON WAY LOVE ESTHER

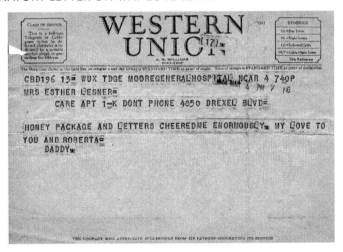

[Editors' note: On Saturday, March 25th, they spoke on the phone. Esther's trip was postponed as noted in both of their letters written March 26th.]

March 26, 1944—"Sitting in the Sun"
My Darling:

I hardly know how to tell you how "wrong" I feel about spoiling your Sunday with the disappointing news that you must delay coming here for a little while yet.

Here I sit in the sun, in only a pair of shorts, enjoying the surprising calm that overtakes this place on Sunday. The whole day has been magnificent and had fate been a little kinder, you would be sitting here with me. Honey, don't think I didn't try to make some arrangement for your arrival. Yesterday I went to Asheville, talked to several people and even contacted a kind, buxom lady who seems to be the local boss of Travelers' Aid. She was most efficient, and promised to obtain a room for you and the baby. That's just the point. A room that's in some moth-eaten boarding house is not for you nor the baby. Honey, the excitement of your coming for a moment blinded us to the fact that the baby would become a real problem for you under any boarding house arrangement. I know your capacity for enduring where I'm concerned, but what do you suppose would happen to me as I struggle through the increasingly difficult days of training while you are confronted with endless adjustments made necessary to take care of the baby's needs? Furthermore, I have no assurance as yet that I will be granted a daily pass, and assuming that I get one, I'd see practically nothing of the baby under her present schedule. I would have to leave camp by 5:30 p.m. to catch a bus, and leave you again about 5 a.m. in order to get back to camp for 6 a.m. reveille.

No, Darling, this isn't for us. Please don't think that I have decided to hold you off indefinitely. You know how I feel and how I choke up at the sound of your voice. I promise you that if it's my good fortune to stay here, and some suitable place can be found for you and Roberta, you shall take the first train possible. This is a wonderful place and the baby will thrive here. The evenings are cool and the days glorious. What I hope to do is get us a place either in the hills, or in some private home. Keep this in mind, Honey.

In the meantime, proceed as we planned. Set up some sort of "housekeeping on a small-scale" at your mother's, and you will feel more secure and certainly more rested when the time comes to join me. Certainly, I shall feel better too. We acted impulsively and hastily but fortunately not without second thought. Undoubtedly, without proper facilities to look after Roberta, you would grow nervous and irritable and we would both suffer. If the arrangement with Sergeant Katz is to our mutual benefit, I shall take immediate steps to set up a household for us. You know that this too must be carefully planned.

Be brave and sweet, Angel, and don't despair. Remind me to tell you that you looked very lovely the last time I saw you, the next time I see you.

Goodnight, My Angel, Daddy

[Editors' note: A portion of Esther's letter follows.]

Sunday March 26, 1944, 7:00 p.m.
My Angel:

Several hours have passed since our hurried and harried conversation—enough time almost for me to have regained my composure and rationality.

Darling, while I am unspeakably disappointed over not seeing you next week, I am greatly relieved by your decision and much more comfortable. My great anxiety to be near you at least and to have you see our terrific baby overcame all apparent obstacles to our precipitous trip to Asheville. However, I must admit I did have misgivings about it too, and under the very uncertain circumstances I was frightened. I kept hoping against hope though that things would work out, as they always have somehow and my burning desire to be near you as soon as possible all but blinded me to reality. I fully agree with your final decision, Precious, and would certainly abide by any decision you might make, whether I agreed or not for the moment. I fully appreciate that you are always sane and thoughtful and much less given to the impulse of an emotion than I. That's why I do nothing without consulting you. That's <u>one</u> of the <u>myriad</u> reasons I need you so desperately.

Needless to say, I am terribly let down now that there is no longer fuel for the excitement generated in me by the prospect of seeing you so soon. That excitement was sufficient to submerge all the anxiety and apprehensions attendant upon my coming down as soon as next week. But, you know, Darling, eventually I do see the light in most instances requiring thought, and I fully realize that all of us will be much better off by simply postponing the move. Were I alone, there would be no problem, for I could endure anything which would bring me closer to you. However, the baby can make no compromises. She can't do without sterilized bottles, diapers, a bed, and a buggy as the barest essentials, all of which imply a stove, hot running water and an address. Without these things for our doll face, I would surely be desperate— even though content myself to sit and wait for you all week. I'm prepared to make great sacrifices toward that end, darling, so please don't be too fussy on my behalf when looking for quarters for us. Just so I have the bare essentials listed above, and just so the place is clean and not too sordid, I'll make it do if it means being near and with you.

March 29, 1944
Darling:

I'm sneaking this one in while Sergeant Pie-face drones on and on. The subject is scouting. I just asked a question, just to keep them thinking that I'm interested in scouting! I got a dumb, evasive answer. By the time you receive this, you will undoubtedly have decided that I either deserted you or got shipped, neither of which can happen. We are being classified this week and by the end of the week I shall know exactly where I stand. I feel sure I will have good news for you, Darling.

This has been a hectic week for me, what with band, choir and column duties, and I spoke up and told the chaplain that I couldn't be expected to do so much on my free time. I put it plainly to him and asked him what I'm expected to tell the interviewing officers, since there is no such thing as Special Service in this type of hospital, although they do carry a Special Service officer. In the meantime, I delayed turning in my column so as to force the issue and, Darling, I won a real victory. Captain Fiorvanti, of the S.P.U. [Stability Police Unit], wanted to know where my stuff was and ordered the paper held up to give me an opportunity to write it. Darling, it has caused considerable comment, even to Col. Lesher, who kidded me during inspection recently. Naturally all these comments fly over the grapevine and speculation about Basic Lesner is lively. I don't think I'm overestimating this business. After all, being seen riding around in a staff car with Major Mering isn't bad either. This is a small, closely knit outfit and all these things are noticed. Honey, I tried to impress upon you the importance of my getting the binoculars. Angel, in the Army such small things weigh heavily in one's favor. Please don't deny me this opportunity to help myself. I know it's a bother, but Honey it's worth the effort!

I got the accordion in good order. I was called upon suddenly to play a small, portable organ for chapel services yesterday and I think I acquitted myself. This may also become a regular function for me as the Sergeant who has been playing is kept very busy in the hospital.

I had thought of asking for surgery technician but on second thought I'll be better off to get myself assigned to Personnel as a clerk and combine it with the Special Service tasks they have heaped upon me. If this works out, I'll be here for months and possibly permanently. That's what we want, Angel, isn't it?

We have a hike this afternoon, a four-hour night operation tomorrow, and in the next week or two an overnight bivouac. I hope it's dry. At the moment, it's pouring and my arthritis is misbehaving but not to the point of making me blue as it sometimes does. I hope the terrible moving job didn't get you down. I don't envy you the job. Soon, Angel, I shall know what's what and you can come here for a stay. It would be wonderful if enough gas could be obtained to drive down here. It would simplify matters so much. Is there any such possibility? Or is the car kaput as usual? I'll write again tonight, Angel, and forgive me for neglecting you for two days. I'm seldom finished before lights out these nights.

All my love. How's my cherub? Love to all.

March 30, 1944, 6:15 p.m.
Sweetheart:

Here we sit burdened down with gas mask, pistol belt from which are suspended first-aid kit and canteen, field pack which includes tent, tent pole, pegs, rope and a rain coat, and in a few minutes we'll put on the tin hats and move out to the drill field to play soldiers. I feel exactly like that clown in the Empire Room [fancy nightclub in the Palmer House Hotel, Chicago], with all this stuff suspended from my body. Of course, preliminary to starting out, we have a hell of a lot of fun getting ready, but by 11 p.m. tonight we'll be dragging our behinds plenty. The Army has a sound reason for everything, and while this seems goofy, actually it's excellent training.

Now for some news. Well, I know at last what the Army expects of me. I'm to be a clerk. What kind, I don't know, but clerk I am. Confidentially, I've been told that this is an excellent opportunity for me since hospital work isn't as glamorous as it sounds. For a moment, I had entertained the idea of asking for surgical technician, but I've heard that since the hospital is well staffed, I'd probably spend most of the time carrying bedpans or some such tasks. I still like the medical phase of our training best but there are so many here better prepared to enter the hospital jobs proper that I'd probably be outclassed even if I got a crack at it. Don't be worried, Honey. I stay right here and the best news I can give you is that my clerk's rating, which will lead to a stripe, is a mere formality. Major Mering is all for me and told me plainly that he knows what he's doing by classifying me as such. He is the interviewing and classification officer, too. He had a twinkle in his eye and it seems to be common knowledge already than I am headed for Personnel and Special Service. I'll have to work hard but it will be worth it. I'm up to my ears in music projects already and if I get a good spot in the administrative setup I'll be well off. Here's what the major said: "Lesner, if I put you in the hospital, I have to leave you there. As a clerk, I am the boss and can put you where I wish." That's all I wanted to hear. I shall take up my pursuit of living quarters now that I know what's what, but don't be impatient.

– Interruption –We have just returned from the night operations and it was very realistic and exciting. Of course, they didn't use gas, but a harmless screening smoke, but it was like the real thing. Boy, that's drama and it gets you. You hit the ground hard and fast and don't look for a soft spot. It's good training but leaves you quite breathless. I guess I'm becoming quite a rugged individual and I admit that I like the rough and tumble phase of the Army although I shy away from judo and such. More tomorrow, Angel. They're hollering for lights out and I'm the guy who turns them out, as the switch is over my bed. Goodnight, Angel. 11:00 p.m. Boy am I tired. Kiss my cherub.

XXX, Daddy

April 2, 1944
Honey:

Well, we had a "little party" in Barracks 733, which will probably bring punishment upon us all. There are always a couple of fools who can't control themselves and the result was that Lucky Knox lost a beautiful front tooth and sustained a smashed lip, while the guy who bit him broke his hand. Poor Lucky, what an awful thing to lose a front tooth! Don't worry about me, though, Angel. I stay out of these quarrels and as much as possible out of the barracks. Last night I practiced on the organ until 10:15 p.m., so you see I have little time for barracks fights. We have some swell guys here, too, and I naturally gravitate towards them.

There is a rumor floating around that the musicians eventually will live in a separate barracks. I hope there's some truth to it. What an ideal arrangement that would be. Honey, hold on to your seat. Your daddy is really getting into the groove. I am the pianist of the orchestra, and you should see me banging the keyboard. It just shows you can do it if you have to. I'm not too bad, but I'm worried about how the hell I'm going to coax any boogie-woogie out of my classical hands. I haven't the faintest notion how to begin even. Time will take care of that, however. The boys will have to dance to slow and moderate tempi until Private Lesner gets into the jive groove. Can you appreciate my situation and poetic justice of same? After getting my ears beaten off by listening to the Hotel Sherman's [nightclub in Chicago] jive and jam murderers, I get into the army and prepare to dish it out now for a change. Believe me, I'll torture them plenty with my hasty chord constructions.

Travelers' Aid called me to tell me they found a room in a boarding house near the bus station. 'It's clean but not fancy,' said the lady. I know what this means and I won't permit you to move the baby into a boarding house room, no matter how much I want both of you here. I shall accept the generous invitation of the Jewish citizens for the Passover, and at that time I'll try to make some arrangement for us. Be patient, Angel, we have so much to be thankful for.

Here is a new GI picture of your daddy.

Kiss my cherub a big luscious kiss. Her daddy is very glad he married up with her mama. April 6 [their third anniversary] should be a beautiful day!

My love to all.

April 6, 1944, 2:50 p.m.
Angel:

By a stroke of good fortune I happen to be free this afternoon while the other Basics are pounding off their feet on a road march, carrying full field pack. I had a dental survey appointment at 1 p.m. and fortunately the clinic didn't start functioning until almost 2 p.m., the scheduled hour for the three-hour hike. Consequently, I arrived back in barracks after the outfit left. Boy, what a relief.

Tuesday night we climbed a mountain and I'm still weak from that one. That was the night operation I told you about over the phone. I am beginning to be alarmed at the little time left me for letter writing, and a daily letter to you has become almost impossible, unless I steal time in class. But this week it is most important for me to be on the alert in class. We have a very important training inspection Saturday and I'm still shaking in my boots. There is absolutely no time to study or go over notes and how the hell they expect us to learn everything is beyond me. In demolitions, of all things, I got 93 and 100 in two written tests. I also fared very well in other tests, but unless I can find some time to really dig in, I'll suffer in the anatomy and medical tests, and those are my favorite subjects. Tonight, for instance, I have a radio broadcast rehearsal at 6, performance at 8, and many things to look after in barracks. However, I won't have to kill myself tonight, since I'm not on the hike.

We were granted a pass from Friday noon until Monday morning for the Passover and I was sorely tempted to have you come down, but the same situation prevails about living quarters and I know you would want to bring the baby, so I have passed up the whole thing. Passover without my own means nothing to me. I've turned down the invitation for the Friday Seder and will go to the Jewish Center on Saturday instead. Furthermore, I'm desperately in need of a rest and Sunday in camp is a bit of heaven. Believe me, Honey, I made an effort to get home but it was no go. The passes are limited to fifty miles and my future here is too promising for me to get into difficulties now. A Basic has no leg to stand on when he gets messed up. Jack Garber went home on a three-day pass, but Jack is in a position to obtain this privilege. I hope he called you. He really is a good friend to me, although I suspect he wishes I wasn't so painstaking with my column.

Well, Angel, the best information I can get is that I am classified as class 3, whatever that is, and unless some law is passed about over age, I'm afraid I am available for overseas duty. I've had a long talk with Chaplain Boyer who is a sweet, helpful person, and he told me that the reviewing board had me slated for a chief clerkship which is very, very good. However, he urged me to make every effort to get transferred if I can, since he frankly states that I'm in the wrong outfit and argues that I should be doing public relations. He is a friend and will help at this end if some action can be started at home. Darling, I'm in no position to do or say much since somebody along the line thinks that I got a terrific break by being assigned to the medics, but I feel sure that your mother can untangle it if anybody can. I'm quite willing to be a PFC [Private First Class] at home rather than a sergeant in India or some such place. Don't be alarmed, Angel, our going to India isn't imminent and is only a speculation on the part of the chaplain. I pinned him down to a statement on furlough regardless of what may happen to the 130th and he assured me that our fifteen-day furlough will be granted unless a major catastrophe occurs to our armies in Europe, and that, to hear the officers, is remote. They are most optimistic about the end of the European phase very, very soon.

April 6, 1944 – HONEY CHIEF CLERKSHIP IN VIEW FOR ME. URGENT. HOWEVER EFFORTS IN MY BEHALF CONTINUE/ INFORMATION REQUESTED FOLLOWING. CONTRACT APRIL 6 1941 [their wedding vows] CONTINUES IN FORCE- DADDY

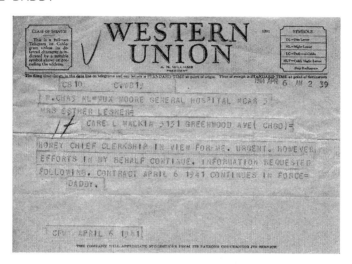

This week, the sixth of our preliminary training, has been a bitch so far, and more to come. I believe that I have made an excellent impression here on all concerned, and this is even more important than high grades, and for that reason the majors may not want to release me without a struggle. I'm not even sure that I can be transferred from the Medical Corps to another, unless it's another hospital, and anything less than a numbered General Hospital would hasten me toward the war zone, so this phase must be carefully considered. It has been said that you can only go to the infantry from the medics, but I don't know whether that's official or not. However, if the public relations job you spoke of is related to the infantry, it still would be better being home than here. I'm not very clear on this and your mother can find out about it. I simply cannot grasp the vast network that integrates all the various branches of the Army. We are not combat soldiers according to the book, but by golly all they talk about here is killing. I can't make much sense out of it.

Another thing: they might make a fuss here about the orchestra. That's a joke and shouldn't stop me from being transferred if such a thing is possible. The orchestra, as far as I can see, has no official standing, and if and when we go over, they'll probably pick up professional bandsmen as well as the new instruments we're promised when we reach a port of embarkation. I'm not kidding myself. I'm merely humoring the major. I'm about as much a dance band maestro as Roberta is, and at that she'd be better at it than I am. I love music but it's grotesque for me to be playing games when I can really do something worthwhile. However, Angel, it's my "ace in the hole." If it's no go on public relations, I'd rather make music on the typewriter as a clerk, and on the piano as a soldier musician than smell the defecations of the poor devils who are less fortunate than I. The chaplain, who looked up the records for me, says other than the clerkship specific number and class 3 classification, he can discover no further symbols such as you described over the phone. Lieutenant Zitlin, public relations officer at Vaughan General Hospital in Hines, Illinois, could be of great help, Darling, and you are free to call him and ask him for advice. Please do this and you will see how much people try to help. He pleaded with his superior officer to get me for Vaughan, but the new ruling at making every soldier take basic prevented such action.

One thing is sure. We will get our specialist training here and that will make everything easier, since a man on detached service cannot be touched, meaning that if I went away to a school, I'd be stuck. Call Lieutenant Zitlin anyway. Get me his first name and official address. I want to write to him. I don't think I told you, but he drove out to Fort Sheridan while I was there to see me. At that time he told me where I was going and why I couldn't tie up with him. However, he seemed sincere when he told me on departing that he wouldn't forget me. Remember, Dear, all these men are ambitious to make a good showing. Their postwar plans are based on their current accomplishments, and if they can get capable underlings, they'll take action, Lieutenant Zitlin, included. I have so much printed proof of my ability and of my prestige. Surely these things should count now. I won't grieve if nothing comes of all this, honey, and you will join me soon, I promise you, but if I can come home to you and my cherub, anything the Army asks of me will not be difficult. My future is secure since I assure you that, God willing, I'll come out of the Army with a good record.

The weather here has been brutal; snow, bitter cold for three days. I wore two fatigue suits, a sweater, and my overcoat yesterday, but it promises to be fair and warm for Easter. My Darling, this is our [third] anniversary. May God grant that another one does not pass without you and Love Lettuce. What can I say? Perhaps to say simply that I love you is enough. Believe me that a waking moment does not pass without some thought of you and there'll be no calm in my heart until this is over and we can start anew. If I don't write every day, don't worry. I won't keep anything from you and hope you will do likewise. Whatever lies ahead has no terror for me as long as you stand by and guard our Angel. I believe the chaplain as a man of God and as far as it is humanly possible to determine, we are in no immediate danger of being shipped out. He cleared up for me many erroneous impressions I had and I feel calmer and more secure than I ever have since I went into service. He has promised to look out for a cottage for us, since he's in a position to do so, and with some luck we shall soon be watching the sunset together.

I have been bolstered enormously by a letter from Roy [brother also serving in the Amy]. I'm going to use it in part in my column, and then I'll send it to you. It's a treasure. He writes: "Everything that happened to me seems to have happened for the best even though at times I griped because I thought I wasn't getting a square deal. I was mad twenty months ago when my outfit went to Africa and I was left behind. What happened to those poor guys in Africa shouldn't happen to a dog. So you see, Sam, it's best to be patient and let Fate do what it will. I've always felt that nothing could happen to us and it's been proven to me many times out here. God has been watching over me and I'm sure He is looking out for the rest of the family as well. Sam, sometimes I think the people back home are worse off than we are. It must be awfully lonely back there. Your mention of the chocolate bar at Northwestern Station brought a lump to my throat until I remembered that we are not alone in this thing. Only one other thing before I close: whatever your job is, do it to the best of your ability although at times it looks as though it's all in vain. I was tempted to give up many times, but I didn't, and I'm sitting pretty right now."

That's our brother, Roy, talking, Darling! There is some good in war!

A bright Pesach to you all, Daddy

CHAPTER THREE

Basic Training: Phase 2—Clerk Training

April 9, 1944
Angel:
    We completed the first six weeks yesterday with flying colors, and tomorrow we start on the second phase. There is little that is new. I miss you and Love Lettuce to the point of distraction and will renew my efforts to rectify the situation. I had another sweet letter from Ruth. She's a peach, taking time to write me. My many friends, I guess, have given me up. I have had no word from any of them. I love only you. I must, else why do I sit here in camp while the rest of my outfit are carousing in Asheville. If Love Lettuce is sleeping when you receive this, go to her crib and touch a kiss to her rosebud mouth for me. If she is up, hug her real hard and I'll know the moment you do it. Dear God, how grateful I am for her.
    All my love, Angel. Daddy

April 10, 1944 – In class
Darling:
    Our technical training started this morning and while I sit here idle, as the interviewing goes on, I'll try to get this off in the second mail so that a whole day isn't lost.
    I filched this piece of paper. It's a sample of one of the tests we had last week.
    Our schedule, due to shortage of training equipment, including typewriters, is to be spread over a twelve-hour day. To my utter disgust we clerks have a class in touch typing every day this week from 6 to 8 p.m.
    One consolation, however, is that we get two hours off in the afternoon and I intend to spend mine sitting in the sun and thinking of you and the baby. The colonel again assured us that a furlough will be granted so we will have two weeks together this summer, when you shall have every minute with me. The chance of your coming here seems to be growing more remote. A cottage is prohibitive with our income and a room is really out of the question with the

Basic Training: Phase 2—Clerk Training

baby. Unless I find something decent and within our means, I'll have to steel myself for the ordeal of waiting to see our angel until furlough. Weekday passes again have been revoked and we have only the weekend privileges. What a life, without a wife! I'm disgusted! Darling, get me out of here!

Your Daddy Forever

---

1. Define a map:
2. The three (3) types of military maps are: 1. _____ 2. _____ 3. _____
3. The colors used on a military map are: 1. _____ 2. _____ 3. _____ 4. _____ 5. _____
4. Grid lines are shown in _____ on a map; water in _____; man made objects in _____. (Name colors)
5. Contour lines are used to: 1. give the distance between hills; 2. show ground form; 3. designate observation points for patrol leaders. (Circle one)
6. Show the conventional signs for the following:
   House: Church: School: Cemetery:
7. There are usually _____ types of North shown on a map. These are:
8. True North is measured to the magnetic north pole.   True   False
9. Name two (2) ways of determining direction in the field.
10. The military symbol for Co A, 145th Inf is:
11. A strategic map is drawn to a scale of 1:21, 120   1:63,360   1:250,000   (Circle answer)
12. Grid lines are usually spaced 2000 yards apart; 1000 yards apart; 750 yards apart. (Circle answer)
13. The color used to designate Enemy troops is _____. Friendly troops _____.
14. A wasted area is always shown in brown.   True   False
15. Contour lines "widely" spaced indicate a _____ slope.

April 11, 1944 – At ease
Darling:

It's 9:07 p.m., to be exact, and I've just come from the phone where I spent several minutes trying to convince a lady that I am not Col. Lesher but Pvt. Lesner. The things that happen to me! The operator got the names mixed and the detachment officer had me running to the phone, thinking all the time my precious was calling and dreading to hear what precipitated the call. Thank God it was a mistake!

Well, honey, the newest phase of our training is really something. Tonight I learned to type "RUG." and "Fur" by the touch system. What do they want from my life? I typed 385,000 words last year by the hunt and peck system and now

(Sweetheart: Imagine, I did this without looking! My goodness, what a way to win the war!)

> Sweetheart! Imagine, I did this without looking!
> My goodness, what a way to win the war!
> fur fur fur fur fur fur fur fur fur fur fur fur fur fur fur fur fur fur fur
> [many lines of "fur" and "rug" repeated]
> I can also top! type, Bunny, Buggs, jug, jugy - etc.
> Some stuff! I'll say.

I'm starting all over to learn how to type. OK. It will be well worth the effort. I can see now the advantage of doing this the right way.

You know my strange manner of remembering a phrase here or there and just where to find it. You have no idea how I miss my ready reference books in preparing my weekly column. These guys around here are appallingly ignorant about literature and I'm always stymied when I want to make some reference to a figure of literature or history. I shall get Kleenex tomorrow. [*Editors' note: While civilians at home were sending necessary supplies to soldiers, in turn, the soldiers obtained items such as Kleenex and cigarettes which were hard to obtain at home due to rationing.*] It poured so hard all evening I didn't go any further than the classroom and back to barracks. Two hours of touch typing has left me exhausted, and I didn't get my sun bath today because the sun didn't shine, and taking a nap in the madhouse is an impossibility. More tomorrow. Love to your mother and dad. I await the new photo of Love Lettuce. Please hurry it along.

Goodnight, Sweetheart. Daddy

April 13, 1944 – At ease
Sweetheart:

The usual pandemonium reigns in Barracks 733, but I'll attempt to write this short letter so that it will go out with the first mail. Your letters received and enjoyed tremendously. I go back to your letters to replenish my vitality, so an extra premium should be doubly effective.

You know I'm strictly *mishuge* [Yiddish for "crazy"], and it occurs to me that it would be just about time for you to discover that more happened than we thought when last you visited me, although I can see how that could be possible. However, it's just the coincidence of time and implication in your letter that set me off thinking back over the divine moments we spent together recently. How I'd really like to get busy on another Love Lettuce. Her little face haunts me and I can hear her voice. I'm going to call soon and you must keep her up and make her laugh. I'll call at 6 p.m. one of these days and that won't upset Boopsie's sleeping schedule. Darling, until you've been away from her any length of time will you know the feeling of a tiny hand clutching your heart. I feel it so certainly so constantly. It isn't an ache exactly, but a steady pulling. You will have a big job to keep me from thoroughly spoiling her. In my present state I'm absolutely unfit for fatherhood. I want only to build a little golden throne and sit her upon it. Angel, you'll have to be a wise queen mother to rule both her and your crazy consort.

I'm sending you Kleenex and "cigs" under separate cover. Kleenex is being rationed here, too, and we can buy only one small box at a time, so I'll start accumulating boxes of them send them periodically. I cannot bring myself to ration your cigarettes, although I know I'm contributing to your downfall, so smoke away and I hope you get ashes in your morning coffee. More tomorrow.

Love, Daddy

April 13, 1944 – At eye clinic, 2:00 p.m.
Sweetheart:

At 8 a.m. this morning I started to sit in this eye clinic where I am presumably to be fitted for glasses. At 11:45 a.m. I went to lunch and at 1:45 returned to my place on the clinic bench, along with a half-dozen other guys. Lunch was very good and my desire to sleep immediately after it almost overwhelmed me in the one o'clock class, from which I escaped into the sun at the crucial moment. The walk back to the clinic was made pleasant further by an ice cream. Now here I sit, scribbling as best I can with my knee for a writing surface, so don't think I'm drunk or in my dotage. My eyes have become slightly irritated from the bad light and extra work I've been doing, so I decided to get GI glasses. That is if they decide I need them. The major in charge of this department is fickle and may decide I don't need glasses. At any rate, I'll probably know in the next hour, or day, or week or so. In the army we all "hurry and wait" all day long.

I've drawn guard duty for tomorrow night (Friday) so I'll be free for the weekend, thank goodness! I'll do some intensive house or apartment searching. Our classes in army clerkship continue to be a positive negative as far as getting any useful information out of them. They serve only one purpose, and that is to keep us from going on road marches, etc., which isn't bad, although I've reached the stage where I relish some exercise. I continue to grow slimmer, apparently, for everything hangs on me and my face is acquiring that cadaverous look you admire so much. If we don't go into summer uniform very soon, I'll have to alter my O.D.s, and there isn't a tailor on the post. The night typing classes are a delightful challenge to habits of years standing, and I still get a kick out of learning to do something new. Why didn't you tell me touch typing is such fun? Now I can write my book, or get ready to write it. That's all that prevented me, not knowing the touch system. Band and choir practice have gone to hell temporarily while I make it fur, fun, jug, bunny, etc. all over sheets of paper. Our young sergeant is a good instructor and just loves to encourage us.

– Interruption –I just popped into the examination room and out again, and now I'm waiting some more. There is nothing new. I expect to take care of my correspondence this weekend. I only wish I got more of it from the gang. Mail call continues to be the daily wellspring of vitality for all of us. I have resolved to write to Roy every week so that he will have at least one weekly letter. How much it must mean to him! If you can continue to make me some of that delicious fudge, that's all I would like. Cake and such similar food stuffs are a burden since there is no storage space for big boxes except under the bed, and that doesn't appeal to me. I'll make one exception. Sometimes, if you can corner some little cheeses, tinfoil wrapped, I'd like to have them. They are an excellent substitute for army mess when the damn stuff starts coming out of my ears. Every now and then I pass up evening mess to get rid of the systemic poisons accumulated as a result of pork, pork, pork, wheat cakes, wheat cakes, and rice, rice, rice. I'm not complaining. The food is good if your constitution and temperament can stand it ad infinitum, but how I'd enjoy a glass of milk and some graham crackers occasionally. Milk is not on the menu, except in the morning with cereal. I eat the stuff fast to get a bowl of milk. The scrambled eggs, however—and they're not powdered egg—are an indictment of army cuisine. I've run out of paper.

Goodbye, my angel. Daddy

April 14, 1944 – At ease (momentarily)
Darling:
I have about half an hour to write this, then I step forth again to protect my buddies in arms while they sleep. In short, I'm ON GUARD this evening,

Basic Training: Phase 2—Clerk Training

a pleasant one for a change. I'm lucky in that respect since the weather has been rotten in this "land of sunshine," if you believe the Chamber of Commerce.

Your letter delighted me. Love Lettuce sitting on your lap while you read my letters is exactly the picture I had of you. What a joy she must be in her present state of well-being. May God grant her perpetual health and happiness. It makes it easier for me, knowing she is thriving so well. Of your exciting plans, [to drive to Asheville with Esther's mother], the one about the car, seems the most attractive to me at the moment. Your mother would be an angel in such an arrangement and one of you could accomplish in a few hours what it would take me weeks to do.

I believe I told you, that to add to my other disgust, we have a night class from 6 to 8 and it will continue for eight weeks. Good God, I'll become a touch typist while my wife and child pine away for their daddy! However, if you three come, I'll crawl to you at 8 p.m. at least five nights a week, and even continue to stay until the morning. The weekends go without saying. You could stay a few weeks and then go home via New York so Ruth could see the baby. I'm sure that if your mother is on hand, she'll find something approximating living quarters. But Darling, I just can't do this systematically as long as I'm tied down. You can be assured of a place for a night or two until something can be found. The baby is a problem, but coming without her would leave us both tortured with anguish at our fate. Damn it, will I ever get out of this basic hell?

The process of becoming a clerk is becoming irksome. You have no idea of how hopelessly enmeshed in bureaucracy has become our democratic government. Writing a military letter becomes a problem for a skilled draftsman. No ordinary person can hope to achieve the marginal spacing and precise structural patterns laid down by army regulations. Honey, they are mad! No wonder government employees shrivel up. No wonder they get ulcers and cancers. They're crazy, Darling. They're crazy. Me, with my temperament! I have to measure margins to a fraction of an inch and then dot the paper with countless commas, colons, Roman numerals, Greek numerals, alphabetical subheads, paragraph numerals, indentations, enclosures, etc. I haven't yet discovered where or what you write in the body of the letter. No doubt I'll get the hang of it eventually, but at what a cost? My long nights in the D.N. [*Daily News*] office were ecstatic joy in comparison!

Coming back to our hope for reunion, I wouldn't feel right in going to New York instead of Chicago just because I'd be a bit more comfortable. No, Darling, if I can get away, I'll come home. In a few moments the call to guard will resound, and I'll go into the night to think of my darling and the cherub she gave me.

Good night, Sweet Wife. Daddy

1944 Apr 15 PM 9 16
HONEY, HAVE RENTED IDEAL ROOM FOR YOU AND BABY STARTING NEXT SATURDAY CRIB NOT NEEDED IMMEDIATELY. WILL PHONE TONIGHT GIVING DETAILS. PLEASE GET READY. SAM

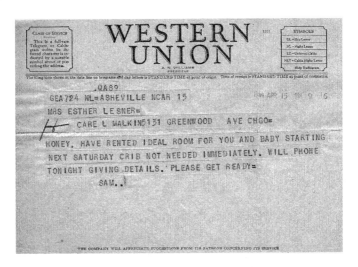

April 16, 1944, 6:30 p.m.—READ THIS FIRST
Sweetheart:

    I told you I'm getting goofier by the minute, but you'll have to put up with me because I think of you and your comfort constantly, so I've altered our plans slightly. Don't get scared, your coming here is planned, but instead of going to Mrs. Hatch's comfortable but uncertain accommodations, you and our angel are going to the Monte Vista Inn, a replica of Turkey Run which in our memory turns us back to happy days. But here's the great news. Monte Vista is only three miles from the hospital and can be reached within ten minutes, while going to Asheville would consume over an hour and make it impossible for me to see you during the week. Adding to our good fortune, the Monte Vista's kitchen is at your service as far as preparing the baby's food, and if you remember Turkey Run, you will likewise have your meals served you in the main dining room and quite likely the baby's food can be brought to the table so you can eat together. This, honey, is so much more satisfactory that I can't believe it's true. Further, Mrs. Phillips, the manager, has a small baby bed which will be placed in our room and when I stay over the extra charge is $.50, whereas Mrs. Hatch wanted $1 every time I stay. I gave Mrs. Hatch a $3 deposit which I think she'll return, but if she doesn't it will be worth thirty times $3 to see you every night and not have to kill myself in the process. Cars going back and forth always give a soldier a lift and I can be at the hotel in a few minutes after leaving camp. The hotel has

Basic Training: Phase 2—Clerk Training

a beautiful stretch of lawn in front, mountains in the rear, a swimming pool nearby. An A & P store is a stone's throw away. In short, everything one needs is at hand. The hotel is on the very edge of Black Mountain, a small but completely adequate town for our needs. My friend Sidney Cantor, a nice Jewish gentleman from Memphis, is also bringing his wife down here Saturday and she's coming to the Monte Vista. He describes her as tall, red haired, thin face. She'll be on the Carolina Special. Is that your train too? And any rate she'll be on the lookout for you. I'll move heaven and earth to meet you Saturday if you are arriving that day. Our reservation also is for Saturday. You'll have a private bath, what's more, and that in itself decided me to change plans. A baby requires this at least.

Now you must be wondering, "what's all this going to cost?" Honey, it's reasonable. Including all your meals, it's $22.50 a week, and considering all in all, that's very cheap. If you don't feel like eating some nights, it's deducted from your bill. (Bring your ration books.) I'm so much happier about this arrangement. So we won't save money this year. Having you so close at hand I can save a couple of bucks on transportation and in many other ways, for under the first plan, I'd be constantly trying to buy food, since knowing you, you would neglect to eat if you had to go out every time. This way that responsibility is removed. And they tell me the meals are excellent at the M.V. Another thing, there's an eight months old baby living at the hotel, the child of the proprietor's daughter, I believe, so they are happily disposed toward children. You will bring only such bed linens as are necessary for Roberta and of course will be responsible for laundering her things. All else is under regular hotel service. I'm sure you'll find it ideal, and don't worry about the money. If things were normal, we'd take a vacation anyhow. I know I can manage to spare $8 or $9 more if you are nearby. I have no reason to spend for anything, now that we are pretty well set. I'll need a few extra summer issue shirts, but will worry about that later.

Darling, this will be a wonderful summer if we'll let it be. The fact that you are actually coming here has completely turned me topsy-turvy with joy and my head is full of plans, some of which no doubt are the machinations of a madly romantic mind such as mine. I dread the thought of you having to face the task of keeping Roberta's feeding schedule up on the train. How this is to be managed, I don't know, but, after all, thousands of people in the same situation travel constantly, so there must be some arrangement for this even in wartime. I suggest you arm yourself with all the information you can get beforehand. Perhaps Travelers' Aid will advise you. They go to great lengths for servicemen and their families.

If you should find it expedient to leave on Friday, I'll arrange to have you met at the train if that is possible. I don't dare ask permission to do it myself. We shall see, however, when I get your telegram. Honey, please take note: I have no money on hand so please mail me $10 in a letter at once. I'll want to get a few things ready for you.

Wait till you see the surroundings! Roberta will see her first cow here. If it works out, sweetheart, we'll stay until my furlough comes up and then will all go home for Roberta's first birthday [September 15]. What an event that will be. Remember, sweetheart, limit yourself to bare essentials, concentrating on the baby's needs, and once you are set, anything we need can be sent to us. By the way, there's a beauty shop near the hotel, so if you want to get a hair curl I'll stay with the baby. Just like at home. You'll love this spot. We had planned to go to Turkey Run with our baby. Well, we'll do it sooner than we planned at Monte Vista.

I can already see myself the instant you hand me the baby! Now that you are coming, I can tell you what it has cost me in peace of mind since I saw the baby last. I didn't look into the bathing facilities in the house, but I am sure they are adequate. At any rate, I'll be sure to find a little baby bath or large bowl in the numerous antique shops here. For the moment, we'll improvise as best we can. It will be fun to see just how good we are providing for our child under difficult circumstances, and certainly, it will be an experience that we'll recall with amusement in the future. Let's face it bravely. We are so much better off than many others, and, at least if it becomes too difficult, we have good, generous parents ready to take up again for us.

I'll try to win some consideration to change in part my schedule for the mighty typing class, but I'm not too hopeful in that direction. It's just my luck that the Army hasn't gotten typewriters and I have to lay around here from 3 to 6 instead of getting through at 5. Saturday and Sunday we shall dine together early enough so that we can take the baby with us. Then we'll return and sit on the porch. It might be a good idea to have the portable radio sent. I'm sure there would be no objection. Some days we can hear the symphonies or spend a day in the park. Honey, don't forget a thermos bottle if you have one. It's the one thing we'll need constantly. Don't burden yourself with extra things. The rest I leave to you. Above all, don't worry and keep calm. I'm so excited and nervous, I better stop now. The address is enclosed. The rest is up to you, My Darling. A safe and easy journey for you is my prayer. Please notify me if there is a hitch so I can act accordingly.

Love, Daddy

P.S. Bring the camera and my sunglasses, if you can find them. All so my khaki bathing trunks!

April 18, 1944 – In class
Honey:

There's nothing doing at the moment. The instructor frankly admitted that he has nothing to say so we are just sitting around until lunchtime. Well, Angel,

Basic Training: Phase 2—Clerk Training

I hope you're going to get off for Asheville this week. I didn't realize at the time that you had so much dental work and that the baby was getting shots. The shots can be resumed here, and possibly free of charge, since servicemen's families are entitled to these things.

I'm so enthusiastic about the Monte Vista. A little later perhaps, if your mother is willing to come down, we can take a cabin if one is available. I had considered a cottage at first, but it comes out about the same, financially, and you have the extra work of cooking. You have a full-time job just looking after "cookie." I'll help you as much as I can with her laundry and things and I'm sure you won't find any obstacles to overcome. If necessary, we can even get a little electric stove, and if you don't feel like going down to the dining room, I'll pick up some delicious sandwiches at the Post Exchange and bring them along.

There's nothing new. I'm collecting Kleenex and chocolate bars for you, and I even had a box of Rice Krispies in my ration. We can have a lot of things sent to us from home. Needless to say, we'll not want for a snack. I hadn't thought about the baby's milk, but I'm sure it can be kept in the hotel's refrigerator. These people here are dumb but they are kind and considerate. You'll experience no difficulties, I'm sure. Praying to see you this weekend, I remain your Daddy (ever, ever loving).

[Editors' note: After this letter was written, Esther arrived with Roberta on Saturday, April 22 and stayed until the first week in June.]

Photos from the time Sam and Esther were together in Swannanoa and Asheville.

June 7, 1944—Somewhere in the Blue Ridge Bivouac Area

Darling, this is a picnic. A picnic with all the ramifications of a mass of men gone native. Tuesday morning broke warm and beautiful, and for a moment I regretted that you departed, but before 2 p.m. I thanked God you were gone. What a deluge. What a mess. No kidding, the canteen cup was a bottomless cup as the rain poured in while the coffee poured out.

Darling, please don't think I'm unhappy or miserable. This is too funny to leave a guy in bad spirits for long. The tent is fairly dry and the dampness is something I have been gradually accustomed to. Sleeping on the ground with just a blanket and newspaper between you and the earth is an experience I'll long remember. I have dedicated my next column to you, describing life in bivouac, and it will tell you more than I can at this moment, since I'm sneaking this during an outdoor class on rights and privileges of a soldier. We give a band concert here tonight and by playing at the officer's club Friday the band gets out of a brutal four-hour hike. That's a break at least.

Must be brief now, dear. Will try to write again later. Got your telegram and was grateful. Call my mother. I'll sneak her a letter today, too, I hope. It's fair and cool today—I hope!

Love to all. Kiss my Love Lettuce. Daddy

June 7, 1944
Darling:

I have a few moments of leisure and will take up where I left off. The day has continued warm and beautiful and I am so exhausted from all the sunning, swimming, hiking, that I'm dizzy. We just finished an hour of playing and may play again in a few minutes. Bivouac such as this is truly a picnic on a grand scale, and equally as tiring. The schedule frequently goes amiss, and no one seems to be bright enough to improvise so we spend hours just wandering back and forth. I'll not gild the lily. My bones ache aplenty from sleeping on the ground, but the time passes quickly and soon this shall be over.

I'm tenting with Manny and the confusion is something. You ought to try keeping house in a tent 6 x 4 and too low to even kneel in. Our mattress is gradually growing in thickness as we acquire dry leaves and newspapers, and speaking of newspapers, how do you like the news [about D-Day, June 6]? May God guide our boys to quick victory. News like that electrifies soldiers in camps everywhere. We get the radio broadcasts, too. If you had stayed, you could visit me in camp on Sunday, a rule they just passed. But I'm glad you are home safe and will be settled when I get there.

Angel, there is a rumor afoot that we might get out in time for the 7:00 train on Saturday [June 17th]. It's only a rumor but I'd like to be prepared, so send me $20 for a train ticket. Our bus fare will be refunded, but not in time to use it for the train. At any rate, if there is no truth to it, I'll bring it home again. Whether train or bus, I'll be in condition for the worst they can offer in way of transportation. Rugged, that's what I'll be.

If I don't write every day, don't be alarmed. I'm "bivouacky" from all this activity and there is still much to do to make the damn tent more comfortable. Details when I get home. Love to the folks. Beg them to forgive me for not writing. Gosh, I'm tired. —A kiss for you and one for our angel – Daddy xxx

June 8, 1944
Darling:
What a day! We put to actual practice all we've learned as medical soldiers, and set up a regular field hospital. It fell to my lot to be a patient, with a hand wound, and so I spent all of the afternoon lying in the woods and then the hospital, simulating a patient as others went through the process of admitting and disposing of patients. It was very interesting. Manny Levin was a psychiatric patient and what a show the boy put on! He had the officers in stitches and has been elected to repeat his performance for tomorrow's class. The kid has had some acting experience and is a natural.

The day was threatening, but now at 4:15 it is lovely and warm. Nothing much to do tonight so I'll go for a swim and then retire to my Spartan bed. God, is it hard! In all, it's pleasant, though. The food is surprisingly good even if served à la mess kit.

Nothing new otherwise. Please don't worry. It is ridiculous to think that we will be subjected to any great danger on the Infiltration Course if this is what they call tough. Really, I'm not rationalizing. Medical soldiers are not commandos. I'm certain Monday will be negotiated with little difficulty. If possible I'll wire you, although this seems a remote possibility. At any rate, don't worry. I'm well and happy in the anticipation of a holiday with you soon.

All my love, Sam

June 10, 1944
Darling! I've run out of writing paper and it's raining so I'm sticking under cover. The dance job last night was very successful and what's more important, we stayed in barracks instead of returning to camp. The hot shower and shave was grand. Now I'm back in my tent. We've done absolutely nothing today (Saturday) and tomorrow promises to be quiet, too. I guess we can't leave before midnight on the 17th after all, but I'll be on that bus, you can be sure.

I called my mother yesterday, knowing that you would understand. If I don't get a letter from you at six o'clock mail call I'll be desolate. Hope all is well at home. Have stockings for your mother. Would you like some, too? They have a much finer brand now, a 45 mesh or something. They look nice. How's Limpid Pools of Limpidity?

Until tomorrow, all my love. Sam

June 13, 1944
Honey:

I got to write fast as I'm taking a break while the saxophones tune up.

Came through the Infiltration Course safe and sound, though today every bone aches. Thank God no mother or wife has to witness the thing. It's ghastly, although not as dangerous as most guys like to make it out to be.

Did you like the "Open Letter to my Wife"? I followed it up with a P.S. which I'll mail to you. Honey, I'm coming by bus after all, but it seems we will be delayed 1 day since they don't want us to travel over the weekend. That's OK though, since it will give me two weekends at home. Will leave the same time, however and arrive in Chicago Tuesday morning.

More later. I'm called upon to make music.

Love to all, Darling. I dreamt the Cookie had a mouthful of teeth. What a bore this band has become. Daddy.

[*Editors' Note: Sam went to Chicago on furlough. His next letter was written July 3.*]

CHAPTER FOUR

Post Basic:
The Wait for Deployment

July 3, 1944 – 9:00 p.m.
Darling:
    While waiting to get my call through, I'll write you this brief note. The trip was tedious but otherwise uneventful. Most of the boys are back and are spreading rumors like mad, but the truth is that no one knows anything. Some of the Basics have been assigned to hospital jobs, but as yet my assignment has not been posted. I guess the next week or so will be one of fretful waiting and hoping, but whatever comes to pass you must have courage and unspeakable faith. I am blue to be away from you again, but I know it won't be for long. Surely this awful thing must come to a final and gigantic finis, and if there is any decency, any common sense in the working plan of our Government, married men won't be too long in reuniting with their families. All my love to you to sustain you in this, our second separation.
    My love to all. Daddy

July 5, 1944
Darling:
    I missed writing your daily letter yesterday so I'm trying to make up by getting this written at 7 a.m. I went to the movies in Asheville last night to see *Story of Dr. Wassell*, a splendid film, but not exactly a morale builder. Barracks is usually quiet as most of the boys now report for duty at the hospital at 7 a.m. I have no assignment yet and I ducked a latrine detail neatly yesterday. I hope I'm as lucky today. Don't be alarmed that I'm not assigned as yet. It's simply that there is nothing to do until we get someplace we can call our own.
    I had a peculiar experience yesterday. Awakened from an afternoon nap, I was told the C.O. wanted to see me at once. Well, you can imagine my excitement and nervousness. I hadn't committed any crimes, but I couldn't figure out what he could possibly want. Transfer, discharge, promotion? It turned out he wanted me to accompany him to Spencer Pines to find John Hunt's cottage. John's kid was sick and the C.O., believe it or not, was making a personal call to see how the kid was doing. The camp has been electrified by this extraordinary

conduct of the C.O. And naturally, since I was his "aide de camp" pro tem on the mission, much explaining was necessary to satisfy the guys. Who knows? Maybe I'll become the colonel's boy. That won't be bad. Well, he gave an otherwise dull day a much-needed lift, to say nothing of my own spirits.

My love and a prayer for your well-being and our little darling's. Daddy

July 5, 1944 – 8:00 p.m.
My Darling:

My recuperative powers are so remarkable, apparently, that my thumb is practically healed although the vast amount of bandage the dispensary saw fit to apply makes writing difficult. I guess that's out as a stopper on the overseas business, which, from the looks of things, is not too far off. Please, Angel, don't lose heart at reading this, but I promised I would conceal nothing from you. I have absolutely no fear. I have only a profound sorrow for the pain it is causing you. There is much to be said but it can only cause you greater anguish. The truth is no one knows and all is based on wild rumor. How cruel this sort of thing can be! No wonder the government strives to stamp out rumor mongers. I will undoubtedly regret having written this letter, but you must find courage to face it when it comes. Enough of this. Someday soon we will laugh at our fears as I relate to you and Angel Face my adventures. Please don't read between the lines and think that I'm leaving something unsaid. I swear on our holy love that I know nothing more and am concealing nothing. When the time comes, if it is possible, you shall know all that is permissible. I pray that we shall meet again perhaps in the East at that time.

I'm doing some extraordinary gold bricking in the meantime. By hanging around the Special Service office I am avoiding all sorts of unpleasant details. I think my luck will hold out until Jack Garber returns and takes over the paper which he left in my care. The trouble is, the typewriter was removed from right under me today for some obscure reason, and even if I got an inspiration for a column, I couldn't write it. Oh yes, while riding with the C.O. yesterday on that strange mission, he told me, apropos of nothing, that he liked my writing very much and that all the officers have commented upon it. So where's the stripe, already? I'll lose my mind waiting for that PFC.

Goodnight, My Angel. I'll write again tomorrow and tomorrow and tomorrow, God willing.

Daddy

P.S. Love to Ruth and the kids and the folks.

July 6, 1944
Darling:

This Special Service office is a nice, quiet spot. It's just 8 a.m. and no one has arrived yet. I expect to stay here all day and read magazines and such, with an eye peeled for interesting bits for the paper. My thumb is "touchy" this morning and I'll go over and have it dressed as soon as I finish this.

Darling, I'm worried now that my last letter made you very blue. Please forgive me for being such an ass. It will be time enough to feel bad when the time comes. In the meantime, for the next couple of weeks, at least, we are sure to sit tight. I feel considerably more cheerful today and pray that you are the same. Honey, in this business of war one makes the best bargain he can. I feel that I have done very well with this outfit. Having the respect and admiration of one's officers is a big thing. Likewise, I find that the enlisted men are on my side. I feel "secure" with them. It would be an awful thing to make a change now. It is not unusual. Most men develop a peculiar sense of attachment and loyalty to their outfits. I feel I shall reap the harvest of my extracurricular activities once we are overseas, or in our own installation. I dare to hope that we may become a permanent installation in this country.

Well, my Angel, I've got to get on the ball and look like I'm busy. The men will be popping in shortly.

Kiss my Love Lettuce. Daddy

July 7, 1944
Darling:

Your letters are like rare wine. They make my head swim with the bouquet of love with which you impregnate each letter. I can never hope to duplicate such beauty of expression.

My luck is holding. My time is mine to do as I wish, and I spend most of the day in the Special Service Office, preparing next week's *Hot Compress* which will debut a new feature of mine, "Fancy Phrase," a compilation of beautifully and cleverly expressed word pictures garnered from various publications. I urge you to get a copy of *Esquire*, August issue, and read it from cover to cover. It will carry you away for a few hours into a land of delight. I am quoting several passages from it in my new column which will be in addition to my regular column for which I am still lacking an appropriate name since we are no longer Basics.

Well, Angel, you can see that when I am doing what I love best, I can be fairly comfortable and in a reasonable frame of mind despite the fact that the North Carolina Chamber of Commerce has sold America a bill of goods as far as the vaunted Asheville weather goes. You could drown a duck this morning, and it's building up to this since we got back. Yes, Angel, I'm glad you are home. I wouldn't have you endure this for anything. I'm just hoping it lets up because I've got a guard detail tonight.

We continue to indulge in the spreading of the wildest rumors which grow more fantastic with each telling. Every little action on the part of the officers, every notice on the bulletin board carries some special significance for someone who immediately starts another one going around. I'm guilty of this too, though

I keep my thoughts to myself. For no good reason at all I got to thinking about India this morning after seeing an orientation film, *The Battle of China*, but then yesterday someone advanced a reasonable argument which pointed straight to Alaska. In all, the morale here is much higher than I believed possible in view of what faces us. A picture such as the China film leaves no room for uncertainty, irresolution. Dear God, how could we have faced it if the Jap bombs had splattered our own helpless Roberta's blood in the streets of Chicago? These are no propaganda films, Angel. This is brutal fact, warning people everywhere that bombs dropped from the air aren't choosy when it comes to defenseless people. How can men walk the streets indifferent to the horror that might have rushed over us too? There isn't a man here who doesn't wish with all his heart that this thing were over, but there isn't a man here who won't shoulder his pack with a real determination when the time comes to move. I'm glad, Honey, that I'm a small part of that movement.

Well, what started out to be a breezy note to my beloved has turned into a heavy opus on patriotism, etc., but it's my destiny to fit into this vast jigsaw puzzle which will eventually spell victory and freedom, and fit I must if I am to return to you an emotionally matured husband and lover. Each passing day brings that closer.

My juiciest kiss for our Daddy-Allergic child. I see her tiny face before me a vision of an angel floating in space. Guard her well, and you'll have done your share nobly.

To you, My Love, all my love. Daddy

July 8, 1944
Darling:

No letter from you in today's first mail and already I'm panicky. It's just 3 p.m. We've just finished a long, tedious showdown in inspection and since no one seemed to be keeping military secrets around here, it's apparently safe to say that we will leave here sometime next week. Some sort of mail censorship will go into effect several days beforehand, no doubt, so if letters stop coming with regularity for a while, just be at ease. It doesn't mean we've gotten on a boat. Troop movements must be protected even for the shortest distance. I can't say anymore since I don't know any more. I can only say, may God grant you courage to face the uncertain future for a short time. I am sending home the suitcase with a few extra things that are extra baggage. The suitcase will be locked but the key will be tied to it. The post office advises this.

My thumb is still pretty sore and I have difficulty writing. Darling, I feel exactly as you do about seeing a fine movie, play, or hearing good music without my only love by my side. Over and over I keep saying to myself as I watch something special, "Oh, if Esther could only see this!" My enjoyment is diminished by the fact that you are not at my side. We'll have to catch up on a lot of movies when this is over, and concerts too.

I'm afraid we'll be restricted to the area next weekend, so I'm going in tonight to a movie with the boys and perhaps a beer. Just one, a toast to my beloved, and then back to camp. I've got to work on the camp papers Sunday. Have courage and faith in our God, My Love. It won't be long. I'll write every day as long as I can. Daddy

July 9, 1944
Darling!

I hadn't intended to make you unhappy with my telephone call of Sunday afternoon, but hearing your voice overcame my resolution to be gay and cheerful. Please, Darling, don't worry. I'm not afraid, I'm just terribly lonely. This is not unnatural. Most of us are reliving those early days after the [Fort] Sheridan nightmare. It means that we are merely making an adjustment for the second phase which will be undertaken very soon. The redeeming factor, however, is that once we are launched on our own, we will be extremely busy which is the best thing that can happen to us. Too much leisure is a very dangerous thing for soldiers, especially those who have wives and children back home. You know that I will pick up the tempo again and make myself useful. It doesn't matter much whether it's here or somewhere else. Location has ceased to be of importance. We want to get into this thing and get it over. I am choked with anguish at the thought of you trying to accept the reality of my departure for foreign shores, but I must save you the torment of waiting for some definite word. While no one knows exactly when, that we are going is a certainty. My Darling, like millions of your "sisters in misery," it's now your turn to "live from day to day" until this is over.

If only I could share with you the hysterical comedy that fills our lives as we prepare for this business! We have all become mad extroverts in sheer self-defense, and wild laughter follows every idiotic prank played on some unsuspecting GI. This is the comedy of war: each guy covering up the hurt that's in him. I have only looked upon the shenanigans from the sidelines, but I'm afraid I'll be drawn into it too. Perhaps that will be better. I need to laugh more. Henceforth I shall try to describe some of our doings, à la Olson and Johnson. Generally, we are a crazy, loyal, sincere bunch despite the clown's motley we wear.

The weather continues threatening. Yesterday (Saturday) we floundered through cloud bursts all day. No wonder my spirits are so low! Please tell our friends to write to me. I feel so funny when there is no mail for me.

My Angel, I love you. Daddy

July 10, 1944 – 10:30 a.m.
My Darling:

The sun has broken through at last. It looks like the beginning of a beautiful day, and I feel bright and cheerful this morning. I know what's the matter with me now. I was worried silly last week that my writing ability had gone bone dry. Try as I might, I couldn't get anywhere with the column, and to add to my distress, the boys kept asking for, and the officers kept repeating that my stuff was very well received. I ducked out of last week's issue because it was hopeless to try to compose anything. Yesterday evening, however, I took the bull by the horns and made it work. My new column will be called "How do you like it?" based on a remark that all civilians make to soldiers home on furlough. I sum it all up with some first-class sarcasm: "How do I like it, Mister? How would you like a compound fracture of the femur?" Writing is my life. Because it doesn't come easy, each word sinks deep into my consciousness. I suffer acutely when mistakes are made in the process of transcribing what I have written. All your life you will have to tolerate my "mishugas" [personal nuttiness] and inspire me to go on when I get into such a mood as I experienced last week. But I will make you proud of me.

[*Editors' note: He sent home one page of "Hot Compress" which is reproduced below.*]

Well, Darling, I want to get the suitcase ready for mailing, and clean out a lot of other junk. There is some talk of a visit to the Smoky Mountain Reservation scheduled for next Sunday. It should prove to be a delightful outing for us, so if we are restricted, we will at least have a nice Sunday away from the area.

To you, My Love, all my love. Kiss Boopsie hard for me. Daddy

July 11, 1944
Angel:

I have just sent off the bag with some of my things, including the new shoes. Guess I'll have to wait a while before I can wear them. I put a big box of Kleenex in too, so open the bag and get it out. I was afraid to send anything else from the PX at this time.

Well, honey, it's come up. We leave here the middle of next week for an eastern staging area. It's small consolation but it's what we hoped for. I know exactly where, but I can't put it in a letter. I wouldn't be an instrument of jeopardy for my buddies, or myself. However, it looks like you will be able to come east (and even stay in Ruthie's house) because I think we will be able to meet. Pray to God that we will be permitted to do so. More tomorrow, Angel.

Daddy

Post Basic: The Wait for Deployment

Page 6   "THE COM-PRESS"   14 July 1944

HOW DO YOU LIKE IT?

BY PVT SAMUEL LESNER

Take away the cold compress. It's a "Hot Com-Press" we've needed to dispel the "Army Daze," the lassitude that ossified this two-pence brain since returning from that 15-day furlough.

Thought we had "jolly, jolly sixpence" worth of brains when we climbed aboard that furlough special. Our valuable and newly acquired staff cartoonist, Tec 5 Lewis E Casady is right. We've been smoking the wrong kind of cigarettes, figuratively speaking, of course. (See the Hot Com-Press for 23 June).

"How do you like it?" How do you like that! There it goes again! Look, mister, it isn't a three-ring circus. It isn't a championship football game. It isn't a major league game. It's war. You do as you're told. You learn, learn, learn. I like it fine, standing in chow lines, sleeping with 35 other guys, shouting to be heard, damning them to pipe down, being damned for turning on the lights or turning them off, yearning for your wife's warmth, missing the "miracle" of your kid's first hesitant step, longing to hear from John in New Guinea, from Bill in Italy and Roy in England, and what do you do but come home and walk smack into a "How do you like it?" How would you like a compound fracture of the femur?

Well, you can see now why we needed a cold compress on the head, but it was a "Hot Com-Press" that did the trick. While we were away somebody eulogized us— "those basic kids"— as the writer put it, and we suspect the heavy hand of smiling Jack "Horace Greeley" Garber in the writing of that laudatory piece, "While They're Away," in the June 23 issue of "The Hot Com-Press." We were away on a "well-earned furlough," wrote Editor Garber. "They've stood up well under all our good-natured razzing and baiting. When they get back, let's all blend ourselves together to make the 130th General Hospital the best damned medical outfit in the ASF!"

We'll blend, make sure of that, Mr. Editor, but somebody's going to have to outloutlaw the word "Basic" around here.

Speaking of furlough reflections, the Chicago contingent kicked that one about "once a Basic Always a Basic" around plenty. "Where's our stuff? What are they calling it?," queried Pvt Patrick Squillace as he grabbed for a "Hot Com-Press." That's when we were shamed into action. Let's hear no more about the rugged basic training at Grant and Ellis. If we made the sergeants laugh and befriended a corporal, that's to our credit.

We've reflected upon our mistakes and boasted about our achievements, and our fatigue hats got too small from laundering. While we were away, we hope you guys had as many nice things to say about us as we had to say about you. To paraphrase that duckwalking martinet's infamous phrase, "We're Not Hell on Wheels. If you don't believe it, try us."

DON'T BE RELUCTANT

Washington, July 3, (AP) - Fighting this global war and getting ready for it has cost the nation $199,940,000,000 since July 1, 1940, or about $140,560,000 a day.

We didn't ask for it, but we can't stop now. There's a terrific job ahead and it takes cash. You can bet your bottom dollar that you'll be paid back with interest so why not invest in your post-war future. After all it will be an honest dollar earned by your own tears, sweat and blood. Don't be reluctant. A War Bond allotment, particularly in that new GI series, will offer more post-war comfort than the memory of a latrine crap game or a marathon beer party. Now is the time to give your Uncle Samuel the O.K. on that pay deduction for bonds.

The New Yorker reports of a GI of Tacoma, Wash., who fought in Sicily and at Volturno River in Italy without a scratch. He landed in France as a paratrooper in one of the first waves of the invasion and was injured when a cow fell into his foxhole!

July 12, 1944
Darling!

It looks like it's going to be a quiet day. Nothing to do, and maybe it won't rain—but that will be too much of a good thing. Well, by this time you have received the final blow to the solar plexus and I can't say as I enjoyed landing the blow. I think all my life I'll be haunted by the memory of the letter which must have crushed the last spark of hope. Strangely, now that the axe has fallen, we are all greatly relieved and are enjoying our remaining days here. I got slightly drunk the other night on beer, just enough to make me glow, and we had a picnic. I'd chattered like a squirrel and the fellows howled at my antics. On top of that I've acquired a pipe and the boys looked at me with the questioning expression, "what goes here?" Well, Honey, you know these are merely harmless surface escapes for a guy filled with anguish over the grief his Angel is experiencing. You must have courage knowing that I am in a splendid outfit, an outfit which will be far removed from any immediate danger, and knowing that my life will be comparatively easy. As long as it must be, I want to reap all the benefits I can from this forthcoming experience. I hope you understood what I meant by "Ruthie's House." That, I believe, can be our rendezvous, depending of course how long we will be at the staging area. If such a thing as a pass is available, I'll get one. Of course, if a strict censorship is maintained, I don't know what method is left to let you know. However, let's wait and see. I have a feeling it will work out.

My love to all. To you, My Love, all my love. Daddy

P.S. We leave here next Thursday [July 20th].

July 16, 1944
My Darling:

I couldn't even figure out what the date is today, that's how my head is going round and round as I wait in the telephone exchange to talk to you. Of course, the anticipation of talking to you is always exciting, but I'm afraid you'll have to take second place to a hangover today. Yes, I was noisily drunk last night and today my head is buzzing. What a party! The officers certainly did right by us, too, in their final shindig. It was a delightful way to earn $5. We have been told that three meals would be served on the train, which means approximately a twenty-four-hour ride. You will be notified where to write as soon as we leave here. It will be a temporary APO number. I have reason to believe we will not embark for a week or two, anyhow, and if a pass is possible, we shall meet, My Darling. Take care of things and try to distract yourself until we get set. Then, I'm sure, I will be able to write you reassuring news about our location and our safety which is a certainty in our type of unit.

To you, My Love, all my love. Daddy

July 17, 1944
My Darling:
Nothing new today as yet, but the tempo is gradually being stepped up and I suppose by the time you get this we will be ready for the final "Fall Out." The Sunday was a quiet, pleasant one. The weather was gorgeous and I had an orgy of sunbathing. I went to the post movie at night and laughed and cried at Andy Bracken in *Hail the Conquering Hero*. It's grand. The fella does some brilliant acting. Tonight we have a Jewish service and a party afterwards. Asheville's Jewish ladies are coming out with refreshments, etc.

I have some new snapshots made on bivouac which I will mail in a day or so. The ones I enclose, I treasure. Put them away safely. Someday we'll laugh over them and amuse our little Angel with tales of her daddy's heroism with nothing better than an accordion for a weapon Maybe I'll find you a treasure in the old world I am going to visit. Believe me, my every thought will be of you and you shall share my every experience even though great distance lies between us.

To you, My Love, all my love. Daddy

July 18, 1944
Darling:
Forgot to send this one with the rest. It's the furlough goodbye pix. Keep it with the collection. What a day this has been. You'll get the details later. I promise you an interesting letter.

Honey

July 18, 1944
Darling:
Just a few papers and negatives to add to the accumulation. Don't know what to say at this point, except that I love you overwhelmingly. It is all I can offer you to comfort you in the days ahead. I know you will do your job, and I'll do my best to do mine, whatever it is. If through my musical and writing activities I can bring even a moment of pleasure to those who will have to suffer pain, I'll consider it time well spent. Be as brave as you are devoted to me and your mind and heart will find peace. To you, My Love, all my love. Kiss Love Lettuce for me. I'll kiss you both every night, even if I have to be content with pictures. I'll write tomorrow again.
Daddy

July 19, 1944
Darling:
This is the last letter from this post. In the morning the big adventure begins. How long we will be in the States becomes daily more uncertain and if the signs mean anything it will be a very short time, perhaps too short for us to fulfill our longing to see each other again. If we should fail in this, remember that I carry away with me a heart filled with love and desire for you. The days ahead without you will be difficult, as they always have been, but the constancy of your love and devotion will sustain me. I love you, My Darling, more than I ever have gotten around to tell you, but what else is this suffocating feeling I get when I think of you? I will resume writing daily as soon as it is possible, so that you shall never be without some word from me. Kiss the Love Lettuce and if you get a new picture of her, send it to me. Maybe her first birthday will be the brightest in our lives. Who knows, September may bring relief to all the world? Pray God that it does. Keep the home fire burning, Angel. I'll be there soon to stretch my tired feet. Remember our fireside romancing? I'll not say goodbye, Angel.
To you, My Love, all my love. Daddy

July 20, 1944 – En route, destination unknown
My Darling:
We are making speed now, after that painful pull over the hills that I admired so much but disliked climbing over. The Southern RR has done its best, having provided Pullmans, but the heat inside our car at the moment is staggering, to say the least. Well, I guess even this will pass in time and some new phase of what awaits us will unfold. I shall try to maintain my reportorial zeal for interesting details (non-censorial ones, of course) with which to amuse you.
One incident occurred at lunchtime. We were served in our own cars. Consequently the feeding crew had to pick their way with some restraint, alien to K.P.s, back and forth through the entire train. The sandwiches and chocolate milk arrived in due time. Then we were informed that canned peaches were on the

next trip. I love peaches, as you know. Imagine, then, my surprise when the next offering turned out to be hot peas, after the sandwiches and drinks had long disappeared. The peaches showed up later, so all was made right by us. The boys are surprisingly undemonstrative. They're playing cards or sleeping, although how they can in this heat is a mystery I wish I could solve. I'll share my lower with another GI tonight. Chummy but not very comfortable. Well, Angel, when we get where we're going, I'll take up the letter writing.

I hope the earrings arrived safely. Somewhere in this mad world there must be a doll shop. They're going to hold up this war long enough for me to find a dolly for our little Angel, or I'm going to protest "long and loud" to those guys in Washington.

To you, My Love, all my love. Daddy

July 21, 1944
Darling:
We arrived at this eastern camp this morning in good order. Had a pleasant, restful night in a Pullman, but we were at the wrong end of the car, apparently. The chow kept running out before it got to us, so I'm hungry and ready to eat. Sure would like to have chow with you in Ruthie's house. I'm hoping, dear. Don't know what the rules are yet, but guess we'll be told soon. I'm well, and housed with a lot of guys I like particularly, and I imagine the bull sessions will really be something when we relax and get going. Write to me, Angel, as I'm very lonely for a word from you already. Why didn't you write in time for me to get a letter Thursday? Mail was distributed en route, and I swallowed hard to hide my disappointment. But I understand that you were confused about our departure. Weren't we all? They certainly can keep military secrets after all. Good bye for now.

To you, My Love, all my love. Kiss the Love Lettuce. Daddy

July 22, 1944
Darling:
The day is beautiful, the food good and the barracks bull-slinging just as distracting as ever. At this point there is so little that can be said that one is left floundering in a sea of uncertainty, so I'll tell you one thing that I'm certain about: I love you, very much, even if you don't write to me three times of day as I have been doing to you. Don't despair, Angel. Just hold on. This thing will come out right yet. More tonight. Love, Daddy

July 22, 1944
Darling:
The enclosed papers I treasure above anything even though they don't impress the army with my ability as a journalist. I'm not bitter, though. Maybe after this I'll be a better, more lucid scribe and I'll make lots of money and buy

you a diamond wristwatch. That's what you want, isn't it? If only I had had a letter from you yesterday, my utter loneliness would have lifted for a while. I'm disgustingly healthy, however, so don't worry. I'm quite ready for anything. Love to all.

To you, My Love, all my love. Daddy

July 22, 1944
Sweetheart:

I don't know where to begin since no letter from you has arrived yet and I have no way of knowing what you think has happened or what you might know. We are still busily engaged in the business of preparation for overseas duty and that, My Angel, is a vast project. One can't help but marvel at the tremendous effort our government makes to protect us. If we make half the effort, we'll have this over in no time. It is permissible to say that we are at a camp on the East Coast. The APO number, of course, reveals that. When the signal to move comes, it will come suddenly, no doubt, so it's silly to guess and only raises false hopes. I am haunted by the fact that we had hardly an hour completely to ourselves while I was home recently, but the hours of peace and contentment we will spend in the future, together, will erase the memory of our inadequate adieu. Have faith, My Darling. You have a big job to do, too, keeping little Pudding Face fat and beautiful for my return. My love to all the folks.

To you, My Love, all my love. Daddy
P.S. Write to the address on the envelope until further notice.

July 23, 1944
My Darling:

Sunday morning in a world apart! But Sunday has its meaning in a place like this too. We slept later, for one thing, and that's a thing to be grateful for. Breakfast was a fulsome, good, old-fashioned meal: cereal, ham, eggs, melon, coffee, bread and butter, marmalade. It was a struggle to clean up the tray since it's against my principles to waste food. My streamlining, achieved through such sacrifice, is going to pot, literally, but I guess I'll slim down again later, if only through "feeding the fishes." I wish I could tell you about some of the goings-on here, but for the moment that's taboo. If we don't have mail call pretty soon, they'll have to take me in a cage. But this being Sunday, surely they'll get around to it. If they only knew how I drink up the spiritual wine from your letters, they would sort mine out and bring them to me on a golden tray, for your letters are the wellspring of being. How is Pudding Face getting along with her da-da-ing? Kiss her for me.

My love to all, and to you, My Love, all my love. Daddy

July 23, 1944
Sweetheart:

The day is finally drawing to a close and for the first time I am glad to see it go, full knowing that there are so few days left before we leave for our big adventure. Mail call came about 4 p.m. and there was no letter from you. My heart sank and I must have turned green under my deep tan because several guys looked at me and asked me if I was suddenly ill. Surely tomorrow there will be a letter! I've got fourteen hours of K.P. tomorrow so perhaps it will distract me for the day. This may be the last letter for a few days.

To you, My Love, all my love. Daddy

CHAPTER FIVE

Post Basic: Deployment to England

[*From Oral History interview with grandson, Edward C. Bernstein, in 1986*]:

SL: *We took a troop ship to England, to a marshalling area where there was a great deal of organization to bring together people coming from various places into the 130th General Hospital, a 500-bed hospital. Some men had training, some did not. But we established our hospital.*

[*Editor's note: To write her book* GI Jews, *Deborah Dash Moore interviewed many veterans, including her father, who served in the army in the ETO. Regarding the voyage to Europe, she learned that*

> "Embarkation is dramatic, particularly the actual boarding of the ship. It is the climax of soldiering in the U.S. . . . It is the beginning of another life. . . . Most of the drama of leaving the United States . . . came from the hustle and bustle of embarkation," which left little time for thought. "Handling all your equipment absorbs most of your attention." The steep gangplank seemed both narrow and precarious, a bridge to another world. But there was more than drama in the details. A vast unknown faced these soldiers. (p. 92)

Undoubtedly, embarkation was rough for Sam also. However, his letters reflect his persistent optimism and purposeful desire to find the positive in all circumstances and to relate only the positive in his letter to Esther.]

July 27, 1944 – En route
My Darling:
   What can I say? Here we are out at sea and wherever you look you see the might that is ours. It makes you enormously proud and the word fear has no meaning. I can't tell you what I see around me, but believe me, Darling, it is magnificent. We are very comfortable while above deck and no worse off than I've been on the several ocean-going ships I've been on. I'm a hardy sailor. No

discomfort so far, and if my luck holds, I'll come through this in excellent spirits. We have an abundance of food but I'm taking it in moderate quantities, Darling. I can't outsmart the censor, but you must believe me on one detail—that is that I'm exceedingly well and in high spirits. I haven't laughed so much in a long time.

You will get this letter, no doubt, after we have debarked safely. I regret this since I want you to share my sense of well-being and security that I feel at this moment, but our safety depends entirely upon the watchfulness of the censors. Wherever we are going, I shall resume writing to you daily as soon as it is possible. Your last wonderful letter I received just now, and I hastened to the sun deck to write this answer.

To you, My Love, all my love and to Love Lettuce too. Best to the folks. Daddy

V-Mail – En route (Somebody forgot to mail this.)
My Darling:

This is an unusual situation. Having shared with you all these months all my experiences in Army life, I find now that I can tell you almost nothing of the things you would like to hear. However, as I said in my last letter, if it hasn't been censored, the voyage is nearly finished and I'm in excellent health and have enjoyed every hour of it. You must believe this. Some things, of course, weren't deluxe, but they had a definite humorous side to them and I have had many hardy laughs. Oh, if I can only tell you! Last night I dreamed that you were with me. I pray that will be true soon. How is our angel, Roberta? Please have a picture made of her for her first birthday.

All my love to you Darling. Daddy

August 7, 1944 – At sea [V-Mail]
My Darling:

We are approaching the end of our voyage in good order and in excellent health. This has been an experience that has enriched my life beyond estimation. Someday I'll be able to tell the story and time will blend the thousand and one details into a tale of romance and adventure. Be brave, my Darling, and soon the mail will be coming with regularity. Perhaps someday we can retrace this course on a ship as seaworthy as this one, but of course, in a stateroom. The troop compartments are designed for rugged men only.

All my love, Daddy

August 8, 1944 [V-Mail]

Somewhere in England at the moment is a setting of such natural magnificence that it is breathtaking. What a country! The great English writers haven't overdone it. It's all here, exuding strength, durability, beauty in its contrasts. I hope it is my good fortune to see much of this country now that I'm here. It fires the imagination. I am well, Angel, and I received your last letters today. My heart burst with loneliness for you and the baby, but I am only one. There are so many of us with the mind and heart turned toward home. Thank God, at least, for the beauty that surrounds us. It helps a wee bit, don't you know! My Love, keep writing, but don't be alarmed. It takes a little time to get things moving again.

    All my love, Daddy

August 9, 1944 – Somewhere in England [V-Mail]
My Darling:
    Next to the day when I left you, this has been the unhappiest. In wartime, friendships, which become so sacred to the soldier, are broken with utter disregard for the feelings of the men. This, in the larger sense, is necessary, but it is painful nevertheless. Thus, as I watched truckloads of my friends depart to join other units today, I was overcome with loneliness. Manny remains, however, and together we talk constantly of our Esther and Betty. The day turned out to be a restful one and as night approaches my confidence has been fully restored. We remain the 130th as before. What the next month will bring for us in this English countryside I can't say, but this is a hearty spot. More tomorrow, My Love. Our home at the moment is an English manor. It's quite something!
    Daddy

August 10, 1944 [V-Mail]
My Darling:
    I want so much to write to a long letter but I'm afraid it will take ages to reach you, so for a time I'll continue with this V-Mail. I have received all your letters, four of them in England, so you can figure out just how things worked out. I am sick at heart to think that official notification of our safe arrival takes so long, but it can't be helped. Someday I hope to make it all clear to you. Indeed, it is important to guard information on troop movements. I kiss you and the baby every night. The English children look healthy and happy. There are a number of redheads around here. They chase the men and ask for gum, only they say "gom," the *u* like an *o* in gone. I get such a kick out of hearing them talk, but as yet miss most of what they are saying. I hope to see the inside of an English pub soon, but don't worry, I'm strictly a beer man.
    With all my heart, Daddy

August 11, 1944 [V-Mail]
My Darling:
    Nothing new to report today other than that I am very well and contented with my lot, which may prove to be a most satisfactory deal after all. The

important thing is that I am remaining with a general hospital, and no matter where we might go, it is the best break. I lost my friend [Jack] Garber and a few others in the shuffle so I don't know how I stand now in Special Service. The band, too, will have to be reorganized. I didn't get to the pub last night as I caught a work detail, but I didn't mind. This morning we got our English money and we're having fun getting it straight in our minds. I have more than I need so I'll buy a bond and have it sent to you. That can be done even from here. I wish you could see the roses in our garden. What a paradise even though it needs pruning. Noble ladies once paraded their charms through the same garden.

Love, Daddy

August 12, 1944 [V-Mail]
My Darling:

This will reach you, no doubt, while you and the baby are inhaling Michigan City fresh air. I'm delighted you decided to go and I'm sure you need the comparative quiet of Indiana. Do you remember? Continue to write as if you are getting all my letters. And they'll all arrive soon. Have mine been censored badly? Let me know so I can be guided by it.

I love you. Daddy

August 12, 1944 – Somewhere in England [V-Mail]
My Darling:

This is the second letter in an hour, so you see I'm right on the ball. We have just been dismissed for the afternoon and I chose to come out in the sun-drenched garden and write to you again. Tonight I shall attempt to find a doll or some appropriate token in honor of our Angel's first birthday. I'm scared silly of my first encounter with an English merchant since I can't make heads or tails out of the money, but I'll ask one of the "veterans" here to steer me around. I wish I could tell in detail the beauty of this place, but that's taboo. I'm curious to know how my letters written on the ship fared with the censors. It's so difficult to be articulate and yet observe all the rules. I hope I was allowed to tell you that the voyage was a pleasure cruise. We were most fortunate to have crossed during the best time of the year. Others less fortunate can't understand my bubbling enthusiasm. Routine has been quickly established again and all is well. I'm anxious to get to work.

Love to all, Daddy

August 13, 1944
My Darling:

Sunday in England: We slept a little longer this morning, had a good breakfast and then spent a pleasant morning shooting the bull with the guys in my particular room. The fireplace has been going all morning and has been fed by the various impedimenta which are periodically discarded by all GIs out of sheer necessity. One really could get along on the original GI issue but few men seem to care to try it. I think it's OK to tell you that we are housed in a manor, the rooms of which still boast of their former splendor. A visit to town last night proved diverting but not exciting. Maybe we picked the wrong pub for our initiation. I don't intend, however, to indulge in a series of initiations. There is no such thing as a toy shop that I can discover. I'll try to get to one of the larger cities if possible. Your priceless descriptions of Love Lettuce's antics keep me laughing and crying with joy and pride. Dear God, hasten the day that I can see her again! We have just been paid, had chicken dinner, and now mail is being distributed. So, My Love, cheerio until tomorrow's letter.

All my love, Daddy

P.S. I just got two letters, yours (August 2) and Ma's.

August 16, 1944 [V-Mail]

My Darling: The English countryside is still lovely but the dampness has laid me low with an attack of arthritis. Thus, for the past few days I have been a patient instead of a medic in training. I pray that by this time you have had some word of our safe arrival. What an ordeal the waiting must be. I must warn you, Angel, there may be another lapse in mail for a short time, but please don't be alarmed. It's one of those situations which can't be revealed, but I swear it's purely military and has nothing to do with my health. The inflammation in my knee has subsided and a short rest should make me as good as new. My heart is with you every moment and the baby's approaching birthday keeps me throbbing with excitement.

Love, Daddy

August 17, 1944 – Somewhere in England [V-Mail]

My Darling: (Use my regular address for the time being.)

Yesterday I wrote you about my misadventure with English weather, meaning a swollen knee. I hope you got the letter since I am desperate with anxiety about your state of mind because of the long delay in my mail. It must be a nightmare of waiting for you. Under my present arrangement with the fortunes of war I am not too badly off. The rest in this station hospital will do me a world of good but I don't know how long it shall last. I may be detached from my outfit, which, frankly, would be to my advantage. If this does happen, you shall have comforting news from me, which is what I pray to be able to send you at all times. The war news is astonishingly good and brings renewed hope to all of us. Please assure my folks that my present status as a patient calls for no alarm.

All my love to you, My Love, Daddy

August 18, 1944
My Darling:

I don't need the telepathic powers of a Dunninger [Joseph, 1892–1975, famous mentalist and magician] to know what you are thinking, and my heart aches to think that the terror of uncertainty is added to your loneliness. But such are the fortunes of war as concerns me that my letters are destined to arrive at indefinite intervals, for a time, at least. At the moment time passes pleasantly in the hospital. The inflammation in my knee is gone but an ache remains in my left leg, a small thing, however, compared to the pain that some of these boys have known. I guess I'm a schlemiel after all. My Darling, I hardly know what address I'm to give you. To be on the safe side, write duplicate letters to both, meaning my regular one and the one below:

Private Samuel J. Lesner
36786054 Department of Patients
4186 US Army Hospital Plant
APO 652 New York, NY
All my love to you, My Love, Daddy

August 19, 1944 – Somewhere in England [V-Mail]
My Darling:

A hospital is certainly a nice place not to be in, even though you get waited on, and there's hot water and fresh towels. At any rate, the M.D. thinks I can start soldiering again, if I don't pounce on my legs too much. Well, I hope a few other guys think so too, but about all one does these days is bounce. There's no end to the conditioning, it seems. Maybe I'm a commando and I don't know it. Again, Angel, I caution you not to worry if letters are slow in coming for a short while. It will all get straightened out soon. Has anyone heard from Roy? Please write him and give him my address. I don't seem to be able to make contact from this side. Write me long, newsy letters.

I love you, my Angel, Daddy

August 19, 1944 – Somewhere in England [V-Mail]
My Darling:

Today, after a week of unbearable silence, your two letters of the 6th and 7th reached me at the hospital. With what joy I read them, but with what regret that up to the latter date you still had no official word of our safe arrival. How can necessity be allied with such mental torture? But I guess it is essential to our safety. This begins to have the futility of writing letters to one's self. I am myself again and await the order to vacate my comfortable bed, an order which I will carry out reluctantly, but others have a greater need for the space I now occupy. I don't know what's in store for my unit, but it won't be less than rugged.

I beg you, My Darling, to hold fast to your faith. We are safe here, and God willing, we will come through without mishap.

Kiss Love Lettuce. Daddy

August 20, 1944 – Somewhere in England [V-Mail]
My Darling:

Another peaceful day in this haven and then back to the business of soldiering. I have read several excellent books while here: Daphne du Maurier's *Jamaica* and Ernie Pyle's *Here Is Your War*. The Pyle book is remarkably clear and accurate. You must read it. The man has written into it bits of immortal prose. *Jamaica* is dark and brooding, but well done. My Darling, it looks like I won't have a present for Love Lettuce on time. Tell her how much I love her, though, and that I'll make it up to her. September 15. What a day that will be for me: a day filled with thanksgiving for you both. Your love is my source of life. Be firm in your faith and keep yourself well and beautiful for the day of my return. My love to all our good, devoted friends. I'll write to them soon.

To you, My Love, all my love, Daddy

August 20, 1944 – Somewhere in England [V-Mail]
My Darling:

Here I go again, writing myself a letter. The awfulness of writing, knowing that days will have passed before you get this, drives me crazy. My darling, if I didn't know you and your extraordinary common sense, I'd go nuts thinking how you are struggling with your emotions while awaiting word. I think it's the cruelest part of this whole business. I could stand anything if I knew that you had some respite from the anxiety that must be your lot these past few weeks. Be as brave as you are true, My Love. I'll come out of this safe and sound. Sleep in peace, My Darling. All your letters caught up with me yesterday.

Love, Daddy

August 24, 1944 [V-Mail]
My Darling:

What a beautiful afternoon! And what excitement. I just talked to [brother] Roy over the long-distance phone. He certainly sounds fine and frankly I think he's completely sold on England. I expect to meet Roy very soon. He says he can fly to where I am, or will be, [censored]. The radio brings us news of all the goings on and the news is really something. We hear all the famous American radio programs (from recordings) and we have American movies. Please save some *Daily News* issues for me for this period of allied victories. I want to see them.

Love, Sam

Post Basic: Deployment to England 81

Wednesday August 16, 1944

Thursday, August 17, 1944

Tuesday, August 22, 1944

Wednesday, August 23, 1944

August 27, 1944 [V-Mail]
My Darling:

Another Sunday in England, and it's a calm, beautiful day. We're going to have a dance tonight and the ghosts of numerous lords and ladies will look down upon a strange sight in the ballroom where once they stepped a gay quadrille, in the flesh. All your letters have reached me but the one of August 14 came before the one of July 31, in which you described the new suit you made. I know it is beautiful, having been created by your magic hands. Tomorrow Roy will come to see me. He is some distance away but he says he can manage it. Imagine, after almost two and a half years we shall meet in a strange land. I tried to buy a dolly for Angel, but the prices are outrageous for the junk available. There has been no mail from you for several days, but Manny doesn't get his daily letter either, so the tie-up must be general. I guess I must learn to live through days without mail. Love to all. I long for you.

 Love, Daddy

August 28, 1944
My Darling:

What a beautiful Sunday. Two wonderful letters from you of the 16th and 17th, and one full of the most wonderful pictures I have ever seen of our remarkable child. I'm surprised that you say they are not very good. True, the photography is faulty, but no camera, or technique, could deny the beauty, the haunting personality of our child. The one in which she stands with legs crossed brought on a rush of tears and laughter. I think I came very near to hysteria, the uncontrollable rush of pride and joy sweeping over me like a wave. Honey, I thank you for sending me the pictures. I shall guard the pictures with my life, you can be sure. Let me keep them all for a while, Angel. I'll find a little portfolio for them. Periodically you must make other snapshots of her so I can see her in every stage of development.

Angel, each morning I wake, thinking "perhaps today the letters will be delivered to you." I have written so many, and I could beat my head against the wall in sheer anguish that you are kept waiting so long before hearing from me. But many of us are in the same boat. Our consolation is that events are moving so rapidly that the war scene shifts constantly. This is good. I can't tell you why now but you will understand later when you learn just what our mission is to be and the kind of work we will be doing. Some changes in our personnel have given the unit an entirely new complexion. My accordion has become a millstone around my neck. Why didn't I listen to my wise wife? The darned thing, at the moment, is at the hospital where I recuperated from my arthritic attack. You see, the band was busted up, which apparently frees Uncle Samuel of all further responsibility in the manner. If I can't sell it, I shall have to forget it because I can't include it in my personal baggage. We travel very light these days. More tomorrow, Angel.

To you, My Love, all my love. Daddy

P.S. Roy is coming here tonight

August 29, 1944 – Somewhere in England [V-Mail]
My Darling:

Just a few lines this time to say that I am fine, the new men in this outfit proved to be gentlemen and good friends, and the outlook in general for our unit is a good one. The biggest news, though, is that yesterday Roy came from his camp and spent the evening with me. Our detachment office was kind enough to ask him to chow and stay for the night, which is what he did. Need I tell you how proud I was? You know he wears a Presidential Citation about which he has never spoken. He looks wonderful, and has all sorts of stripes and ribbons to show for his splendid work. He was the focus of all eyes in camp. He promised to write to you. Our meeting, of course, was most dramatic. More later.

Love, Daddy

Letter from Roy describing the encounter.

Sgt. R.H. Lesner
HQ. & HQ. SQON
1st Bomb Division
APO 557 c/o PM
New York City
29 Aug. 1944
Dear Esther:

This is your long lost brother-in-law speaking to you and bringing the news that you've been waiting so long to hear. I saw him last night—yep! I spent the whole evening with Sam and stayed at his camp overnight. Wish I could have stayed much longer but most of my time was used up in traveling. You see, he's stationed quite far from me. Esther, he looked well. Of course he's in a new country and is still a little green and confused, but that only lasts a short time. I was the same way when I first came over here. He's been quite worried about you not receiving mail for him but I assured him that all the new people who come over have the same trouble with their mail. I want you to know that he is in a very beautiful part of the country and has everything he wants. In a short time you will be receiving his mail regularly and normally.

Esther, I don't know whether you can picture those few moments when we first met. You know how emotional he is, and when I saw him the same thing happened to me, and we just stood and looked at each other, neither of us being able to say a word. I guess we both had great big lumps in our throats. But after a while we settled down and then the questions began to come from all sides. I don't think I've ever talked as much or as fast as I did last night, especially when his friends found out that I had been here over two years. They all showered me with questions and I felt like a big shot pioneer or something.

He showed me the pictures of the baby. I never realized that she is so grown up. She's really beautiful. Esther, I must close now as I have many other letters to write, but before I do, I want to assure you that Sam is quite safe and will never have to see the things that I've seen. Manny says hello and sends his love to Betty.

Give my love to all and to your mother and dad.

The kid brother Roy

P.S. I'll bet the phone will really catch hell tonight.

September 1, 1944 – Somewhere in England [V-Mail]
My Darling:

Just time for a short one to say that all goes well in a rugged sort of way this week. Wish I could tell you just what's cooking, but that would be cut out by our so far tolerant censors. When you get this please call the folks as I have time for only one now. That pause that doesn't refresh you will prevail again for a few days and then maybe we can get down to some real letter writing. It's peaceful as usual in this spot and I discovered some new vistas of magnificent beauty. I know now that you know we have arrived safely and a great weight has been lifted from me. I look at Angel's pictures every hour or so and get hysterical all over again. That one where she stands with her feet crossed gets me. Roy said, "How do you rate such a beautiful kid?" Well the Lesners agree that she is a beauty, and cute too. That's all now, Love. Be brave and be fortified with my profound love for you.

Daddy

CHAPTER SIX

France: Killing Time

[Editors' note: After the liberation of Paris from August 19th to 25th, Sam's unit was moved to France, crossing the English Channel the same way the D-Day troops had done on June 6, 1944, as he mentions in his letters. Following is a description of the D-Day operation from The Illustrated History of WW II by John Ray (London: Weidenfeld and Nicolson, 2003).]

At 9 a.m. on 6 June 1944 the BBC announced that "Under the command of General Eisenhower, Allied naval forces supported by strong air forces began landing Allied armies this morning on the coast of France." D-Day and Operation "Overlord" had arrived. Eisenhower, the Supreme Commander, and Montgomery, commander of the ground forces, had earlier fixed 4 June for the start, but bad weather caused a short postponement for what was to be, in Rommel's words, "The Longest Day."

During the night, paratroops from three Allied airborne divisions, and glider troops, were dropping inland to seize strategic points. Then, at dawn, landings commenced on five Normandy beaches. Three were attacked by the British Second Army: "Gold" and "Sword" were tackled by British troops, while "Juno" fell to the Canadians. The other two, "Utah" and "Omaha", were assaulted by the US First Army. The landings were preceded by heavy naval bombardments and bombing. Overall, the Second Army suffered few casualties in getting ashore, but the Americans, particularly on "Omaha", met fiercer resistance. ...

The men on shore pushed forward, gradually managing to scratch a toehold in France. More ships and landing craft arrived, so that during D-Day 156,000 troops were landed from over 2700 vessels which crossed the Channel. The cost that day was 11,000 casualties, including 2,500 killed. A blessing for Allied forces—and a curse for the Germans—was the strength of air support, with the Luftwaffe almost entirely absent. British and American aircraft flew over 25,000 sorties by 9 p.m. on 6 June; the once powerful German Air Force managed only 319 on the same day.

The Wehrmacht's reactions to the landings were confused, helping the invaders. Rommel was in Germany for his wife's birthday, von Rundstedt still believed that the main attack would come later near Calais, while Hitler, who had slept late, refused to release extra panzer divisions into Normandy. By the

France: Killing Time

time the German forces moved forward from reserve, the bridgehead was being firmly established.

Over the following days the Allied armies were reinforced and their positions extended until all the landing sites were combined into a bridgehead forty miles across yet only up to ten miles deep. Progress was slow. . . .

. . . the human price continued to rise. In six weeks the Allies suffered almost 100,000 casualties in killed and wounded. . . . (p. 176)

Although the Americans captured the port of Cherbourg on 26 June, the great break-out did not come until 56 days after the first landings. While the bulk of the panzer divisions faced Montgomery's army in the east, US forces launched Operation "Cobra" and swept out from Avranches. Some moved west into Brittany, while others turned east to trap the Germans who were being pushed back by British and Canadian forces near Falaise. This area, the Falaise Gap, then became one of the war's great killing grounds. The Germans attempted counter-attacks and made frantic efforts in the early days of August to escape, but all to no avail. As well as pressure from Allied ground troops, fighters and medium bombers of the Tactical Air Force had a field day. By the end of the battle, the German Army B had been shattered. Some 50,000 prisoners were taken and 10,000 killed. Hundreds upon hundreds of lorries, cars, carts and tanks were smashed, so that only about 110 tanks and assault guns escaped to retreat to the river Seine.

Thus the great invasion and subsequent battle of Normandy were completed, with the German Army retreating eastwards in some disarray. American forces swept forward at panzer pace, especially General Patton's Third Army which aimed toward Paris. The capital was taken on 25 August when General de Gaulle and French units entered the city, whose humiliating occupation had lasted just over four years. At the end of the month Patton's men reached Verdun and the battlefields of the First World War. Further north, British and Canadian units, under Montgomery, advanced along the Channel coast, while the American First Army took Amiens on 31 August. . . .

Hitler was assailed on all sides. He barely survived an attempt on his life made by German plotters on 20 July. . . . Between June and August 1944 the Germans lost 600,000 men at the very least. It appeared that the whole fabric of the Nazi state was bound to collapse within a short time. (pp. 177–78)

September 5, 1944 – Somewhere in France
My Darling:
At the moment my prayer is that the ink holds out so I can give you something of the events that have transpired since we left the "luxury" of an English countryside. You recall the catchphrase I taught you about the three S's. Well I did the first one this morning, to my enormous relief, and since we are promised "washing water" this afternoon, I am almost overcome with joy in anticipation of a shave and perhaps a vigorous toweling over "putrid carcass." After a very wet night, the sun promises to break through and dry out our pup tents, which

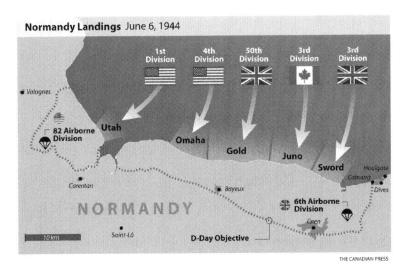

Reprinted with permission from The Canadian Press

stand in magnificent alignment in a grassy meadow "somewhere in France," a meadow which, not too long ago, was a battlefield. My Darling, read this letter objectively. It is not my intention to make you feel my discomfort, or to weigh down your spirits. Frankly, you get so used to all this it doesn't bother you one bit. I want to give you a fairly accurate picture of our life, and thus I tell you of the incidents pertaining to it. I don't know when this will reach you, nor how the picture will change by then, but at the moment, I am doubled up in my tent, directing all my thoughts and all my love to you and Angel Puss. My great regret is that I have no way of sending her some token of my love for her first birthday. You can, however, deliver a special birthday kiss for me.

Several days ago we left our English manor and moved to a port where we boarded a splendid ship in which to make the channel crossing. I imagine the details of the crossing are still a military secret, but I believe I can say that sometime later we climbed down the side of the ship, jumped into a huge landing barge and rode to shore in a stinging spray of salt water. The barge rode right onto the beach and we piled out on a scene of desolation that would do justice to a DeMille movie. Angel, I still think this is a movie in the making. I see myself as another person and acting a role in this vast spectacle. Can you get the feeling of this thing? I never believed, until now, that this thing can be real and yet so unreal. The ship, the barge, the beach still showing signs of a great struggle, and the extraordinary peace and quiet that now blanket this scene. Nowhere is there a sign of war, only the scars of war. Cows are pasturing, berries are ripening on the hedgerows that once were barriers between

France: Killing Time

enemy and allies, and farmers are slowly taking possession of their lands again. You must bear in mind, Angel, that many women, nurses, Red Cross workers and WACs, are going through exactly the same motions that I am. They climbed down the same ladder on ship side, they rode the same barge, and they struggled up the same beach. They didn't trudge the five and a half torturous miles to our campsite as we did, but in all other things they face the same rugged life that we do.

[*From Oral History interview with grandson, Edward C. Bernstein, in 1986*]:

SL: *I don't know where we were at the time—maybe still in England—when we were told that an invasion had taken place over the Normandy beaches, but until we got there we didn't know that we were coming over the same route as the D-Day landers. We were disorganized and disoriented by the process of being ripped out of civilian life and shipped across the Channel at night. It was awful. We were hustled down into the hold of the ship in the dark. There were huge wooden tables for eating but no sleeping accommodations. I had a hammock which I strung under and tied to the legs of the table. Everyone showed a brave front. Jokes and vulgarity kept us from focusing on danger, fear, loneliness and the miserable conditions surrounding us. But we were lucky that we got into this medical outfit. We were non-combat medics with Red Cross armbands.*

We were moved to France and went up over Utah Beach close to Omaha Beach, tamping through the water and onto the beaches, to Carentan in Normandy. Moving up to the top you could see the vast destruction; the bombardment must have been absolutely fierce. We were warned that there were many unexploded bombs. You had to be careful where you stepped. You followed precise patterns and never wandered off anywhere. The bomb squad—the detonators—went through first to clear paths.

[*Editors' note: On the 40th anniversary of the Normandy Landing, June 6, 1984, Tom Brokaw relates his experience interviewing veterans visiting the site of their landing:*]

> There on the beaches of Normandy, I began to reflect on the wonders of these ordinary people whose lives are laced with the markings of greatness. At every stage of their lives they were part of historic challenges and achievements of a magnitude the world had never before witnessed.... This trip to Normandy was their first time meeting each other and their first journey back to those beaches since they'd landed under very different circumstances forty years earlier.

Brokaw spoke to two veterans. "I remember all the bodies and all the screaming." Brokaw continues: "Were they scared, I asked them. Both men had the same answer: they felt alternating fear, rage, calm, and, most of all, an overpowering determination to survive." (The Greatest Generation [New York: Random House, 1998], p. xxix).

I thought they did a remarkable project, the way they set up the camp in Carentan and started to instruct us in how to conduct ourselves as combat soldiers even though we were not engaged in combat.

In Carentan, we were in an open area; there were fields all around; the farmers had abandoned their fields and their crops; there was no tilling of the soil going on, just all abandoned. But there was a fringe of heavy, deep forest all the way around which was obviously areas that the farmers had not cleared away for farmland.

We established the 130th General Hospital. A peculiar thing happened. According to all the rules and regulations of war, it had to be a certain distance behind the battle front—I think fifteen kilometers—but it was a good distance behind the battle zone. However, our hospital for some strange reason kept moving up closer and closer to the battlefront, and at one point we were actually ahead of the designated zone of battle.

[September 5 letter continues]:

The mess tent is taking shape rapidly and perhaps before long hot food will be available. That doesn't faze me, though. I had hot soup last night, and hot coffee this morning by the simple expedient of using the little heating tablet provided us. The K-rations are palatable, though unimaginative. I continue to wonder at the lack of common sense in the packing of the K-rations. Such a thing as a plain soda cracker would delight any soldier, but instead they put those horrible "dog biscuits" in every package. What good is the nutrition in them if the boys throw them away? Well, one has to have something to gripe about. Despite the wet, I was quite warm and comfortable last night, our first night in this new camp. We have no idea of how the war is going since for several days we have had no papers or radio reports. But a memorable day in our lives will be Labor Day, [September 4] 1944, the day we "hit the beach" of France and made a successful landing. Darling, I am reaping some good from all this. I ask only that God grant me health. To go through a physical breakdown under such conditions would be a disaster; thus one is constantly on the alert to protect life and limb. We move so rapidly, and with such loads on our backs, that the guy who isn't up to par suffers truly. I'm happy to say I can take it. The utter exhaustion and soreness of feet and body pass quickly with a night's rest.

Perhaps I get more out of this than most men. The long hikes are made less painful for me as I "drink in" the romanticism of the scene. We wound our way through several villages yesterday and the settings were unbelievable. One tiny farm village sported a magnificent church. Everything is of stone structure, defying time and bombs, although the scars of war are plainly visible. It's all very old, substantial, romantic and appallingly unsanitary, from our point of view. The few inhabitants we saw ignored us as we passed in a long single file, or gave us a timid V sign. I guess they're tired of greeting troops by this time. One little French lad plainly astonished us by asking for "any gum chum?" My one concern

France: Killing Time

is for your peace of mind, so believe me, Darling, that we are very safe here. The war keeps running away from us. I've got to clean out the tent now. Red ants are appearing on the scene. My love to all. Tell them to write.

To you, My Love, all my love. Daddy

[*Editors' note: On the Internet, we discovered a website with photos about Carentan—then and now—authored by Erwin Jacobs, Senior Project Leader E-mental health at Trimbos-institut, Soest, The Netherlands. He maintains this site about interesting places from World War II that he has visited. On one occasion he and his wife traveled to Carentan, where they visited historic sites in Normandy and took many pictures. He kindly gave us permission to use his text and photos below.*]
Background:

> I am Erwin Jacobs and I am living in Soest (Soestdijk) near Utrecht, The Netherlands. My family roots are in Arnhem where as a young boy I became interested in the role Arnhem and surroundings had played in the World War II. My family had to evacuate Arnhem during the Market Garden operation and my mother was born in the same month this took place. . . . After the war my grandfather fought against the Indonesian freedom fighters and eventually returned to the Netherlands in Arnhem. It's hard to imagine what all these persons have gone through and how it is still affecting their lives up till now.
>
> Today there are few visible remains of these conflicts and a lot of places are forgotten where sometime heroic or tragic things have taken place. With my family background, to search and remember such places has received much interest of me. It is remarkable to see so many places where everyone is passing by but where striking stories can be told. Searching for the same exact place where a picture has been taken then and to make a comparative picture now is an opportunity for me to give these places more meaning. Furthermore it is fun to visit places where you would normally not go.

CARENTAN created on Wednesday, 13 February 2013 10:01

> Four major highways and a railroad converged in the city of Carentan to make it one of the strategic points to link the 2 beachheads Omaha and Utah. 5 days of fierce fighting made Carentan a difficult objective to meet. On June 13th the Germans counter attacked Carentan in which the 506th held their positions just long enough to let the American tanks stop the attack. This part is seen in the episode of *Band of Brothers*.
>
> Carentan was defended by the 6th Parachute Regiment, two Ost battalions and remnants of other German forces. The 17th SS Panzergrenadier Division, ordered to reinforce Carentan, was delayed by transport shortages and attacks by Allied aircraft. The attacking 101st Airborne Division, landed by parachute on 6 June as part of the American airborne landings in Normandy, was ordered to seize Carentan.

In the ensuing battle, the 101st forced passage across the causeway into Carentan on 10 and 11 June. A lack of ammunition forced the German forces to withdraw on 12 June.

GI´s pointing to a sign post at the center of Carentan. Photos courtesy of Erwin Jacobs from his blog http://www.wwiithenandnow.com/index.php/france/normandy-d-day/carentan

When the 101st Airborne entered the town of Carentan on June 12, 1944 (D-Day + 6) after heavy fighting on the two previous days, they met relatively light resistance. The bulk of the surviving German defenders (from the 6th Fallschirmjäger Regiment) had withdrawn to the southwest the previous night after a heavy Allied naval and artillery bombardment. Both sides realized the importance of the city: for the Americans, it was a link between Utah Beach and Omaha Beach, and would provide a base for further attacks deeper into German-occupied France. For the Germans, recapturing Carentan would be the first step towards driving a wedge between the two U.S. landing beaches, severely disrupting and possibly even destroying the Allied invasion.

Just before the crossing of the railway. Photos courtesy of Erwin Jacobs from his blog http://www.wwiithenandnow.com/index.php/france/normandy-d-day/carentan

The railway of Carentan now has more protection due to the high-speed trains crossing the town. The roads leading to the crossing of the railroad now has dead ends.

France: Killing Time

Photos courtesy of Erwin Jacobs from his blog http://www.wwii thenandnow.com/index.php/france/normandy-d-day/carentan

A Carentan street, then and now. Photos courtesy of Erwin Jacobs from his blog http://www.wwiithenandnow.com/index. php/france/normandy-d-day/carentan

The 17th SS PzG Division counter-attacked the 101st Airborne on 13 June. Initially successful, its attack was thrown back by Combat Command A (CCA) of the U.S. 2nd Armored Division. The severe casualties suffered by the 3rd/502d PIR, estimated at 67% of the original force,[10] resulted in the nickname "Purple Heart Lane" applied to that portion of the Carentan-Sainte-Mère-Église highway.

Carentan 101st Airborne in front of town hall and the town hall today. Photos courtesy of Erwin Jacobs from his blog http://www.wwiithenandnow.com/index.php/france/normandy-d-day/carentan

September 7, 1944 – Somewhere in France
My Darling:

It's a half an hour to noon chow and I'm anxious to get started on this since I didn't write yesterday, the day being full of activity and troublesome inspections. Soldiers always gripe about inspections, but only reluctantly admit that out of each one comes some good, such as yesterday's, for instance, the result being more room in the tent which is something to cheer about. I can work up no enthusiasm, however, about the sanitary facilities, the like of which should stir inventive minds to great action. But nothing happens. We merely moan and groan. What a subject for a Rabelaisian discourse on the Ways and Means of Crapping in a Bivouac Latrine! I need, with great urgency, to seek the nearest "accommodation" every morning, rain or shine. Ponder upon my state, then, when, delighted with my new and most beneficial habit, I trip hastily to my rendezvous with Mother Nature, only to find a vulgar straddle trench surmounted by a narrow board, elevated to the approximate height of a regulation stool. Now, by suspending one's rear well over the board and imitating a diver in a "jack-knife" turn, one gets enough traction for the final act, which is satisfactory despite the shifting of said traction from front to rear instead of side to side of "hung hole." This board arrangement, however, is a vast improvement over an even more primitive style which we employed earlier this week, namely, the simple squat over a long, narrow trench. Here, indeed, was a delicate problem that would have stumped an Emily Post. Suppose you enter the latrine which is only a canvas screen around the trench, and a GI already is squatting at one end of the trench facing you. Well, if you count him as a friend, you squat at close interval, facing him, and thus you can discuss world affairs while mustering for the final "ugh". If you don't know him so well, you can still face him by taking over the other end of the trench. Now a third GI enters. I have observed that even the crudest GI hesitates in this impasse. No matter which way he faces, one guy is going to get a spouting rear in his face. Of course, if number 1 is enemy and number 2 is neutral he can seize the opportunity to make a new friend and enrage an enemy. Motivated, however, by neither animosity nor friendship, he can take a middle position and pray that the next guy to enter isn't a bosom pal of the guy he has elected to face from his middle spot. So the whole thing becomes complicated and smelly, to say the least.

Chow was good but hastily eaten as a sudden shower hurried us back to our "rabbit holes". I hope that my last letter wasn't censored. I took in some of the surrounding countryside last evening and came back refreshed and mentally stimulated, though a little sad that such rustic beauty and calm must periodically give way to the blight and blemishes left by war. Where farmers used to greet each other over the hedgerows, now soldiers shout in passing, "Hey, where you from?" — "Chicago!" — "Here's your Chicago!" — "Here's your" (this or that)— is the stock reply or rebuttal to everything, the remark being companion piece to an obscene gesture. It's all very funny, apparently, because everybody laughs and pulls the same thing at the first opportunity. Another idiotic expression used without rhyme or reason, is "never happened." No matter what you say, it's always—"never happened."

When your mail catches up with me I'll be able to discover what I've told you so far and what I've missed. I'm completely mixed up, but your letter should be some clue. Angel, if I alternate these long letters with short V-Mail forms, don't be disappointed. Most often a letter has to be written on the run. Your preparation to meet me at the gang plank is a bit premature, Angel, but my arms ache for you and I'll know no peace until I am with you and the baby again. Love to all.

To you, My Love, all my love. Daddy

September 8, 1944
My Precious Darling:

I could kick myself all over this beautiful French countryside for having written you about my sojourn in the hospital. Having just this minute received your letter of the 25th, I am ashamed of my lack of judgment since I should have known that from such a great distance the very word "hospital" would be terrifying. I swear that it was nothing more than an attack brought on from too much hiking, possibly, and after the rest in the hospital, which was the only sensible place since we had no proper place in our own area, I felt refreshed and renewed in vigor. Our first sergeant, a prince of a fellow, saw to it that I did no hiking for a week afterward, and it was only on my own that I resumed the hikes and exercises because I felt the need for some exercise to absorb the great amounts of food which is shoved at us. Speaking of food, we have resumed regular rations now and I must say this stuff is excellent. I'm afraid you'll get me back a well filled-out Daddy.

Honey, your mail is not censored so write what you please. Only mail from overseas units is censored.

You must believe that I write you the truth, and when I maintain that we are safe from danger, I am being truthful. If you look for trouble, you'll find it here, but I have only one ambition and that is to return altogether sound to you. It so happens that we will have to live bivouac fashion for a while, but it's not too bad. At least you get plenty of fresh air. Perhaps someday some guy will discover a comfortable position for sleeping on the ground and then the soldier's life will be all clover.

I'm delighted with our daughter's progress in teeth sprouting. I devour her pictures at every rest period and always stop at the one with the feet crossed. Our child's personality radiates even from a picture. One week more and she will be a year old. It will be a beautiful sunny day even if it rains for my heart will be filled with joy. I am never away from you both in thought, Angel. I know how you feel about the heroes who are sitting out the war in the good old USA, but I know that like myself, millions are sharing my fate. There is a very bright side to my being in the 130th at this moment. I wish censorship would permit me to tell you all the facts but all I can say is have faith that this will turn out right.

Since we have had to strip our packs and luggage to bare essentials, I had to discard your precious letters which I frequently reread and so kept on the ball in answering them. If I've forgotten anything it's not because I didn't get your letters, which incidentally will be slower in reaching me now since ammunition has priority on all space these days. Mail call, like your mailman, has become a source of my day-to-day survival. The sun is hot. I'm going to sunbathe my rickety knee. Goodbye, My Love.

Until tomorrow, Daddy. Love to all.

September 9, 1944, 4:15 p.m.
My Darling:

It's a bright, sunny afternoon and I have contemplated on the pleasures of a bath, to which end I placed a helmet of water in the sun beside me in the hope that it will warm up sufficiently to be used for the purpose. This is the standard method of bathing in this area. Also at my side is a neat pile of long grass which I plucked with my hands in the past three days and which now, like a clucking hen with a nest of hatching eggs, I keep turning over and over to dry in the sun. The resulting hay, stuffed into my laundry bag, will make a swell mattress for my old bones. When I finish my ablutions, I shall use the soapy water to rinse out socks and underwear. You see, water isn't just thrown away. There is no tap to turn on at will. I have made a unique discovery.

– Interruption –

The damned bugle blew for assembly. The first sergeant wanted a detail of twenty men for something or other. I had to grab helmet and fatigue jacket and run like hell to the other end of the field. But I wasn't picked, thank goodness, so I resume to tell you about my discovery. It's Life Buoy soap! No, dear, I haven't conquered B.O.! It's a new miracle. It's the most ideal soap for washing clothes. What it is that makes it so I can't say, but it's good. You, too, would marvel if you saw the two handkerchiefs before and after. The kerchiefs should have been buried, they were so putrid, but now they're snowy white, and what's more, I washed them in cold water! We buy the soap at about three or four cents a bar, so I'm not being extravagant. It certainly is the all-purpose soap for a GI.

– Interruption –

Just ran out of ink and had to beg some from a guy in the next platoon. You can't get ink here, so any day now I'll start using a pencil, if I can steal one. In a minute, I shall have to stop to take care of some pressing matters. I'm still unwashed, it's near chow time and my duffel is spread over an acre of ground

France: Killing Time   97

being aired and sunned, and a big, black cloud is overhead. I'll be a busy guy in a few minutes. More tomorrow, the first Sunday in France. My love to all and to you, My Love, all my love. I am well and quite rugged it seems. No ill effects at all so far from the tenting and exposure, of which there is plenty.
   Love, Daddy

Sunday, September 10, 1944 – Somewhere in France
My Darling:
   I'm starting this while waiting for noon chow, after which I am going sightseeing, so forgive me if this is shorter than usual. It's a magnificent day. All my belongings are airing and drying nicely, and I, shaved and bathed, am absorbing sunshine. Yesterday afternoon was a full one, what with taking a sponge bath in my tent. It's a story in itself and I'll devote a letter to the preparation and execution of the same. I waterproofed my shoes, so I'll get a measure more of protection against dampness.
   The sanitary boys are right on the ball, having now provided "box seats" for the morning (and frequently afternoon) performances. The board and bare-ass contraption is still present but is totally ignored by the boys, a fitting fate for so ignoble an "accommodation."
   We were paid in French money this morning, so now francs are flying all over the place, changing poker hands rapidly. My bank notes—they are quite attractive—are safely tucked away. I'll keep a couple of the small four-cent and ten-cent notes for souvenirs. The colors will intrigue Roberta. Her birthday will have passed by the time this reaches you. I fervently hope that you hold some little festivity to mark the occasion. I am with you every moment.
   One of the peculiar aspects of living on the ground is the sudden and overwhelming desire to urinate which overcomes one. At first I was alarmed, but comparing notes, I learned practically every guy here makes sudden and precipitous trips to the urinal. It is mainly due to the fact that we consume considerable liquid and do almost no perspiring. In a way, it's a good thing. It keeps the kidneys flushed. There is humor in the thing in that guys in the midst of doing one thing or another, suddenly start crossing legs and "holding in" just like little boys who forgot to make "wee wee" when they should have. "French cleaning," My Dear, is an American intervention. There is no cleaning of any kind available here. Consequently, woolen O.D.s are washed, with disastrous results. I changed my mind at the last moment and didn't send in my woolens. I'd rather stink then be choked to death. You should see some of these guys struggling into their "washed garments"!
   We see many planes, and some put on a show for us, but they are all ours heading out to give the enemy well earned hell. The brutality of the Nazis is appalling, but their end will be all the more conclusive. There goes the bugle.
   To you my love, Daddy

September 11, 1944, 9:45 a.m. – Somewhere in France
My Darling:

Another beautiful day is in the making and in half an hour we fall out for close order drill and calisthenics, the latter of which I could do without. I wrote you that yesterday (Sunday) was devoted to sightseeing. Sites such as I hope mankind will never have to behold again I saw a-plenty! I can't tell you where we went, but the scene is so vividly burned into my memory that I'll remember it all when I can tell you, in person, I hope. From our beautiful pasture in which we camp, to the awful scenes of destruction is like moving from heaven to hell. Angel, don't think I expose myself to needless danger in viewing these scenes. The armies have long passed by and all is now a beehive of restoration activity. What amazed me was that some of the French people view the destruction with something of a sideshow curiosity. Maybe they've become used to this sort of thing. I wonder how we would take it if an American city were leveled by bomb and shell. I am afraid that our people have absolutely no conception of war, let alone total war! No wonder men return home and refuse to talk about what they've seen. Why our government consoles and protects the "home bodies" from the awful truth is beyond my comprehension. Every American, young and old, should be compelled to view the films which undoubtedly are made. It should be driven home now, not later when these films will be shown sandwiched in between Mickey Mouse and *Hot Love in Sumatra*. My Darling, it is appalling how half of America sweats it out in ditches, while the other half sits it out in nightclubs, theaters and down-filled fireside chairs.

You can get emotional about many things here, but there is no exact way of summing up one's feelings on seeing, day and night, the great, overwhelming motorized might of America roaring down the road in every direction. It's all American and American-built equipment, doing every conceivable kind of job of supply, reconstruction, communication, transportation, salvation. I have used the word "magnificent" lightly many times. How can I ever use it again except for something like this miracle of American motors. The ships are another story. The trip across the Atlantic was another miracle of coordination of brains and might.

It's drawing near to calisthenics time, Dear, so I'll end this with, to you, My Love, all my love. Give the "Love Lettuce" a huge kiss for me, and please give my love to all the family and my promise to write to them very soon. Darling, call my folks and tell them I'm feeling grand. I'll try to write to them, too, but may get stymied by one thing or another. Call Mayme, too, and give her my love.

Daddy

France: Killing Time

September 12, 1944 – Somewhere in France
My Darling:

I have just cabled to you, at government expense, 3,965 francs. Don't faint. I didn't rob the Bank of France. 3,965 francs amounts to $80, which is the money I mentioned in an earlier letter, and which I thought to deposit in a soldier's deposit account. But thinking it over, I decided it would be best to send it home. I have one request which I hope you will fulfill. Put the money in the *Daily News* account which we still have. It is interest-bearing, and gives me sort of a claim on the *News*. Unless you need the money urgently you will see the wisdom of doing this. I haven't actually saved $80 out of Army pay. Most of it was money I brought from the States, but I'm not depriving myself. Our weekly PX rations amount to 25 francs ($.50) and occasionally you can manage to spend 5 or 10 francs. Beyond that there is nothing to buy, and gambling is strictly out of my field. Last night's mail call brought me your letters of the 18th, 22nd, 24th, and 28th of August. But Manny Levine scored with thirty-six letters! How that Betty can write! It should happen to me!

Darling, if you can find a good fingernail file, I'd like to have it, also a jar of your favorite cream. The cold-water ablutions are pretty rugged and drying. You could get these into a very small package. I don't need candy or food. There is more than enough to eat, and the sea air just about spoils anything in transit unless it's vacuum packed.

I count on you to maintain as many contacts with the "profession" as is acceptable to you. God knows, it will be a struggle to get back to a point of effectiveness in the newspaper business. Don't be afraid of "taking advantage." I have a right to professional survival, and by golly, I'll fight my way back.

Well, I seem to be getting a bit "testy" this beautiful morning so I'll sign off. You must believe me, I am very well and my only regret and sorrow is that the effect of our terrible separation is so devastating to your nerves and health. I pray that you will find the courage to see this a bit more objectively, if only so that our future will not be beset with shattered nerves. I know how thin you get when you bear a grief and I'm terrified by it. Truly, Angel, it's rough here, too, but I guard against anything that will bring us grief in the future. It may help if you continue to think that the scene, at least, of our encampment is one that gives me spiritual comfort. I love the countryside to the extent of overlooking the inconveniences. The sun and clean air fill me with vigor and above all hope. It always has had that effect on me. An hour in the sunshine and I'm cleansed of all despair. Believe that I have rare moments of pleasure here and it will help you. How can I tell you how much I have longed for you and hope that through a miracle you could be here to be my guide. Through your knowledge and your complete accord with my feelings, France would be a great adventure for me. I get nowhere with my French book. Perhaps because I know that in that department you are my ears and tongue. It's chow time.

To you my love, Daddy

September 13, 1944 – Somewhere in France
Sweetheart:

What am I doing? Nothing. I'm still unassigned since the whole outfit is waiting for orders to move to a permanent post. I'm not worried, though. When the time comes, I'll make myself useful. Naturally the band and newspaper are things of the past. The European Theater doesn't allow such shenanigans.

Now, you can do me a real service. I have been noticing the extra-fine stationery you use. My supply is exhausted. I'll have to beg some for tomorrow's letter. If you put two or three sheets in every letter, I can build up a supply. It is not available in any form at the present and I agree that V-Mail is not the most satisfactory way of writing to one's wife. Ink is also not available, but I can always resort to pencil. This situation will right itself later, but it's a pain in the neck at the moment.

What do I want for Christmas? I want to be home, but that isn't likely. Also, I need my shaving mirror, which I foolishly sent home. There are no mirrors in France or England it seems. Also, those nice heavy sox which I sent home are a crying need here, if I'm to spend the winter in Europe. It's not my fault honey. They threatened us with immediate execution if we took any of these things along. They maintained everything was available in the E.T.O. Available my eye. Where are you going to get ink in the middle of a cow pasture? I must go begging writing paper now, so adieu, My Love, until tomorrow. Kisses for "Cookie."
Daddy

Sunday, September 14, 1944, 11:30 a.m. – Somewhere in France
My Darling:

Your warm letter of September 5 reached me yesterday, which is very good considering the difficulties to be overcome. I'm delighted. It seems to shorten the distance, getting a letter that isn't almost a month-old.

Labor Day, as you now know, was a "not unpleasant" one for me, too. At least it had the element of adventure and drama, and culminated in bedding down in this spacious pasture which besides sporting foxholes to explore, also has a thick border of black raspberry bushes. Yesterday I picked a pail-full and had a feast before wiggling into my homemade sleeping bag, more commonly known here as a "fart sack." Forgive the vulgarism. There is no other way of saying it and retaining the flavor of Army humor.

I wrote to Bulliet, Lloyd Lewis, and Pence James yesterday. Perhaps Pence might carry an item about me. It won't do me any harm. Watch his column. I put it squarely to Lloyd that the *News* never leaves my mind and that I'm coming back and expect full recognition.

The night sessions here are devoted to long walks and discussions on music, literature, etc. My pleasant comrades are a Cleveland social worker, a swell lad; and a Harvard man from Boston; both of our faith and intellectual, but primarily intelligent. The Harvard guy overheard me talking about the

France: Killing Time

recorder to a British Red Cross. He knows all about the thing and we hit it off. Both men are in this outfit, of course. Tomorrow (Friday, September 15) [Roberta's birthday], I think I'll devour the baby's pictures.

To you, My Love, all my love. Daddy

September 15, 1944 – Somewhere in France
My Darling daughter:

Just a year ago today, at almost the exact time of this writing, I was told that you were born, a healthy, lovely girl child. To the doctor, and to the world in general, the birth of another child was a routine thing, but for me your arrival was the hand of God bestowing upon your mother and me a gift, the most precious that man can receive.

You should know that your sweet mother and I speculated and wondered much what you would be like before you came. We even had misgivings, doubts. We couldn't see how we two ordinary mortals could achieve anything but a nice, ordinary baby. And then you came and we knew we were blessed. A cherub, an angel had come to our house. We thank God for you, Darling, and this day, so far from you, I am still sharing your mother's joy.

I know you are having a birthday party, and I am sure a wonderful cake. I shall have my sweets too, little "Love Lettuce." I shall eat a dish of fine blackberries which I picked this morning. I picked them because they symbolize more than the sweets for your party. The berry bushes conceal the foxholes in which men fought and died for our wonderful country. They were hard and green when those brave men crouched in their holes and tossed death at the enemy. But even as they knew those bushes would bear rich fruit, so did they know their heroic efforts would bring victory which is so near for us.

Thus, it will be all through our lives, angel. We will find the sweets of life only through first winning the battles of life.

I am not sad today, little "Love Lettuce." I am lonely and my own "battle" may be a long one. But I know when it is won, I'll find a double measure of sweets awaiting me, you and your mother. The day is ending as my daughter's natal day should—beautifully. Good night, My Lovely Daughter. God bless you and your mother.

Daddy

September 16, 1944 – Somewhere in France
My Darling:

I didn't write you yesterday as I was bent upon writing to our angel child, and then it got so dark I couldn't do else but go over and join the men at a huge bonfire and songfest. It was our first social get-together and it seemed more inviting than the dark tent. We are now in huge ward tents which will be far better than the "rabbit's hutch" we have been calling home for almost two weeks. At least you can stand up in a ward tent, and what's more, we have cots to sleep on. So I figure on drying out some of the arthritis from my bones. Yes, it bothers me continuously, but certainly not to the extent of knocking me over.

Did you get the birthday card V-Mail letter I sent to Roberta several weeks ago? It should have arrived days ago. I sent it early so that it would come before the 15th. My birthday letter to Roberta may have been a bit profound for a one-year-old child, but perhaps in years to come she may find it in her "book" and know anew how she fills our hearts with pride and joy. I made what may seem a possible error in the letter in stating that I was writing it at almost the exact time she was born. What I meant was that since here we are six hours ahead of American time, and allowing for the differences between Chicago and Eastern time, I was actually writing it at the time she was born which was 12:40 p.m. Chicago time.

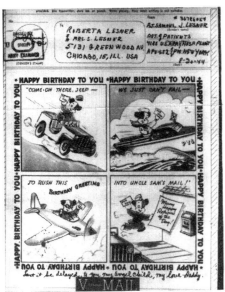

The day again is beautiful and a bunch of us are sitting in the grass writing to our wives, sweethearts, etc. One guy is breaking off his engagement, via V-Mail, and is writing it in better English than is his custom, since he asks the spelling of almost every other word.

Not much that's new or interesting today. We seem to be settling down here for a spell. The afternoons are ours to do as we please, but time flies here and you don't venture very far lest you miss chow and must go to bed hungry. You see, there are no canteens or PX's in a cow pasture, and one can't go looking for food from the natives. Forgive the brevity of this one, Angel. I'm lazy, mentally and physically. My love to all and to you, My Love, you know what! Don't forget to enclose the stationery in your letters.

Daddy

September 17, 1944 – Somewhere in France
My Darling:
[Editor's note: In her book GI Jews, Deborah Dash Moore writes of the importance of Jewish holiday observance for the Jewish soldiers, and how much the U.S. Armed Services encouraged such observance in 1944 in Europe.]

> The rapid retreat of German troops in the summer of 1944 brought large sections of Belgium and France into Allied hands by the Fall. And September brought not just the first taste of freedom for European Jews but also the Jewish New Year, the beginning of the year 5705. This would be the first Rosh Hashanah openly observed without fear since the German occupation of the continent four years earlier. . . . The Army encouraged Jewish GIs to observe the holy day, offering passes and occasional furloughs that promised a break from routine. (p.209)]

This is the hour (11 a.m.) daily when I span the great distance between us and bare my every thought to you. I'm sitting plumb in the middle of our pasture and writing as the good sun warms my bones, and what a warming we all need since the nights are appallingly cold. Tonight, no doubt, a "great" contest will be held to see who can devise the warmest "sleeping bag" out of the various blankets, newspapers, tent ropes and canvas shelter halves we possess. My own creation, designed for last night, looked so good it was widely copied, but this morning I had to admit to a lot of cold GIs that it wasn't so "hot." I have another "design for sleeping," however, and will try it out. What good are blankets, though? What one needs is one's nice warm wife to fortify oneself against the cold. Remember the incident in *For Whom the Bell Tolls*? I'll bet that sleeping bag was warm!

Tonight, My Darling, I'll voice publicly my whispered prayers for you, our angel, and our loved ones. Jewish services for Rosh Hashanah are to be held in a nearby town for us. I expect to go to all the services planned for today, Monday and Tuesday. Yom Kippur, too, will be observed here. It is a great moment for us, Darling. Freedom of worship is fast being restored to Nazi paganized Europe. How that monster will rave and rant tonight in his own hell he has pulled down around his pointed ears. How can we ever doubt that there is a righteous God?

In his own strange ways he lets the mad dogs destroy themselves. Yom Kippur may be the great day of reckoning. [Editor's note: In her book GI Jews, Deborah Dash Moore echoes these sentiments: "American Jews were coming to fight both an American and a Jewish battle against Nazism" (p. 93).]

Happy New Year and love to all. Daddy

[*From Oral History interview with grandson, Edward C. Bernstein, in 1986*]:

SL: *On Rosh Hashanah, 1944, we were stationed in Carentan. A notice went up on the bulletin board saying all soldiers of Jewish faith were invited to attend a High Holiday service in the adjoining town. We had to sign up on the bulletin board and we would be collected at a given time and taken in a truck to the area where the service would be held. Two or three of the boys who recognized each other as Jewish talked about it and we speculated how many guys would show up for this ride. The estimate was maybe six, seven, ten at most. After all, how many Jewish soldiers are there? To our amazement, when the appointed hour arrived, such a crowd of soldiers showed up that it took two trucks to transport us. When we got there, there was a delay in getting things organized. It was a beautiful afternoon. We were standing out in the fields near the tent where the services were to be held. You couldn't help but be aware that off in the distance, in the forest area, you would see figures darting out from the trees. We wondered what this was. One person ran up to us and identified himself as an Israeli underground fighter. He was very neat and trim. That's when we discovered what this was about. There was a whole group who had heard about the services, and, as French Jews, they wanted to come to the service. There was an undue delay. The sun was setting. Finally, when we were all called in to the improvised synagogue—it was an Orthodox service—it was discovered that the lights on the altar had not been lit. As you know, according to tradition, after sunset no Jew strikes a match. This was a dilemma. They wanted to start the service but the candles weren't lit. Somebody had a bright idea: they got an armed guard and marched down to a POW compound behind the installation and got two Nazi prisoners whom they marched to the tent to light the candles. Then they marched them back. The rabbi, a colonel from New York, proceeded to lead the service. It was a very touching moment. It went through me and held me in thrall for weeks after that. How ironic this was that here these Germans who had persecuted so many Jews had to light the candles for the Jewish service.*

[*Editor's note: It was common for Jewish services to be held outdoors, in the woods: services were held in a clearing in the woods for Passover, Rosh Hashanah and Yom Kippur. Deborah Dash Moore wrote: "When celebrated overseas, the traditional round of festivals resonated with Jewish reasons for fighting the war" (p.141). Further, she explained that "Jewish soldiers discovered contemporary relevance in public worship. In France in 1944, after landing at Cherbourg, one medic . . . went into the fields with other Jews in his regiment 'and used a German 88 as a pulpit to conduct the holy services commemorating the New Year.' Without a rabbi, 'on a*

France: Killing Time

battle-scarred field,' they prayed 'using the equipment of the persecutors of their faith'" (p. 141).]

September 18, 1944 – Somewhere in France

My Darling:

Two of your letters, August 29th and September 1st, arrived yesterday just as I was leaving for the first Rosh Hashanah service. Since we have been in France I have tried to write you daily, long letters which will reach you (or have) eventually. I can't explain the inconsistency of the mail and can only accept the situation stoically. You will note that the period in which I wrote hasty V-Mail letters was one during which we were either moving, being held "incommunicado," as it were, or during my illness. For the next few weeks, I am sure, I will be able to fulfill your dearest wish—a daily long letter, since I think we'll stay put for at least that period.

The service was poignantly beautiful. My heart ached for the loss of our dear friend Moe and I was overcome with the futility of trying to span the great distance that lies between us. Life is cheap on the battlefield, and some aren't even accorded the "nicety" of a common grave, but eventually the world will have disgorged its brutality and we'll resume living by conventions.

This morning, having again attended service—there are more than twenty-five officers and men of the Jewish faith in our outfit and all attended—I discovered that the young, fine-looking lad who warmed our hearts with his cantorial brilliance is a Chicagoan and lives at 4300 W. Van Buren St. Bill Blumenthal is his name. He worked in Mark's Jewelry Store on State St. It might be a "mitzvah" [Hebrew and Yiddish for "good deed"] to see if you can find his family listed in the phone book and convey to them the great spiritual pleasure their boy gave us. He is a pal of the Lind Brothers [famous family of cantors in Chicago] whom we got to know and like so much. I'm going to the service tonight again, and perhaps tomorrow, too, just to hear the fellow.

Service is held in a tent with an improvised, though beautifully decorated, altar. Gorgeous petunias flank the altar, and, ironically, are kept fresh in huge shell casings filled with water. The shells were retrieved from the pasture battlefields. The censor informs me that it is permissible to say that [word excised by censor] is within an afternoon's visiting distance. Yes, I've been there, and on the road to [word excised] you see some sights to remember. [excision], as undoubtedly you have read in the papers, was not seriously affected by the ravages of war and is quickly being restored to its former industry and activity. Incidentally, more than four hundred men and women in the service gather for the services, and it does one's heart good to feel this brotherhood so far from home. We have no regular rabbi to assist the cantor, but several high-ranking officers from the various units in this area fill the bill intelligently and efficiently. Our young "cantor," though, is the messenger of our prayers.

Jewish identity could not easily be ignored or repressed in Europe. Although Jewish GIs had left their country as Americans, crossing the Atlantic into the shadow of the Third Reich involved specifically Jewish issues that would complicate further their quest for fellowship.

Crossing overseas thus initiated journeys that encouraged American Jewish soldiers to explore not only new and foreign worlds but also more personal ones. Integration into the military forced Jews to search hard for comradeship. They could not take for granted the friendship of the men in their unit. Loneliness and isolation often accompanied their military service overseas.

In the European Theater . . . the German enemy's presence meant that their Jewishness, even if buried, could not disappear from their consciousness. They were American Jewish soldiers fighting for respect as men, both individually and collectively. (Deborah Dash Moore, *GI Jews*, pp. 91–92, 116, 198)

Honey, I understand that certain small parcels can be sent without requests. Inquire about it. It would be ideal for getting small things to me that might strike your fancy or that I might desire. One thing I want is a couple of good wash cloths and a dish rag. The wash rags are necessary with all this cold-water bathing, and the dish rag is sorely needed for my mess gear. Unless it's wiped dry each time it rusts and makes for arduous cleaning. Small delicacies, of course, are most welcome, but please don't go shopping like mad. You know my tastes, and small things in small packages would add spice to the "pièce de résistance" which nourishes me when mail call brings me your letters. That you have all of me, you may be assured.

My love to all. Your, Daddy

September 19, 1944 – Somewhere in France
My Darling:

Your letters of Sept. 6 & 9 received with joy. We're catching up with time. But I've decided to answer systematically, starting with the oldest one.

The great enthusiasm with which all of you greeted the news of my meeting with Roy pleases me, of course, more than I can say. It seems my army career will be filled with dramatic moments. All Roy says about my health and mental attitude is quite correct. I feel fine, am brown as a chestnut (all I do is sit in the sun) and it seems I'll be caught up in a whirl of activity before long. You ask what I am doing. The answer is nothing. But look what's happened! You know our band was broken up when we reached England. I was sadly disappointed, but I was in no position to question the decision. Soon after, I went into the hospital. Lo and behold, one day Jack Garber comes lumbering into the ward with my accordion and deposits it under my bed. I fumed at the utter indifference of those whose duty it was to await a more opportune time to burden me with an accordion. So I left it with the chaplain upon leaving the hospital, instructing him to sell it or send it home. Yesterday, however, having already written to

France: Killing Time

inquire about the instrument, I was told that the American Red Cross had bought it for $50. But here's the payoff. It was the unit attached to our outfit that had bought it. Thus, at seven o'clock tonight, a messenger will deliver it here and I've already been asked to join the small musical [word torn off] of an adjoining hospital unit. I frankly declined to make any solo appearances and gave only a weak promise to join anything. I want my $50. That's all. I'll send it home as soon as the money is turned over. The sale is final, and no money-back guarantees. If they want to let me play around with it, OK, but no more four-hour rehearsals for me.

I am tickled that you had a party for "Love Lettuce" with all the trimmings, and by now you know that I was "there" too. I can imagine her excitement in having so many kids around. I could have told you months ago that our child would be a "world beater."

The cantorial work of our fellow Chicagoan, Bill Blumenthal, was remarkable in its power to sustain the spiritual mood of the great occasion throughout the three days. We all were moved by his eloquence and spiritual power. I hope he will be able to "sing" the Yom Kippur service too.

The point system, My Darling, is as yet a nice bit of political vote-catching, but if we are completely victorious in Europe this year, I think a more intelligent plan will be formulated and carried out! I continue to hope that this will happen. My love to all, and to you, My Love, all my love.

Daddy

September 20, 1944 – Somewhere in France
My Darling:

In answer to your letter of Sept. 8, again I am sorely distressed that it has taken so long a time for you to learn that we are safely set up in France. I hadn't thought of the initial shock you would experience in learning that we are in France since all is so blessedly peaceful and quiet here. But it is beginning to sink in that you and the family must have received this news with great misgivings. I beg you to believe that we are perfectly safe.

I'm sorry your bad luck in picking a movie still prevails, but I think most people these days are noticing the tripe that's dished out as entertainment, but for something better to do, they continue their habit of going to the cinema. Even we who are starved for entertainment notice the awful lowering of movie standards. A certain Mickey Rooney–Judy Garland film we saw before leaving England had me beating myself over the head. The director didn't know how to polish off the darned thing and didn't stop until the whole cast wound up by waving bullrushes or something, in a mad frenzy.

We did get a fine show last night, though, from a neighboring unit. They brought over a swell bunch of "live actors" to put on most of a musical show which they had written and produced some time ago. Our guy, Cpl. Dash, proved to be a find as the M.C. and chief laugh-getter. I told him he'd rate an eight-column overline in the *News*. He's a former professional actor and entertainer, now acting as Special Service for his unit. We had a huge bonfire, a pickup orchestra, and a lot of laughs. No, I didn't play. An old, wheezy accordion was brought over as a substitute for mine which hasn't arrived yet and I felt it was best to decline. I must make a clean and positive break with this awful, time-devouring "hobby" for the rest of my GI life. It was forced upon me in the States, but by golly, there'll be no more "pressure" performing for me. It is no longer my concern to provide entertainment. Where the hell are all the entertainers who are supposed to be over here? If they're not in France, where then? Yes, I am bitter. We got a royal "screwing" once, and that's enough. I'm an Army clerk and that's what I intend to do. I'll close now to do the "next best thing," go to chow.

Love to all, and to you, My Love, all my love. Daddy

September 21, 1944 - Somewhere in France
My Darling:

Our days are busy and full despite the fact that we have no actual tasks assigned to us yet. The morning, for instance, flies. We're up at 7, dress hastily, make a mad dash for the latrine, which is quite a dash away from our tents. Rush back, grab steel helmet, towel and soap and rush halfway across the field to the ablutions stand for a quick, cold water wash. Fall out for first formation at 7:30. Rush back to tent, tear down bed, meaning the improvised sleeping bag which daily becomes more complicated as each man adds a new trick. Fold and stack blankets and display same with all other field equipment in precise arrangement on bed, and take off for the chow line which forms a block away. After chow, we police area, slowing working our way to the now commonplace "front and rear" traction defecating boxes—those cute "rear suspension" jobs have vanished, thank goodness—make a hasty deposit and fall out for calisthenics and drill. If you draw the first shift on this you have an hour in which to shave, wash clothes, and draw your P.X. rations after the drill. If you draw the second hour, you disappear since you aren't allowed in or near tent during the "Bitching Hour," which means inspection of entire area. Then there is that precious hour before chow in which I write your letter. This morning, however, I had to delay it. I wanted some apples. I got same. No detail after the afternoon formation, so here I am soaking up regular July sunshine and composing a letter out of mere nothings.

I hope you'll forgive me, Honey. There is so little that can be told. We are becoming very comfortable, and the "management" of this sprawling establishment is really going all out to keep us happy little non-combat warriors. I have even acquired a pipe and to all intents and purposes, I'm quite the country gentleman. Yesterday, I "harvested" a helmetfull of luscious berries. Today, apples; tomorrow—well, tomorrow! A calf was just born in an adjoining field, and yesterday a huge bull was brought into the pasture. One day, and soon, I hope, we, too, will be allowed to go home and start life anew. Start planning for the future again. Don't despair, angel. I am well and have again found this routine stimulating in several respects. The urge to converse again in other than GI "language" is with me and fortunately there are several men here who "speak" that sort of language. My complaint of yesterday about the absence of live entertainment in this area has been voided. Tonight, we get a USO show. A spacious tent has been set up and a fine stage is being hammered together. That's all for now. I must straighten out duffle, wash underwear, and go for a shower two miles down the dusty road. Love to all. Kiss our wonder child.

Love to you. Daddy.

September 23, 1944 – Somewhere in France
My Darling:

Time for a short one. More later today. Received yours of Sept. 3, which isn't much since it's three weeks old and merely reminds me that I was lax in writing to you in the period between the end of August and our arrival in France. Actually, it was physically impossible to write on some days during that period, particularly during the channel crossing, and I checked with Manny and his letters to Betty during that period were as infrequent as mine. Since arriving in France, I have written you daily long, long letters. Honey, you've missed a day or so yourself. I know how you must feel, and believe me I walk around in a daze, too, when I get no mail for two or three days.

I tried several times yesterday to take pen in hand. Caught a pick and shovel detail in the afternoon to dig a six-foot trench for defecating, and wound up in the evening with a headache that floored me. Haven't had one like it for at least four months, but I thought I got smacked with an axe. Just like one of your "swell" migraine heads. I was out for an hour. Four aspirin fixed me up and after an hour I fell asleep and had a restful night.

– Interruption –

I was called out to go to the showers, which is a real treat. Had one yesterday, too, and luxuriated in the warm spray for half an hour. Returned to an elegant lunch of turkey, potatoes Milanese, corn, chocolate pudding, etc. Really swell chow today. I'm resuming this at 1:30. I am lucky enough to duck an afternoon detail. I'll wash towels, air blankets, and write you an intelligent letter. Darling, my ink is still begged for this one and that so, call my folks and explain that I'm limited to one letter a day until I can get some.

Love to all. To you, you know what. Daddy.

September 23, 1944 – Somewhere in France
My Darling:

As I promised, this is No. 2 for today. My towels and socks are slowly "boiling" in a helmet set over the grate which is used to heat up a huge can of water for ablutions. Yep, we're catching up with modern conveniences. You get hot water for shaving if you're fast. I can't draw this water for laundry, so I sit and watch and wait. With a little effort it's not difficult to keep clean.

I've made a number of requests. More than I should, perhaps, but what I've asked for will serve me well wherever we are. If you can't get a flashlight, I'll settle for a couple of candles. Don't forget the warm socks. I think they'll give us a muffler, but if not, you can knit one for me. I wear the sweater every day. I must go to my laundry now.

We'll have Yom Kippur service here Wednesday. I know only one prayer: a prayer for a quick reunion with my beloved wife, our angel child, and our good families. Keep your chin up, Sweetheart. God is good. So many others are looking at death every moment while we are in this quiet, beautiful area. We're having a blackberry feast in our tent tonight. You should see the size of them. Love to all.

To you, My Love, all my love. Daddy.

September 24, 1944--- Somewhere in France
My Darling:

Sunday morning. The entire day is ours to do as we please, but there isn't much to do, so I'll get my duffle in order after finishing this, take a walk, and then spend the afternoon reading. It's one of those beautiful autumn days: brisk, sunny, and conducive to vigorous walking.

We had quite a delightful live show here last night, brought to us by a regular GI unit, and a band that could rate with anything I've heard in the course of my café meanderings. The boys set up an outdoor stage and Manny, who has his moments, festooned the supports with toilet tissue, appropriately enough since the review was dubbed "Blow It Out." The berry feast, which I prepared, having hoarded the lump sugar from my K-rations, and to which I also added some canned cream which I acquired on board ship in the channel crossing, came off nicely, too. Each guy in our tent caught about two heaping tablespoons of berries. This we topped off with candy bars drawn from the mobile P.X. which visits us weekly.

My labors with towels and other items was for nothing. I forgot them on the line last night. They were blown hither this morning. It will be dry in an hour, though, with this sun and air.

My deep coat of tan is the envy of all. They can't see how I do it. Well, if they would come out of the tents long enough to see the sun they might discover how it's done. Each man to his own liking. They like cards. I like sun.

The boxes with the front and rear traction got a workout all through the night. I guess the guys ate too well on turkey yesterday. I wasn't affected and feel quite rugged this morning. Haven't collected the $50 yet so I shall ask for it. The

France: Killing Time

Red Cross likes to receive but is a little slow when it comes to giving. I'm afraid this pen will run dry in a minute so I'll close with a request that you continue to write me detailed accounts of the baby's day-to-day actions, and, of course, about all your activities. It helps to bridge the great distance between us.

Love to all and to you, My Love, you know what! Daddy

September 25, 1944 – Somewhere in France
My Darling:

Still no mail from you, but there's a very good reason for it. The ships that are coming in are loaded with food, and the mail bags have to wait. Well, I'll have one delicious afternoon reading all the letters that surely will come in a bunch.

Yesterday (Sunday) turned out to be a bit blustery so I stuck close to the tent and read a few short stories. Your recommendation of "Razor's Edge" is certainly inviting, but I doubt if the book is available. We have set up a small library of the GI series which are issued to the Armed Forces, so maybe it will turn up. In the evening we had a movie, *Sensations of 1945*, and I must say it made me homesick. In it are Sophie Tucker, Dorothy Donegan, Cab Calloway, and Woody Herman. It was like a typical roundup of the night clubs for me. Tucker looks marvelous in the film, and Donegan is still the amateur. Her playing shows its defects even more on the screen. I wonder where Tucker is now. I'd like to write to her and tell her how she pleased the boys in this tent theater in the middle of a cow pasture.

Darling, don't worry too much about the requests I've made. If certain items such as flashlight and camera are not available, forget them. If you think of it, put a couple of candles in the fruitcake package. They will come in handy. I've got an old shell casing and perhaps I can fashion a holder for a candle. Even the little bit of light would be cheering in the tent. Don't forget the wash rag and dish rag.

I have checked with Finance about the bond deductions which began in August. Laundry service has been resumed here so the washing detail will be considerably lightened. Washing a pair of fatigues in a helmet is quite a trick if you can do it. The GI laundry, however, does it better. The boys are all busy fashioning ashtrays out of the shells we have found in the fox holes. The finished product is really handsome, and if I can get my hands on the hack saw, I too will have one for my sweetheart. When it's my turn to go to Cherbourg [north of Carentan; see map with letter of Sept. 5]. I'll try and take it in to a machinist's shop, if such a thing exists, and have it done. I'm afraid I wouldn't get far with the overworked hacksaw we have. Now don't go to worrying about my picking up shells. They are harmless, having been exploded. We use them for trash cans and I believe I mentioned that in the synagogue I saw them being used as altar vases. When they're shined up they're beautiful. Wish I could send a whole one home for a vase. It would look elegant on our round coffee table. Maybe I will. I'll look for a matching pair.

There isn't much else that's news at this time. I am enjoying very good health, eat like a wolf and enjoy the companionship of some really nice guys. They are all friendly, and I must say, on the whole nicer than the original bunch. I think this outfit will do some good here, once we get going. Don't worry, Angel. Love to all. Kiss "Love Lettuce" for me. Daddy.

September 26, 1944 – Somewhere in France
My Darling:
This is the hour for which I wait each day, from 11:30 a.m. to 12:30. It's my hour to talk to you. No mail yesterday, but I'm hoping today will bring me something that I can carry with me into the synagogue. I will ask the Lord's blessing with the letter in my hand. I have acquired a bottle of ink through the generosity of a swell guy here, and I hope to snag some writing paper, too. The Jewish men here expect to fast all day since we will be away from our camp. I shall not mind it too much. I've acquired a few extra pounds with the heavy eating around here.

There is nothing new except another innovation in latrine comfort. You must be wondering why I indulge in so much latrine description, but such matters become of great importance when living in a field. At any rate, the whole "project" has been placed under a large ward tent and I must say we now have comfort and privacy. Approaching the tent, however, is like entering the sideshow tent of a circus, the big attraction being the row of GIs sitting in various positions of distress, bliss, open pleasure, meditation, and hopelessness.

We have found a new apple tree with excellent apples, so the berries have been getting the go-by for the time. The day started wet and miserable but the sun has just broken through so all is well for the start of a great New Year for us all. That's all for now, My Darling.

Love to all, to you, Daddy

September 29, 1944 – Somewhere in France
My Darling:
A blustery morning, so we're congregated in our tent awaiting a break in the weather more suitable for drilling and calisthenics.

The Red Cross has paid off so at the earliest opportunity for sending money home, I will forward the $50 which I received for the accordion. I hated to part with it since it is a good instrument, but I can't see myself worrying about it and dragging it all over Europe and heavens knows where else. We seem to be "digging in" here so I guess nothing will happen for a time at least. A recreation program for us is well under way and, coupled with our boondoggling, we have enough to occupy us.

I have finished one ashtray, but it's so attractive I think it would serve better as a cigarette tray. To that end, I left the patina on the inside as Nature designed it and polished only the outer surface. I also left the stem which was in the shell. The stem which is part of the detonating cap is perforated and I thought it would

France: Killing Time

be an original idea to stick old fashioned matches in the little holes, thus adding utility to the general decorative effect. You will see what I mean when the thing arrives. I expect to send it off in a few days. It may tarnish en route, but a little metal polish will quickly restore it to its original beauty. I think you will appreciate why I left the corrosive effect inside. It adds an antique beauty to the thing, whereas the boys who shined theirs inside and out have achieved only an ordinary ashtray, in my opinion. You will notice the little curled screws also inside. Into these can be inserted small match books. At any rate, I fashioned the thing all by myself. If I get my hands on some tools I can make a few other gadgets of beauty and usefulness, but tools are not being thrown around. I want to fashion a little dinner bell.

That's all for now, Angel. Love to all. Kiss my cherub daughter and find peace in the knowledge that I love you more than the written word conveys.

Daddy

September 30, 1944 – Somewhere in France
My Darling:

Just a few minutes to get off a fast one lest the day go by and no letter gets written. In twenty minutes we take off for the hot showers which really are a treat after the dabbling in cold water which is my morning ritual. I like to wash before going to chow so it means using cold water, as the GI can we use for heating shaving water, etc., doesn't get going until 9 a.m. or so. Besides, the hike to the showers is stimulating.

Caught a carpentry detail yesterday afternoon so I couldn't do much with the ashtrays, but if I'm lucky, I'll be free today and possibly even get to send one off to you.

No mail from you yet, and my heart is sorely tried, but since it is a general condition, I find courage to believe that all is well at home.

Dreamt of the baby again and this time she appeared in all her cherubic glory. You too, Angel, appeared well and happy. I pray that is so.

The war seems to have hit a stalemate. From now on I'm afraid it's going to be hard, bitter fighting until the end. No more amazing advances. We are meeting the enemy on his own ground. Perhaps it's what we need most. This time we should learn what war does to young hearts and old, and truly make this a victory to end all wars.

Well, Angel, the whistle is blowing. We saw *Arsenic and Old Lace* (movie) last night and I recalled our evening together in the theatre.

Until tomorrow, my love to all, and to you, Daddy

October 1, 1944 – Somewhere in France
My Darling:

At last, one letter, Sept. 17, arrived and when I'll get the preceding ones that you must have written, I can't say. You speak of France, so you know at last, but

I'll have to wait for your letters in which you tell me of your reactions to the news. Again, I swear that I have written every day since we've been in France, and on several occasions, two letters a day. I hope the mail has not been lost.

I am very well, Angel. You must believe that and not let yourself worry on that score. There is very little to do here and our amusements run largely toward rough talk and bull shooting. It's hard to read with the constant racket of shouting voices, and of course bedtime is very early. Believe it or not, we are usually asleep by 9 p.m. and sleep until 7 a.m. That's some sleeping. Frankly, we'll all welcome a little activity which may soon demand all of our time. But that's what we're here for.

Love to all. To you, my Darling, a heart full of love and devotion. Daddy

October 2, 1944, 3:30 p.m. – Somewhere in France
My Darling:

No mail yesterday, and no promise of any today, but I'll carry on as I promised. The day is one of those rarely beautiful ones. I missed my usual before-chow letter-writing interval but will be compensated for it. The whole bunch of us went on a berry-picking expedition and tomorrow's chow will produce delicious berry pie. The cooks here are really unusual for Army mess personnel. The pies are excellent.

Now to the main business: At last I have finished the ashtrays as best I can with what tools are available. They are packed and ready for mailing which I will do tomorrow since I missed the censoring officer today. Also, in your carton will be several small items of interest. So look for them as I am filling the boxes with straw. I have a beautiful key from the castle in which we lived in England, some coins, French notes, and a piece of parachute silk for a handkerchief. I think you'll like it. The tray, though, I hope will win your admiration. I really think it is handsome and as I explained in the other letter, useful as a cigarette dish rather than a butt dish. It may tarnish en route so take some steel wool or metal polish and rub it down a bit, in a circular motion, so as not to scratch it. It takes a beautiful luster. The shell itself is part of a huge one which was fired in great number in the storming of the beaches and final drive inland.

There is very little of news, except that we should start functioning very, very soon. I beg you to be a brave, Good Wife and Sweetheart, and not worry no matter what happens. The uncertainty of the mail may continue for a time but you will understand that the safety of all, as well as the uninterrupted flow of supplies, are the contributing factors. I wish I could send you something really beautiful from France, but under the present circumstances it is impossible to get anything worthwhile. So, Darling, accept my bits of junk as token presents which some day I shall redeem with things more worthy of you.

My love to all and to you and our angel a heart full of love. Daddy

P.S. Darling, mail call just brought me letters for Sept. 8-11, and two of the 19th. Still a lot missing apparently. Now to read them with joy. Daddy

France: Killing Time

October 4, 1944, 9:00 a.m. – Somewhere in France
My Darling:
   I am passing up a shave with hot water to get this written since I didn't write yesterday.
   My mother told me in her letter that at her party Roberta kept repeating, "Daddy, Daddy," while pointing to my picture. I haven't received your version of the party yet. Give me a word picture of it.
   I'm glad you finally caught an entertaining movie. I mentioned having seen *Arsenic and Old Lace* here. You know the crazy character who thinks he's Teddy Roosevelt and who blows a bugle at the damnedest times? Well, you can just imagine what goes on here now every time the bugle blows. Everyone hollers "charge" and dashes like mad for the assembly area. Thus, we amuse ourselves. Everything becomes an occasion for a demonstration. We just "charged" out and back again as the skies opened up. I see I can't finish this in place as a half dozen guys are hovering around my one-inch stub of candle which I found in a garbage pit and by which I am now writing.
   My love to all, and to you. My Love, all my heart. Daddy.

October 5, 1944 – Somewhere in France
My Darling:
   Your most wonderful, delicious, newsy, inspiring, soul-satisfying letter of Sept. 21st at hand, and now I feel guilty as hell about complaining at the lack of daily letters. Yours are so super that one carries me along for several days. But, Honey, a daily lift is so good, too, that I can stand it just fine.
   My boondoggling kept me quite busy all day. Now if I had some tools I could send you some nice candlesticks. My experiment turned out quite well so I guess I'll cut the parts and send them home. You can have them finished in any machine shop. All they'll need is a couple of screws or some simple welding. Looks like I have my work cut out for me. More tomorrow, Angel, after I reread your superb letter.
   Love to you, My Love, and to the rest, my best. How's my cherub?
   Daddy

October 6, 1944, 3:30 p.m. – Somewhere in France
My Darling:
   I just reread your letter of the 20th-21st. It's the kind of letter I like to get. Full of news, and, what's more important, an indication that your spirits are high, which is the one thing I want more than anything.
   The tent is empty except for myself and one individual who is asleep. The boys are all attending an afternoon movie. I've seen three this week and doubt if I can stand another one without either becoming a moron or going nuts. If that's what we get, I can imagine what the civilian stuff is like. Most of these

have been shown in the States, though, so all one can say is that Hollywood certainly has set a new low in the art of cinema making. I'll go to the evening showing, but only to kill an hour or so of the long nights we have, since there is no light by which to read.

Seriously, Angel, I'm not depriving myself of things material. Later, perhaps, when we get located near something like a city, I'll certainly require more funds and shall use my money accordingly. What little I can save now will go for the luxuries we are doing without now. At any rate, I'll need a coat, at least, and certainly you'll need personal as well as household things when we are on our own again.

My love to the folks and to you, My Love, all my love. Daddy

October 6, 1944, 6:00 p.m. – Somewhere in France
My Darling:

Certainly, you can appreciate the fact that we can't sit in the middle of a cow pasture for the duration. Angel, we are only "waiting" here. Our real work must of necessity be done elsewhere, but that doesn't mean we are going to "do battle" with our bare hands, nor does it mean that we will be in any more danger than we are now, if picking berries is considered dangerous. Naturally, if one looks for trouble, he'll find it. I've told you that this was a battlefield not too long ago, but I swear if one minds his own business and does as he is told, no harm can come to him. I'm not one to go looking for trouble, you know that.
Your wonderful letters have given me enough material for several days' letters. Thank you, Angel. Much more tomorrow. It's getting quite dark. Good night, My Love, good night, My Cherub.

Daddy.

October 7, 1944, 10:30 a.m. – Somewhere in France
My Darling:

A dull, gray morning and not much to do. I can't undertake to write to all those I'd like to since the paper and envelope shortage is a real one, and I must conserve my little stock for you and the folks. One guy just told me he paid 8¢ per sheet of writing paper. That gives you some idea. I mentioned that you might put a couple of sheets in each of your letters. It would help me enormously. This stuff I'm using is hopeless, but it's all I've got.

That's all for now, "Sweet." Tomorrow I shall compose an "opus" for you.

Best to all, and to you and our cherub, all my love. Daddy

October 8, 1944, 10:30 a.m. – Somewhere in France
My Darling:

As I promised, this beautiful Sunday morning is yours and I'll try to give you a summary of the hectic past two months. To this end, I dug around in my

France: Killing Time

duffle bag and found some of the ship papers for which I wrote daily columns, on the way across. I believe I never mentioned this to you in the anxiety of the days that followed after landing in England. At any rate, our ship got out a daily two-page paper, the staff of which was composed of members of the ship's passengers on each crossing. Garber and I, therefore, along with a couple of intellectual paratroopers and two of our "Hot Compress" cartoonists comprised the staff for our crossing. We had it nice, indeed. The paper's office was on ship's deck which was otherwise off-limits to enlisted men. I was provided with a yellow arm band, "Special Duty," and I roamed the ship at will, looking for "news." Believe me, on a ship loaded with GIs there is much to see and report, and much that you can tell only in private to intimate friends. I don't think I told you about the paratroopers, for instance.

Here's an excerpt from my column of August 2: "Those blond hussies—they're doing it right out in the open now, rubbing peroxide in each other's hair! Those handsome paratroopers throw their weight around plenty but at least they don't throw their dandruff around. The peroxide, if nothing else, keeps their scalps clean, according to a medical officer whom we asked about the paratroopers' promiscuous hair bleaching." The crazy guys apparently carried along bottles of peroxide which they brought up on deck and rubbed into each other's hair. In a few days after the application they would blossom forth as "beautiful blondes." I must say they were startlingly handsome, some of them. They always looked dashing, and how they kept their boots shined in that madhouse was a complete mystery to me. A peculiar aftermath of the paratroopers' influence is that now every medic who can acquire a pair of paratrooper high-tops, by hook or crook, polishes them like mad and wears them with all the dash ever achieved by any airborne devil. I even know of one medic who removed the Armed Service Forces insignia from his jacket so that he would be able to masquerade even more successfully as a paratrooper. I know because it was my "combat" jacket he was wearing on that date. The new jackets were issued to us before we left the States. They are very dashing and we were the first medics to get them. So when the guys who had been over here for a year or so spied them, we were offered all sorts of bribes to loan them for a night of dating. The character who borrowed mine claims he didn't remove the ASF patch, but I know better because I had just sewed it on that very day.

Here's another crazy trick that they pull around here. It's one for the books. The Army, as you know, doesn't indulge in any polite discussion on sex. The facts are faced frankly, and consequently every means is taken to prevent infection and spreading of infection. Thus, rubbers are available to every man. In fact, it was "compulsory" to take a "Pro" packet along when going out on pass. Well, as I explained before, living in the middle of a cow pasture makes these things quite useless. But someone discovered that by fashioning the "thing" into an elastic band one could "blouse" the bottoms of the trousers to make them look just like paratrooper pants. Darling, believe it or not, everyone is doing it, wearing rubbers on the legs! At first it was a strange thing to hear one GI ask another, "Hey, have you got an extra rubber for my pants?" Well, they tell us to "improvise." If you don't have the proper materials, improvise, they say, and these days we do that aplenty. My candlestick which was born out of sheer necessity now has started a dozen guys off on various lamp-building projects, etc.

Coming back to the ship, I don't remember if I told you about how we "sweated out" every meal. The food was excellent, but it meant taking a steam bath with each meal. For some unexplainable reason, no one thought to put steam traps over the mess gear washing vats. The water was kept at a terrific temperature and so as you dipped your gear, steam arose in a solid column, hit the colder air above, and descended upon you in a torrent of rain. You were wet through and through when you emerged from that inferno of a mess hall. Yet we "endured" it and got hysterical with laughter after each bath-meal. To see the guys pop out of the mess hall gushing sweat from eyebrows and ears was really something. It brought to mind the Turkish baths we used to go to as kids. Here's what I wrote:

> "Sweat Without Tears"
> If Turkey would make up its mind, this item would be more to the point. We could give credit where credit is due, equally and impartially. We're thinking about the Russo-Turkish bathhouse we used to visit once a week to "sweat it out." Once a guy told us the temperature of the sweat room was 140°, but it took both Russia and Turkey to achieve that. Imagine our disappointment, then, when we found the temperature in the ship's mess hall a mere 120° yesterday morning. Looks like the US-Russo steam bath business isn't up to par. Hence we urge Turkey to come in and show us how to make up that difference of 20 degrees.

So it went, Angel, many events that I shall always remember and relate to you when God brings us together again.

In succeeding letters I'll try to give you word pictures of other phases of our GI life. Mine has been, so far, a pleasant life, if being away from one's loved ones can be pleasant. But each man here carries the same burden of homesickness. Alone, it would be unendurable; together we offer some release and comfort to each other in our exhibitionism, our bull-shooting, our brusque, often crude expressions of friendship, and our tying of these bonds in the reading of excerpts from the letters we receive. No playwright, Darling, has yet caught the full drama of those rare moments when letters are opened and everyone suddenly starts bidding for attention. "Hey, listen to this!" "Hey, read this!" A guy gets a letter at last from his girl who, he thinks, has thrown him over. Another one reads (with mockery) a phrase from his girl's letter. He's been trying to shake her. Another hands over a letter. We read, "Son, perhaps some boy you know won't receive a

France: Killing Time

Xmas package. Let us know. We'll send it. That will be our Xmas." That's all for today, My Darling.

Love to all, Daddy

October 10, 1944, 10:30 a.m. – Somewhere in France
My Darling:

It's so nice to have some good writing paper. I hope you will continue to send me a few pieces in each letter. The situation may improve very soon now. At any rate, letter writing may be physically impossible en route so I will have the advantage in that those of your letters which will reach me before then will help to build up my meager store of writing paper.

There is absolutely nothing to worry about. We are fast becoming as bovine as our four-legged friends which graze in the surrounding pastures. My spirits sagged and even a movie, *Casanova Brown* with Gary Cooper, didn't refresh me.

That's about all for now, Angel. I'll try to get back on the ball for tomorrow's letter. Wish you could see the astonishing blackberry bushes. We have picked them until we're dizzy, and still there are millions. What jam they would make! Love to all.

To you, My Love, all my love, Daddy

October 11, 1944, 10:30 a.m. – Somewhere in France
My Darling:

Yesterday's letter, assuming letters are arriving in chronological order, may have given you some idea of the state of things with us. I hope that is permissible to repeat at this time that we can't stay in the middle of a cow pasture indefinitely. When we are going is the Army's secret, but that we are going soon is very, very certain. It is said that the mail will improve considerably in our new location, once we are established, and that prospect alone make going desirable. We are also assured that living conditions also will be considerably altered for the better, which is only reasonable to expect since a hospital requires at least a vestige of permanency to function. The winter months, I hope, will pass quickly, and the spring may at last bring an end to the war in Europe.

I beg you not to worry about my safety, health and mental state. Safety, beyond the point of a favorable location, is up to the individual, and I don't forget for a moment that I want to get home in good order some day. My health, apparently, is good. I haven't even had a cold despite the night dampness. I confess my bones ache at times, but that seems to be due to "old age." My back troubled and worried me. Consequently, I had it checked thoroughly. The pain is entirely muscular, due to the hard cots on which we sleep. I guess eventually I'll become accustomed to it. Basically, I am sound. Good heart, lungs and all that. I am pleased. Our swell shower tent has been dismantled and moved away, so again the problem of bathing must be met. This is only temporary, no doubt, and something will be available before long. Since we don't sweat, we don't' stink and don't alienate friends, but I would like to get washed all over without getting my shoes wet.

I gave up the book-end project for the time being, but my design is an original one and perhaps later I can carry it out. Our P.X. has provided Mounds instead of the tiresome Sky Bars and at least I have a piece of candy I can enjoy. But no Hershey's as yet. The Hershey's, they say, are going to the front. Well, that's small compensation for being at the front. I thought I was gaining weight rapidly but apparently I'm not. I can tuck a woolen undershirt, a sweater and a fatigue jacket in my pants and still button up comfortably.

Here's a little news. I have grown a mustache, simply because shaving the upper lip is an ordeal with cold water. It's a trim, handsome hirsute adornment and the boys claim it is very becoming. What amused me most, though, is that the mustache came out definitely light brown, with a touch of red! I'll remove it, of course, before we meet again, since you have such an aversion to mustachioed gents. Every other guy here now sports a "dirty upper lip" and Hollywood could pick up some movie villain types cheaply here. That's all for now, Sweet. Tomorrow, if possible, more, and tomorrow and tomorrow.

Love to all. To you, My Love, all my heart. Kiss the cherub for me. Daddy

[Date torn off. Seems to be between October 11 and October 16]
My Darling:

Possibly before this day is over we will be in Paris. A magical word. Everyone is excited by the thought of it. We left our cow pasture earlier than was expected, but we went willingly, joyously. This time we are traveling by hospital train, a unique experience. Crowded and uncomfortable as usual, but fun for all of that. I was lucky for the first night; I got a bunk—a litter laid across braces suspended from the walls. If we spend another night on the train, perhaps I'll have to take my turn on the floor. Well, the spirit of comradeship and congeniality is so contagious that no one notices the inconveniences.

Paris, I'm afraid, will offer most of us only that which is free, since we sent our money home before we realized what was happening. It's silly, of course, to even think about this since there is always the likelihood that we will be rushed right through Paris. I lost my treasured identification bracelet in the excitement of leaving the pasture, and then I cut my hand on a K-ration tin. It was treated immediately on the train and now is only causing inconvenience in writing. That right hand of mine is certainly taking a beating, it seems. I hope the mail will catch up with us in the next few days. I'm so lonesome for a word from you. My Darling, how much nicer it would be if we could see Paris together. Someday we will. The city of romance, of love. Yes, someday we'll go together.

My love to all. To you, My Love, you know what. Kiss the cherub. Daddy

CHAPTER SEVEN

Belgium: Building the Barracks

[*From Oral History interview with grandson, Edward C. Bernstein, in 1986*]:

SL: *We moved on to Belgium, to the town of Ciney, and took over a long-standing hospital that had been occupied by the Germans. After they were driven out, we moved in. It was beautifully equipped. Most of their stuff was left. We built our own living quarters. It was winter and we worked outdoors, pouring a concrete platform—we were knee-deep in concrete—on which we erected permanent residential tents, thirty beds to a tent.*

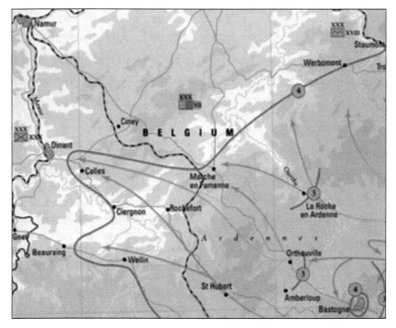

Reprinted with permission from John Ray, *The Illustrated History of WWII* (London: Weidenfeld & Nicolson, 2003), p. 181.

Street scene. Public domain photo from History of Medicine Collection, National Library of Medicine, NIH, Bethesda, MD

130th General Hospital exterior from Sam's postcard photos.

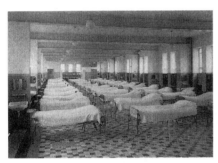

130th General Hospital ward, from Sam's postcard photos.

130th General Hospital dining hall from Sam's postcard photos.

 According to the international rules of war, the hospital had to be a certain distance behind the battle zone, but ours kept moving closer to the front.

 I was called in by a Classification Officer who asked me, "What do you want to do?" I replied, "Sir, I don't know." The officer said, "Well, we don't have any need for a night club critic in this army." And I said, "Well, sir, you could put me in the dental corps." —"Why?"— "Well I married the daughter of a dentist." I figured he can't bust be for being impudent as I couldn't be any lower than a Basic. But apparently he wrote that down on my chart. Meanwhile they sent me out on a work detail to dig trenches, polish the brass in the latrines, do the cement work and all the menial dirty jobs. I managed always to romanticize everything I was doing. I got a good kick out of it because it inspired me and I wrote back some letters describing the use of the slit trenches which were the toilets for soldiers. I always managed to see the humor without becoming indignant because I kept thinking, I've got to survive; I've got to get home. I have a child and a wife at home.

Belgium: Building the Barracks

October 16, 1944, 10:30 a.m. – Somewhere in Belgium
My Darling:
Take a look at the date-line, take a deep breath and say, "Thank God," for truly there is much to be thankful for.

We are as near to the front as we'll get for a long, long time, and all I can say is that extraordinary peace and calm prevails here, a condition which is unlikely to change. Believe this, Darling, if ever you believed and had faith in me. To top it off, our hospital is being rapidly set up in a structure that defies description. Censorship, undoubtedly, prevents me telling just what it is, but it is a magnificently modern and useful structure. We won't be housed in it, of course, but our lot will not be a bad one. More about that later. Soon we must fall out for a formation, so I'll close this now and resume tonight.

The Paris thing was a total flop since we had exactly one hour in Paris, and that was spent in the station. It was long enough, however, to get you some perfume (I think I got gypped) and a cute doll for the baby. I don't know how soon I can send them home, but I will as soon as possible. Love, more tonight and every night, without interruption, thank God. Belgium will be another great experience. Got your letters of Oct. 3, 4 last night just before bed. We were up at 5:30 a.m. today. But we are happy, very happy.
Love, Daddy

October 17, 1944 – Somewhere in Belgium
My Darling:
A scribbled and hurried note just to let you know that only now, 5:15 p.m. Tuesday, am I able to mail the enclosed letters. If I get a break tonight, you'll get a mighty long letter. Believe it or not, my bracelet was found and brought to me by a lad who came with a later group to join us here. What luck! My hand is fine. Don't worry.
Love, Daddy

October 18, 1944, 6:30 p.m. – Somewhere in Belgium
My Sweet Angel! Where shall I begin? There is so much to write about, both pleasant and very unpleasant. Well, here we are again, in the middle of a Belgian cow pasture, added to which is a sea of mud such as I never knew could be "churned up" by human feet. This is the moment for which I have waited all through a trying day, preceded by a night which I shall long remember with a shudder of recalled anguish.

Now I know the full meaning of the word "son of a bitch". It's a guy who gives an order for five hundred men to struggle through a sea of mud in a bitter, driving rain, to occupy cold, wet tents in utter darkness. I kept thinking of the lamebrain who stupidly declared to you that "we were having fun seeing the sights of France." I hope that moron never crosses my path! I declare to you,

My Love, that I am not going in for confession of the true facts. All that I have written before was true, but also much that I did not write was true. If that moron thinks going unwashed, living in darkness, getting soaked, washing latrines one day, waiting half of one's life away in chow lines, doing a thousand dirty and back-breaking jobs on any day; if that moron think that's "sight-seeing," may all his life be a perpetual "sight-seeing" tour.

Now about the present situation. As I said, briefly, in yesterday's letters, we have a magnificent structure for our hospital, but that's all as far as we are concerned. In that building we will really put in some long, hard-working hours. That's OK. That's what we are here for. Also, when I said, "our lot will improve," that is also true. Eventually we will get into wooden barracks. At present our tents are not uncomfortable except we all are straining to write by candle light. No doubt lights will be strung through our area in the next few days. My detail for the next few days is on a carpentry job. We are laying floors in the tents.

My only candle is burning down. I hesitate to ask you to send any since things may improve here rapidly. I am glad you didn't send the twelve bottles of ink. My Darling, one bottle goes a long, long way, longer than I wish to stay here and write letters. The other things are most welcome. If any item is unavailable, forget it. There is a vast amount of supplies here, left behind by the Germans. Maybe we can promote some of the necessary items. Specifically, all I want are the heavy sox which I need badly, the wash rags, the camera, the face cream, and a bottle of good after-shaving lotion. I haven't received the stationery yet, but I have augmented my supply adequately, at last. The packages now on the way will be welcome if only for the excitement of getting a package from home. In tomorrow's letter I will send you one of the Paris souvenirs. The poor doll took an awful beating in our "terrible exodus" last night, but I'll send it, regardless. Also your perfume. Out of my next pay, I'll try to get some nice things as souvenirs of Belgium. My Angel, I go to sleep now, refreshed and at peace. Tomorrow I'll write about our "hour in Paris." Love to all.

To you, My Love, all my heart forever. Kiss the cherub. Daddy

October 19, 1944, 6:30 p.m. – Somewhere in Belgium (written by flashlight)
My Angel:

Here and there a candle flickers, boys are busy writing, the pot-bellied stove is going full blast, others are talking quietly. It is not yet 7 p.m., but it is almost the end of a day for us, a day in which we accomplished much in bridging the seas of mud, making our tents fast and warm and generally beginning to envision the "tent city" that will soon spring up in this Belgian cow pasture. I haven't the slightest idea when I'll get something to do in the hospital, or what. Well, it makes very little difference now. I suppose one has to sink to the very lowest ebb of morale before things begin to happen. Roy warned me about this very thing when I talked to him. He sensed my feelings of disappointment and despair and followed up his warning with a letter, the message of which I shall always cherish in memory of these pointless days.

Honey, I'm having difficulty focusing the light on the paper and can't see an inch ahead of the beam. I'll try and get a candle for tomorrow's writing. I am enclosing a souvenir handkerchief which I managed to snatch up in the mad rush of the hour we spent in the Paris RR station. Darling, the days will go better and already I have returned to the "circle of GI camaraderie" which I left momentarily yesterday. How tired I was! Please, Angel, don't worry. I am amazed at myself. Despite all this exposure I haven't even got a sniffle while others complain of all sorts of things.

Love to all. Daddy

October 20, 1944 – Somewhere in Belgium
My Darling:

Now that the crisis is passed, I wonder how I allowed myself to "blow my top" as we say in the army. The day was full of activity, as will be the next week or so, but out of our efforts will come about a new tent city. Lights are being installed now, and the floor of our tent should be finished tomorrow. Thus, Sunday morning I expect to greet the day with renewed hope and enthusiasm.

I should have explained what brought about my blowup. You know how fussy I am about keeping things looking neat. And I have never been able to accept the fact that just about everything GI is expendable over here. Thus, I hesitate even to discard a shoelace. Well, then, as we dragged our huge duffle bags through the blinding rain and total darkness I found that it was physically impossible for me to manage mine, plus blankets, pillow and numerous other things that one acquires. I was dragging mine on a two-wheeled cart which repeatedly upset. All this came after a day of mopping acres of tile floors. I was in no mood to wade ankle-deep in mud after that. Well, mood or no, I did and finally crawled up to my tent, about a third of a mile from the main building, a sorry sight to behold. It was a night I shall long remember.

Enough of that, though. With additional winter clothing, which will be issued soon, we shall manage nicely. At any rate, if it's my good fortune to work in the hospital in one capacity or another, most of the day will be spent in beautiful and comfortable surroundings. There are many things I want to discuss with you, Angel, but I beg you to wait a few days until we get proper lighting, or until an hour in daylight is a free period. After a few minutes of this candlelight composing, my eyelids begin to shimmy. Please, Angel, tell my folks not to worry as I can't manage more than one letter a night for the present.

The war news is very good again. Maybe, maybe, soon—who knows? Love to all.

To you, My Love, my heart. Daddy

October 21, 1944, 8:00 p.m. – Somewhere in Belgium
My Darling:

I feel like a millionaire again. I have had a very hot shower, a shave, and three letters from you, dates Sept. 12, 14, 15. Where they have been wandering all this time I don't know, but a letter a year old would fill me with joy. Now I know why I haven't had your report on Roberta's party before this. What a report! It was worth waiting for. These three letters, I think, bring yours up to date.

My Darling, I know exactly how you feel when I notify you that a new move is in the offing. Well, perhaps now I won't have to write such news, except the one time when I start for home. We have a wonderful hospital here and our "slavery" this week has produced marvels. Our own area is quickly assuming the neat, efficient contours of a well-planned town, even though we are under canvas. My carpentry has contributed no small part to the near completion of "our town." Tired? Yes, very, very tired at the end of a day, but there is a real satisfaction in seeing this materialize under your very eyes. It won't be so bad, Sweetheart. Getting a bath or a shave is complicated business, but it can be accomplished.

One thing I am delighted with is the pot-bellied stove we have. It gets red hot, will dry anything in a few minutes, and best of all, I can have a cup of coffee in a jiffy. I saved a number of coffee packets from my K-rations and it was well worth the effort. I have about a month's supply. No packages have arrived yet and I'm becoming a little anxious. None of the boys have received any, although their folks write that they sent them. So I guess the packages will all arrive in a heap. What a night of sampling and noshing that will be. Our electric lights have been installed—two to a tent, but Manny had to beg a couple of candles so that we could get enough light by which to write. A candle is a useful item here. They will be welcome at any time, so throw in a couple in the next package. Also, Angel, you don't mention the heavy sox I asked for. If this terrible slogging through mud is to be our daily ordeal, heavy socks are a must. I refer to the ones I sent back from Swannanoa. They were of unusual length which is what I want. If you still have them, send them, although I'm afraid it will be months before they arrive. Darling, I hesitate to ask for anything since I know what a job it is to get anything. Perhaps it might be best to hold up all other parcels until after the Xmas rush. That will be a madhouse this year for sure.

Now a little about this new phase of my career. Here we are in the same mud, confronted with much the same difficulties as faced the men in the First World War, apparently. French is beyond me. I've tried one or two words (with success), but it is difficult for my tongue. If the natives speak or understand German, they don't let on. I wish they would though. German would be a cinch for me. I don't know just what the Belgian language sounds like, but apparently most of them speak French. Some of our boys who can handle language get along very well and act as interpreters. My own "conversation" with the natives is a riot. "Scramyvoo" means get out when the kids come around the tents. They are friendly and ask constantly for gum. I gave one kid a piece of chocolate and he jumped up and down with glee. I'll never forget the tiny little devil of a French kid (in France) who learned to swear like an adult in a few days and saluted everybody with a vile greeting that used to "kill" the guys who taught him the words. I know that when I have had a chance to relax a bit, much that I enjoyed hearing and seeing will come back to me. Then I shall relate these impressions to you.

One of the funniest things to happen in the last two days, however, tops anything I could imagine could happen to a bedraggled, unshaven, unwashed, unhappy gang of "engineer medics." We call ourselves "engineers" now, in keeping with our daily toil and general non-antiseptic appearance. Well, here we are, grunting, bitching, hauling, pushing, digging, sawing, nailing, and we return at last to our tents to plop down into beautiful, striped canvas beach chairs. Five such "lounge lizard" contraptions to each tent. We know not from where they came. We care not. Perhaps more such incongruous luxuries are in store for us. We have a "select" group in my tent, pleasant fellows, intelligent, good company. I hope it lasts.

Love to all. To you, My Love, my heart. Daddy

October 23, 1944 – Somewhere in Belgium
My Angel:
Before me I have your letters of Sept. 12, 14, 15, 29, 30 and Oct. 2, 3, 4, 5, 7, and the 9th, which arrived this evening. I started to read right through and write a long letter based on them, but I got as far as the treasured one of Sept. 15 and decided that if you are to get a letter at all, I'd better wait for a better time. Our feeble light bulbs will blink out promptly at 10 p.m., and I must get several letters written tonight.

Truly, we are attuned to each other. It is uncanny how you catch my unspoken, unwritten thoughts. Well, Angel, as I said before, certainly we couldn't sit in the middle of a French cow pasture and make ashtrays all day long. We should have moved out of there long before we did, and my contradictions were not amiss. On one hand we were poised for movement on an hour's notice, while on the other hand we were stringing electric wires all over the place. I must say my army career has turned to engineering with a vengeance. I may never carry a bed pan or wield a hypodermic needle, but by golly I've done some mighty strange things as a medical soldier. And we are the guys who were supposed to be the "limited service" bunch, the imperfect, the "too old for combat" jerks. The legitimate engineers around here have overshoes and boots and warm coats. We medics wade through the same sea of mud, sans boots, coats or overshoes. They don't' think much of us back home, but you should hear what the combat boys here have to say about the medics.

I have thought of so many things that you would enjoy hearing about, but when I start to write, the thoughts elude me. The physical exertions of the day leave me fogged. Things should quiet down very soon and maybe I'll get a hospital job of some sort. This at least will be a new experience and will revive me again. I swear that I am well. I've suffered only a sight head cold and bruised hands from hammering and dragging planks. I sleep with a new determination though. Our wooden floor, good stove, fairly comfortable cots and sufficient blankets make for all the comforts a guy can ask for in the army.

Your wonderful descriptions of the baby's brilliance fill me with unmeasured joy. Through your letters I see her grow day by day. I, too, have thought about the day when I come home and you and the baby will walk up to me. That thought, My Darling, is not exclusive with me. There are so many men who have yet to see their children for the first time. That's all for now, My Love.

Love to all, Daddy

October 23, 1944 – Somewhere in Belgium
My Darling:

A full day of hard work in the open, I find, leaves me tired but not unhappy. It was a nice day compared to what we have had to contend with atmospherically the past week. That our detail is actually producing something, rather than, like the typical army detail, moving a pile from here to there and back again, is encouraging. Also, I'm learning something about building construction which is useful information. Who knows, perhaps we may want to build a home someday and at least I'll be able to follow the architect's plan with something approaching intelligence. I still haven't the slightest idea of what they are going to do with me here, but I'm resigned to anything. I'm afraid I'll never conform to army standards which, apparently, spring from the well of confusion. I have seen so many "carts put before the horses" that I'm beginning to believe that there is no beginning and no end to anything. In the army, you plunge right into the middle and hope it comes out right. No, Angel, I'm not just bitter, nor disillusioned. I'm just still disturbed (and often amused) by the astonishing method by which we win wars. It's all very chaotic, seemingly, but there's no denying that the job gets itself done.

I'll admit, My Darling, that each time we moved, I experienced these days of loneliness and uncertainty for I knew that heartache and worry were in store for you. How I wish I could spare you that. For us all this moving about is time consuming and even interesting, but for those at home all this moving about stirs new fears and apprehensions. Thus, the doubtful "pleasure" of seeing Europe is even further minimized by the regret of causing one's loved ones hours of worry and uncertainty. If only one could put in a few facts, something definite. I suspect that the censor has at last used his knife on my letters. Has he? Let me know.

I did take a good look around the countryside today, while leaning on a shovel, and I must say I was excited for the first time with this "mud flat." The surrounding countryside is beautiful. The first snowfall should turn it into a Xmas card scene.

Well, Angel, I've succeeded in writing a very dull letter. Tomorrow I shall lean on that shovel a little longer. Maybe my dull brain will be sharpened to the point of observing something of the life and activity around me. I know I will, for I must not fail to record my impressions of the Belgian phase. I'm tempted to remove my shoes and socks and squish the mud between my toes. I think that will do the trick.

Love to all. To you, My Sweet Wife, my heart. Daddy

October 25, 1944 – Somewhere in Belgium
My Darling:

Well, here I am, all set to enjoy a quiet, pleasant evening around the pot-bellied stove, writing to my favorite girl and what happens? The generator goes on the fritz and there is no light. There is a bit of candle, though, set upon an upturned cup, so I'll try my best to finish this without getting the eyelid twitches.

It was a warm, pleasant day and my day of digging sod left me tired but not unhappy. I sleep with a vengeance and am ready to get out of the "fart sack" at 5:30 a.m. By keeping "right on the scrotum," as they say here, one gets his bed ready for inspection, cleans up his portion of the tent, makes the trek to the hospital for chow, gets washed and tooth-brushed while there, and returns to the area in time for a 7:20 formation. By that time I'm already worn out since everything here seems to be on the top of a hill. Oh, my aching back!

We were issued overcoats today and I managed to draw a nice, new one, size 38S. Now if I can find some way of driving a nail into canvas, I can hang it up. I'm clever, though. I'll find a way. The boys are always wondering what I'm going to do with the various pieces of junk I pick up here and there. For instance, what was once a very beautiful pull-up chair was thrown on the pile. I took the back, which was in good condition, and fastened it to the head of my cot. Thus I have an elaborate "head board" for my bed. It really looks "exotic." The trouble is, there is no time to sit in bed and rest. When one goes to bed here it is strictly for sleeping. Another contraption I have was once an odd-looking litter. I discovered the iron framework of it on the pile and dragged it to the tent. There was a howl, but I showed them how it could be utilized. But doubling the frame at its natural joints, and wiring it down, it became an excellent clothes rack. Unfortunately, it sets too low for an overcoat, but already I have an idea for an addition to it to accommodate the coat.

My helmet laundry service, however, suffered a setback. I put handkerchiefs and socks together to boil. The helmet just fits into the stove lid opening. Well, my laundry came out sterile enough, but you should see the color of the handkerchiefs! Our laundry, however, will be going full blast this week and henceforth it will be the Army's responsibility to keep us in sterile (and white, I hope) handkerchiefs.

Just for the record, Angel, since you think I'm so easy to please on food, the chow has been dependable, to say the least, but good days are ahead. Hospital personnel are known to rate superior chow. Our evening "toast and tea sessions" are enjoyable, though. In a few minutes, I'll put on some water for tea. I wish I had some lemon. I checked the contents of my duffle bag this evening. The doll still has her hair, though somewhat mussed. I wrapped her in a soft muslin cloth and at the first opportunity, I'll mail her to my cherub daughter. The town nearby is still off-limits but one of these days we'll be allowed in and then I'll look for appropriate presents for my two greatest possessions—my wife and my daughter.

Hershey bars (the giant size) turned up on our P.X. rations this week, but my two are gone already. Devouring them bit by bit made sod digging just a bit more bearable. The shovel-leaning periods today were filled with loud lamenting for the good old days when one could go to a Turkish bath. My fellow shovel-leaner and I carried on so, we talked ourselves right into taking a hot shower before evening chow. Thus, when we were dismissed from further labor, I rushed to gather towel, soap, etc., and hobbled to the fancy tile shower stalls which are numerous in the hospital. So did several others. Partially undressed, it occurred to me to turn on the shower to test the water. I turned in vain. The shower nozzle produced only a miserable trickle. What to do? Scream, curse, collapse? I stripped. Wash I would, cupping my hands to catch the drops of warmish water. I managed to wash ears, nose, arm pits, privates and finally feet, hoping all the time that the trickle would continue to trickle until I got the soap off. A guy in the next stall, less wise, worked up an all-over lather and then didn't even have a trickle in his nozzle. They say now that come Friday the nozzles will spout again.

Well, Sweetheart, I've bitched enough for one day. What new wonder has our angel performed? Put her hand print on a letter and I'll kiss it a thousand times. Love to all.

To you, My Love, my heart. Daddy

October 26, 1944 – Somewhere in Belgium
My Darling:
The generator is working tonight, but even if there was no light, the three letters I received from you today would be my light by which to answer.
Sweetheart, your praise has made me self-conscious. I really don't see my letters as being anything unusual. There is no time for subtlety in the army. Everything is said and done in a broad, uncultured manner. If you don't notice these things

Belgium: Building the Barracks

and retain impressions of same, you are dead and don't know it. I can't bring myself to write some of the things that are said and repeated a thousand times a day.

Our nice town nearby is still off-limits, an irksome business to men who are herded from one miserable detail to another all day and all week, including Sunday. To travel so much and to see so little is what gets me down. How I want to see Europe and not cow pastures!

I'm afraid we'll have to do without the vases and candlesticks. My whole supply of shells was left behind when we left for Belgium, and there are no foxholes or shells here. I hated to leave the stuff. I even completed a striking pair of bookends and had to leave them behind. That's all I needed in my duffle bag for that nightmarish trek through rain and mud that horrible, horrible night when for the first time I completely forgot that millions were in even a worse plight than mine. I promise that will never happen again. Goodnight, My Love. My "fart sack" still has to be made ready for the night. Kiss my cherub.

Love to your Dad and Mother. Daddy

October 27, 1944–- Somewhere in Belgium
My Darling:

Another extraordinary day of cement pouring, etc., has passed and it's near bedtime again. I have wanted very much to reread your letters at hand but the day is so full, and the evening so short, I must again put it off to a more leisurely time. This evening, for instance, after chow, I prepared to shave, which I needed badly. One heats part of his precious drinking water; adjusts the mirror so as to catch the most light; spreads out the necessary shaving tools on the bed; props up helmet containing hot water (on bed, too); and then proceeds to lather and shave while being acutely aware of the danger of upsetting the whole business right in the middle of the bed, thus rendering it unfit for slumber, which, at the present rate of energy expending, is very, very important.

After shaving I sorted and marked my laundry for tomorrow's delivery to the Q.M. laundry which finally is accepting all of our stuff. Happily, this will leave a wee bit more of leisure for us. This life is rugged, but it is not without its compensations. It is good to work outdoors. The work we are doing also makes us realize how easy it is to get out of condition. Those six weeks in France made lazy bums out of us. The tent is warm and comfortable. Most of the fellows are out to the movies which are shown at the hospital. I haven't gone yet and do not intend to do so until the heavy details are over. Furthermore, it would rob me of the hour in which I write to you.

To you, My Love, my lonely heart. Kiss "HER" tiny hands and feet for me.
Daddy

October 28, 1944
My Darling:
This will be a short one since there is nothing new to report. I am now an accomplished plaster-finisher, having been given a trowel this morning and told to finish off a concrete floor which we poured yesterday. Since this trowel finishing is the most lucrative job in the world of construction, I can count on a secure future, it seems. At any rate, the sergeant in charge was very pleased with the work. My mazel [Yiddish for luck]! There are half a dozen floors to be poured yet.

Mail call just this minute brought me your letter of the 16th. Pause while I read it. My darling, a beautiful, interesting and even a little bit frightening letter. Frightening because of the uncanny way you have of "knowing" much that I can't write. Your "troubled sleep" was a prelude to days of waiting again since no mail could have reached you for more than a week by my way of figuring. Also, your "easterly direction" fear was not entirely groundless, as you know now. You are wrong, though, in thinking that we are in an unsafe area. It is a cruel phase of security in wartime which prevents us from telling our loved ones just how safe or unsafe we are. I can only beg you to believe that danger such as combat units face is totally unknown to us.

Our "city" is coming along splendidly. The place looks like an architect's nightmare at the moment but there is a plan after all.

Sweetheart, it seems we are going to have an airmail stamp shortage. If you think of it, drop one in an occasional letter. I dread the thought of being caught without an airmail stamp. I await with barely restrained emotion the new pictures of "Love Lettuce." Love to all. Don't worry.

To you, My Love, my lonely heart. Daddy

October 30, 1944 – Somewhere in Belgium
My Darling:
Two letters, Oct. 14 and 19, arrived tonight. News that cookies as well as fruitcake are on the way made me drool. How I wish I had a box of cookies tonight, since I passed up supper in order to get a shower. The shower was tepid, as usual, but I was refreshed.

The day was a pip. I troweled concrete from 8 a.m. to 4:30 p.m. What a business! Yesterday, My Darling, I didn't write to you. I beg you to forgive me. If I had known how troubled I would be for not having written, I would have forced the energy to do so, but Sundays here are work days. What a Sunday! We finished off the day of construction work by hauling heavy beds to our tents, and here's the payoff. With the beds came magnificent innerspring mattresses. Thus, this Belgian cow pasture which is fast becoming a thriving community now sports innersprings and lounge chairs. This may sound ungrateful but really, I'm not. The new bed is heaven. If only one could "lounge" on it for an hour!

Sweetheart, I don't know when I'll be able to manage more than your letter. I count on you to convince my folks that all is well with me. Eventually, this heavy detail work will be over and I'll resume writing daily to all. Another day has passed which always means it's a day nearer to the end and the beginning again for us. Love to all.

To you, My Love, my lonely heart. Daddy

October 31, 1944 – Somewhere in Belgium
My Darling:

No letters from you today, but I know that a lot of mail has arrived and will be sorted soon. Another day of troweling. The construction project begins to look like something. The mud, however, is terrific. A steam-shovel can make an awful mess of a once peaceful and even beautiful pasture.

I forgot to mention yesterday an incident which occurred during the day that was quite amusing even though it caused me some discomfort. I was pulling a grading board over the newly poured concrete. I was moving backwards while a man on either side of the board was applying the pressure to level the cement. Suddenly the wire I was pulling broke and down I went into a sea of cement. I was a sight but it struck me funny and I laughed along with all the men who viewed my perfect movie fall. The Detachment Commander, who saw it, laughed like hell. At the first opportunity, I told him he owed me a Purple Heart since my pride was "wounded" in action. Thus, by the "trowel and error" method I have become a regular "Christ in Concrete."

At the end of the day, today, for instance, I dragged myself into the tent thinking that I was a sorry sight. I prepared to shave and upon looking into the mirror I got a shock. My ruddy, outdoor complexion surprised and delighted me. Actually, I have been thriving on all this outdoor activity, despite my aching bones to the contrary. The innerspring mattress (this is no joke) is marvelous and a night on it refreshes me and renews my hope. At least our new beds are splendid and at present we have plenty of blankets. The tent is warm and hot water can be had in a few minutes with the coal fire going constantly. The weather is still mild and Sunday was a beautiful day. The sun really can shine in Belgium.

I have inquired about a Belgian doll from one of the natives. Perhaps I can get one. All the little kids around here wear the cutest white fur coats on Sunday. I suppose its Belgian hare or something. I know you'll think I'm crazy but if it's possible to buy a tiny white coat for Love Lettuce, I shall do it. At least I can hug the coat before I send it off. These things, of course, are rationed and I may not be successful.

We were paid today and I find I have more than $20 which I can't spend on myself. If only we were permitted to go to town! Angel, I must also write the folks

tonight or you'll have a real job on your hands. So with love to all, and to you, My Love, my lonely, loving heart, I close.
    Daddy

November 1, 1944 – Somewhere in Belgium
My Beloved:
    Today the pictures of our Angel arrived, just in time to turn a dull, tiring day into sunshine for me. What can I say? When I came to the "V for Victory" picture my heart melted. What a child! How does it happen that a child so young can register so many different expressions? Dear God, what a blessing you have bestowed upon us. Thank you, My Darling, for producing such a lovely child. How truly you must love me to give so much beauty from your heart and soul to produce such, I know. Instead of spending hours on my hands and knees smearing cement, wouldn't it be more sensible for me to be home and trailing my daughter on my hands and knees, picking up after her? I am more determined now to find a way to get that little white fur coat for her. What a sensation she would be in it.
    We finally saw the training film which was made about the work of our type of hospital. The film was made in England and clearly depicts what this thing is about. I feel now that there is a purpose to all our labor and troweling. I haven't been placed as yet and feel a little disturbed by it, but it is my nature, I guess, to worry about such things. Manny was assigned to switchboard duty today. It's a good break from many angles. He is well liked and has a knack for making friends and playing "army politics," talents which I lack utterly. Maybe I'll be a bedpan commando after all. I won't complain, however. I know what great treasures await me at home.
    Mail must be coming to you slower than ever. I can write only at the end of the evening. Thus, the letter stays uncensored until the following evening and apparently isn't mailed out until the third day when the mail clerks go to pick up our mail. There isn't much we can do about that, though. I had another thing or two to say but the chatter in the tent has driven the thoughts from my mind. Eventually, we'll get a day room and a bar and the chatterers will leave me in peace.
    The C.O. gave us a very nice talk this afternoon and I must say he is a man to be admired. The wounds of the past weeks were healed in the few minutes he talked. I guess we are prone to forget that this is no time for personal issues. A man in his position has tremendous responsibility, and the individual soldier—as an individual—only gets hurt if he decides he rates special attention. I don't mind admitting the adjustment hasn't been easy on me. I'm afraid I enjoyed too much individualism and freedom of expression to accept readily the mass functioning and mass reaction that makes for a well-disciplined army.

Sweetheart, don't start thinking I've done something to get in bad or anything like that. I'm just expressing in a crude way the effect a recurrence of the army blues has had on me recently and I know exactly what brought it on. It's the distress I experience in being unable to save you the pain of my "gadding about" Europe. Oh, to be free to tell you promptly and completely the what, when, and where of our European "tour." At last, I believe, we have come to a halt. We are really "digging in" now. And I beg you to believe that we are safe. The town, which we saw too briefly, is charming and has many shops into which I would like very much to go hunting for presents for my wife and child. That's out, of course, since the town is "off-limits." Well, Angel, it's way beyond my usual bedtime, so goodnight, My Beloved. Kiss the cherub. Love to all.

Daddy

November 1, 1944 – Somewhere in Belgium
My Beloved:

A short letter but a cheerful one. Just returned from the movies, having seen a film of such awful stench that my own unwashed person is perfume in comparison. Going to the movies was a pleasant break in the routine, though, and the chatter and good will that prevail among our boys is always a tonic. Thus, a fairly easy and pleasant day draws to a close. In tomorrow's letter, I shall try to describe some of the conversations we hold with the children who flock to our area to watch us work. Sundays, of course, brings out Papa and Mama too, and they stand for hours on end watching us from their roadside "grandstand." It's very funny indeed. My French is hopeless but I manage to get along somehow. Everything apparently takes place "tomorrow at two o'clock," an expression which we use when we are stumped. We tell the kids to return "tomorrow at two o'clock" for chewing gum, candy, etc. It's no secret, of course, that numerous little deals are consummated in this manner, but on the whole the kids are primarily interested in getting "gum, chum" (yes in Belgium too) and begging for "chocolat" which of course is devoured by us as soon as we get it from the P.X. Chocolate, here as in other European countries, seems to be worth a fortune. And to think that Belgium has turned out some of the finest chocolate known!

Sweetheart, after a day of "negotiating" and thinking it over, I've decided against the white fur coat which I have learned is prohibitive as to price considering our child would too quickly grow out of it. How I wanted to indulge in this luxury just once, but common sense prevails. The coat, a good one, plus a bonnet would run about $50. I don't understand this since most of the kids seem to possess them. Well, that's the way it is. But I won't be moved on one thing, I'm going to get a fur bonnet, which will be useful for several years, and maybe I can get a little muff to go with it. At any rate, a Belgian doll, dressed correctly by one of the kind women—the wife of one of the civilian workers—has been promised me. I don't know how soon I'll be able to get it, but get it I will. All this "negotiating," of course, is carried on in the most atrocious French and "hand-waving" English you ever heard. What gets me is the way we unconsciously adopt a "foreign" accent in speaking English to the natives. I showed the "V for Victory" snap to my civilian friend who understands a limited amount of English and I said, "See, this is my 'babee.'" I wish I could get some of this down on paper. We are so busy making ourselves understood, we miss the great humor in all this. The kids, though, are delightful. They are all very "wise" and can be awful shrewd when it is to their advantage. One little devil pretends to understand nothing of English except the word "cigarettes." He always answers "non compré" but if you mention cigarettes, he perks up and shouts, "Ah, cigarettes, compré." I really am going to apply myself to learning a little of the language. Our guide books are good and it requires only a little daily application to learn enough to get by very well.

Darling, I have been completely revived and feel fine. You must believe that. I learned today that my assignment has been set. It's exactly what I wanted, and as soon as it is official I'll feel free to tell you more about it. No mail today, but perhaps "tomorrow at two o'clock." The baby's pictures brought me many compliments on our wonderful child. My own pride and joy in her is unmeasured. What a radiant face she has.

Love to all. Darling, to you, my heart forever. Daddy

November 3, 1944 – Somewhere in Belgium
My Beloved:

Today I received your letter of the 13th in which you mention mine of the 4th, 5th, 6th, and the great pleasure you got from them. To keep on remembering that the letters following caused you anguish is what drives me daffy. The day you wrote the above-mentioned letter we were on our way again, and you know the rest through the letters that followed. Thus, I hardly know what words will set your heart at rest and make you believe that all is well again. We have much work to do before we can really be comfortable, and by that time the hospital will require all our time and energy, but at last we have a job to do and a real contribution to make toward ending the war, a day we all desire with all our hearts. There isn't a soldier here who doesn't want to get home as much as his loved ones do. We talk of that day constantly even though we know there is much war yet to be fought here and elsewhere. I am still on the cement details and am actually beginning to "enjoy" it. Time flies as I dwell upon the "trowels and tribulations of a medical 'engineer.'"

Nothing new to report, Angel. I guess I'm so good at troweling they forgot the Army spent much time and money making me an Army clerk. We get *Stars and Stripes* and *Yank* regularly so we are well posted on the war. We devour the headlines even as you civilians do and each day hope that "this is it, at last," but the old war machine just keeps rolling along.

What's going on at home? How do people act these days? Are there many shortages besides cigarettes? Ha, ha, we get them for 3 francs a pack, but I'm not tempted in the least. The pipe is my only vice, and it doesn't stink, not mine! We have been blending our own tobacco by sweetening and moistening it with apples. It's very aromatic. You shall see! If I can get some Worth perfume, would you like it? I think I can but know nothing of such smelling things. Chanel, I'm afraid, is not available at any price. At least I haven't heard of anyone getting any.

Again, Sweetheart, I stop writing for this evening with this letter, so please explain to all and sundry relatives and friends how badly I feel in having to neglect them for a while longer. My laundry must be prepared for tomorrow and other things readied for a busy day. Goodnight, My Love.

Love to all. To you and our "Pride," my longing heart. Daddy

November 4, 1944 – Somewhere in Belgium
My Darling:

What do you know? An airmail letter dated Sept. 22 reached me today. That's a new record for airmail—five weeks. Well, it's a letter in my beloved's hand and that's what's important to me. You mention those fireside heroes who think we are "seeing the world." How I'd like to have a couple of those guys here for some "sightseeing." How I'd love to see them slip and slide through this terrible mud. How I'd like to see them shiver at 5:30 a.m. and struggle through darkness. How I'd like to see them labor seven days a week, and for entertainment, flop dead tired into bed at 8 p.m. because it's too damn dark to see anything, and anyhow you have to allow the shoes to dry out so you can put them on the next day.

I'm not writing these things to cause you distress, My Darling. We get quite used to all of this and manage to have fun in the intimacy and companionship which makes barracks life far from dull. I'm merely giving you a written account of how much "sightseeing" we are doing and the next time one of these morons enrages you with his stupidity, jam this letter down his throat. The day of reckoning is coming, My Dear. You are right, My Love. As you put it so beautifully, "Our sacrifice will net us a richer, more understanding, fuller life. We will always be able to live comfortably with ourselves and certainly with each other." I miss you and the baby more than I dare attempt to say, but I'll never regret one moment of all this. It must end soon and I know what sort of person I'll be when I come back to you. I can't promise you wealth in material things but in love, respect, and devotion I can promise you all that one person can show another.

To my great delight, my Belgian friend has already produced the doll, lavishly (and somewhat luridly) dressed in red velvet. It's cute, though, and typically Belgian. Tomorrow I shall hunt up a box and send off the dolls (I still have the French one which looks very cheap by comparison). Perhaps you can get a snapshot of the baby with the dolls. Angel, I hope you are keeping a complete photo album on our child. I safeguard all the pictures I have, but you know, most anything can happen to one's personal possessions, and I'd be heartbroken if I thought mine were the only ones we have. I don't like to carry all of them in my pocket for fear of breaking them up. At any rate, keep all of the negatives and someday we'll prepare a real collection from them. Who cares about dishes or Japanese prints or furniture when one has such a living doll to photograph. That's a worthwhile hobby.

No packages have arrived as yet so I'm resigned to waiting until Xmas. I read in *Stars and Stripes* that the *Daily News* has been sold to a newspaper chain. See if you can get me some news on how the thing will function now. Is Lloyd Lewis still in? Also, any news on departmental changes. Also, inquire whether John O'Keefe is still in. I didn't answer his nice letter and feel that I should even at a late date if he is still in the executive office. I'm even entertaining a few ideas for articles if I feel I still have a sympathetic ear at the other end.

In your letter of Sept. 22 you wonder if I have become a bed-pan commando after all. No, I haven't, nor have I become anything else as yet. The next week or so, however, will bring me a summons to be interviewed again. Perhaps this time someone will remember that I'm a "Joe" named Sam Lesner who was a pretty good journalist once. How they can use that here, I can't say, but in the army very funny things happen. One thing I know. Whatever it is, I'll apply myself and try to be useful. I close now, Angel, with all my love.

Best to all. A kiss for the cherub. Daddy

November 6, 1944
My Darling:

Election Eve, a wartime president is again to be elected. You'd think we who long for some assurance that our future will not be beset with terrible disappointment and longing for the day of reunion with our families would show some interest in the election. Well, somebody asked somebody else this morning, "What day is it?" "November 6," was the reply. "Oh, tomorrow is election day." "Yeah." That's all. That's about the only comment I heard on the election. What's the matter with us? I don't know. Maybe it's just that we feel that you at home won't let us down.

I didn't write yesterday. Though I hated to pass up my nightly letter, I allowed the boys to drag me off to the movies. The film proved to be a fairly entertaining one, starring Charles Laughton whom I like very much. Your letter of 22 October came yesterday. Why my letters suddenly slowed down only the Post Office Dept. knows. Knowing that our new move was imminent, I wrote every day so that you would have letters over the fruitless period of travel which turned out to be a nightmare in that a fairly short distance took "days" of travel. I raged at the delay knowing that even after arriving several days would pass before our mail "took off."

Belgium: Building the Barracks

Well, My Darling, I was interviewed again today regarding my place in this setup. It went something like this:

– Private Lesner reporting as directed, Sir.

– Thank you, Sir! What did you do in civilian life, Lesner?

– I was a newspaper columnist on the *Chicago Daily News*, Sir. (Pause for general laughter.)

– Ha, ha, that's a fine qualification for the Medical Dept. Let's see, maybe you can write a gossip column (more laughter). Well, Lesner, you've been around a hospital for a time now. What would you like to do?

– I was trained as an Army clerk, Sir. Guess I haven't much choice since clerking would be about the same in any department of the hospital.

– But you have some preference?

– Well, Sir, maybe since I married the daughter of a dentist, the dental clinic could use me.

– Well, we'll see, Lesner. I'll try to place you somewhere as a clerk.

End of interview. Thus, again the rumors one hears turn out to be rumors and I return to my trowel detail to await the momentous decision that the army must make sooner or later. Yep, it's all for the best, or something. Je vais bien; comment allez-vous?

Love to all. Kiss the cherub. Daddy

November 7, 1944 – Somewhere in Belgium
My Darling:

I wish you could hear what's going on in this tent at this very moment (7:45 p.m.). It's terrific. For no reason at all, a political debate got under way, with everyone yelling and no one listening. Come to think of it, someone did make a passing remark about the election, and bang! And after I innocently wrote yesterday that the election stimulated practically no discussion up until this moment. We have a remarkable young man in our tent, a George Friemark of New York, a highly cultured Columbia U. man who held a professorship in a college before coming into the army. His forte is political history. But he speaks brilliantly on many subjects. It's a joy to listen to him try to set some of these lame-brains straight, but they are incredibly stupid and through their ignorance glares the baleful light of bigotry.

Well the debate died down as quickly as it flared up. The boys are now on their favorite subject—women. But about all they can do about it is talk about women.

Our building project is coming along splendidly but I wish you could see the incredible mud we have churned up. I got a good break today. I was issued a pair of rubber overshoes and am I glad. I celebrated the event by washing and shining my shoes, the first time they have been clean in weeks. We who are working on the project are known as "field" men. Coffee is brought into the field about 10 a.m. every morning and it gives us a welcome break. I don't mind being outdoors all day. It certainly leaves one feeling tired, but full of fresh air. Angel, I wish you could see how flat my stomach is. My, my, would you rejoice. I don't think I lost weight. I merely tightened up some sagging muscles. My mustache went off with last night's shave and this morning several guys expressed regret that I did so. They seem to think I'm the type who can wear a mustache. Maybe I'll try again.

Angel, I'm a little worried about my folks' correspondent "resigning." Is that the truth, or am I being spared? If only they could write to me themselves. Please, Honey, urge my father to write just a couple of words. He can, you know. I'll know his handwriting and be reassured that everything is okay. If he just signs his name on a scrap of paper, I'll be satisfied.

The dolls will be mailed this week. I have a good box at last. The chaplain is going to town and maybe he can get me something to send you. Love to your folks. Please beg them to be patient with me. I will answer their treasured letters. Kiss the baby.

To you, My Love, my heart. Daddy

November 9, 1944 – Somewhere in Belgium
My Darling:

Again, I passed up my daily letter to you yesterday, because the Army sent us a mile of vehicles piled high with supplies, which according to the best tradition, had to be unloaded in the pitch dark with an icy rain making Popsicles of the unloaders. I can understand the terrible necessity for unloading the vehicles promptly and sending them on their way, perhaps to carry supplies to far more important localities, but there is much in the way of doing things that leaves one wild with rage. Well, each day I learn to be more sparing with my mental expenditure. Each day, I learn better how to become detached. Each day it gets easier to go through the day forgetting for long moments that I am I. It is a strange feeling, suddenly realizing that the trowel going back and forth in wide arcs is the most absorbing thing in your life. Then, a warmth fills me and I start dreaming. I see myself troweling my own cement, stopping to go into the house for a cup of coffee or lunch with my wife and child; explaining to you my darling, in my dogmatic fashion, just how it's done and why; even planning to be even tempered and still locally industrious and repairing any damage that the kids might do to the fresh cement; and all the time enjoying the sympathy showered on me by a loving and wholly understanding wife.

Thus my mind goes round and round and always comes to a perfectly balanced stop on the wave thought—*wife*. Mail call just came, but I netted nothing for the third day. How I dread these "barren" days. Yet I am not alone in this. The mail is a hopeless muddle.

We had a beautiful and heavy snowstorm today but the rain has started again. It is washing it away. Oh well, my sturdy overshoes got me through the worst of it and I feel quite careless as I go sloshing along.

At last, I have accumulated enough wrapping material to pack a few things I have acquired, including the dolls. I intend to make the package tonight but may hold it for day or two. I want very much to send your mother something, but I won't insult her with some piece of tourist's junk. The boys have told me that very sheer and attractive scarves are available in the nearby town. Angel, what can I give you for your birthday? To date I have only that bottle of doubtful perfume so far. I know that you would not deny me the dubious pleasure we get out of spending our hard-earned francs for the junk which most soldiers buy, and it is really an unforgettable experience to bargain for something in a strange language, but I consider that the same amount of money in the hands of a wise shopper is productive of greater value, and certainly to more useful and lasting things, so I have a proposition. I have 1000 francs, $20, in my possession, money that I had planned to spend for you and your mother. Since the money won't arrive in time, I beg you to draw that amount and buy for both of you any item or items you desire. The money will be cabled with next month's surplus and thus you will be able to replace it in our account.

Angel, please don't dissuade me in this. It might make the proposition more interesting if you have the packages mailed to you from the store and you can even put my name on them as the sender. I think Fields or any comparable store would fall in with this plan.

Perhaps tomorrow's mail will come and I'll be revitalized. Kiss the baby. Love to the folks. Make my dad and mother put their signatures on a scrap of paper. Then only will I be at ease. May God grant our reelected president the strength and wisdom to lead us to a quick victory and a speedy reunion with our loved ones.

To you My Love, my heart. Daddy

November 10, 1944 – Somewhere in Belgium
My Darling:

Another day is drawing to a close. Mail call brought me no letters. Today I mailed the package including the two dolls, the perfume, and some other items of a more useful nature. I hope the package arrives in good condition, and it is conceivable that it will arrive by Christmas. The Belgian doll is quite gay and with luck should arrive looking in good health. When will I have a letter from you? Mail has arrived here from the States dated October 27, which would be swell if I got one. Maybe tomorrow I'll have some luck.

We are to have a brief Armistice Memorial Service in the morning so the day at least will be less arduous. The boys are staying in tonight, it looks like, and since this is the birthday of one of our most popular guys, it promises a party at 8 p.m. when he comes in from guard duty. Some of these guys are very enterprising and always manage to turn up the ingredients for a good party. This is the nicest part of this whole distressing business, the companionship and intimacy of living in crowded quarters with a gang of extroverts. Last night, for instance, after a few sips of grapefruit juice, we conversed in French and German only for hours. It sounded like the Tower of Babel at its worst. Our beautiful snow has been washed away, and we now face the prospect of living in even stickier, deeper mud. How I enjoy my overshoes. I slosh around unmindful of the pitfalls, and I mean PIT-falls. Well, Angel, the "tone" of this tent is becoming anything but conducive to letter writing. I think joining into the light-heartedness prevailing at the moment will do me some good, although pinging away in a corner of my heart is that little devil worry because I have had no word now for the fourth day. Only until I again put my arms around you will I be entirely free of that fear.

Give my love to all. Tell the cherub Daddy sealed the package with the kiss.
Love—Daddy

November 11, 1944 – Somewhere in Belgium
My Darling:

The hot-stove league is going full blast already and its only 6 p.m. I don't know what it is about the guys in tent 15, but we certainly attract visitors. The traffic through this place is terrific. Six of us, being involved in a deep discussion, ignored chow call. We shook our duffel bags, found enough tins of C rations to go around, made coffee, and thus without leaving the tent we dined in the best army style.

It was a pleasant day, in that I didn't trowel today and found well-spaced details to do. Saturday night in the Army for us means sitting around the stove and discussing the day's activities, rumors, injustices, and damning the more privileged in the setup. At the moment, we are all awaiting the mail, which our tent representative is gathering. He just returned empty-handed. So we are all in the same floundering ship "Morale." There is still Sunday, which should start nicely tomorrow, as there is to be no reveille, the first active human understanding on the part of the "Management" since we arrived here. At least tomorrow I'll have time to shake out my blankets, and with luck, even get a shower. Oh, how I need a shower. Most of the guys are taking off for various places. I welcome the calm that is descending. I'll inch up to the stove with a batch of your letters and plan tomorrow's letter to you.

Goodnight, My Beloved. Kiss the cherub. Love to the folks. Your Daddy

November 12, 1944 – Somewhere in Belgium
My Darling:

A pleasant morning (we slept until 9 a.m.), a not-too-difficult afternoon. And now the hot-stove league is gathering round the potbelly for the usual "blah." No movie tonight, so it's to be expected that most of them will stick

Belgium: Building the Barracks

around tonight. Our day should be finished before long, and most of them will go there, leaving the tent a place in which one can think again. Incidentally, we are soon to be housed in excellent wooden barracks which we are constructing. One is completed and it is very warm and comfortable. Our nice beds go along with us. You can't imagine what an innerspring means to a guy who has slept on the ground.

No letter from you today, but no one got any so it must be that the mail is being held up somewhere along the line. Peculiarly, though, a V-Mail from my folks, dated October 28, arrived tonight and as yet I have no letters from you within a week of that date. I am beginning to wonder if a series of V-Mail letters wouldn't be better under such prevailing conditions.

Last night I reread a batch of your letters. My Darling, we must both learn to take these mail lapses with less stress. It seems that every time our armies move or are about to move, the mail gets shot to hell. The countryside is magnificent and makes the terrible mud even more terrible.

Goodnight, My Love. Kiss the cherub. Love to the folks.

To you, My Love, Daddy

November 13, 1944 – Somewhere in Belgium
My Darling:

I held my breath as the bugle sounded mail call tonight. How I needed some word from you to make the long black night bearable. Yes, I received two letters, October 18 and October 31. I am appalled that as late as October 31 you still had no news of our move. That is the one thing that tears at my heart like the claw of a wild beast. How I would want to spare you this mental anguish. Letters written en route and upon our arrival should have reached you by the 31st. I don't know what to do. I have just heard that all airmail this winter will be carried across the seas by ship. If that's the case, V-Mail will be better since it requires less space to carry it in bulk. I'll try a few again, and we'll see how they go.

My last letter from Roy was dated October 9. He said nothing about leaving Europe. My heart is filled with joy for him, but at the same time, the news inspires in me a sense of loss, of utter loneliness. Knowing that he was here was a sort of "anchor." Now I'll be here alone. He has done more than his share. I pray that nothing happened to change his orders and that he's already home or well on the way. He worried a good deal about me and I feel that he's "pushing" the boat, the sooner to tell you that in our meeting he found me in good health and accepting my lot with fairly good grace.

My darling, I suggest that you get a batch of V-Mail and at every opportunity just write a few words in addition to your regular letters. Angel, I ask this because just a word from you and your signature saves me days of distraction. My Darling, how can I disguise what I really think from one so astute, so discerning, as you?

We have been depressed by the turn of events here, too, and a winter in Europe is certainly in the cards for us. May God grant that it is to be the one and only winter here. To save ourselves long hours of heartache and disappointment we must now make a less emotional estimate of the situation. If I were alone in this I would cry out to our God and ask "Why?" Why must I endure the separation from the ones I love so profoundly? But, Angel, all about me men are beginning to ask, "How much longer?" There is a tremendous job to be done yet, and it must be done without any regard for the personal factors involved.

But no matter how distressed I may become about all this, I remain unshakable in my faith in a righteous God. He has given me a Queen Esther and a divine child. I'll come out of this whole, physically and spiritually. You, My Darling, are my light in these black nights. Whenever you are beset by fear and worry over me remember that the light of your love for me must shine above fear if my courage is to be unfaltering. What more can I say? How else can I say it? Here we are violently shaken down to fundamental emotions. The knowledge that you are mine sustains me.

Tonight we moved into our new barracks. It is warm and comfortable. You are right, My Beloved. You belong at home with our Angel. Good night, Sweet. Keep well for me. My love to the folks. Tell them to write whenever they can. Kiss the cherub.

Daddy

November 14, 1944 – Somewhere in Belgium
My Darling:

I don't know how many times this scene is being duplicated tonight. But there is something to be said for it. How I wish I were skilled with pencil and sketch pad. All day, as I worked, I kept thinking of your letter in which you said you prayed that we would remain on the continent and far back from real danger.

Yes, Darling, we are to stay "on the continent" for some time, it seems, but "somewhere in Belgium" in itself implies that danger here is a passing thing. The war, as you know, is being waged on a wide front. Thus, we hear and see much of the passing danger, and yet, coming back to the scene which I started to describe, all is serene here. The lights haven't been hooked up yet in our barracks so for light, tonight, there is the glowing red stove, a flickering candle here and there, a lantern slung between my bed and a buddy's, and a flashlight throwing its beam on this writing paper. There are three stoves in this long barracks, but currently all the letter writing and the quiet discussion is going around our stove, meaning the one nearest my bed. Mine is about seven feet distance from the stove and is an upper. Yes, we are using double-deckers now. We still have the swell mattresses. The upper, I find, is warm and a less apt to get stepped on by a muddy shoe.

Belgium: Building the Barracks 145

Well I'll try again. Maybe this time, I can get the "scene" which for some reason intrigues me, even though the dominating theme is shoes. Many shoes, muddy, twisted, "weary." The shoes are "resting." They are resting in a grotesque circle around the stove. The feet are at rest too. Mine are resting on my upper and from my elevated perch the scene immediately in front of me is one that will be etched in my mind. Some packages have arrived, and the lucky recipients have handed around the candy contents. Perhaps next it will be my turn to pass around. There was no mail today, only packages and newspapers. So we are all moaning tonight about the T.S. we have been getting recently on mail. I should make a pretty good haul when the mail does arrive. . . .

My Darling, because of certain new restrictions, I dare not attempt to buy you a birthday present here so I beg you to accept my plan for purchasing yours and your mother's. The plan I mentioned in an earlier letter which I hope you'll get in time to act upon. Good night, My Angel. Kiss the cherub. Love to the folks.

My heart, so full of love, is all yours. Daddy

November 16, 1944 – Somewhere in Belgium
My Darling:

No letter from you yesterday but Manny's letter of November 1 informed him that his people know we are in Belgium. Thus, I assume that you know too, though I long to hear from you. I know how you must feel and that to say "don't worry" is small comfort since I can't tell you what and where. You must believe, though, that our hot-stove league holds forth every evening without undue interruption. I mentioned "passing danger" in another letter. That was no double talk. It is comforting to know that the enemy is on the receiving end of the passing danger. I'm writing this in the brief interlude before noon chow. With luck I should be able to manage my usual airmail tonight. Love to all. I am well and in good spirits. Keep well, My Darling. A kiss for the cherub.

Love, Daddy

November 16, 1944 – Somewhere in Belgium
My Darling:

Today I also wrote you a V-Mail. It may have arrived before this one. I shall continue to do this for a time. Perhaps that way some word will come from me more frequently than in the past. Mail call will be in a few minutes. I hope I'm lucky tonight.

No mail! What in the world am I going to do? What can I write? It's only the fact that no one got any that keeps me from exploding. It's colder now and no doubt the rain will be less frequent and the mud will dry up somewhat.

How I wish the camera was here. I'd like to have a pictorial record of this project and the guys who are building. It is hard to distinguish the men from the mud. We blend "beautifully." It's no use trying to clean your clothes. You just dry them out and put them on again, stiff with clay. Well, it's not bad after you fail to remember to wash. How quickly we drop the "must" of civilized society. Yet on the whole, we are a healthier lot than when we came into service. I look into a mirror only when it is necessary to shave, and I must say it always surprises me when I see the reflection of a pretty healthy-looking guy. I think I'm a little older in appearance, but still have trouble convincing guys that I'm 35 going on 36. My arthritis bothers me a bit but the outdoor work requires considerable muscular exertion and sleep comes easily as a result. The morning finds me rested and ready for the day's toil.

The project must surely reach completion soon, and then we "field men," as we are now designated, will take our places in the hospital, which actually doesn't require all of us as yet. This doesn't make me unhappy since it means that our boys are holding up magnificently in their front-line jobs. Thank God that is so. The news is looking up again and hopes run high. That's all for now, My Darling. Love to all. My heart is filled with warmth at the thought of you and our cherub.

Love, Daddy

November 17, 1944 – Somewhere in Belgium
My Darling:

I wish you could hear the hot-stove league at this very moment. The war bulletin received this morning tells us the big push is on. We are excited and we are sitting around the stove and guessing at the strategy being employed on the front. This is the welcome pause before noon chow when we all become great generals. But in fairness to these boys on our own "front," we are striving and accomplishing too. History should record that the medics of the war "are on the scrotum" in the ankle-deep mud, as well as on the tiled floors of hospitals. No matter how rough it gets, there's always loud laughter when the shoes are at rest around the potbelly. Going to chow now.

Love to all. Here's all my heart, My Darling. Daddy

November 17, 1944 – Somewhere in Belgium
My Darling:

I am high and dry on what approach to take in this letter since today again there was no mail. I realize now, however, that this is unavoidable since the holiday mail being moved to the ETO this year is without precedent. Only a letter or two seems to trickle through, and I suspect that nothing will be forthcoming until Thanksgiving. I would gladly pass up the packages for a letter but I guess I have to wait. No one else here seems to be getting any mail although a few packages have come through. This subject must be boring by this time, Sweetheart, but there is so little else to write about at the moment. Also by the end of the day I'm dog tired and can't think straight. I am well and eat the constantly improving food with sharp appetite which is stimulated by the outdoor labor. Believe me, Angel, this is doing me no harm that I can discover, except that heavy fatigue overtakes me by the end of the day. I pray that all is well at home. Forgive me for the brevity, Angel. I'm so sleepy.

Here's my heart. Daddy

November 18, 1944 – Somewhere in Belgium
My Darling:
No mail again today but my heart tells me that all is well with you so I await the day when all your letters will arrive.

A warm, fair day found us moving rapidly toward a completion of our project. And even the mud will cease being a problem soon as sidewalks are now under construction. I wish I knew what was going to happen to me after I serve my turn in the "chain gang," but I hate to go prying. They don't like that sort of thing around here, I've discovered. Well, it's something to know that I can adapt myself even to slave labor, if necessary. I am not unhappy, My Darling. Building something does give one a real sense of accomplishment. This being Saturday night, with the town definitely off-limits, no recreation of any sort available, we sit around the stove and shoot the bull. Yet there is no resentment, no bitching. The boys are quite content to sit quietly. What gets me, there isn't even any card playing in this barracks. Tomorrow (Sunday) is a regular day for us, but it doesn't matter, since there is no place to go.

We devour the news from the front, and we express loudly our hopes and prayers that this time it will be the knockout blow. How those monsters can resist so long is really beyond comprehension. How little we knew of them and how close we came to disaster in preparing to meet them. I can't keep our cherub from growing up (how I'd like to see her as she is now) but I can keep myself from changing and I promise you I'll come back strong, enthusiastic, hopeful for the future, and, above all, with a heart full of love for you, My Darling, and a most indulgent parent. I warn you, I'll spoil that child.

Love to all. Your Daddy

November 18, 1944 – Somewhere in Belgium
My Darling:
The hot-stove league, now in action around the stove during our brief pause after noon chow, is circulating the rumor that twelve bags of mail arrived. That's a very nice rumor. Maybe it's true and I'll get a few of your precious letters tonight.

All is well here. I feel fine. Had a morning in the hospital on patients' baggage detail. Maybe I'll get back there for the afternoon. It's interesting. I'll explain later. I am anxious to get this in the box so it will be censored tonight. I had my tooth fixed again this morning so I shouldn't have any more trouble with it. I hope your dry socket is just a memory. I guess you stood it with more grace than I did. It is a hell of a pain. Love to all. Kiss our cherub.

Your loving, devoted, Daddy

November 20, 1944 – Somewhere in Belgium
My Darling:

At last the mail came bringing me your letters of October 26 and November 1. You should have had letters earlier than October 19, as we arrived here several days before that date. No doubt the missing letters have arrived by this time. Your disbelief in my ability to "take it" is not justified. I'll admit we have been through some mighty rough days, but I have weathered it without mishap and now await my opportunity to serve the hospital in some capacity. Along with your letters have come letters from Roy, [sister] Mayme and the folks. It is Roy's last letter to me from Europe. He should be home by now. I can imagine the scene when he walked (or walks) in. I am enormously relieved that he is out of the area that has been the target of the Nazi "Flash Gordon" terror devices. My last letter to him apparently did not reach him in time but it will follow him as will the fruitcake your mother sent him. No matter where you go, the mail ultimately reaches you. I have seen some rare examples of this.

No packages have arrived for me as yet, a pleasure which I anticipate daily. Sweets are at a premium here. And I doubt whether the situation will improve. Cigarette rations, too, have been cut down by more than half and some of the boys are feeling it. I haven't acquired the habit so remain unconcerned as I have sufficient pipe tobacco on hand. We have been reading in *Stars and Stripes* about the cigarette situation in the states. The prices some people are paying doesn't surprise me. Our hour in Paris left us speechless at what goes on in the cigarette black market, which was flourishing quite openly in the station. I'll save the details for some treasured evening when we are together again. How many stories I shall have to tell you!

I did receive your letter describing Roberta's [first birthday] party, and I shall always keep it. Also, I know that the August bond arrived, and now the September one. Our daughter's development continues to enthrall me. You describe her antics so delightfully. But I am not pleased with her penchant for throwing eggs in your mother's face. You must tell the young imp that her Daddy and several million other Daddies would give a great deal to taste a fresh egg again. Ours are strictly the powdered variety, which I have given up entirely. While on the subject of food, our chow gets better and better and then lapses again for a while into that tasteless state. Seriously, Angel, I shouldn't like to come home to a child who throws food. Is she being indulged a little too much? Or is this just a phase of every child's development?

Well, Angel, I am going to attempt a shower tonight. How I need it! I have only to don raincoat, overshoes and various other garments, and slosh a third

of a mile through the stickiest mud I'd ever encountered. When I get to the hospital, the water, no doubt, will be even less than tepid, so I'll turn around and slosh back to a welcome bed. Goodnight, My Love. Best to all. Kiss the cherub.
 Your Daddy

November 21, 1944, 7:45 p.m. – Somewhere in Belgium
My Darling:
 Just a few hurried words in lieu of a regular letter tonight. In a few minutes, a USO show is about to begin. It is my first night "out" since we arrived here. And as long as I had to come to the hospital building tonight for choir practice and a tetanus shot, I decided to remain and see the show, which played here last night, and which the fellows urged me to see. I am writing this on my lap while sitting on a mess hall table next to Manny, who true to his childish exuberance threatens to tip us all over as he wiggles and giggles. The show is starting, Angel, goodnight. I am as well and happy as one can be without a wonderful wife whom I love and long for very much. More tomorrow. Kiss the cherub.
 Love, Daddy

November 22, 1944 – Somewhere in Belgium
 My Darling: Just a few words to tell you that as of today, 12 p.m., all is well with me. Am resigned to the labor details for a while longer. Everyone is very busy now, so it really doesn't matter what you get to do. A band might be started here and I might get in if doesn't demand too much of my few moments of leisure. But I'd rather be making music than listening to the hot-stovers who use that four-letter word as a noun, pronoun, verb, adverb, adjective. It gets awfully monotonous. I shall give thanks tomorrow, Thanksgiving Day, for the blessings bestowed upon me. Love to all. I'll share your Thanksgiving dinner by dreaming about the incomparable Malkin [wife's parents] table.
 Love, Daddy

November 22, 1944, 8:00 p.m. – Somewhere in Belgium
 Yes, Darling, three letters, Nov. 3, 4, 6, arrived tonight and I'm as high as a kite, having drunk deeply of the contents, best of all, the heart-warming wine of our daughter's talents and angelic nature. Her response to you, My Angel, chokes me with an unspeakable pride and joy. It is hard to put into words just how I visualize the picture of you two, now that she is at a stage of development in which each person about her has an identity. You plead that you haven't the power to put into words all she does and says, yet I shall never forget how my heart bounded when I read your words recently how Roberta coming up behind you, as you knelt, stroked your back and said "nice Mommy." That, my darling, is what makes the bad days endurable. I'm sorry if I "conveyed" more than I had a right to in my letter of Oct. 18. That "terrible night," for me at least, was

a test of human endurance comparable to infiltration, but there was no danger involved such as you mentioned. That sort of thing is as remote here as it was in France.

"That night" was the doing of someone whose sadism left no room for even a vestige of common decency. It is forgotten, however, and we have resumed a norm of GI living and working which has much that is interesting and even wholly entertaining.

Tonight, for instance, a hub-bub of letter reading out loud followed in the wake of mail call. We who mailed our ashtrays from France at about the same time were pleased to hear that the parcels arrived, but we, meaning Len Goldhammer of Cleveland and Sam Lesner of Chicago, were a little confused by the reception said ashtrays received from wives of above-mentioned senders. Mrs. Goldhammer wrote, "And the desk piece is very impressive. I'm sure it weighs a ton." Mrs. Lesner wrote: "the ashtray is antique and useful." We have come to the conclusion that we have very polite, very loving wives who just couldn't say "what sort of junk is this?"

Maybe we are all wet. After all, you did say you "adore it." I have the feeling, however, that the excitement of finding the shells in foxholes and sweating over them with inadequate tools made them seem like "rare objects" in our eyes.

Tomorrow we are to have a real feast after all, including wine. Tomorrow, I shall reread your letters and close the day with an opus to you. Bon appétit, My Darling. Kiss the cherub.

Love to all, Your Daddy

P.S. Enclosed is a picture of dubious distinction.

November 23, 1944 – Somewhere in Belgium
My Darling:
Having just returned from an excellent dinner with a warmth in the head from the splendid wine served, I can think of nothing better to do than to write you of the day's events. The weather did not allow for too much outdoor work. So we field men had a comparatively easy day for a change. The boys in the hospital are beginning to envy us. Their workday is considerably longer than ours. We had breakfast as usual at 6 a.m., but dinner was served at 2:30 p.m. I fortified myself around noon, however, with anchovies and crackers. The

Belgium: Building the Barracks

anchovies, I readily accepted from Manny, who received them yesterday from home. He doesn't like them, he says. I hope he meant that because I have yet to inform him that the anchovies are no more. For dinner the mess hall was made festive with table decorations, and at our table we even had a charming lady, one of the Red Cross girls attached to our unit. She hails from Oak Park, Illinois, although she hasn't lived there for a number of years now. The boys are returning one by one, and before long, this barracks will rock. Unofficially, we have called it a day, though it's only a little after 4 p.m. There is to be no evening meal tonight, but I couldn't look any more food in the face. I'll have my evening coffee later and call it a day.

In chapel this morning we sang a hymn, "Count Your Blessings." I counted mine, as I do every day, and my spirit is high. An Army hospital is a good place to look around and take inventory of your blessings. I am well, I am safe, I have rare treasures awaiting me at home. I have a promising future. I am thankful. With God's help, we shall find peace and contentment and success. Be of good cheer, My Darling. You alone have the power to inspire me with confidence. I can't fail as long as the warmth of your love radiates even at this great distance.

Tell our cherub that next Thanksgiving we shall break the turkey wishbone and wish for another one, just like her.

Love to all. Your Daddy

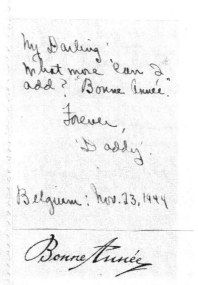

[Card enclosed: "My Darling: What more can I add? Bonne Année. Forever, Daddy. Belgium: Nov. 23, 1944]

November 25, 1944 – Somewhere in Belgium
My Darling:

Again, I shall have to write briefly and hastily so as to get this into the box in time for tonight's censoring. I failed to write you last night. I went to the movies directly from chow, and it was quite late before we returned to the barracks. The film was *Marriage Is a Private Affair*," with Lana Turner, who astonished me with her fine performance. I have always thought of her as a sweater girl and for one fleeting scene it was revealed why she has enjoyed this dubious distinction. Yes, I looked too and uttered an appreciative gasp of delight. The story, though, was deftly handled on the screen, much to my surprise. I would recommend the film to all young married people, and old ones too. There is a message in it for everyone, and I admit that it made me feel ashamed for my sins of omission. I was reminded of several occasions on which I was too dumb and blind to catch the exquisite overtones of a good wife's love. I have been guilty, My Darling, of thoughtlessness and I have caused you pain. I hope I shall return with more wisdom. [*Editors' note: After the war, Sam became the film critic for the* Chicago Daily News.]

We have sunshine today. We are all delirious with joy over this fact. This speaks for itself.

The war news is good. Our hopes are high. Our morale, and mine in particular, is excellent. Today we enjoyed the spectacle of seeing our batch of war prisoners take over most of the difficult field work we've been doing the past weeks. I'll write more illuminatingly on this subject later.

No mail from you for three days now, but I guess it will arrive before the week is out. Must return to the field now, Sweet, and watch the "supermen" work.

Love to all. To you, My Love, all my love. Kiss the cookie. Daddy

November 25, 1944 – Somewhere in Belgium (Delayed) [An unfinished letter]
My Darling:

Our joy was short-lived. Our "charming guests" [German POWs], however, continued to work in the rain as we watched them from under canvas. They have no choice, but they do work steadily, doggedly. When they first appeared, the blood rushed to my head. But as the day wore on, we began to single out faces and study them. There is nothing super about them. The faces range from stupidity to middle-class smugness. We are forbidden fraternization with them. That is very wise. They are being treated fairly. That's sufficient. Since, by their own "admission," they have done no independent thinking, for many years, they can't possibly understand our good-natured bickering, which is so much a part of our daily lives. They can keep their "Order" through which they have accomplished so much mass murder and suffering. We have nothing to learn from them. We can teach them something, though, but only through refraining from prying into their empty minds. They are no enigma. They invited in the gangsters and then fell in love with the business of playing "Robber Barons." Very well, they have played the brutal game long enough. Trap them and squeeze them and they turn out to be small fry, indeed.

There is one "redeeming" trait in them, and that is the ability to do things in "ordered order" as compared to our organized confusion. But we do get things done. I must admit this is the one thing that amazes me. I was lost as only a lonely, heartsick, sensitive, imaginative guy can be in the early weeks of our organized confusion here. It was exactly like a bad dream in which you try to scream and can't or that even worse sensation of falling without ever landing.

But from day to day something was happening. Little by little laughter came easier. The bitching lost its note of bitterness and became again the banter of our acquired exhibitionism. Perhaps I'm seeing the sunshine again a little prematurely, but I do know that today I feel better than I have in a long time.

In the back of my mind a little devil keeps repeating, "Ah, ha, you feel good and superior now because you are now the superman. You can stand and watch the slaves labor for you. You can snap a finger and bring them a-running. You can shout and strut and play the conqueror."

Well, one thing is clear. We must make them understand we mean business. We can't help treating them with contempt for as long as they live they will remind us of the horror they visited upon the world. But gradually, we will temper our feelings as we continue to come in contact with them. As I explained, you find yourself searching for the monster in their faces and you find ordinary faces differing one from the other as do those of other people. They wear faces of very young lads, as arrogant as those of young boys anywhere, or they wear the faces of the undistinguished middle-aged. They could be absorbed and eventually no one would know the difference. That is wherein lies the real problem. Shall they be absorbed and "lost in the shuffle"? Or shall they be set up again as a people? In barracks we argue that problem by the hour. That is good, too. Perhaps this time we will not pull up stakes when it's over and say, "So long, Europe. Straighten out the mess yourself."

The Nazi poison is working even now in the face of their total defeat. The Medusa head has entwined its serpents on victims in every compass degree. Unlike the Oriental problem, where we have to overcome the mass strength of a common enemy, here we have to find and destroy the cesspools of treachery and political intrigue as well without diverting the main force of our armies. It's a big headache, my dear, but we must apply a more definitive treatment this time than the aspirin with which we bowed out last time.

November 26, 1944 – Somewhere in Belgium
My Darling:

For two days I have been "sweating out" a letter about our guests, the POWs who are working for us now, but I got nowhere with it, although I am saving the six pages I have written for mailing at a later date. No mail from you today, again, but Eureka! Two packages. Gosh, what a delicious feeling it is to get a package: the fruitcake and your box of utilities which I requested. Both parcels arrived in perfect condition. I am writing your mother about the cake, but I do want to say to you that your mother has the hands of a great artist; only a Horowitz could play a rhapsody as a companion piece to that cake. I mean that, Dear. I don't care what my buddies think of me. Half of that cake I keep for my own great pleasure. But half I had to pass around.

Your package, My Love, was welcome, too, although, as I feared, most of the things I needed badly have been made available at the P.X. in the interim. Ink, for instance, this very afternoon I was able to get, and two hours later your package arrived. Well, My Darling, I promise I'll use it up in letters to you, and I am happy that you sent it because the inferior grade obtainable here has been playing havoc with my pen, which I treasure. I let no one use it. It's that swell Waterman which your mother gave me. The socks are wonderful and welcome. The Army persists in issuing me size 11½ for a size 6 foot. The damn things bunch up in my shoes and drive me wild. The cream, also, is welcome, although I obtained some last week through . . . . Maybe I shouldn't say how. The nail file I shall use tonight with vigor. In all, I'm a very lucky guy to have such a wonderful wife and such a remarkably creative mother-in-law (in matters culinary). The day was pleasant as to weather and very interesting as to occupation. I did little more than play "straw boss" on the cement detail, and I've reached the end of the day, feeling very good, indeed. This feeling is elaborated upon in the unfinished letter I mention. I will send it to you.

My Darling, I must write your mother's letter, and then take off for the showers. Oh, how I need a bath! Goodnight, Love. Thank you for the things. I love you very much. Kiss the cherub.

Love to all. Daddy

November 26, 1944 – Somewhere in Belgium [to Hattie Malkin, mother-in-law]
Mother, Dear:

The cake arrived this evening in perfect condition, but even if it had crumbled, I assure you I'd lick the pan, which I intend to do when the last Ambrosial morsel is gone. Mother, I'm not applying "suction" as we crudely put it in the Army. The cake is one of the very best in the long list of culinary masterpieces you have turned out for the gasping delight of the fortunate ones who have sat at the Malkin board.

Thank you, Dear. I am as proud as I am delighted. As you know, we call our dining room the mess hall. The chow lives up to the name. It's a mess, you can be sure. I shall have to discover food all over again when I return. I hereby draft

Belgium: Building the Barracks

you as my guide to good eating when that happy day comes. I owe you a letter in answer to your splendid one, "My Day." I shall answer it before long.

Life here is becoming less difficult day by day. The hard, dark days of the past few weeks [working in the cold outdoors to pour the cement foundation for the barracks] have left no mark upon me. I am well and high in spirit. We do have that in common, Dear. We can take plenty of hell and come out of it smiling. I hope you are well.... Give my love to Dad and tell my daughter that she's expected to throw kisses, not eggs, at her doting Maga. Remember me fondly to those you may tell of my whereabouts.

As ever, Sam

[*Editors' note: At this point, Sam's "trowels and tribulations" came to an end, and he was assigned to work in a ward in the hospital.*]

CHAPTER EIGHT

Belgium: Medical Clinic

PART 1
HOSPITAL WARD ASSIGNMENT

[From Oral History interview with grandson, Edward C. Bernstein, in 1986]:

SL: *After the initial construction phase was over—it was very difficult, the next steps were much easier because we occupied existing buildings that had all the living quarters and the working quarter, the laboratories. What happened was that for a long time, although my specialty was as a ward corps man, it took some time before they got around to using me in the hospital operation itself. Finally, I was assigned to a [psychiatric] ward of thirty beds, and single-handedly I had to manage somehow to keep thirty [battle-fatigued] patients from tearing the place apart. I had a knack for it. I've always had a warm spot in my heart for young people who were in trouble, and so I treated them very well. I was very kind to them; I wrote letters for them. They wrote poems and I would mail them back to their families. As a result of that I won a citation as the best corps man in the 130th General Hospital, and my reward was a trip to Paris, which was a disaster.*

November 27, 1944 – Somewhere in Belgium
My Darling:
    While the doctor is seeing the patients, I have these few minutes for a brief message. I am very well and delighted with what I'm doing. Of course, I'm still in a ward where there is none of the usual bed-panning, etc., but in time I suspect I'll graduate to the bright aspects of ward man attending. This morning, for instance, I was suddenly switched from one ward to another. It's better for me to get my bearings in the new ward as the other called for more skill than I possess at the moment. I hope they let me learn, though, and not keep me as a "straw boss." I've just applied my first bandage, a simple thing but it was a debut. More tonight.
    Love, Daddy

Belgium: Medical Clinic

November 28, 1944 – Somewhere in Belgium
My Darling:

Lest I fail to get this in the mail in time for the 6:00 censor, I write briefly, though happily of the day's activities. Having been transferred to another ward, minor wounds and injuries, I've spent a most engrossing day tending my charges, making solutions, conferring with a nurse, a charming gal, and a ward officer, an understanding, patient man. He has kindly offered to explain as much as he can and guide me in acquiring a working knowledge of ward work. My head is spinning with pharmacy names for the various medications, and all the professional abbreviations that are used in the record books. Tomorrow, it will all be blank to me again, but I know that the next day and the next it will all become clear to me. I'll write more when I return to barracks tonight. It's so comfortable here, I hate to leave the place for that noisy, smelly barracks.

Love, Daddy

November 29, 1944, 1:30 p.m. – Somewhere in Belgium
My Darling:

No mail from you for several days now so I suppose since very little is coming through, we are again in for a period of waiting and hoping. The evening letter has come to mean so much to me. A bad day is made brighter at the end and a good day, ending with a letter, makes me downright gay. The past three days, however, have been wholly absorbing, and I have found my assignment most satisfactory.

Naturally, until I establish a routine, much reserve energy must be expended in the numerous tasks to be done, tasks which eventually my patients will take over. I could have enforced this immediately, but in order to know what the jobs are, and how best to do them, I'm first doing them myself. It may be a futile approach with these GIs, but I believe an intelligent approach will net me results. I may be wrong, though, very, very wrong. Then I shall have to get tough. The day is filled with the usual administering of medications, preparation of various solutions, and, of course, the many cleaning and washing details necessary to maintain a ward up to standard. I don't mind this at all. To acquire knowledge, one must start from the bottom. You might ask, "what good is all this?" It is good. The Army, Dear, commands the best and the most revolutionary results of medical research. It is a liberal education, just being exposed to the workings of the "miracles." I wish you could hear the discussions in barracks when after a day we gather around the stove. These boys, who didn't know an aspirin from a horse's behind before they entered service, now talk with astonishing authority and scientific awareness. I don't mean that we (they) strut around playing Louis Pasteur, or anything like that, but it is astonishing what they have learned and how much they can do. Mind you, most of these guys are not ex-medical students. As a matter of fact, in our final manpower distribution in this hospital, some of my buddies who were trained as ward men are now clerks, and I, a clerk, am a ward man, sans experience of any sort. Yet I feel that I can do it, and apparently the Army does too. Tomorrow, of course, this can all come to naught. I may be switched to something else. At the moment, though, the medical atmosphere in which I work is not without compensation for the trying days of "engineering." My feet hurt from bouncing around but it's the hurt of accomplishment. I may not write tonight so I've used this momentary break to "talk" to you, Angel. I hope all goes well at home. Love to the folks. Kiss the Love Lettuce. I await your letters, so full of love and faith.

God bless you, My Darling. Daddy

November 30, 1944, 3:00 p.m.
My Darling:

My education is proceeding by leaps and bounds. In an hour or so, I shall have a difficult ward in which work of real importance is to be done: a new and probably radical treatment, which is producing fine results. I am to learn this treatment, as I understand, and I'm excited and pleased. It will mean hard work, but it will be most revealing to me. That I know. Here is where I shall gather the knowledge, a microscopic view of the human body and the most remote workings of his mind. I wish I could tell you more.

[From Oral History interview with grandson, Edward C. Bernstein, in 1986]:

It was a psychiatric hospital. They did experiments with questionable treatment methods giving insulin shots to wounded and combat fatigued soldiers who were brought in from the front lines in shock and deposited with us. The experimental theory was to take combat fatigue soldiers, almost comatose, and awaken them [with the insulin shot] so that they could be sent back to the front lines. . . . We were getting combat casualties into our unit. I witnessed some bloody messes. I was heartsick when I saw the condition of some of the soldiers. But one develops a strange protective covering in these sickening situations.

Angel, I will answer your sweet letters (I received November 15, October 28 and 29 last night) more fully, tonight, perhaps. In a few minutes my patients will be arriving and I want to look prepared even if I am scared silly.

They can keep their clerkships! This, I really believe, is what I want. I wake up smiling and ready for the day's tasks. I hope I'm right. A package just arrived. More later.

Love, Daddy

Belgium: Medical Clinic

November 30, 1944, 9:20 p.m. – Somewhere in Belgium
My Darling:

What a day! If my letter of this afternoon reached you in chronological order, you know that I'm in my third ward in as many days, but this one should prove to be the best from the standpoint of learning something about the work of this hospital. This afternoon, the package including the camera, soap, wash rags and mirror arrived in good order. All the items are useful and most welcome. In fact, having failed to achieve a shower in over a week, I dipped washcloth in helmet and washed all over tonight. But my day had yet another glorious surprise in store for me: Love Lettuce's new pictures! I beg you to get the negative of that one and save it. I want that for our future home. It has all the beauty and innocence of childhood in it. It is the kind of picture that will give her pleasure, too, when she grows up.

Love to all, to you, my heart, Angel. I'm so sleepy. Daddy

December 2, 1944 – Somewhere in Belgium
My Darling:

I have reread your wonderful letter of November 14. I am happy, My Darling. Through the crazy chain of events that has led me here has run a tiny rivulet of purpose. How can I tell you what it means to be doing something, to be playing a part in this dramatic, ghastly business of war?

For the second day now I have treated men who have given so much of their hearts and bodies and have come almost to the end of their endurance. After all this roaming around, suddenly I am catapulted into the very heart of this thing we are doing. I can't tell you much, Darling, but what I shall carry away with me when this whole business is over perhaps will bring me closer to that apex of writing power, which you so generously, though prematurely, ascribe to me now. My Angel, only in this single thing do we disagree. No human being is uninteresting to me. I'm glad now that I have always felt so. Here the (human) mice and lions lie side-by-side and each has a right to demand your attention—and sorely needs it.

What I give of myself, beyond duty, renews my strength and determination for the following day as no other experience has done. It is my spirit, my warmth, my willingness to do that must be as patient and effective as any medicines we use.

Today I experienced the extraordinary sensation of giving someone else a shot in the arm. Without any previous experience or knowledge whatsoever, I handled the needle with good skill. I trembled inwardly but my patients never suspected it. Fortunately, there was no time for a reaction in me. There was much work to be done immediately after, and the day closed for me with a cheerful bunch of boys bidding me a warm goodnight. That, My Dear, is what gives one strength.

A friendly, highly intelligent nurse has been my teacher in the preliminary stages. The rest is largely up to me. Pray with me, My Angel, to find the strength, the patience, the kindliness to do this work until I am no longer needed.

Before me, spread upon the table, lie the baby's pictures. From the nose puckering disdain to the face of cherubic loveliness in the exquisite portrait study, I view our Blessing with such an overwhelming sense of joy and pride that I repeatedly pick them up and plant kisses on her button nose. . . . She will know and love me the moment I pick her up again for my heart sings out to her every day, even as it does to you. I must end now, my darling, if I am to include the unfinished letter.

Love to all. To you, My Love, all my heart. Daddy

December 4, 1944 – Somewhere in Belgium
My Darling:

A few hurried lines just to let you know I feel wonderful. I'm still excited about my job, and it looks like my enthusiasm will last. I never seem to get tired, watching, waiting on, and serving my boys. As fine a bunch as I've ever encountered. They are also grateful and appreciative. They've been through plenty of suffering, and they know how to appreciate the little extra things we do for them. Gosh, you get attached to them after a while and sending them back to duty isn't always easy. They're brave boys, though, and if in some little way I've added to their reserve of strength and courage, I feel compensated for the tired feet I get. What's important is that I'm thoroughly happy doing what is necessary to get them back into top condition. More tonight.

Love, Daddy

December 5, 1944, 2:30 p.m. – Somewhere in Belgium
My Darling:

While the boys take their afternoon snack, I take my nourishment in writing to you. All I need to keep me well and happy is the constant assurance that you and our Angel are well. Letters again are being held up, but I know that all is well. It must be a real comfort to you that I am exceedingly satisfied in what I'm doing as long as it proceeds along this line of work. In a day or two some of my first patients will be leaving and it will be with a real sense of regret, because they are such splendid boys. But I allow myself the satisfaction of knowing that in the past few days I have contributed to their renewed energy and enthusiasm for going on with their work, which is far more significant than what we medics are doing. Give my love to all. All my heart is yours.

Daddy

December 6, 1944 – Somewhere in Belgium
My Darling:

I must beg you to be satisfied with V-Mails and perhaps unfinished letters from time to time. I must use the brief breaks in the routine imposed upon me

now to write what letters I can. But it appears that at the end of each series of treatments there will be a day or two of leisure. These opportunities, I shall seize upon to write you long letters. I usually get back to the barracks quite late and quite tired and the past two nights I have gone to bed without writing. Please do not feel alarmed at this routine. It boils down simply to fatigue at the end of a long day and sleep restores quickly. What is important is that I am very happy in what I am doing. A survey of the patients yesterday produced high praise for me. It caused some stir since I'm so new on the job. I'll try to write tonight.
    Love, Daddy

December 6, 1944 – Somewhere in Belgium
My Darling:
    What is this thing that has come over me? After all these months of despair, of loneliness, I have found myself. This is the thing I needed to see, the suffering and pain of others, to realize that my lot is not a bad one. I'm still too excited about this new avenue of thought and experience that has been opened up for me to give you an accurate picture. But I do know that someday I will be able to say to myself, "Little man, you've been through some busy days. But you've done a good job." May God grant that all these boys will live to return to their homes.
    Sweetheart, forgive me for not writing my usual lengthy pieces. I have suddenly become alive, objective. I can say in so many words I love you. You are my strength. I can do no other than my best with that in my heart. I am well. I'm happy. God bless and keep you, My Wife, and our angel child. More tomorrow.
    Daddy

December 7, 1944 – Somewhere in Belgium
My Darling:
    It has been a day of accomplishment, but also there were moments of sadness as well as moments of pride in a job well done. This morning, I sent several of "my boys" back to duty. They went away, renewed in vitality and with hope for a safe continuance of their duties. Soon more will go and finally the last of the original bunch upon whom I "practiced" with sympathetic though untried hands. It frightens me a little now that it is over, but that first shot left me shaking like a leaf, although the patients did not notice. There is so much more to this business than the purely mechanical acts of giving medications and shots.
    Each night, I have sought out men here of more experience and urge them to discuss their approaches and reactions to this particular phase of our work. I keep asking myself over and over "Am I on the right track?" This thing may prove as much a healing for me as for those who are treated.
    The moment I enter the ward I become a swift-moving, smiling, sympathetic, helpful individual. Throughout the day, it doesn't even occur to me that the "drive" necessary to carry out the job could bring a frown to my face. It's a very good feeling, winding up the day with the face that is still smiling. I can't

explain. Perhaps I should wait a bit. Army rules and regulations aren't very easy to live by and one day I'll probably get slapped down for some oversight. Then perhaps the little crack will appear and out of it will slowly trickle the warmth, the compassion, the desire for knowledge which fills me now. I hope on that day the courage doesn't fail me.

Tomorrow, we expect a fairly easy day since treatment has run its course with the current group and there's not much to do until we start over again. Darling, don't think that the job has become "my all," although I admit there is little else that holds my attention as much.

We have a splendid day room now (yes, I troweled most of the concrete floor in it) and it is in this comfortable room that I am writing now. Good light, proper chairs and tables, and those canvas desk chairs add to the comfort of the room, which more properly could be called a hall. Beer is sold, but I can't drink the stuff. We hope to convince the first sergeant that enough of us are interested in good music to warrant cutting off a small section of the room for good music. Through radios and phonographs, which we possess, this could be arranged easily. Oh to hear a good recording! Angel, I hope you are building up our library from time to time. Please allow us this extravagance, for when I come home, we are going to load the machine and make love.

I bought you some very attractive wooden shoes. As soon as I can get a tiny pair for Roberta I'll send them off. No mail again today. Perhaps none tomorrow and tomorrow, but I'll wait because when they come finally they will be full of the love and devotion which has sustained me in this long separation from you. Give my love to all. I got a nice Christmas box from the Block captain (apparently, the friends and neighbors of local board 123) the other day. Nice of them, eh?

Love, Daddy

December 8, 1944, 4:30 p.m. –Somewhere in Belgium
My Darling:

As I expected, it has been a fairly easy day, and with luck I'll get this in the mailbox in time for tonight's censorship, thus saving a whole day. Your letter of November 19 came a few minutes ago.

My last letter from Roy was dated November 9, I believe, and he said he was leaving soon. So I assume he is home by this time. He must have sent his clothes far in advance. Undoubtedly, he was held up a few days to be "processed." There is no end to the checkups every time a guy moves.

Most of "my boys" are still here so today we just sat around and talked. They're still at it as I write. I have shown them your picture and the baby's. And they all agree I'm a lucky guy and a very good picker.

I'll certainly be on the lookout for [the movie] *Laura*. I haven't been to any of the movies for two weeks since they show the film for us at 9 p.m. That means

Belgium: Medical Clinic

getting to bed at midnight or later. Not for me! I'm in bed by 9:30 or soon after that, and do I sleep! It's fun to sleep so soundly and to awaken knowing that you have an interesting job to go to.

Tomorrow, perhaps, may be fairly easy too, but by Sunday we should be in full swing again with a new group. What will they be like? I keep asking myself, giving birth to the wish that they are as swell as these guys to whom I shall say au revoir tomorrow. Can you understand this thing that has taken hold of me? For a week, I have "shot" them daily, then sweated out two hours of anxiety after each treatment, watching them react, which isn't easy on the nerves. I have found myself praying over each one. Well, they're all happy and laughing now. That's the important thing. I await your letter all about Love Lettuce. This must go to the mailbox now, Sweetheart, or else.

Love to all. To you, my heart, Daddy

December 9, 1944, 5:15 p.m. – Somewhere in Belgium
My Darling:

It is very quiet in the ward at the moment. The boys have gone to the show. My dwindling flock continue in their happy frame of mind. This is the phase of the job that is so pleasant, getting to know the men as they really are before they take off for old or new assignments. The day has been pleasant and easy. We hit the jackpot today as to food, and I'm full of the things I like, chicken, salmon, stewed tomatoes, salad, etc. I must hurry, if I am to get this in before six. So I close with the heart full of love I bear you. I'm going to sing at the GI party next week. Had a solo in chapel last week and expect to be a soloist for the Christmas service.

Love to all, Daddy

December 10, 1944, 5:35 p.m. – Somewhere in Belgium
My Darling:

I must write very quickly in order to get this in by 6:15 p.m. for the night censoring, thus saving a whole day. Your wonderful letters of November 25, 26, 28 just arrived, as did a gem of a letter from your dad. I certainly appreciate his taking the time to write to me. The awful gaps that have to be filled in, that you may get a fairly accurate picture of what I do and think and feel, also applies to your hopelessly unchronological letters. You mention Roy several times, yet I have no letters telling of his actual homecoming. You'll discover, though, Angel, that every soldier comes home with a hurt in him. That will be a problem confronting all families and all friends of returning soldiers. What I have learned of war in this past week makes the postwar problem seem enormous indeed.

I have pipe cleaners, thank you! You poor civilians! . . . The V-Mails, My Darling, were only in addition to the regular nightly ones which apparently have

gone to Constantinople. I'll write again tonight. I'm bursting to tell you the story to date of the career of "Dr. Lesner."
Love, Daddy

December 11, 1944 – Somewhere in Belgium. Our new APO is 350
My Darling:
Today, again, we started anew with another group and it was well beyond mail-censoring time before I could get started on this letter. I deplore the loss of a whole day as a result of it, but I beg you to make this sacrifice for me. Let your heart and mind be at rest if a day or two passes without word from me. Try as I might, some days do pass by without so much as a pause for a long breath. Thus I have taken to scribbling hasty V-Mails. If I were permitted to describe in detail what transpires in any given day during treatment, you would understand why I beg you not to fret. It is easier to ask such a thing, of course, than to accept a like situation, for I am desolate when there is no mail from you. Since our mail call is after 4 p.m., mercifully, I have only a few waking hours in which to fret, while for you it means a whole day must pass before the next mail.

Angel, I have indicated our new APO number (350) at the top of first page. No! We have not moved. It was a change which should have been made some time ago as the old one was in conflict with another outfit. Mail, undoubtedly, will be speeded up, so begin to use it at once: 130th General Hosp. APO 350

Please point this out to my folks, too.

In your letter of Sunday, Nov. 26, you say: "This will be my dullest letter of the week." On the contrary, it was the most exciting of the three I received because of the reference to Bloch's "Schelomo". I wish I could have heard it with you. How differently things would have been. Knowing you, loving you as I do now, how quickly I would have poured out my heart to you, where on another occasion I was frozen with fear and disappointment that you didn't sense my echoing of that tragic music. For me, "Schelomo" is the ancient heart-rending cry of our people sounding down through the ages, a cry that has burst from the pounding hearts of other millions in these bitter years that have passed.

All day yesterday, I felt a weight upon me, a feeling of troubled excitement. In part it was the anticipation of starting anew today, and in part it was a sense of despair. No one wants this terrible war (except those stiff-necked bastards and those slant-eyed monsters), but we'll have to go on killing and being killed for days upon days. You hear from those around you what it's really like "at the front," and while on one hand it hardens you for a bitter vengeance upon those mass-murder maniacs we face, at the same time it sickens you to learn that we have no other choice but extermination of the enemy. From the youngest to the oldest of those who are sent here, you hear the same cry, "Kill those bastards."

Belgium: Medical Clinic

This time we must put the fear of God into them for good. For indeed they are a godless horde in their suicidal march to doom. Do they really believe that we'll get tired of this business before we finish the job? They have diabolical war machines. We have men who remember with a shudder that they had to shoot women who killed other mothers' sons with the snipers' guns. The bastard sons of those women, however, knew only Hitlerian wrath when they turned their guns on their own kind. Thus, your reference to "Schelomo" was like a release spring for the ache in my heart. In recollection I heard the climactic moment of the music when the single horn cries out in imitation of the ram's horn, O hear, Israel! That very brief musical passage in "Schelomo" is at once a cry of despair and a prayer of hope.

All day I longed to tell you how I felt about saying au revoir to "my boys," knowing that they had no choice but to return to duty. There is no such thing as taking up where you left off in war. In war, you just plunge in from one dark abyss into another. I thank God they went away feeling that in us there's still something of civilization.

We feel these things so deeply, My Darling, because we have our "Schelomos". We need no formal religious concepts. Our religion springs from deeply within us. I often wonder how deeply they feel their Christ as I participate in the regular chapel services. I hope he is as comforting as are our "Schelomos."

More tomorrow, My Love. Kiss the cherub.

To all, my best wishes for the Holidays, Daddy

December 13, 1944 – Somewhere in Belgium
My Darling:

I had intended writing you a long letter tonight, but I am, in turn, so disturbed by the stupidity of the American press that I want to puke. Imagine the utter crassness, the wholly unbelievable callousness of the Associated Press in releasing for general consumption the news of the hospital to which your enclosed clipping refers. I don't get it. We are not supposed to talk about these things even among ourselves, but the American press strikes terror in the hearts of many people who were concerned with the welfare of their loved ones in Belgium.

No, Sweetheart, it wasn't ours, thank God, and you must believe that it isn't likely to happen to us. More than that I can't say. While it was a tragic business, it was not deliberate, we believe. The hospital's proximity to other targets, it is said, brought about the bombing. At least that is what we know of the affair.

I prayed that the news item would never fall under your eye when I learned the AP released the story. Since facts cannot be given, why in Heaven do they print such stuff? Isn't it enough that the families of the victims are notified of their loss, without stirring anguish and fear in many other hearts? I say — Shame. Shame on the American press for its grossness. It's the one time I feel sick to my stomach at the thought of returning to work for the *Chicago Daily News* someday.

My Darling, I'm on the spot as are all of us here. Whatever I tell you now, you will always think I'm concealing the truth. I believe, though, that you do have faith. Real faith in a merciful God. I believe that I will come out of this safe and sound. You must believe that with me.

We are very busy, and I'm still engrossed in and excited about my job. If I don't come out of this a sort of male Florence Nightingale, it will be only because the Army will suddenly decide to make something else out of me: My new bunch of boys are turning out far better than I dared to hope after giving them the onceover.

One drawling, drooling, 1st-grade moron said to me yesterday, "Sammy, how do you put up with such a bunch of boys?" So my method, I dare to hope, is right. This bunch, if I succeed, will be my real victory.

Be brave, have faith, and believe that I am safe and well, as I truly am. My love in unmeasured quantity to assuage the pain you have suffered from that terrible clipping.

Love to all, Daddy

December 14, 1944 – Somewhere in Belgium
My Darling:
I'm delighted with what the mail call brought me, even though one of the four letters was of rare vintage, dated Sept. 26. Isn't that the limit? The others are of Nov 7, 8, 12. Also had a V-Mail of Nov. 26 from Roy, which again proves that V-Mail is coming through far more regularly than airmail.

There's little new at this point, My Darling. We work very hard and by the end of the day, I'm a "sad sack," although I swear to you, I enjoy every minute of the day. The work is interesting, and each day some new phase of this treatment is revealed to me. We have been promised a half-day off very soon, and then I'll sit myself down and write you a comprehensive review of all that has transpired. I have some notes, which I hope will help me put it down intelligently.

Roy writes that he is on his way to California. That one word made my knees buckle. I'm afraid he'll see the Pacific Ocean from the other shore one day soon.

We have much work to do here, and I feel safe in saying that our stay here will be for the duration. True to form, I got myself involved in various things again. I'm the only soloist for the Xmas service, I'm to sing at a GI party this coming Sunday, and further, it looks like I'm again a dance band musician, my ex-accordion having turned up here as property of the Red Cross. Well, it's a busy life, if anything. The music for the Xmas service is of a really high caliber and I'm excited about being chosen to do it.

Ruth's [wife's sister] nice Xmas box arrived yesterday. It is very sweet of her. I will send off her wooden shoes this week, as I will do with yours, too. I have a souvenir pair for the baby, but according to your description of her tiny feet, it

Belgium: Medical Clinic 167

will be years before she can go clumping around in them. Maybe I can find a real tiny pair, too. I must close, Angel. A dozen chores must be done before I call it a day.

Goodnight, My Love. Love to all, Daddy

December 15, 1944, 7:30 p.m. –Somewhere in Belgium
My Darling:

Just a few more lines to augment the letter I wrote at supper time, but which you will get before the first one, no doubt.

At any rate, again, I repeat, do not worry about the change of our APO number. The change, coinciding with the news you read in the *Chicago Daily News* about that other hospital, probably has you believing all sorts of things. This coincidence occurred to me after I had written you advising about the APO change, and I could have kicked myself for not making this clear to you then.

At the moment we are gathered in the Day Room, where we are to hear a talk on Sex Morality, and a rereading of the Articles of War. Never a dull moment in the Army. I've also been to a choir rehearsal and practiced hard for next week's service. My solo, with chorus, is a moving, inspiring piece of music, and I'm thrilled to have the chance to sing it.

My patients are all fine as of today, and I'm beginning to feel like a "miracle doctor." This is a strange, engrossing business. They run me ragged doing things for them, but even when they're very sick, they're conscious of my presence and "come around" very quickly when I start soothing their shattered nerves. I am fortunate in that the two nurses and the ward master are in agreement that our combined kindness and constant attention is the best approach to the problems confronting us. This makes for a smooth-running ward and responsibilities are equally shared. The boys respond quickly in such an atmosphere of cooperation and consideration.

Please, Angel, explain to all and sundry that I am hard-pressed for time and can't write now without torturing myself with lack of sleep. The first break I get, I'll make good on all the letters, even those I haven't received from some of our well-meaning pals.

Give the Love Lettuce a huge kiss from her adoring Daddy. My arms ache to embrace you.

Daddy

December 15, 1944 – Somewhere in Belgium

My Sweet Darling: The mailman is making amends even though the letters are slightly old, but they are wonderful bracers for me just the same. Today I got those of Nov. 9, 10, and 13. I am sad in the knowledge that this period of writing these sweet letters was such a fruitless one for you. How this grieves me to know that you are worried. But, Angel, we'll both have to learn to accept the situation.

I know how you feel about the war news, but I beg you to be a little less responsive to those horrible purveyors of half-truths. I don't quite understand what has happened but the wave of pessimism is too phony to be a real indication of the true situation. Undoubtedly, we are getting the post-election "treatment" now to counteract some of the fine promises which were made so freely. I'm not criticizing the Administration. No one man can change the course of things. I am criticizing you folks at home, who had the war over last Sept. in the face of facts which were there for the examination. With Xmas just around the corner, there is very little likelihood that Peace on Earth will prevail on that day. We know as little about what the situation is as you do at home, but there is no pessimism here. Our job is a big one, an all-consuming one. No time out for strikes, for discussions. If it is true that we are rationing ammunition on some fronts, it's not that our boys are wasteful. Rather it's that you at home are wasteful of our boys' lives in your infernal strikes, your false optimisms, and your downright indifference. We read recently, that a bonus would be paid to the war-workers who stayed on the job. That made me feel very bad in the pit of the stomach. The boys upfront aren't getting their nerves shattered and their bodies torn to bits with a bonus in view, nor are we carrying urine and fecal matter for a bonus. What I'm doing here, I'm doing with all my heart and strength. There is no bonus for me in the thousand things I do beyond the line of duty. I, too, will have many stories to tell you, My Love.

While our separation is cruel in the aches it inspires in our hearts, which are so wonderfully attuned to each other, our acute awareness of what is going on in this unhappy world now will make greater our joy in each other in a happier day. For this day I live and strive to make myself worthy of my great treasures awaiting my return.

Here is my heart, My Beloved. Daddy

December 16, 1944 – Somewhere in Belgium
My Darling:

What a rugged morning! And what an education I am getting this is the interval between my return from lunch and resuming of activities about 1 p.m. So I hasten to let you know that I am well and very satisfied with what I have been given to do.

I'm afraid I can't write you an airmail tonight, as I have a dozen things to do of an urgent nature, so forgive me, sweetheart, and except this V-Mail as today's message of love. To think that I might have been stuck in a dull office with even duller individuals. This is exciting. This is work that gives you strength. Believe this, my love, I am truly engrossed in this particular phase of hospital work. Love to all. Will have some new pictures for you soon.

Daddy

Belgium: Medical Clinic

December 16, 1944 – Somewhere in Belgium
[Letter to Mrs. Hattie Malkin, mother of Esther Lesner]
Mother dear:

Today your wonderful box of Huyler's cookies arrived while I was very busy with my patients and I knew that now I must answer your treasured letter of October 10: "My day." I had planned at first to outline a full day as you did so interestingly, but what I'm doing is of such a nature that only a lengthy discourse upon a subject which is very new to me would result. I can repeat only what I have just written to Ruthie who has filled my barracks with bags of delicacies: "In these past two weeks I have lived a lifetime for my heart has been pierced by the tragedies of war. War does far more than shatter bodies. It also shatters nerves. It is our job to restore these nerves, but it is also our job to put forth faith and courage back into their hearts. This is my penance. Never again can I be guilty of impatience, of intolerance. What a strange thing is the human mind!" In "my day" you wrote: "Maybe it would interest you to hear about that which occupies all almost all of my waking hours. Roberta is her name, with whom I am much engrossed and whom I find interesting to say the least and a godsend for what ails me." Why is this power taken away from us as we grow out of childhood? How much more we need this power as adults. The contents of your letters sank deep within me for what is happening to me must have its roots in the heart-glow of your letter. I too start my day at 5:30, impatient to learn more of the simple lessons of human relationship. This is such a unique experience. I arrive at my ward in high spirits, and I leave at the end of a tiring day, smiling and excited in anticipation of tomorrow. I don't know how all this came about. I do know, though, that an hour after I started the job, I became "another person." We are no "miracle doctors," though. Certain proven laboratory products, combined with unending patience and understanding, are our tools. The medicines I have learned to give with a calm, professional flair. The other tools are used instinctively, for I am not conscious of a calculated move to make these unhappy men more comfortable in their temporary haven of warmth and safety. I do know, though, that going away is being made easier for them. You, with your enormous capacity for doing things for others, would be revitalized in this work as I am daily. Thus, I have linked you to these boys today by making their supper festive with the Huyler's cookies from you. Nary a morsel they left me, but they filled my heart with their chorus of thanks. Goodnight, Mother. Keep warming your heart with the light in Roberta's eyes. Sam

December 18, 1944 – Somewhere in Belgium
My Darling:

Having dispatched an airmail letter to you this morning, I shall augment it with this brief V-Mail and I'll bet you two francs you read this before the airmail.

It is very quiet at the moment. The boys, now permitted to leave the ward, have gone to choir. The weather is extraordinary in that at this advanced date it is still like spring. I haven't worn my overcoat yet. We are waiting for "the snows" which the natives speak about. So far all we have had are "the rains". The war news has caused a stir of excitement here, but then we "relish" a chance to get emotional about it once in a while, since more often than not, it is very peaceful here. Hope to have a letter from you tonight.

    Love, Daddy

December 18, 1944 – Somewhere in Belgium
My Darling:

    Just a few words to beg you not to be alarmed if I don't write for a very few days. I have been selected to do a few days of detached service in a place I long to see more thoroughly than the last visit permitted. It should prove a most satisfying experience. Please, please, don't worry. I expect to be back for the Christmas service for which I have been practicing very hard. I hope it will be some of the best singing I've ever done. My love to all. The memory of past Christmas holidays with you will fill my mind with thoughts of you. My heart is overflowing with the love and longing I feel for you.

    Merry Xmas, Daddy

December 19, 1944 – Somewhere in Belgium
My Darling:

    A dull, dismal Monday morning finds us waiting for the bunch to be made well again and if the incoming ones respond, as well as this bunch, I shall get some personal satisfaction from it. If all the boys live up to their promises to visit Chicago after this is over, we shall have to keep perpetual open house. Naturally, I don't expect anything like this will happen, but it does feel good to know that all these guys remember that "ward man" in their days of remembering their war experiences.

    Instinctively you single out the ones of high caliber, and while complete impartiality motivates me in my feelings with them, it is unavoidable that some appeal to you strongly, and you spend extra hours talking to them. What stories they tell. How little we know of war here, and how utterly uninformed you at home are. I have always maintained that keeping the true facts from those at home is one of the major catastrophes of this war. I have always felt that Americans can "take it" and arise to the occasion, but as long as the home front gets only the periodic palaver or paid propagandists and melodramatic news casters, America will continue to go about its "business as usual" and receive the headlines and broadcast the usual "tsk, tsk," and pseudo-tragic head shake. Then some, aroused to action, will buy another bond and make a reservation at a nightclub.

Belgium: Medical Clinic

You may read again some of that stuff which caused you so much grief and anxiety. Be assured, my love, that it does not apply to us. The good Lord is with us and we are safe and very busy. Let your heart be at rest. I am well and continue to be engrossed in this fascinating job.

My love to all. To you-my heart. Kiss our cherub. Daddy

Part 2
The Battle of the Bulge

December 23, 1944
My Darling:

Where shall I begin? So much has happened in the brief interval of going to and returning from Paris. How each thrill, how each stirring sight tortured me in that you were not by my side. The Eiffel Tower, the magnificent Trocadero Palace, the Arc de Triomphe, the eternal flame at the head of the unknown soldier's tomb, the palaces, the Louvre, the Place de la Concorde, and many other historic spots which suddenly became a reality for me.

What's more, My Darling, I could hardly check the tears of longing and loneliness for you as I sat enthralled by a performance of *Othello* in the magnificent National Opera House. Red plush, My Darling, makes the galleries as beautiful as the main floor seats. I have a program, which I am sending you.

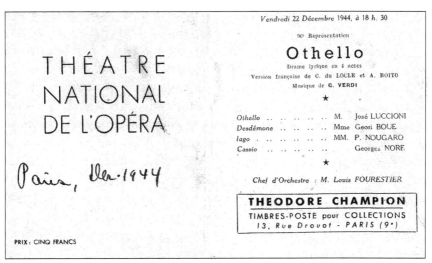

How did this all come about? Well, to begin, my work at the hospital has been so satisfactory, I was given the opportunity to go to Paris on the mission related to our work. My companion and I, having completed our mission, were to wait in the city for available transportation back to our post. We browsed around, trying to find a place to stay, which is next to impossible due to the influx of combat men who have priority on hotel accommodations during their forty-eight hours rest visits to the city.

Will, my companion, and I wandered into a music shop, where film is also sold. We were intrigued into making phonograph records of our own voices. A very kind lady, sensing our language difficulties, stepped up and helped us negotiate. She turned out to be Madame Brand, an English teacher at the Ecole Jules Terry. Before the day was out, Madame found us a pleasant room, had us to lunch, took us on a tour of the city, and turning us over to her son, John, 21, and soon to be a teacher of literature, departed for her home, only to return later for the Opera. We were her guests for that, too. My Darling, these are people to whom I shall be eternally grateful. Madame will send you children's French books for the time when our angel will begin to learn. I beg you to write to Madame and express your thanks for her kindness to me. There is also a young girl of eleven who is studying ballet at the Opera, and I can honestly say the child has talent and personality. John took us to many parts of the city we would have otherwise missed. We found a moment's rest in the unbelievable interior of Notre Dame Cathedral. No wonder these... wonder of the great city. You walked by my side, because while I made conversation automatically with my companion, deep inside of me I was seeing Paris with you. I tried pronouncing the French names of places very carefully so that you would be pleased with my heavy-tongued French. As I "talked" to you, I would chuckle, leaving my friends surprised and uninformed. The record I made for you, I may never be able to send you, but you will never need such "irrevocable testimony" to hold me to my vow. I'll repeat it to you a thousand times over.

The shadow that has fallen across our path this Christmas is only a warning that we must not be shaken in our determination to finish this terrible job that is war. I believe that you at home, as well as we here, know now that there can be no more division of strength to finish this. Christmas, 1945, my Darling, will find all of this just a memory, I pray God. Love to all. Kiss our angel.

Love, Daddy

December 24, 1944 – Somewhere in Belgium
My Darling:

I augment the enclosed letter with the urgent plea: "Please do not worry." I am well and safe despite what you may be hearing and reading about the war. Your letters of December 1 and 11 were awaiting me, as well as the scarf. It is beautiful, warm, and, more important, it is a symbol of your comforting arms and magic hands caressing me with the warmth of your love.

At present, ours is a hectic life, but we are safe and warm, by the grace of God.... You must send me no more valuables or packages until further notice.

Love, Daddy

Belgium: Medical Clinic

[Editors' note: The 130th General Hospital was evacuated to Namur on December 23–24 because of the close approach of the Germans in the Battle of the Bulge. Due to Army censorship rules, Sam deliberately avoided describing the terrible dangers he had just experienced, which were part of the battle. He will finally tell that tale in his letter of May 13,1945, V-E day, when censorship ends. [See chapter 11.] Following is a historical account of the Battle of the Bulge from The Illustrated History of WW II by John Ray (London: Weidenfeld and Nicolson, 2003).]

In mid-December came a totally unexpected counter-blow to the Allies which for a short period forced them on to the back foot. On 12 December, several German generals were summoned to Hitler's headquarters and learned that he intended to launch a surprise offensive in the West. To sit back defensively, the Führer reckoned, would bring inevitable defeat. "It is essential to deprive the enemy of his belief that victory is certain," he told them. "Wars are finally decided by one side or the other recognizing that they cannot be won." He hoped that the Allied coalition, composed of nations with totally different backgrounds and ambitions, would disintegrate.

His aim, resurrecting memories of 1940, was to drive forward through the Ardennes with panzers, which would then swing towards Antwerp. In his reckoning, the loss of that port would lead to a second Dunkirk, with a rapid evacuation of the Allies from mainland Europe. Afterwards he would turn his attention to the Eastern Front and deal with the growing Russian menace there. It would be an understatement to say that his generals were surprised at the news, but orders were to be obeyed.

Two powerful armies had been gathered and re-equipped for the offensive and included nine panzer divisions. A cloak of bad weather covered them, preventing Allied air assaults and helping their secret movements. The blow fell on 15 December on four American divisions holding a front of some 90 miles and had rapid initial success. Soon **a bulge** appeared in the Allied line, with a consequent "Battle of the Bulge," as mainly American, then British, troops fought to stem the attack. By Christmas Day the offensive had lost momentum. For the Germans, there were shortages of fuel and, as the weather improved, increased intervention from hundreds of Allied aircraft. The Panzers were slowly forced to retreat and by 16 January 1945 were back at their starting point.

The unexpectedness of the offensive shattered any complacency on the Allied side. There was still far to go. The cost to the Americans was 19,000 dead and 15,000 men taken prisoner, but the Germans had sustained 100,000 total casualties, as well as losing 800 tanks and 1,000 aircraft. "It spelt bankruptcy, because we could not afford such losses," stated General von Manteuffel. As the pincers closed on Germany from east and west, total defeat was in the offing. For Hitler, nevertheless, there would be no capitulation. "Never! Never!" he told his generals.

[Summary]
Hitler's quixotic decision to launch a full-scale counter offensive in the west

in December 1944 played into Allied hands. Although, against all the odds, the attack achieved some initial success, the idea the panzers could break through to the Channel was no more than a fantasy. German commanders knew they would be lucky to reach the river Meuse. When the skies cleared at the end of December, and Allied airpower could intervene again, the game was up. The battle cost the German army its last armoured reserve and hastened the end of the war. (pp. 180–81)

December 25, 1944 – Somewhere in Belgium
My Beloved:
Christmas Day is practically over. While to our faith it has no religious significance, there is no denying that in a larger sense it has become part of our lives. It is the reminder that another year has really run its course. It is the time in which to pause, to take inventory of one's friends, to reestablish broken friendships, to consolidate other human contacts; in short, to recognize the fact that the future holds only terror and loneliness for him who has been so selfish, so self-sufficient that he has neither loved ones, nor friends with whom to embark upon the unknown, unchartered sea of the new year.

The day started with a solemn, deeply moving service this morning. How solemn the occasion was you shall know soon, I hope, from my own hand.

My Darling, if ever you felt my presence, you must have felt it this morning as out of my heart poured a silent prayer that you would find the courage to face the grim news that must have filled the papers and radio lanes these past few days.

You must believe that we are safe and well, no matter what you hear or are prone to believe because of the news. There will be much work to be done here and all of us will have to exert ourselves to the fullest. This is a good outfit, and I must add, a very lucky one.

You related a dream you had recently in which we relived our Turkey Run "honeymoon." That was no dream, My Angel. That was a vision of our "rebirth together," as you put it so exquisitely in your letter of December 1. We will have that rebirth, My Angel, because I do focus all my "attention and thoughts on the end of all this war."

I hope my Paris letter reaches you before this one, for I want you to know that the prelude to this Christmas, for me at least, was a happy one in that I could turn my thoughts to you completely as they drank in the beauty and [*rest of letter is missing*].

December 26, 1944 – Somewhere in Belgium
My Darling:
Not much to report today except that the Christmas boxes are becoming a problem, which proves that our eyes are bigger than our stomachs. My problem

is not so acute, since I used most of my stuff to treat the boys in my ward, but the mountains of food that Manny has accumulated is typical of most of the fellows. There is no denying the thrill of opening a package. But more often than not, the disposition of said contents becomes a bother. I do appreciate a box of candy once in a while, but that's all! History is being made in this phase of the war, and all of us are a vital part of the making. The story will be told someday, and our pride in our current accomplishments will have been justified. You must promise me never again to give way to an agony of worry. Letters will always be slow, it seems, from this area.

Mail call just now brought me no letters and no packages. . . . I just ran out of ink and can't get at mine at the moment. So I'll close with the abundant love I bear you. Tomorrow I'll write to our Love Lettuce on some special stationery I bought today. Love to all. Did you get my Christmas card? Did your mother get her birthday card?
Daddy

December 28, 1944 – Somewhere in Belgium
My Darling:
It is very early in the morning and I'm writing hastily so as to finish before I'm caught up in the activity and hub-bub of the day. That I am writing to you with regularity—though I wonder at what painful intervals my letters arrive—should be a real assurance to you that all is well. From a point of the health and safety that is true. I can't be an ostrich, however, and bury my head. The grim reality of war sweeps in ever-widening circles. The peaceful valley is no more. The poppies will be well nourished again. It's a great wonder to me that Mother Earth doesn't belch in agony with her gullet over full with blood.

My Darling, to you alone can I say these things which stir me so deeply, but I am painfully conscious of the fact that you will believe that we are directly concerned. You must not read into these words that which is not so. Every moment of living in peace or war has its particular dangers, but when intelligence, consideration, and common sense direct that living, danger remains "a thing of the moment." We have successfully by-passed the grimmer aspects of this titanic struggle and are enjoying conditions conducive to good work. Hope, springing eternal in the human heart, thus carries us from one critical point to another. The New Year, let us hope, will bring us to that turning point in the fortunes of war, and never again will the beast break out from the steel trap. The trap was set carelessly, perhaps, because the hunters were more concerned with the "the furry skin for Christmas" than with giving this tortured Earth a long measure of peace. My love to all. I will write to our angel on special paper.

Here is my heart, My Beloved, Daddy

December 28, 1944 – Somewhere in Belgium
[Letter to Roberta Lesner, daughter, fifteen months old]
My Little "Love Lettuce":

Mama writes me so many wonderful things about you. How you walk, smile, sleep, talk. Oh, the wonder of it! When I left you, you were only a smiling butterball who had to be lifted up every time I wanted to press my face into the sweet warmth of your ambrosial body. When next I see you, you will run into my arms and you will know that it is your Daddy, who is "kissing you to pieces."

This terrible war, my sweet child, robs us of all that is decent, but it can't shake from our souls the last remaining spark of hope which is inspired and fed by the love we feel for our children.

Mama and you have been at my side through all this nerve shattering business. I have wanted to send you many pretty things, but now we must wait for a more settled period in this great struggle which must bring us many years of peace and happiness. This special stationery is reserved for you, my sweet Roberta. Kiss Maga and Papa, and your adoring Mama for me.

Daddy

Belgium: Medical Clinic

December 28, 1944 – Somewhere in Belgium
My Darling:

Just a few extra lines to augment my airmail of the same date. We are sprawled out in various postures of letter composing, meanwhile eating salmon salad on crackers which Len Goldhammer, my Cleveland social worker friend, is dispensing as he extols the virtues of his wife, Rose, who sends him all sorts of sandwich spreads. No, Darling, I'm not jealous. It's ridiculous loading a guy down with all that stuff. We get plenty of food. I have made a New Year's resolution never to load myself down with anything and that goes for the time when I return to civilian life, too. I shall tell you why someday soon. Please, Darling, don't worry. All goes well despite the threat to our position here.

Love to all. Daddy

December 29, 1944, 9:00 p.m. – Somewhere in Belgium
My Darling:

I have packed a pretty souvenir of my recent Paris visit and shall mail it tomorrow. I believe you will be as enchanted with it as I am since it will remind you of the many delightful evenings we spent together at the ballet. I shopped for hours, but could find nothing approaching it for its power to evoke the fond memories. I wanted very much to buy you something practical, too, but the prices were staggering for merchandise which differed in no way from typical American Christmas suggestions offered for purse-heavy Gullibles. I will refrain from describing the souvenir for I think you will relish it more as a surprise. I only hope its delicacy will not be marred in transit. I packed it very carefully, though.

There is very little that is new. We are stemming the tide of the Nazi counterattacks, apparently, and perhaps the New Year will see us again on the road to success. Received a gift from the office today and some luscious candy from your kind, loyal father. I'll thank him in a personal letter. The office gift would delight a gambler but is useless to me. At first opportunity, I'll write of the past few days' unusual emotional experiences.

Love to all. Kiss the Love Lettuce. My heart to you, Angel. Daddy.

December 31, 1944 – Somewhere in Belgium
My Darling:

At long last, your letter of November 22—the epic one describing Roy's homecoming—has reached me. I laughed and cried and came very near to a hysterical outbursting of all the pent-up emotion within me.

Yes, Angel, Roy was scared. Even as I will be and as all others are in anticipation of that moment when we will step over our own thresholds again. All these overtones of the greatest drama of all—"The Family"—you played with matchless skill in your letter, one that I shall cherish.

I know that it was more than a personal issue and Roy's homecoming was a symbol, a great promise, an irrevocable fact that we do come back, by the grace of God.

Our clan has been spared and though I promised to write you about some of the things I have experienced and seen in the past weeks, I hesitate because of their grim aspects. But to know how fortunate we have been and continue to be is to know and face the realities of war and the unspeakable grief it brings to the less fortunate.

I have seen terror; I have explored the chaotic minds of those who lived through terror; but they lived. I have also seen those who died and I have seen a youthful, naked body turned to alabaster by the hand of death, but not without its crimson décor. Where once was a sturdy spinal column, the alabaster figure "wore" a huge "petunia" gouged out of human flesh.

Tonight, we'll find some way of celebrating the beginning of a New Year, although we hardly need the usual stimulants. We are so ready to laugh, to bolster each other, to assume a little of each other's emotional burdens. In the slaughterhouse of war, human life is ghastly cheap, but to the surviving, the living, the loss of a buddy leaves a void that is crushing. We dare not think of war in terms of these "unimportant" personal tragedies, yet the very fountain of strength, determination, and devotion springs from the dark subterranean passages that are the brotherhood of Man.

But why must we sink to the level of beasts to discover the essence of that brotherhood?

True, we didn't ask for this role we are playing in the crucifixion of civilization, but will enough of us remember the "petunias" in human backs when this is over?

We *must* remember, for the next time it may be our sons who will "wear a petunia in death." You and I and all of us who have known loneliness, anxiety, despair in this tragic year about to pass must resolve that with victory will also come a never-dimming flood of light through those dark dormant passages of human relationships.

For us, My Angel, the year has not been a tragic one despite the great anxiety we have known. For this we must be thankful. May God grant that, in passing, it has been the worst year in our lives. I have come through many difficult days without mishap. I am well and in good spirit. I have learned much in this year, much that will make me less unworthy of you and the precious child you have given me.

At the moment, we are enjoying some leisure and unexpected divertissement. We are comfortable, well fed, and regarded with a little more esteem than many equally as worthy, perhaps. I am letting the old year pass without regret, though, because the new year will hasten the day when I shall embrace you again.

Belgium: Medical Clinic 179

Love to all. Here's to 1945, and the fulfillment of the wish that is foremost and ever in your heart.

Love, Daddy

Set of postcard photos from 1944, labeled Charleroi, a town near the 130th General Hospital in Belgium. These cards were found among Sam's letters.

CHAPTER NINE

A New Year

January 1, 1945 – Somewhere in Belgium
My Darling:
The first letter of the New Year! And I am happy to say it can be a totally cheerful one. The close of a beautiful day of unusual warmth and sunshine brought me your letter of December 13, and though you plead that it is composed of trivia, it is a source of real pleasure for me in knowing that all is well at home.

Apparently, some of my letters describing my work are coming by mule pack, or else yours commenting on same are coming by broken-down carrier pigeon. At any rate, at the present, we are concentrating on general hospital work, due to the emergency, and it may be some time before I get back to the job with which I fell in love on so short acquaintanceship.

A neighboring city has a splendid operetta company, so last night, New Year's Eve, several of us attended a performance of Franz Lehár's *Paganini*. The chief singers were notable, though the staging, orchestra, and direction were mediocre. They are to do *Manon*, with Belgium's leading diva, in the near future, and we are going if it is physically possible. I am saving all the programs for you. I don't believe censorship will permit my sending them at this time, but later, I believe I shall be able to send them. We even found the opportunity to swim in a wonderful pool in the above-mentioned city.

The Belgians are splendid people—friendly, courteous, generous. An incident in the theater last night thrilled us. About fifty people seated in our immediate vicinity, lined up at the final curtain to shake hands and wish us luck and victory in the New Year. It was all spontaneous and very heartening. We (my Cleveland buddy and I) were asked to join them for supper, but the curfew for GIs and the necessity for returning to quarters made this impossible. I haven't written to sweet Madame Brand yet but expect to do so tonight.

With your letter today came a sweet one from Ruth. She is a good soul. I am haunted by the fact that I haven't yet sent the kids anything, although I've tried to find suitable presents. Some beautiful wooden shoes, which I bought for them at the same time I bought yours were stolen and I haven't had a chance to replace them. I hope the package containing yours and the baby's gifts arrives. There was considerable confusion at the time I mailed them. I can't tell whether they went out or not. I hope the Paris souvenir arrives. I mailed it yesterday. I think it will delight you, Sweetheart. I am having a time finding something suitable for your mother. The junk they show here would be an insult. Please believe me that I am constantly on the lookout for a fine bit of lace, or some such useful item, but so far, what I have seen is not to my taste. It is wise to wait for just that opportunity when good fortune will produce something worthwhile.

I hope the dolls have arrived by this time. Our active daughter, I suppose, will prefer the adventures on a rocking horse to playing with the doll, but tell her that when I come home, I'll build her a whole gymnasium in which to expend her excess energies. It is hard to imagine her bouncing around. Does she still press her adorable head against the bars of her crib when she sleeps? How that used to worry me. Do you know that I used to get up three or four times a night to look at her? Oh, My Darling, it's so good to be a parent to such a child, to say nothing of being the husband of such a wife. That's all now, Sweetheart.

Love to all. Love, Daddy

January 3, 1945 – Somewhere in Belgium
My Darling:

Last night's letters, December 19 and 21, gave a wonderful pickup, but at the same time brought home to me the full realization of how distressed and worried you must be. What can I say to ease your anxiety? As long as you have letters from me in my hand you must believe that all goes well with us. I have never known you to indulge in false sentiments or prop yourself with phony religious concepts, but I do feel that in this great time of distress you are finding a measure of hope in our Gracious God. My Darling, how can I explain this without sounding like a streetcorner soul-saver? We curse, we will give voice to all sorts of blasphemy, but in the moments of danger we have known we have found coverage in the silent prayers. To know that you have the strength is to find the courage. I have known these moments and I have known how blessed I am in having loved ones who inspired that courage. I can tell you no more now. The facts are of no importance anyhow. They will be interesting only in retelling them in days to come. <u>What is important is that we are safe and well</u>. This you must believe with all the strength you can muster.

[From Oral History interview with grandson, Edward C. Bernstein, in 1986]:

The war turned around and Belgium was attacked again. The Germans invaded at Christmas, 1944. We didn't know that much of it was a bluff. They had inadequate supplies, shabby uniforms. But the madmen in Germany tried one more time in France and Belgium. But they lost. The US finally pushed the Germans back.

Perhaps it is well to tell you that all of our personal belongings have been lost in one of the accidents of war. Why am I telling you this? Because, My Beloved, we have been spared and we know that the sudden and peculiar proximity to danger can't be our lot again. I am very humble, My Darling, and very thankful. Angel, don't go thinking of all sorts of imagined horrors. The whole thing was just a dramatic moment of very small significance in the overall picture, one that I shall delight in relating to you someday.

Let us look about and see how lucky we are. So far this has been a picnic with the usual inconveniences of picnicking for me. I have had as many moments of laughter as I have had moments of loneliness and fear. This is a maturing experience that will pay off big dividends for us someday. Angel, you must believe that there is a day-to-day challenge in all this that makes for an exciting game. The little things that we took for granted before are now occasions for rejoicing in their accomplishment. Comfort is a forgotten word, but in the endless adjustments we create little islands of contentment for ourselves that only a soldier can appreciate. I'm afraid you would be shocked at what we come to think of as satisfactory, but we soon learn the art of improvisation, which we often carry to a fine point.

Darling, please, please, don't worry about me. I swear on our sacred vows to each other that I am safe and well. Tell Betty that she will be doing Manny harm in worrying so about him. We are together and have numerous laughs over numerous things that have transpired. Tell Love Lettuce that her "nighty-night Daddy" doesn't go unanswered. I kiss her goodnight every night. Please call my folks. I haven't time now for another letter.

Here's my heart, My Angel, Daddy

January 4, 1945 – Somewhere in Belgium
My Darling:

We have our "trivia," too, and feeling very gay and having little else to tell you, I'll indulge in a little bit of small talk. First, though, I did get out for a few hours yesterday and found some lovely handkerchiefs for your mother and mine, which I will mail in a day or so. They're colorful, inexpensive things, but are so much nicer than the fancy, machine-made lace things that look very cheap despite the prices. The handkerchiefs may not be "Belgique," but they are nice, and I hope our mammas will understand. We have walked our feet off and found only ordinary stuff at fantastic prices. The things I'd like to buy would take a half year's pay at Army rates.

The people here are very friendly and as you go along the street you hear "bonjour" all the way up and back. Some of us are going to a French vaudeville show tonight. I found that the good diction of the actors makes it possible to catch a word here and there. I also think that hearing as much French spoken as possible will be an incentive toward attempting to speak the language. I seem

A New Year   183

to understand some and, of course, can figure out most of the painted signs and instructions. In Paris, for instance, we got along famously by just reading the signs.

Speaking of books, I've just finished Albert Spalding's splendid autobiography, *Rise to Follow*. If he wrote it he is first a brilliant writer, and secondly a pretty good fiddler. Read it, if you can. It's most enjoyable. Now I'm on *A Tree Grows in Brooklyn* and next on the list is Walt Whitman.

Speaking of movies, like King Bruce who suffered defeat in despair "six times" and then upon seeing the spider spin his web for the seventh time and succeed, likewise won a victory on the seventh try, so I suffered, but persisted in trying and at last succeeded. I have seen the best movie of all I have suffered through in the army. The film is *Saratoga Trunk*, with Ingrid Bergman and Gary Cooper. Wow, what a picture. It's a must that Bergman is a combination of Helen Hayes, Louise Rainer, and Katharine Hepburn in this delightful film. Besides the excellent cast, the direction and particularly the backgrounds are terrific.

I must get ready for the "theatah, Old Dear." I found some delightful ashtrays with appropriate French sentiments inscribed on some, which I'm sending to Ruth. I know this will please you.

Kiss the Love Lettuce. Love to all. My heart to you, My Beloved, Daddy

January 5, 1945 – Somewhere in Belgium
My Darling:

Just a few lines to assure you that all is well. Am going on duty in a few minutes and lest the day slip by without another opportunity to write, I resort to this unsatisfactory method [V-Mail]. The weather here is astonishingly good. No snow yet. Some fog and dampness, but an overcoat threatens to make you swoon with the heat. I suppose they get snowed in here when you at home start looking for Easter bonnets. I'm not complaining though. The vaudeville show last night was bad, amateur entertainment. Once is enough for that. No mail from you yesterday. Perhaps today.

Love to all. Kiss the cherub. My heart to you. Daddy

January 7, 1945 – Somewhere in Belgium
My Darling:

I failed you yesterday, but you'll have to excuse it due to excitement of receiving seven letters, five of which were from you. They ranged from November 14 to December 27. I think those are the dates. I don't have them with me at the moment as I am writing this while on duty. But I'll reread them a dozen times more and note the dates more carefully.

At any rate, the autographed book of the Durants [Will and Ariel] and the contents of that autograph thrilled me. I don't deserve such praise, but I will try to live up to the future the Durants predict for me. I read the "inscription" as you noted it to my friend [Len] Goldhammer of Cleveland. When I told him what our relationship is with the Durants—and being a learned young man, he certainly knows the importance of the Durants—he was silenced with surprise, and I suspect a little envy. I wish I could read Durant's *Christ and Caesar*. I'm sure it is a great work of literary art. It is quite likely that an overseas edition of it will be printed and will be available. The greatest surprise I have had in the Army is the excellent literature which is made available in this unique overseas edition. I told you I'm reading *A Tree Grows in Brooklyn*, and I have several more fine books stashed up. These are not "compressed," but the complete text.

Your marvelous descriptions of the antics of our precious child move me to such emotional heights that I get slightly goofy thinking about her. I knew that she would be an exceptional child, but I can hardly believe our great good fortune in having such a remarkable child. I do miss her growing up more than I can say, but I know that the years to come will compensate. Oh, the great privilege of directing the early years of development of such a child!

Angel, there is something out of the ordinary in our lives. At almost the same time that you were observing Roberta's reaction to pictures and her ability to recognize objects, I was shopping for just such a book for her. I found a treasure, exquisite color printing. The book is a series of fables and the plates are worthy of framing. I'll mail as soon as I can get a good folder or cardboard. The book is in simple French and is readily translated for children. . . . I wrote to Madame Brand. I hope my letter passes the censors. There is some question about soldiers writing civilians in the occupied countries.

Speaking of French, another reason I didn't write yesterday was because I was getting a French lesson. Now don't get excited. Goldhammer and I met some fine Belgian people in the theater. They invited us to visit them. So at the first opportunity we went. They speak only French. Goldhammer muddled his way through, and I just kept my ears open and concentrated. I think it did much toward helping me to understand the language, though I ventured nary a "oui." I shall do this as often as it is possible, and each time try to construct a sentence or two.

[From Oral History interview with grandson, Edward C. Bernstein, in 1986]:

In Belgium we occasionally got a day off, especially on Sunday. I went walking with Max into town. We wondered if there were any Jews left. In talking to townspeople, we had heard stories of atrocities that were perpetrated upon them and how families were pulled apart. But now liberated, whoever had remained there felt free to come out. We walked down the Main Street. Our orders were never to walk on the sidewalk next to the buildings because you never knew who was there to grab you. So we walked down the middle of the street. As we walked, we noticed a little shop to the right where a little man was repairing shoes. I said, "let's go over there and see who this is." Max spoke French to him and found out he and his family were Jews who were hidden all through the war by some Belgians in a house. Now that the war was over, he had come out and reestablished his store to fix shoes. He had just a few scraps of leather, no whole pieces. He fixed some boots for us. We turned the regular shoes into combat boots. We learned their story, the way they were hidden out for a long period in an attic, this man and his wife and their little girl. She looked to be 2 years old, but she should have been 4 or 5 by this time. But because of being hidden away with no light, no sun, the child really didn't grow.

To add to my linguistic difficulties, we made the acquaintanceship of a poor little Jewish shoemaker, and his nice little wife and child. The man has lived in Belgium for twenty years, but the past five have been lived in the particular hell Hitler designed for all European Jews. Now, of course, after years of torture and terrible privation, they have found some peace and security in their hovel of a shoe repair shop. The little cobbler discovered us. We were passing his shop after leaving the swimming pool when we realized that someone was frantically beckoning to us to come in. Being four strong, we went in and discovered this harmless little man who somehow sensed that two of us were of his faith. My Yiddish, of course, is very rusty, but I get by. They are glad to be alive. I wish you could see the orgy of handshaking that takes place every time we come and go. I had some shoes fixed like the paratrooper boots and feel very dashing.

Angel, they do amazingly good photography here, and the first chance I get I'll have some pictures made. I have mailed the little presents to our mothers, and to Ruth I sent the ashtrays I bought. I think I'll get some for us too. They are nice. I must end now.

Love to all. My heart to you, Daddy

January 8, 1945 – Somewhere in Belgium
My Darling:

Your letters received yesterday were six in number, instead of five as I stated in an earlier letter. The dates were November 15, 16, 17, the precious one of November 23 "from Roberta"; November 24 and December 26. Tonight there was nothing for me, so I'm rereading this wonderful batch. How much has happened since November 15 and how I long to hear from you in answer to my letters of a more recent date.

You must be very confused by what must appear evasiveness, but as far as it is permitted, I tell you all I can in the best way I can. You must wonder how we happen to have so much leisure at this time for swimming, theater-going, etc. Frankly, I began doing another type of work, which makes this possible. I can't tell you at the present time what it is, but it's not a "bad deal," all things considered. The two things that are foremost in your mind, my safety and health, I can assure you need not give you a single moment's worry. I have every reason to believe that army life will become increasingly more pleasant and interesting as time goes by.

I await your package containing the shave lotion, etc. You asked me what I want for my birthday. I'll tell you. A hairbrush, like the one I took with me when I left home. The brush, which was a "loyal friend" through many a lonely evening of cleaning up for the next sordid day, has been lost along with other of my personal items. In fact, I'm starting from scratch. Yes, Darling, you can get me a couple pair of heavy woolen socks if you can manage it. . . . There are numerous lovely pieces of Belgian glass I would like to send home, but packing material isn't available, and I'm afraid to take the chance with it.

Our little Jewish cobbler is delighted with having discovered us, and I, too, am glad to talk to him for an hour. One of the Gentile boys and I dropped into his shop today. The lad speaks German haltingly. While we were there, two French-speaking Belgians dropped in. Then true democracy went into action. The cobbler speaking French to his customers, translated their replies in Yiddish for my benefit. In turn, I enlightened my friend through English and German so that he would get the full flavor of what was said. There we were, a small group of men, worlds apart in background, education, purpose, finding a bond of brotherhood, of understanding. Why, dear God? We are the same men, the sons of men who have died and are dying for just this, and yet it works without all this terrible killing.

The boys have just brought in some beer. I'll join them for short one and then to bed. Be of good cheer, My Angel. I am well and safe and adjustments now are made readily and with a minimum of inconvenience.

Love to all. Kiss the cherub. To you my heart, Daddy

January 9, 1945 – Somewhere in Belgium
My Darling:

Nothing new to report, but I must assure you that all is well. I'm in very good health and I'm enjoying to the fullest a few hours of leisure that are now ours every other day.

I'll tell you a little story. One night, back in the cow pasture, in France, a Special Service group put on a show for us. One of the skits was a very crazy one about three sad sack Joes who were assigned various duties. One of them was placed on duty guarding a warehouse. His reply to an officer who inquired, in great imitation, what he was doing was, "Ahm ona Gotta Dootie" (I'm on guard duty.) That crazy line caught on and for weeks everyone was "ona gotta dootie," no matter what he was doing. I, too, repeated that idiotic phrase many times, little realizing that it could happen to me.

You will say, "Oh my God, how could such a thing happen?" Well, these are critical times, and if clerks and cooks can hold off the Nazi horde, as they helped to do in the defense of Bastogne, I, critic, artist, nurse, can stand in a nice warm building and direct the human traffic for a few hours each day. That's all it amounts to, and I tell you this so that you will not start to imagine all sorts of things because I no longer write about "my boys." I have comfort, I have leisure to read, I have pleasant companions. I can ask no more. Things will right themselves soon, and again I'll be in the work that I approach with a religious fervor.

No mail again today and it looks like days will pass before we get any. I don't know how that letter dated December 26 got through. It got here in about ten days. Oh, if only all our mail could travel at that speed! These nightmares of waiting would be banished from our lives.

I just finished *A Tree Grows in Brooklyn*. Angel, it's a real treasure. Our childhood was not unlike that of the Nolan kids in many respects. How well I remember the poverty, the anxiety, the cold, miserable dwellings, the few pennies earned by running errands, the hand-me-down clothes, the excitement of getting a new pair of shoes. I remember the violent games we played. We dug trenches and battled it out with rocks. We tormented the goat by putting pop bottles on his horns. We "sling-shotted" at birds. We tied a can to the cat's tail. We played dirty games and learned about sex behind the chicken coop. We gave much pain and some pleasure to our poverty-enslaved parents. We exchanged our smoky, smelly kerosene lamps for the naked glare of un-shaded electric light bulbs, and we talked to Aunt Mashie for four hours straight the first day our telephone was hooked up. I even remember our number. It was Kildare 5204.

Thus, the book carried me back more than a quarter of the century, the period in which another war was fought and won. We'll win this one, too, and come home to a better world, perhaps. Well, I should've written my novel first and collected $55,000 for the screen rights. Guess I'll have to pick another subject. Love to all. Kiss the cherub. To you, my heart, Daddy

[From Oral History interview with grandson, Edward C. Bernstein, in 1986]:

ECB: *How was growing up with your siblings and other relatives?*

SL: *I was crazy about Roy. He was a little guy. We always went together, wherever, in the prairie with other boys. Like all kids we got into mischief. We had heard about smoking corn silk. They went into the cornfields and pulled the tassels, wrap them in toilet paper and smoke them. The only time I ever did anything naughty and I felt guilty (I had to steal the toilet paper). I was always a gentle person. Sometimes Dave would try to get me to stand up to someone but I would just walk away. Dave was always stirring up things for us to do. We'd race around the block, Foster to Lawrence.*

January 10, 1945 – Somewhere in Belgium
My Darling:
All day I pondered on the theme for this letter, but for the life of me I can't hit upon an interesting subject. I could, of course, tell you about what is going on in our quarters at the moment, but it would make pretty rough reading.

Inhibitions? No such thing in the Army. Ironically, in the midst of this titanic struggle to determine whether democracy or tyranny shall rule, we have only a purely localized view of this whole business and we are surrounded by people who go about their business in an orderly manner. The crisis is definitely over, and we feel foolish about the fears that took hold of us several weeks ago.

The day has been uneventful. I've shined my improvised paratrooper boots twice today, and my buddies think I'm strictly psycho. It's such fun, though, to wear clean shiny shoes and a pressed uniform after the long weeks of cement-splashed fatigues and water-swollen shoes. The snows have come, but not with the violence we expected, and our immediate surroundings lie peacefully and beautifully under the lambs-wool cloak of snow.

In my several off-duty hours today I have rediscovered the joy of reading, a pleasure which I had all but forgotten through the hectic months that have passed since war became part of my day-to-day existence. No matter what happens, I must find at least an hour a day to read something worthwhile.

Angel, if we have a French–English dictionary handy, send it to me by first-class mail. Perhaps you can find a pocket-sized one which I can carry about with me. A desk-sized one is out of the question. It would become a liability and I would hate to leave it in any precipitous move.

I'm writing this before mail call, so I'm still hopeful, but if I'm disappointed, I have half a dozen of your sweet letters to read again and again.

How is our Boopsie? What new miracle has she revealed? Be brave and be at peace with your heart and mind. I am well and safe. I love you. There is no fancier phrase that expresses it better.

Yours, Daddy

January 11, 1945 – Somewhere in Belgium
My Darling:
I have a painful confession to make. What will you think of me? I've forgotten whether your birthday is the 12th or the 16th of January. I have been struggling to recall some one thing that would put me straight and all I can remember is that tomorrow, January 12, marks the first year of my Army service. Maybe that's why I've forgotten your birthday. I hate to associate it with the terrible fact that on that day we were torn apart. I do remember, though, that I marked your birthday with a remembered title of a play, "The Night of January 12," or was it, "The Night of January 16"? Darling, you must forgive me. Get me straight and I swear it's a day I'll never forget again as long as I live.
[*Editor's note: In 1970, Esther makes an appearance on stage in a production of "The Night of January 16," directed by her second daughter, Judy, at Lyons Township High School. On January 16, 2009, Esther's namesake great-granddaughter, Esther Bernstein, is born.*]

A New Year

I don't have a birthday present for you. What a stinker I am. I've looked everywhere, but can't find anything distinctive or worthy, but, Sweetheart, 12th or 16th, or any other day for that matter, my heart is yours. I am hoping that since I sent the dancing figures by first-class mail, it might reach you in time to make your birthday, but I have wanted to send you something personal, some one thing that you could wear and enjoy every day even as I wear the sweater and scarf every day. Those two items are coming home with me to be worn until they are threadbare.

The news gets better daily, and our lot becomes increasingly easier. You asked that I make specific requests so that you can send various items. Well, Angel, I'll confess that such a thing like a plain soda cracker would be relished. Fancy cookies are nice, but at night when you want to snack, a cracker, a little jam, or a piece of cheese seems to go better than sweets. Fine candy, though, is more than welcome. I don't seem to get enough good candy. I just can't get a treat out of the cheap candy bars the P.X. dishes out.

I have a small calendar and all your letters from 1945 will be marked off as they arrive. Thus, I can tell which ones are coming via Afghanistan. Upon returning from a bad movie last night I found your letter of December 27. Now that's what I call mail delivery. It took actually twelve days from the day it was posted, instead of the weeks we have waited for word from each other. My letters still seem to take several weeks in reaching you. I think, however, the situation will improve and ten days will soon be the "maximum" for letters going both ways.

I am very pleased, but a little overcome by your comments on my "POW" letters. Such letters, dealing with things of the moment, may seem very much out of focus later, but I do appreciate your decision to keep them. Angel, I have a most immodest request to make. If anything in my letters, or any part of them, can be used as "letters to the editor," or as excerpts to be used by my colleagues, I'd be very grateful if you would make them available. I know it is "bad taste" for you to advertise me, but there may be other ways of doing it. The Durant endorsement has given me courage and hope, and I can't help showing off just a little. [*Editors' note: Hence, this book, although seventy-plus years later, in response to Sam's request.*]

Enough for now, My Angel. I go on duty in an hour and must straighten things up a bit.

Love to the cherub. My best to the folks. My heart to you. Daddy

January 13, 1945 – Somewhere in Belgium
My Darling:
I didn't write yesterday, a day of leisure, but a day of activity, nonetheless. We slept late, went swimming, visited our cobbler friend, and had a hell of the time jabbering in a new language, which I call "Beljudofranglaise." We ate

"kichlach" [cookies], drank chicory, and hurried back to the hospital for chow. Then we took off for the Cafe de la Bourse to celebrate our first year in the service. In our toasts, though—and one was in 1916 Nuit St. Georges Burgundy (550 francs per bottle)—there was a single theme, "that another year shall not be marked in this theater of death and destruction." And I drink a toast to you, My Darling, and humbly pray to God that no more birthdays would be "celebrated" away from each other.

The Bourse has an all-girls band, musically not bad, but heavens, what a collection of bags. The leader, a fiddle player, is the payoff, though. At first you think it's some kind of masquerade she's employing, but soon enough you discover that she's quite serious (and painfully self-conscious) about her getup. Some misguided designer, who apparently believes that all Americans are wild cowboys, has dressed up the band in orange and black "cowboy" suits replete with sombreros that, having failed sadly to line up the Mexican or American Wild West influence, make all the gals look like any moment they'll pull out broomsticks and take off. I'm only hinting, of course, that they look like witches. But the leader, wow, a long platinum blond Dutch-boy bob frames her pinched face and her expression of anger and frustration is exactly what I would "paint" on the face of the witch in "Hansel and Gretel" as she makes little Hansel stick out his finger through the cage. Hansel, of course, sticks out a little chicken bone and the squinting witch can't figure out why Hansel isn't getting fat. The whole "picture" is dirty. Well, that's Mlle the leader who has discovered only the E-string on the fiddle and with her bow belabors the poor innocent E-string with a mad vigor that produces extraordinary vibrato and tremolos, all painfully off pitch. The drummer—ah, there is a gal—clean-faced, unselfconscious, a perpetual wide-mouthed smile, and pretty in the bargain. She has such a hell of a good time hitting all the gadgets, including a pair of symphonic kettle drums. She has no technique, but she has charm and salesmanship. If I had my way, I'd regroup the band around her or, better still, find some other gals for her and ship her to America. She'd make money for her manager. A singer also appears. Approaching middle age in appearance, unskilled in the art of stage deportment, nevertheless she made the evening a big success for me singing the jewel song from *Faust* with a warmth, a glistening locality, and a sense of phrasing and adornment that was most gratifying. What a pity, singing her heart out in a saloon. [*Editors' note: After the war, Sam resumed his position as the nightclub critic (in addition to becoming the movie critic) for the* Chicago Daily News.]

Thus, the evening passed too quickly, as there is a ten o'clock curfew. In my particular job at the moment, I am thrown together with a group composed of men I admire individually, so we have many laughs and the tiresome detail is over quickly. There is little else to report at this time. The news is good, we are well, safe, and contented with our lot, so we have put the complaint department on the roof, where it is quite cold, and in consideration for our swell chaplain, we don't ask him to take his hands out of his pockets to punch our T.S. cards.

    Love to all. Kiss the cherub. Here's my heart, Angel. Daddy

January 15, 1945 – Somewhere in Belgium
My Darling:

    Forgive the anemic fountain pen with which I am writing. I borrowed it from my good friend Max Neiburg of Philadelphia, who is a pal par excellence, but his pen stinks. Angel, this week, I hope to write the opus of all opuses. Oh, how much there is to say now. Briefly, though, all is well again, and I have a number of tasks to perform to get settled down comfortably, and within a few days I expect to be back at my favorite job. The weather is grand, cold as hell, but invigorating and clean. Last night, a flock of your letters caught up with me at last. They were dated December 3, 4, 5, 6, and 7, I believe. . . .Love to all. Hug and kiss our cherub. Here's my heart, Beloved. Daddy

January 17, 1945, 8:15 p.m. – Somewhere in Belgium
My Darling:

    You will notice the time of this letter and doubtless regret it as much as I do since it means another whole day lost in the mailing of this short but happy letter. Yes, Angel, I am happy. I'm back in a ward as of three o'clock this afternoon. But before I describe the day, let me say that Monday night, after having written and mailed my letter, I received your most wonderful package of lotion, candy and those sensational cookies. The guys around my bed were not very polite, and neither was I. They just kept diving in after the cookies. Really, Sweetheart, that's the kind of cookie I like best. Not too sweet and very tasty. Yep, I'll have some more.

    The lotion was a gift from heaven as that morning I had used up the very last drop of a bottle I had been nursing along ever since we left Swannanoa. And that candy! Yum. That's really fine stuff, and we've enthused over it on other occasions, I believe.

    Now, let's see. Yesterday (Tuesday), a group of us went to a neighboring city for the day to help out at a smaller hospital than ours. This morning, we spent a pleasant few hours, dragging in a pile of rubble. Len Goldhammer and I searched diligently, but found very little worth saving of the many souvenirs we had accumulated. I found a few bits, however, and was very satisfied. Here's a surprise. The phonograph record I mentioned in an earlier letter is as good as new, and as soon as I can get it censored I'll mail it to you. Then you shall hear my voice. But to mar that little pleasure is the painful fact that in one of the recent goings and comings I lost the beautiful book I bought for Roberta. I don't know when or how I'll be able to try to replace it since it is quite unlikely that I'll be in the city where I bought it. I found another little gem, though, and shall mail it before any more accidents overtake my hard-accumulated souvenirs.

I'm so anxious to know whether the dolls have arrived yet. No letters now for two days, and all the others received were of the first week in December. But tomorrow, I expect mail call to be very productive.

We are caught up again in the old crazy, exciting business of running a hospital and until I get my wind, my letters will be "catch-as-catch-can," but I promise to get one in every day, even if it's a V-Mail. This morning, for instance, I was guarding some "supermen" who were cleaning up the area. After lunch I resumed the fresh-air diet, but was interrupted shortly after by a "call to arms." My ward was being reopened. There were beds to make, sweeping to do, stores to make, patients to check in. Tomorrow morning my day starts at 7 a.m. I don't regret a moment of it. I'm nuts about the whole business. If they'll only let me continue to approach the job with a little show of common sense, I'll be happy. I'm not expecting too much interference, but in the Army, one never knows. Angel, that's all for now. Tomorrow, a more coherent epistle.

Love, love, love, Daddy

January 18, 1945 – Somewhere in Belgium
My Darling:
It is just a few minutes past mail call, and since nothing came, I'll proceed to make up a letter out of a number of things. First, though, if I don't make sense, nor seem to reply to letters which I have received, it's because I carry a batch of them around with me thinking that an hour will be found in which to reread and answer them, but no such luck.

This morning, for instance, I stuffed about seven in my pocket, hoping for a break during the day, but I just remembered where I put them—on a ledge in one of the three wards I worked in today. With two of our "charming guests" we three managed to get three wards ready for patients. And that's some job when you have to build fires in twelve cold, wet stoves, straighten out some ninety beds, sweep, wash and put in order a thousand things. I don't mind, Angel. As I said many times before, I still feel that at last I'm making some real contribution. A clean, a warm, comfortable ward goes a long way toward making your patient well and whole again. I don't know how true it is, but I heard that I would soon be made ward master of my own ward. It's an empty honor, though. It means you catch hell if there's a speck of dust. Actually, I won't be mad if it happens. I like responsibility and it will leave me free to use my initiative in getting things done, rather than wait to be told to sweep the floor.

So much for my work. Now, I don't know what you have been able to deduce from my letters of the past three weeks, but whatever you think, it's not that. I had used phrases and words such as rubble pile with hesitancy, lest you imagine terrible things. Frankly, Angel, we had to go away for a while when things got very hot. That going away, and all that it cost us in spiritual, emotional, and material things, I cannot tell you now. It was rough, it was tremendously exciting, and it was terribly frightening at times. If you will reread my letters of the past weeks you will now get a clearer picture of what took place. You know there are no swimming pools and theaters in a cow pasture.

We are prone to accuse you at home of laxity, indifference, smug contentment. I think I can say now that not a one of us feels that way anymore, for no man worthy of his uniform would want to see his loved ones subjected even for a moment to the terror of a raid, a post-Christmas present from Adolph for us. But he got it back with interest. We have seen many Allied planes going and coming since we hit the Normandy Beach., but what we saw in the skies of our Allied aerial might, in those days when the tide was turned, will live in my memory forever.

Darling, why am I writing these things? Because I know you are no ostrich. I know you possess a great intelligence and comprehension of what goes on in the world. I would be a fool to maintain that all was serene and uneventful here. I write this because I trust you will believe me when I say that I am safe and well; that the danger is definitely over, and that unless we are utter fools and bunglers, the Nazi beast will soon be bled to death.

The weather has suddenly become treacherous and all I can think of is the misery that is the lot of the brave men who are pushing the Huns back to their beer hall dens of intrigue and outrage on humanity. Dare I complain? I'm warm, well fed. I sleep on an innerspring mattress. I can bathe and shave when I want to. I can even step out across the Company Street and order a beer, or I can stay in a nice warm barracks while the storm rages.

I made a few notes in rereading some old letters tonight. On November 24, you said something about lemons, I believe. Are you sending me lemons? That's an excellent idea. Tea and lemon at night. You know, I haven't seen a lemon or a banana since July. We are getting very good apples now in our regular diet. The Belgian grapes and pears which one can buy are tasteless, according to our standards.

I've been at this letter almost two hours, Sweetheart, and I haven't washed up yet. Good night, My Beloved. Kiss the cherub. Love to the folks. A short letter to the folks and then to bed.

Love, Daddy

January 19, 1945 – Somewhere in Belgium
My Darling:
Another day of stove making, bed making, and still no patients. For this I am very happy. It's good to know that our men are so sturdy, so able to take punishment without breaking down in great numbers, which otherwise would flood us. I'll scrub and clean every day for the duration gladly, if it will keep our

casualties to the minimum. I've got a half-hour break now and want to assure you that all is well. I am quite OK. I have just had a wonderful shower. I'll take off shortly to get shaved. One crowds a thousand things into these half-hour breaks, for once we get going, there is little time for personal attentions.

The prisoners assigned to me are good workers, so I find I can keep orders to a minimum. I think they are a bit surprised when I tell them to do something in fairly good German. Frankly, I wish we were rid of the whole lot of them for good. You know that you dare not give in even for a moment to their smiles and boyish attempts to ingratiate themselves, but damn it, maybe they can be reeducated. They're an unkempt, unwashed bunch in their ragged uniforms, but there is no evidence of the monstrous sadism with which they have been imbued, sticking out on them. You can't be neutral in handling them. You either snarl and treat them with contempt or else you find yourself being moderately patient and tolerant. That's the rub. We have boasted how we will reeducate them. But snarling contempt isn't a very good educational medium. So I keep asking, "Well, who is going to take over the job?" Wouldn't it be logical to start now and here? Now we can win the peace, too. Later, we'll only win the war.

It's too much for me. I know only that those who persist in prolonging this terrible struggle, in the face of defeat, should be mowed down. They are the diehards, the "seed" of future German outrages. Those who give up, realizing they are licked, may be still in possession of an ounce of reasoning power. We cannot play the Nazi game. We can't wipe a people off the face of the earth. The Nazis tried it with the Jews. It didn't work. It will never work as long as a handful, even two, survive. That is our job, then, as I see it. We must make them go back to living as a people, not as a menacing horde. It's a big job, but we are bigger than that task and we can do it, if we are worthy as the keepers of the flame of democracy. We nearly let it go out for good.

Love to all. Here's my heart, Angel, Daddy

January 20, 1945 – Somewhere in Belgium
My Darling:

No mail again today, and I was feeling very sorry for myself, and then my name was called at the package mail call to which I had been paying no attention. Guess what? A beautiful box of rarely tasted stuffed fruits from Sophie Tucker. What a thoughtful person she is, and I hope she will feel even at this great distance, how truly appreciative I am, to say nothing of being highly flattered. After all, she is not bound by professional courtesy to keep sending me Christmas packages. Angel, you must relieve me of the responsibility of acknowledging it.

So, Angel, Saturday night in the Army isn't altogether a bust. I'm feeling the cold weather a bit, and am inclined to be grouchy, but I know as soon as I get going again with patients instead of stoves, I'll be OK. Some of the boys, privates like me, who have been overseas a year, were made PFC [Private First Class] today. Time flies. I've been away from you more than a year. Yes, I count from January 12, the day we stopped living, and I've been overseas over six months, believe it or not. Well, I hope I don't have to sweat out a PFC overseas. You are quite right about the Army's inability to recognize and reward integrity and unfailing attention to the job, no matter how disagreeable it might be. I live by only one standard: to do whatever I'm told to do with as much intelligence as possible, and to hell with the honors, although I'm human enough and sensitive enough to feel badly when honesty and integrity go unnoticed. After all, we are not professional soldiers. We were torn from our jobs, where merit and ambition counted, and given another kind of job to do. Thus, you don't turn off all human feelings like a faucet. You go on caring and trying and at each turn you meet heartache, indifference, insolence, selfishness—in short, apple polishing, "bucking," ass-kissing, if you please.

I find that I become unbearably homesick when I hear or listen to any classical music, so I have come to avoid the radio. Only when I am with you again will I be able to open my ears and heart to the music I love. Well, Darling, I've managed to write a "blue" letter without meaning to do so, but it's best to let it come out and get it over. Surely tomorrow I'll read again your beautiful letters which must be piled up somewhere along the line, awaiting clearance. We are excited tonight by the news of magnificent Russia's efforts. Dear God, grant them the strength to move on to their objective, Berlin. You see, we, too, "bloom and wilt" with each success or throwback of our Allied armies. Good night, My Beloved. Kiss the cherub. Love to the folks. Remember me fondly to all those you encounter on Cafe Row.

Here's my heart, Daddy

January 22, 1945 – Somewhere in Belgium
My Darling:

This has been a lovely day. The sun shone brightly and made even whiter the walls of my semi-private room, and turned the festoon of icicles which framed the outer ledges of the windows to a glistening, dripping row of huge eyedroppers.

Speaking of icicles, it was only when I discovered myself pressing one to my brow several days ago, that I realized it was more than the cold weather which made me grouchy, a state I had not been in for some time. It was the strange thing to do, this pressing of icicles against one's head, considering that it was quite cold outdoors. Then it suddenly dawned on me that I was acting a little goofy, so I went on sick call, then and there, leaving a bunch of patients in the midst of the confusion of getting checked in and settled into their beds.

Yep, that vampire, La Grippe, had tapped me on the shoulder and my own diagnosis proved correct. So I'm in a lovely white room, looking out upon a cold, snowy scene, and since Mlle La Grippe touched me ever so lightly, I'm already having misgivings about leaving this nice warm, clean atmosphere of our hospital proper. It is an excellent place, indeed.

While this gives me a sorely needed rest, the thought that any prolonged illness would make you ill with worry, precludes any intention tolerating the Mlle any longer than necessary. No, Angel, I'd be fretful and ill at ease if I had to stay in a day longer than necessary. I can't help it. I'm nutty as a fruitcake. There's work to be done and every man is needed. I have been entertaining the business of the icicle on the forehead incident with secret amusement. Why did I do it? It was a peculiar thing to do in the midst of frenzied rushing about. Yet it was the one little instinctive act which told me what to do without further hesitation.

I do solemnly promise you, though, that I'll slow down and take things at a more even pace. With all my apparent talents for adaptability, I can't quite accept the Army's deliberate, almost apathetic way of getting a job done, but I've come to the painful realization that my tempo is out of keeping with the Army's. It's one thing to sweat out an ordinary cold; it's quite another thing to sweat out a nervous breakdown. Again, in writing like this, I am giving you cause to worry. I beg you to believe that I'm quite OK now. If I didn't have you to "talk" to, what would I do? I have plans for a long "opus" which I mentioned earlier. If possible, it will contain the highlights of the past year. Maybe I can get started while I have this forced leisure.

Love to all. Kiss the cherub. No mail yet. Here's my heart, Daddy

January 23, 1945 – Somewhere in Belgium
My Darling:

An uneventful morning of resting and storing of energy was suddenly interrupted by the appearance of a young officer (second lieutenant) in my room, accompanied by my good friend Max Neiburg. After the somewhat hazy introductions, it developed that the lieutenant, in the hospital to have a certain foot condition corrected by Max who is something of a young genius in this department, expressed surprise that so skilled a fellow should only be a private. Max, bless his heart, said, "Look, Lieutenant, I'm not the only one around here dogged by the onus of rookie. There's my friend Sam Lesner, a writer of some accomplishment who recently earned a flattering endorsement by Will Durant." "Sam Lesner? Why, I know his writing," said the lieutenant. "At Ohio State, where I studied journalism, his columns in the *Daily News* were analyzed and studied by the students." Well, that's the story, Honey, and it took me some moments to overcome my embarrassment. I begged the lieutenant to come back later in the day and talk some more. He promised he would and probably will show up after supper.

I've had lots of company and plenty of attention. You would think I'm something special. I used Sophie Tucker's candy to good advantage around here, though. Angel, the lieutenant has urged me to write freelance and record my experiences even though I have no contacts now for publishing. I explained how my hopes were shattered after being assured in the States that I was going over as "tabbed for public relations." You see, sending a story in is not the simple matter it was in peacetime when I had access to any wire at regular newspaper rates. Then I was an accredited reporter, and I had the right to file stories for the *Daily News* as I saw fit. That isn't so here. First of all, war imposes a very strict censorship. I have no contacts whatsoever, and I don't even know how long stories would be held up. I admit, though, that for the first time I'm interested and will make some inquiry about the process involved in getting some of my observations on the wire. I don't know why I haven't done so before. That's why in a recent letter, I urged you to make available to a few of my colleagues some of my best letters, in the hope that someone would find them strong enough in universal appeal to reprint them in part at least. It is the surest way of showing what this emotional young feature writer is doing "Somewhere in Belgium."

Lt. Stevenson just dropped in, talked for an hour and took off for chow. He's coming back later to hear me rave some more about the excitement of my job. He's a good listener, and he has promised to come to Chicago someday. I guess we'll have to acquire a hotel to accommodate all the guys who are coming to visit us after the war. He's a fine-looking, sincere fellow, though, and I do hope we'll meet again someday.

My ink isn't available at the moment, Dear; hence, the pencil scribblings for the finish. Love to all. What new wonder has our cherub displayed?

Here's my heart, Love, Daddy

January 24, 1945 – Somewhere in Belgium
My Darling:

Late last night the ward man brought me your letter of December 20 in which you mentioned mine of December 6. Think of it, a whole month for an airmail! When I shall have your first letter of the New Year, I dare not guess. Darling, I wish I could tell you just where I am in Belgium, for it would convince you of our safety, but since I cannot, you must believe that again our valley is serene under its mantle of snow. I know it is hard to believe in view of what has transpired in the past month, but it is so. No more theaters, no more swimming pools. Just the interesting routine of the day's work, followed by the painfully dull evenings, which pass quickly, however, since I go to my innerspring quite early. If one does have to take time out for a "slight indisposition," it's just as well there is such a nice hospital handy in which to recover. I've had numerous visitors, all of whom were quite willing to serve me in one capacity or another. Thus, my few humble possessions are being looked after, and the records over which I have fretted so much are in safekeeping. As soon as I'm discharged from the hospital I'll get them mailed out. I'm praying hard that tonight's mail call will bring me news from you. I feel an afternoon nap coming on so adieu for now, Sweetheart.

Kiss the cherub. Love to the folks. Love, Daddy

January 26, 1945 – Somewhere in Belgium
My Darling:

There will be no letter from me dated January 25, since the one I started, I did not finish. Your letters of December 23 and 24 reached me yesterday, as well as a V-Mail from Major Albert Jenkins [first cousin, an M.D.], so you see, your airmails from the States take as long as a V-Mail from the Netherlands East Indies.

Just this moment, a ward boy brought in some mail for me and my hopes soared, only to be dashed again on the rocks of hopelessness and futility. Nothing from you, but two from two boys who were my patients recently. A number of my patients have written to me, and one, a nice lad from Illinois who was tormented by lack of news as to the impending birth of their first child, also sent me a picture of himself recently. I cherish these, of course, since they are the sincere though self-conscious expressions of gratitude at having found a few days of warmth and humanness in so formidable a place as an Army hospital. Oh, how I'd like to take some of these young snots working around here and bang their heads together!

Well, Angel, I am distressed to the point of illness at what the news of the past month must have done to you in view of the fact that there was no mail to reassure you. I won't try to deceive you, for to do so would be to deceive myself. Even with the gallant push of the Russians toward Berlin, there is no optimism here. The near catastrophe has sobered all of us to a marked degree. What lies in store for us, no one knows. Starting on my second year in the Army under such a cloud of uncertainty has been difficult, to say the least.

Well, tomorrow or Sunday I get back to the old routine, and then I'll have less time to get fretful with homesickness. Work is a good antidote for that and the days of waiting for mail seem shorter somehow. There is little else to report. The town is strictly off-limits, and even if one were inclined to go in, there's nothing to go in for. Sleep untroubled, My Beloved. Outside of a mild case of blues brought on by my acute longing for you and the cherub I am quite well and intend to stay that way. This cold at least gave me a chance to rest a bit.

Love to all. Kiss the little lady. Here's my heart, Daddy

January 27, 1945 – Somewhere in Belgium
My Darling:

Mid-afternoon of a very beautiful day finds me trying my legs, which I discover are none too steady. This grippe certainly takes it out of you, and the stuff they give you completes the job. So I feel exactly like that cartoon ostrich with legs wound around each other like a corkscrew and neck and head going round and round. I am having fun, though. Evenings, and afternoons, too, my room has been filled with visitors. They sprawl all over the bed as they fill the room with shouts of laughter. There are Max, Len, Manny, Al, Abe, Lt. Steve (who is a constant admirer), and assorted other GIs who pass the door and drop-in. The kid sharing the room with me is a Chicago boy who just came over. He came down with a very bad cold, so they shipped him to our hospital. Laddie and I ran a neck-and-neck race on temperatures for a couple of days, but he being half as old as I, reminded me sharply that there is no substitute for youth. He's a good boy. I hope this thing will be over before he's been scarred and bruised by the brutality of war. I'm late in finishing this because suddenly I've been called to get my feet treated, something I asked for, but did not hope to get. Max is doing it and I'm sure at last I'll get rid of the troublesome warts. I'll close now, Angel. It's chow time. Later this evening perhaps I'll get another letter written.

My love to all. Kiss the cherub. Your Daddy

January 29, 1945 –Somewhere in Belgium
My Darling:

Oh, what a wonderful feeling! A letter dated January 13, the first one of the New Year, and five others, December 11, 12, 15, 16, 17, from you yesterday. As a result of such a tonic, I jumped out of bed this morning and demanded my release from this "GI home for the Aged and Decrepit." You must be wondering that I'm still in, and lest you become alarmed and think that I'm hiding something, I hasten to add that only the extreme cold weather has been the deterring factor. I appreciate this consideration, and am thus enjoying a nice warm, comfortable room for an extra day or two. I mention to you that I'm having my feet looked after, as long as I'm here and it's just as well not to go into high gear considering the treatment necessary.

Where shall I begin? You have my letters of the period December 15–31, and you are quite right. "Critical" is the word for that unforgettable two weeks. "Somewhere in Belgium" for that period meant "somewhere in hell" for the fighting boys and "somewhere in purgatory" for the rest of us. For our fighting men, the issue was clear: "Dig in and hold and fight as you never fought before." How well they fulfilled their mission is told in the reduction of that monstrous bulge to a pimple and finally to a mere discoloration. The part we played in this great pageant of death and destruction must remain unknown for the time, but that this hospital earned very high praise is a matter of pride with all of us, even though in the final stage only a small group could continue to function.

You may recall that some time ago I summed up an interview I had with the assignment officers. You may remember that I am on record as having said, "Well, I married a dentist's daughter so maybe I'm qualified for the dental clinic." That may happen yet, despite my good record as a ward man. While my former sergeants keep a careful eye on me as I convalesce, the dental clinic, making a belated bid for me, apparently will "absorb" me as soon as I'm released to duty. This much I have learned via the grapevine, and my confusion mounts accordingly. What the dental clinic wants is a receptionist, not a bad deal, but what the wards need are crazy guys like me. Frankly, it doesn't matter anymore. What will be will be. I have no more illusions about the Army. For me, Army life will continue to be a series of near catastrophes, fleeting successes, and the never-ending grimy, sweaty existence it has been so far.

My Dear, you often say that you marvel at my adjustment. There is no adjustment, Angel. There is only a grim, dogged determination to survive, to escape this as soon as possible. There is no dimming of the longing for family and home. The ache grows more acute daily. Time passes and you mark time every second, moment, hour, day, week, month, and year.

But the passing of time, robbing us of life together on one hand, fashions a third life in the image of an angel on the other hand. Our sweet child. How your letters about her fill me with a warmth, an unspeakable pride, a tranquility! I'm afraid to think of the moment when I will catch her up in my arms. Darling, we must not let this moment escape us when it comes. It must be so. First, she will come towards me, alone, and then she will take my hand and lead me back to you, forever, forever.

Now to answer a few questions and make the few comments. First, your guess as to what I was doing (formerly) was quite accurate, except that it went even further. I believe I mentioned in other letters how much depended on certain drugs and medications, and how much on common sense, consideration, kindness, and service. That was a phase of my Army career which gave me material for many hours of discussion with you. I'm afraid that kind of work is over, at least for me, since the need is not so great now, thank God. While I would have liked to stay in that field until I learned to express myself intelligently pro or con on the method, treatment, etc., I do feel relieved to know that our armies are "taking it" and holding up under the cruel punishments inflicted by war. Perhaps I'm being too optimistic, but I can see only what comes within our view, and have no knowledge of what may be happening at other points.

Now for your birthday. Now what must you think about me hesitating as I did over whether your birthday was the 12th or the 16th? My Beloved, I can only add to my defense by saying that my mind rejected so bitter a recollection (my induction day) in association with so beautiful an event in my life, your birthday. Truly, Angel, I was confused and bitter over the irony of it. On my birthday, you gave me your heart, your soul. On your birthday, I gave you a vast nothingness. But there will be many other January 12ths, and God willing, that vast nothingness will be full to overflowing with the joy of living again. That is my promise to you, My Angel.

The loss of the wooden shoes and many other things was not through the deliberate marauding of fellow GIs. Perhaps through letters of the more recent date you were able to piece together the story of those painful days before Christmas. Every one of us sustained some loss, but that's a story to be told in a happier day. That it was "made necessary" to lose many of our personal possessions was unavoidable in the events that transpired at that time. It belongs in the past, however, and all is well now and again I have things galore. I must end now.

Love to all. Kiss the cherub. Here's my heart, Beloved, Daddy

January 31, 1945 – Somewhere in Belgium
My Darling:

Lest the day go by without producing a letter to you, I'll take these few minutes to say at least that I'm OK. I went back to duty yesterday and am again busy in a medical ward, largely ambulatory patients, so the usual routine is kept down to a minimum of running. There is little else to report except my dental clinic deal is so-and-so. They know they have a willing slave in me as a ward man and may be reluctant to let me go. It would be nice to do a job in which you don't swim in your own sweat, but I do know that this is no time to look for "soft spots."

The boys we have this time are fairly regular and cooperate, which always makes it easier. We have a radio in the ward and the good news and pleasant music are fine accompaniments to the day's tasks.

More tomorrow, Angel. It looks like no mail tonight. I'll cable some money this week. It's impossible to spend the damn stuff in this forsaken cow pasture.

Love to all. Kiss my cherub. Your Daddy

February 2, 1945– Somewhere in Belgium
My Darling:

I was lifted up after a weary day yesterday upon receipt of much wonderful mail. Three from you—December 29, January 2. I was lifted, but I didn't answer last night, as I had hoped, but went to bed very early. My recent cold has left me a little weak in the knees. This morning, however, I was repaid for my caution. I felt like a new person.

Your letters, of course, gave me much material for thought and even greater pride in having you as my wife. I know now I never have to write you detailed accounts. You understand what I mean from the sketchy letters allowed by censorship. Your great consideration of my folks, even though you are often torn with worry, leaves me humble. I thank God that you succeeded in talking them out of their anguish for the situation, which, while warranting such worry then, has now resolved itself into the calm and security we enjoyed for so long a time here.

I was amused by your reference to a General Hospital as being far behind the lines. That works on paper, perhaps, but in this war, there are too many front lines. I am not "self-effacing," My Beloved. I did get a break as you will learn someday. It might have been a "foxhole," as it may well be for others who haven't reached the age of 35. I thank God that I can spare you this.

Your January 2 letter: I feel like an awful goon. The presents were so trivial and yet you made so much over them. Honestly, honey, I'm an awful greenhorn, and a "scaredy cat." When we were in the Paris station that time, I could have possibly found something finer than Bouquet de Paris, but unlike a lot of the other guys who did a lot of shopping, I returned to the train when ordered and thus had no time to shop. The cologne, which you so loyally call perfume, was all I could get with my limited time and even more limited French. The ashtray, I can't tell you about in detail. Let's say I found it and let it go at that. Certainly, it's for your mother, and for heaven's sake, use up the perfume. When I come marching home, I'll have something worthy of the occasion. The napkins, well, if you examine them carefully, you will notice the peculiar corner marking. I can't tell you about them now, but they will have some "historic" significance one day. Keep them. The dolls: I'm glad the cherub likes them. They, too, are cheap and ideal for dragging around the house, so let her do so. I had the romantic notion of starting a collection of fine dolls for our child, but I soon learned that it's impossible. The famous doll factories are no more, and toys of real value are nonexistent here. Oh, how you appreciate America, the more you see of Europe.

Incidentally, there is another package on the way, containing wooden shoes. There's also a small gift for your mother on the way, the lovely dancing figures for you, and yesterday (February 1) I cabled you $45. There is no way of spending it here, Darling, so please use it for some Easter finery. You do not answer me on my plan to buy you and your mother birthday presents by remote control. I wish you had done this, Sweetheart. I wanted you to have something special for your birthday.

Love to all. Kiss the cherub. Your Daddy

February 2, 1945 – Somewhere in Belgium
My Darling:

After having written to you a long letter this afternoon (and having mailed it), I received two from you, December 31 and January 4. I was overwhelmed with disappointment when I learned from your letter of January 4 that Mayme [sister] and Ma heard about Paris before you did. What shall I do, Beloved? God is my witness that I share every joy, every experience with you first. I wrote three letters that lonely Christmas Eve. The first was to you and I still remember the text. What I would have given to have had you at my side in Paris. This mail business will make a real nut out of me. First, how the devil did letters of December 24 get to Chicago by January 4? And what the hell did that lousy no good bum of the mailman do with yours? Darling, I've really got something to worry about, what with the moron depositing my letters in your neighbor's boxes. I've even heard a story about a mailman who threw a whole batch of Christmas mail in the sewer because it was too heavy. I'm even ready to believe this in a world gone stark mad with hatred, brutality, selfishness and utter indifference to sorrow.

Angel, you aren't an actress. I could read the hurt and disappointment you've felt as clearly as though you had written it down. I can only beg you to understand how sorry I feel about this miserable mail situation. I have resolved to allow a week to elapse between your letter and those of the family when I have something special to write about. That's the only way I can be fairly sure that you will know first about what goes on here. Your artwork (Self-portrait of a Lonely Wife on Silver Platter) is atrocious, though, and wouldn't even make the grade in the poorest art stall on the left bank of the Seine. I heartily approve of the word pictures of our cherub, however. Really, sweetheart, you have a flair for describing her and her activities that gives me a great thrill. I wish I could save every word you have written about her, but alas, I can't. Did that stupid mailman ever deliver the letters to Roberta (on special paper)?

Sweetheart, Len Goldhammer just tapped me on the shoulder to tell me about a list of names on the bulletin board, of which I was unaware. It seems I have just been awarded a good conduct medal. Yippee! So I'll close now and go get my decoration.

Love to all. Kiss the cherub. Here's my heart, Angel, Daddy

February 4, 1945 – Somewhere in Belgium
My Darling:

I'm not only a good soldier (I have a declaration to prove that!), but I'm also now a PFC, a Private First Class, a first-class private, a Private First (F...ing) Class, as the boys characteristically refer to this distinction. As a matter of fact, I don't feel cynical about it. First, if a guy can behave in this Army for a year, he deserves some sort of a medal. Secondly, while I'm not an Army career man as you well know, it does give a guy a boost to know that he isn't a dog altogether, and that eventually a bone with a little meat is tossed in. In time I may even achieve a 7/5 (corporal) rating. Certainly, the kind of work I do should be dignified by such a rating, at least, but it certainly will make no difference to me in my approach to the job at hand. This is a golden opportunity to learn much that will always be of real value. I find I am genuinely interested in this phase of work, and I can say now that when it came to a final decision, I chose ward work over the more "dignified" dental clinic assignment. Yes, the choice was mine, and I made this one.

It is a very dull, rainy day. At 1 p.m. the brief ceremony of award will be held, and then I return to duty a PFC. I'll close now. I will write tonight again.

Love to all. Kiss the cherub. Your Daddy

February 5, 1945 – Somewhere in Belgium
My Darling:

It's certainly nice to be inside a warm ward tent. The boys are cheerful and satisfied for the moment, having just returned from lunch, and seemingly content to sprawl on their beds and listen to the rain. If you ask the Belgians, they reply, "Oh yes, the snows are gone, and now it's time for the rain." If it isn't doing one thing it's doing another here. The "muds" are next on our list of tribulations, no doubt.

Oh, how I long to tell you just what goes on here and how I am related to the whole thing. I'm not entirely satisfied with what I'm doing at the present, but I have plans. I would gladly spend every working hour with the patients if I could make some real contribution toward their comfort, but there are those who, having only very minor ailments, real and fancied, consume one's energy and time. Yet all these men are important to the scheme of things and must be attended faithfully, the sooner to get them ready again for duty. In a sense, they are even more important than those for whom there will be no returning to duty. Our credo is "to conserve the fighting strength of our armies." Your heart goes out to the human form barely discernible under the massive bandages and casts, the figure unmoving, burned, bruised, the eyes unseeing even were you to remove the bandage. That figure is through. No more guns, no more terrible noise. He can only help himself by clinging to life so the doctors can continue with their work. He can't help the doctors beyond that. But the others—the guys who develop aches and pains, the guys who acquire things, the guys who catch things through no fault of their own—they have to be healed fast, and much of the treatment depends on their cooperation. Well, a GI with a sore toe, or an itch, for instance, is still a pretty active guy even though he's pulled out of the line. So the tug-of-war goes on. You pull them towards completion of treatment while they pull in the opposite direction with their childishness, mistrust, stubbornness, and plain and simple griping. They would toss all medications in the stove; they would banish laboratory tests; in short, they would smash the whole science of medicine back to the dark ages. I know, Darling, that while they act so, they don't really mean it. They are lonely, they're tired, they're scared, even as I am and most of those around me. As long as there is still much war to be fought, these boys will continue to complain, "Gee, I'm getting well, dammit!" It's an honest reaction and it's wholly understandable.

Well, I don't think the prevailing peace and quiet will last much longer so I'll sign off now. Give my love to all. Kiss our "Love Lettuce" many times for me, and know that every waking moment for me is a steady consciousness of my love and longing for you, My Beloved.

Daddy

CHAPTER TEN

Belgium: Dental Clinic

PART 1

EXIT THE WARD MAN, ENTER THE DENTAL CLINICIAN

February 5, 1945 – Somewhere in Belgium
My Darling:

I apologize to the United States mails. Today, I, too, received in chronological order your letters of January 6, 7, 8, and January 11. Since I already have those for January 2, 3, 4, and January 13, I now have a fairly good picture of what's cooking at home. Now I'll put them in order and read all the way through again. Incidentally, I'm religiously checking off the dates on my little calendar.

First, a few comments about your letters. In that of the 6th, you referred to the muffler you knitted. Darling, memorize the lines of my letter about the scarf, for someday I'll be able to tell you the real story about the scarf. Because you made it for me would be reason enough to treasure it, but because it reached me when it did, it became an unforgettable event in my life. It is a story that will thrill you and perhaps "chill" you a little. Thus, My Darling, I store up the memories of experiences which one day I will share with you.

In yours of January 7, you remarked that "Love Lettuce" wants to write a "lellah" too. Take her tiny hand, Sweetheart, and guide it over a piece of paper. No matter what comes out, it will be a manuscript of rare value to me. I am proud and very happy that you acted so quickly in writing to Madame Bland. I have since had another nice letter from them and they are genuinely interested in my welfare. I must answer them this week. Your letter to Madame Bland reads beautifully even though I can guess at every tenth word. I'm sure, though, that it is in exquisite French. I'll figure it out for myself, with the aid of my little dictionary, and shall write you a free translation. The memento of Paris I mailed by first-class mail, so I hope no more than a month will elapse before you have it.

Now for a bit of news. I'm qualified for the dental clinic after all, it seems, and tomorrow morning, exit the ward man, enter the dental clinician, or what have you. It's a long story that goes way back, so I'll save it for another letter after I see how this shapes up. Momentarily, I'll lose my contact with the boys for whom I've expended so much energy, but I'll never lose consciousness of

those less fortunate than I, and I'll find some way to make their days here just a little brighter. Love to all. Kiss the "Love Lettuce."
Your Daddy.

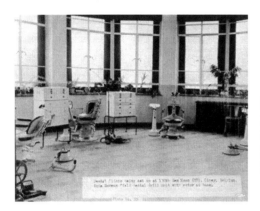

Public Domain photo from History of Medicine Collection, National Library of Medicine, National Institutes of Health, Bethesda, Maryland

[*From Oral History interview with grandson, Edward C. Bernstein, in 1986*]:

Sometime later they decided to assign me to a dental unit headed by a major from Chicago. But dentistry in the Army at that point was largely involved with extracting abscessed teeth with a minimum of preparation for the extraction. And you must remember that according to the war regulations, the covenants which were established by international agreement, we had to take care—medically and physically—of prisoners. We could not just dump prisoners in a compound and forget them. So we were required to do this and since we were a hospital that was receiving wounded—both prisoners and our own troops, we didn't differentiate between who was going to get treated, although the prisoners themselves who got medical attention were kept in a separate POW compound and they wore the striped uniforms so that they could be seen at all times.

I was assigned to this major as his assistant. He was lazy and wouldn't get there before nine o'clock, so I didn't have to hurry either and I could always be well dressed and clean looking. My job was to get to the office and sterilize the instruments, have everything ready, lay out the medications. But before I did this in the morning I had to go down to the POW compound and fetch a young German there who had worked as a dental technician in Germany. So he was skilled in making appliances. Since at some point the Army had to do something about the terrible condition of the teeth in the mouths of some of the prisoners, this young man would be taken out every morning and escorted to the laboratory where he worked. As a prisoner, he couldn't just go scot-free and walk around, so I was given a pistol and I was told to carry it in front of me all the time—up—and go down there and get Fritz or whatever his name was and then march him up to the dental laboratory by holding the gun at his back.

The first time, I was so humiliated by this whole thing, so embarrassed by it, because this poor kid wasn't going to go anywhere. He was young but he was so beaten down, so malnourished, such a mess. I felt terrible about it. I figured if he starts to run I'm not going to shoot him, a defenseless human being at that point. But he didn't. He never gave me any trouble. He seemed like a nice, intelligent young person. I would have liked to have known him in another situation. When they would come in as patients, these Germans were in a deplorable condition. Their uniforms were paper thin, their shoes nonexistent, their teeth in atrocious condition, their health rundown. I'm not making a case for them. As far as I was concerned they were devils. But individually, you could not feel that way about them. They had nothing to sustain them except for the Nazi push behind them.

The major would get a German prisoner now and then as a patient. Since we had to take care of them, he'd put them in the chair and some of these situations were really desperate. They needed Novocain or something before you could do anything. But he absolutely refused. He would say in German, "You shwein hunt." He had such hatred for these people. He wouldn't consider using Novocain on them. He was wrong. He was violating the code of ethics, but I could see that he was terribly disturbed. At one point, we got a guy in there—a great big guy—who had a very bad abscessed tooth in the front. The major decided he was going to remove the tooth but he had to chip it loose before he could remove it. I don't know how this man stood it. He never winced once. The major handed me a mallet and he held the chisel on this tooth and he said, "Hit it." After I hit the major's hand two or three times, he forgot that and pushed me aside. I don't know how he got that tooth out of there. It was a very horrible experience. It showed the ugliness of war on both sides. It brings out the worst. War brings out the most basic animal instincts. In the barracks after working hours you'd see what was happening to decent young American boys. They were becoming so vulgarized, rotten in all their behavior.

February 6, 1945 – Somewhere in Belgium
My Beloved:

Since I wrote you two letters yesterday, I'll be brief today as I must write several more tonight. If the letters arrive chronologically, you will know by now that I am now a dental "clinician." Actually, I assist at the chair. "But how?" you will query, "you don't know a thing about dentistry." That's quite so, and my ignorance was even more apparent today as I staggered through a day of amalgams, oxyphes and amalgam, silicate, calculus occlusion, caries, burs, etc. The dental officer whom I assist is a prince, but a perfectionist, and things must run without a hitch. He explained the necessary routine carefully, and then I promptly forgot all he said due to nervousness and anxiety. But I am not worried. In a day or two, it will all become clear and meaningful and I hope to acquire a good technique in this new field. I have a dental manual and a little application will make things easier. It's really not a difficult routine, considering some of the characters who have been chair assistants, but I am to be a "specialist" in this field.

The clinic, as I once told you, is in the nicest part of the building. It looks like a large and beautiful semicircular solarium. It's really the show spot of the hospital. But here's the payoff. I wear a long, white gown and look very professional, intellectual, and very sanitary. Your dad [Louis Malkin, DDS] will get a kick out of this, no doubt. My ex-ward playmates were very sorry to see me depart, but I think this new setup is going to be very, very nice. The hours are outrageously short, as compared to other departments, and the whole thing has "tone." I can't tell one instrument from another, but I piddle around and make like I know, and eventually I hope I'll know what the officer wants next as he proceeds with a case. My boss, for instance, likes to use many types of instruments in each case, and I wind up with a sterilizer full after each patient. Two of the dental officers are old friends from our Swannanoa days. One is a Chicagoan and the other, formerly our Special Service officer, sponsored me as columnist on our camp paper. They are both friendly and made me feel most welcome. In fact, some months ago they expressed a wish to have me assigned to the clinic. Well, let's hope I'll have a chance to settle down this time.

Your French letter to Madame Bland was translated to me by one of our French-speaking boys, and he was full of praise for your good French. To me it was very beautiful. Your short, but sweet letter of the ninth, plus your wonderful valentine, and the baby's treasured valentine reached me today. I'll write my daughter a letter this week.

Now I must close, Sweetheart. Keep writing me long, beautiful letters. How I need them. Strangely enough, your valentine was delivered to me this morning very soon after I started on the new job, and I couldn't help but feel that you stretched out your hand to give me a pad of encouragement. The day went very well and I have no fear of the morrow.

Love to all. Your Daddy

February 8, 1945 – Somewhere in Belgium
My Darling:

Another day is coming to a close and even though I am a recent addition to the clinic staff, I will join in the festivities tonight at a party to be given for the staff by the highest-ranking officer in the clinic. I don't think I'm permitted to say why he is giving a party, but I do feel pleased that I was asked to be a guest.

The work in the clinic is interesting, but I feel like such a dope. Unlike a ward where you minister to the patients after the diagnosis and the main work has been done, in a dental clinic you are part of each actual diagnosis and operation, and I'm so very green about it all. This is an exact science. There is no time for uncertainty. My officer has a remarkable technique, and with my terrible ignorance of what is going on, I find myself acting like a dumb yokel as I watch in amazement instead of anticipating his next action and having the proper instrument or medication ready for him. He's very patient and very quiet when I do miss my cue, as I do frequently, so learning becomes a little easier. Considering the years I've spent in the dental chair you'd think I'd know all about it, but it doesn't work that way. I still wince with recalled pain when he goes to work on a sensitive tooth with a sharp instrument. I can see the patient's toes curl, even as mine did a thousand times. I think I'd rather witness a bloody appendectomy than watch that little drill bore its way into an unsuspecting tooth. Well, I'm really not too dumb. Each day I've managed to retain a little acquired knowledge, and perhaps in a few weeks I'll take this calmly.

I had no mail from you yesterday, and none today, so I'm let down a bit, but I guess it will arrive in a stack. I have Sunday afternoon off and one thing I will do will be to send you a few things I've accumulated, including the records.

The weather is unusually warmish. No snow, but lots of mud puddles. What new miracle is our daughter performing? Kiss the cherub. Keep well, and don't worry.

Your Daddy

February 10, 1945, 8:30 a.m. – Somewhere in Belgium [V-mail]
My Darling:

I have a few minutes before the first patient is seated, so a few words to assure you that I am in excellent health and am enjoying the new work. There is much to learn, both at the chair and at the receptionist desk. The paperwork in the Army is staggering, and very confusing. There are two ways of doing a job—the Army way and the right way, but the Army way is the "right" way for the present, so one doesn't question the method. One merely gets acquainted with the various forms, their numbers and breakdown of the main forms into countless other divisions. I will write tonight as usual. Love to all. Save that new wisdom tooth until I get home. I'll assist in its removal, while holding your hand, which is more than I do for the GIs around here.

Love, Daddy.

February 10, 1945, 6:15 p.m. – Somewhere in Belgium
My Darling:

As is my custom, I talk to you as soon as evening chow is over, and it was really something to run away from tonight. I don't mind too much, however, as it's a good excuse to eliminate that extra bread and potatoes. I feel a little thinner around the middle, and I'm delighted, of course. Even on a steady diet of Army chow, one can spread out to enormous proportions.

There is practically no news, unless you find it interesting to know that our building project still goes on. Fortunately, I can look out of the clinic window and watch the project as the POW's busy themselves. What we are to do with all the buildings, no one knows, but it goes on just the same. It may be worth mentioning, also, that yesterday we were issued nice sleeping bags. I need mine like I need a hole in the head. Since no passionate Maria came with the bag, I have even less use for it (see Ernest Hemingway's *For Whom the Bell Tolls*).

Here's a bit of news. Yesterday, I received a Christmas card in which was enclosed two dollars. It was from Mr. and Mrs. W. J. Curran of Verona, Pa. I never heard of them. Did you? A message on the card read, "Please let us hear from you and if you get the money tell us all about yourself." It must be a mistake. I never knew any Currans, and I never heard of Verona, Pa.

You mentioned in a recent letter the desire to do some war work. I'm not familiar with the work of the Gray Ladies, but if you feel they are doing some good you can give some of your time to the cause. What most GI patients miss and crave the most is personal attention, which is physically impossible even for those who have no regular hospital duties besides this work. If that is what the Gray Ladies are attempting to do, it's worthwhile

I used to see only what came into my ward, mild ailments and superficial injuries. Now, from my vantage point behind the reception desk, I see the daily parade of human wreckage as they roll out of the elevator, which stops directly in front of me. It's not a pretty sight. Since the regular receptionist had the afternoon off, I doubled today and scooted from desk to dental chair most of the day. The strange dental terms seemed less confusing today, so I guess I'm learning. One of the clinic technicians just returned with a bottle of Ciros Parfum, "Camellia," 500 francs (something over $10 for about an ounce). What do you think? I wish I knew something about cosmetics and perfumes, so I could shop intelligently for some. I'm scared of the stuff because the sale of it is a universal swindle.

Well, Sweetheart, it is quite possible to achieve a bath if I go now, so I close, wondering how I can be more emphatic than just saying I love you. Kiss the cherub. Best to the folks. No mail today, but maybe tomorrow.

Daddy

February 11, 1945 – Somewhere in Belgium
My Dear Maga: [Esther's mother, Hattie Malkin]

Let it be twelve times and twelve blessings upon you for your wonderful letter, "Another Day with Stinky."

I need no better assurance that she is in good hands than your refreshingly honest observation: "that she surpasses all children is hardly justified, but that she possesses everything that is necessary for endearment is obvious." Your collection of Belgian glass is worth a fortune now. You should see the junk they offer for sale. And I doubt if they'll ever get around again to turning out anything as fine as you possess.

Now for this Bruce business. Everyone I've asked says, "Seven times did Robert Bruce try and finally won." If I'm wrong, so, I'll take you to the Yar and we'll drink borscht in honor of the great and victorious Russian armies who are making our earlier return a possibility. God give them the strength to go on and on to total victory. With that, I'll sign off. My love to Dad [Louis Malkin, DDS]. We'll have some hot dental discussions when I get home. In the twelve blessings are included good health and happiness to you.

As ever, Sam

February 11, 1945, 6:45 p.m. – Somewhere in Belgium
My Darling:

It has been a good day in all. With the afternoon off, I made the most of the opportunity. I got a haircut, a sun-ray treatment to tone up the winter pallor, and, believe it or not, a HOT SHOWER. I'm still pinching myself to make sure it's me and that it really happened. Then came the sweetest delight of all—two letters from you, January 25 and 29. My calendar tells me that the letters from January 14 to 20 inclusive, are still to be received, so you see your void of January 8 to 16 isn't any worse than mine.

We are going along at a fairly even pace now, and the exodus is practically forgotten [*Editors' note: He refers to the Hospital evacuation to a different location during the Battle of the Bulge.*] My writing case, which contains your photo and all of the baby's photos I clutched to my heart that terrible night. I haven't let it out of my sight since. I have a small album and am going to mount all of the baby's pictures. I have my watch and bracelet, but just about everything else, including all the Christmas goodies and the request packages were made unusable—just in case. Don't fret, Dear, I have a duffel bag full of stuff again. I miss the camera most of all, though, now that I have film. Don't attempt to replace it. Perhaps I can borrow one long enough to get a few shots for "the records."

The dental clinic is working out very nicely for me. I'll devote a letter in detail on it a bit later. I wish your Dad could see this equipment. It's wonderful. The laboratory can turn out anything, and remember, these men are all Army trained. And the dental officers—it's a joy to see them work. None of that opening up a tooth and packing it with wax for ten visits. The caries are cleaned out and filled and that's that. It saves time, energy, and certainly the nerves of the patients. I don't know whether civilian dentistry has dropped the hokum of keeping a simple caries open for three or four visits, but I do know that dentistry would be "painless" if they adopted the Army method. I do know that where there is infection or abscess, it is necessary to treat a tooth, but oh how I remember the innumerable visits I used to make just to get a small decay cleaned up. And what a bill I'd get at $2 per visit. See what I mean? I really believe that if people in general were convinced that they wouldn't have to spend ten nights in a dental chair for a simple decay, dentistry would be popular and very profitable. Well, I almost wrote that separate letter on the dental clinic, so adieu. Request: I want some cookies. There. Stick that in your postal clerk's face. Yes, Darling, you are always on my mind even when I write to others.

Love to all. Kiss the cherub. Your Daddy

February 12, 1945– Somewhere in Belgium
My Darling:

Talk about luck. Ten days ago you wrote me a letter (February 2). Today I received it, plus yours of January 30. All is forgiven, Mr. Postman. It is a wonderful feeling to know that as recently as ten days ago all was well on the home front. That's the real morale booster. But I can imagine that your visit to the dentist was made even more painful by the letters you must have received from me about my sojourn in a hospital bed. It was stupid of me to write about it since there is certainly nothing unusual about getting a cold. I was afraid, though, that Manny might have mentioned it to Betty, and thus be relayed to you, thereby giving you cause for worry. It is the policy of the unit to hospitalize a man when he is not up to par and get him in shape. That's a very sensible idea and the poor sap who doesn't report on sick call when he is ailing is a sap and a liability. Actually, I felt I would be a menace to the patients with my runny nose, watery eyes, etc. I feel very fit now and enjoy a too-hearty appetite. You should see me struggle with temptation as the bread and butter are passed back and forth. We are enjoying touches of civilized living in our mess. The POWs are bus boys. They keep the long tables neat and see that the tables are provided with trays of bread, butter, sugar, cream. We still use our mess kits, which is the one major nuisance, but it would be a big job to wash dishes with our limited facilities. Thus, it falls to each man to clean and wash his own mess kit, and keep it polished or suffer the consequences—the "GIs."

Now, Darling, I have a mission. There are a few Jewish patients I would like to visit. Perhaps I can find some little thing to do for them. Love to all. Kiss the cherub.

To you, my love as always, Daddy

February 14, 1945 – Somewhere in Belgium
My Darling:

This is my Valentine letter to you because I know that it will make you feel good to know that I am very well, quite pleased with my new job, and at last I can say that I have a dry, warm place to sleep. It may surprise and shock you to know that for the past few weeks I had been living in a damp, cold, frightfully depressing tent at the foot of the slope. To get to that hovel one had to plow through water and mud. It was unavoidable, but of course it had to be me.

Since a group of us returned from our "Gotsa dooty" service, too late to get a bed in the then existing barracks, we found ourselves the forgotten battalion down in those tents. The inspecting officers never ventured down there. We did have many laughs, though, consoling each other. The coal pile was so far away we just did without it most of the time, but we burned our refuse and garbage and everything else that would burn. This morning, though, our last morning "down yonder," we had nary a gum wrapper to burn, but we did have Mrs. Miniver, who warmed our numbed fingers page by page. Bless her heart! Well, that's over. I'm in a nice barracks with some of my good friends. It's warm, cheerful, and comfortable. In the Army one is grateful for these essentials.

Now for the mail. Having received your February 2 letter before that of February 1, I knew only that you received the dancers, but I worried about how they looked. Then yesterday yours of February 1 arrived, and I knew that the souvenir arrived in good condition. I hope that is the truth. It is a delicate thing to send through the mail. Perhaps I led you to believe that the dancers were china figures, which was what I had in mind when I went shopping in Paris. But this little group, made of wire and wool, caught my fancy so strongly I couldn't resist. Somehow they reminded me of our beautiful picture, *The Dancers* (Cezanne—our picture is a Cezanne, isn't it?), which has its greatest appeal in its almost crude execution. [*The artist actually is Degas. A print of the painting hangs today in the living room of Roberta's home.*]

I didn't write last night because a good movie was available. It was *In Our Time*, with Lupino and Henreid. It is based on the rape of Poland soon after Chamberlain, returning from the Munich conference, said, "There will be peace in Europe in our time." The picture falls short of being a great film, but it's well made and timely and reminds us again of the treachery of the Nazis, who approach the eve of their destruction, we hope. What pleased me most was the Chopin music of the background and a good scene from "Les Sylphides." So you see, although I didn't write, I talked to you as the picture unfolded. It's worth seeing just to see Ida Lupino in a splendid performance. Her role calls for a complete reversal of the technique which has made her so important to the screen. The change was a welcome one and very interesting. About *Arsenic and Old Lace*, which we saw in France, I agree with you emphatically. Leave it to Hollywood to snafu a good play. The satire was stretched to the point of the imbecility.

Sweetheart, I must end now. I want to write a short letter to the folks. I received a V-Mail from them today, expressing their loneliness. My calendar says that you still owe me twelve letters for January. Assuming that you missed two nights, I still have ten coming.

I gave you my heart and my hand when we were joined together. They are yours forever. What more can I say in closing this Valentine letter?

Your Daddy

February 15, 1945 – Somewhere in Belgium
My Darling:

The mailman was very good today. Here's my "take." Yours of January 14, 15, 17, 19, and February 3. Your good dad's letter of Jan. 15, Roy's of Jan. 19, and a birthday card (Jan.16) from the folks. Am I happy? I'm delirious. So I know all about the baby's bottle-less nights, the wonder of her nimble brain and your unfortunate accident with your glasses. I also know that you have gone without mail from me for days. This grieves me more than I can say because I do try to write long letters to help you over the dreary days of waiting, waiting. The day has been a beautiful, sunny one. It's fantastic. I thought these countries were snowed in until Easter but the natives assure us that winter is over. I'm not sucker enough to fall for that. I'll keep the "long johns" handy for a time yet.

I had a snapshot taken of me in the clinic today, white gown and all. I hope it turns out. Also, tomorrow, if all goes well, I have a date with the photographer to "sit me" for a portrait. I'm curious to know how I look to others on my 36th birthday. I hope to have some little celebration tomorrow. We are allowed a ration of liquor per month, and while I do not use mine, I did draw my card for this month and shall let a few friends drink it up tomorrow night. Personally, I prefer a Royal Crown Cola which we get here.

Darling, you express regret at not having a birthday present for me. Knowing that you and the baby and all the folks are well is present enough for me. What bothers me is the inability to find suitable things to send home to you. This is so irksome. Money means nothing to us. I would spend every franc on something for you if it were available, but I refuse to fall for ordinary things and cheap perfumes and cosmetics. I beg you, I implore you to use the money I sent you to buy what you want or need. I feel like such a phony. I promised to get something nice for the baby, but I'll be damned if I can find anything out of the ordinary. The fur coat and hat deal proved impractical, so I abandoned it but haven't been able to find a suitable substitute. Here's the situation. The little town where one can buy a few things is a two-minute walk from us, but since there is a curfew and blackout, the shops close very early. At best I could leave the hospital about 4:30 p.m. and run to town before things close up. I'd gladly go without chow for this except when you get there you can find little for your trouble. All I can hope for is a furlough or a pass sometime in the near future, which would get me to one of the big cities. Towards that end I shall hoard my next pay (I got a raise with that PFC) and hope to find a few nice things, including Worth or Chanel or "Paris de Smellow."

Believe me, Angel, I got a wonderful break with this dental clinic assignment. I'm almost afraid to talk about it, so good it is. Such hours, such a beautiful environment, such congenial men and officers! I have reason to suspect my particular officer likes me in his own reserved manner. He feels that I am interested in learning and consequently is interested in teaching. My job was formerly filled by a series of misfits who had no interest and showed it. Thus, I had to break down a certain amount of aloofness and suspicion. I can hardly blame him if he thought, "Is this guy going to goof off too?" What an artist he is. Darling, I know talent, yes, genius, when I encounter it, even if I am ignorant of the medium through which it is displayed. This captain of mine is superb. He works with a deftness and purpose that are astonishing. Today he scared the wits out of me by telling me to mix a portion of oxyphes and amalgam (mercury and alloy) for a "silver filling" he was doing. I ruined the thing but he was very patient and explained why. In mixing it I lost some of the mercury; thus, the mixture got too dry. A little later, however, I mixed another batch which he declared "excellent." I must keep my hands immaculate since it appears from now on I'll even get them into patients' mouths. I'm still confused by which instruments are used for what—there are so many of them, but by golly I'm going to get this thing. I'm going to ask to do prophylaxis eventually. It looks simple. If only we will be allowed to do our work here until this horrible business is over. Things are running so smoothly here now we are almost scared to comment on it. Really, Darling, we have this to be thankful for. I know you pray to God with me that my present lot will be the pattern for whatever time I must yet endure away from you. As it is now, there is no room for complaining. There are so many less fortunate than I.

Roy's letter tells of the shameful treatment of those boys who suffered through the worst of the European hell, only to come home again for K.P. and stove details. Shame on those responsible for such an utterly disgusting display of authority! With thousands of Nazi prisoners housed in considerable luxury in the States, our boys have to go home to K.P. duty? What a mockery! Is this what we are to expect from civilian employers, too, after the war? Will we be allowed to wash dishes in some cheap slop house? I don't think Roy is exaggerating. It's just what I expected would happen. They gave him a ride in a Pullman, they wined and dined him, they showed him the sites, and then they called off the "honeymoon." "See here, soldier, you're just another guy in uniform. So get busy on those dishes." I have seen picture spreads in *Life* about how the prisoners of war lived in the States. I assure you theirs is luxury compared to ours. Why the hell they can't be used to do the details in the camps and posts at home is beyond comprehension. Maybe that's being inhuman to them. I believe Roy speaks the truth and I am furious. What goes at home? I hate to close on such a note of distress, but if those armchair commandos don't get over here and get a taste of this, too, there is going to be a hell of a battle fought between those who came and saw and conquered and those fat asses who wore out their own O.D.s on swivel chairs, when this is over.

Goodnight, My Darling. God keep you safe and well. Kiss the incredible Love Lettuce. Daddy

February 17, 1945 – Somewhere in Belgium
My Darling:

How much better it would have been if I had found a few moments to write you a letter last night, but alas it seemed like bad manners to go off to a corner while ten "guests" celebrated my birthday. It was a surprise. I came down to Central Supply, where my good friend Max Neiburg works, to write my letter, only to walk smack into a surprise party. I'm enclosing the list of guests. Please preserve it for me. Refreshments were Royal Crown Cola and later a huge birthday cake with a candle glowing cheerfully. The cake, a large double layer affair smothered with chocolate, was procured somehow by Manny Levin. There's a pal for you. I happen to know that he went to considerable trouble to get it. I don't know why all these boys are so thoughtful of me. There is so little time and so few opportunities for real social living that I'm a little surprised at finding myself with such genuinely good friends.

On another occasion, when I was in the hospital, my room was crowded nightly with three or more visitors. They sat on the bed, on the floor, and on the other patients' beds and stayed all evening. "Steve," Lt. Stevenson, about whom I have written to you, spent all of his convalescence in my room. Incidentally, he popped into the clinic tonight about 4:30 and we fell upon each other like old pals. He's a nice guy and so enthusiastic and full of the joy of living. May God grant him safety and health. We'll certainly meet again when this is over.

Angel, tonight we're having a dance in our Day Room. No kidding, a band, women, ice cream and all the trimmings. And tomorrow I have a half day off and now it's permissible to go a good distance from our post. Gosh, I can't stand all this "civilization" all of a sudden. Also, tomorrow evening I expect to see the movie *Laura*, about which you raved so much. So, Monday night my letter should be "pregnant" with news. But that's the only kind of pregnancy I'll be responsible for, you may be sure. There'll be some hot times in the old town when I get home, but until then I'm strictly kosher. Request: send me some soda crackers, some cookies and a hairbrush.

The dental work grows daily more interesting. This morning, during a break, I asked my captain to look at my R-13, which I suspected had a caries. Fortunately, it did not since it's one of my sensitive teeth, but he found one in L-5, so tomorrow morning I'll adjust the light, lay out the basic instruments, put a towel around my neck and climb into the dreaded chair. I hope I don't disgrace myself, but oh how I hate that drill.

Goodnight, My Love. Kiss the cherub. Love to all, Daddy

February 18, 1945 – Somewhere in Belgium
My Darling:

A quiet Sunday morning in the clinic gives me this opportunity to write a "quickie" and take advantage of tonight's censoring instead of letting it lie in the box until tomorrow. The weather is dull and gray, but we are going on a little trip this afternoon anyhow. Manny and Max and I have the afternoon off.

That dance last night was a nice affair. The music, by an American GI band, was excellent, but the awful shortage of females left most of us standing around to ogle the few gals who were busy changing partners every two or three steps. But the refreshments were something: chicken sandwiches, real ice cream and coffee. The ice cream was the real treat. The Belgiques can talk about ice cream, but what they sell is a hopelessly watery, mushy culinary mistake which is neither cream nor sherbet, so when I tasted real ice cream, made at the direction of our mess, my mouth did justice. I even had French coffee by floating a spoonful.

I forgot to mention in yesterday's letter that my sitting at the photographers didn't "sit." When Manny and I got there, we learned the guy was in custody for something or other. So I'll have to try again somewhere else. They say there is another photographer in town. No mail from you for two days. I guess airmail is again giving space to other things. Maybe the spring offensive will do the trick this time. I will write later if we get home at a reasonable hour. Love to all. Did you ever get the wooden shoes?

Kiss the cherub. Here's my heart. ♥ Daddy

February 19, 1945 – Somewhere in Belgium
My Darling:

No mail again today so I'm up a tree, as it were, for a theme or two. My work goes along very well. I'm learning many phases of dentistry, and in the knowledge I found new courage, apparently. My captain filled my tooth today and I just sat there as calm as a cucumber. He did "Procainize" [use anaesthesia] it, of course, but even the dreaded needle didn't phase me. He is a remarkably fine dentist and his gruff "exterior" is only a veneer for great sensitivity, I suspect. He had me mixing cement and alloys again today and accepted my mixtures without comment, which in this case is a mark of approval. Tonight, having found a willing victim, I'm going to do a prophylaxis. Learning to do this will make me much more valuable to the clinic.

Our trip to the picturesque nearby town yesterday was partly spoiled by rain, but we managed to have fun, drinking cheap beer, eating luscious small cakes, and buying cheap souvenirs. I bought a little smiling Buddha. One of these days I'll ship it home. Guess I'm going to use most of my pay for sightseeing now. I wish I could get a week's furlough to Paris or Brussels. Well, we have settled down to a pleasant routine and all goes very well. Angel, I must close in order to get this censored tonight.

Love to all. Kiss the cherub. Here's my heart. ♥ Daddy

February 20, 1945 – Somewhere in Belgium [V-mail]
To: Mrs. Esther Lesner, 5131 Greenwood Ave., Chicago, 15, Ill. USA
From PFC Samuel J. Lesner, 130th General Hospital, APO 350 1pm, New York
My Darling:

I implore you to forgive the V-Mail brevity but I'm writing this just before the six o'clock movie starts and since that is almost exclusively our only diversion, I allow myself to be led to the movie hall occasionally. I have your letter of February 6, but that's all. Got a beautiful letter from Ruth today and as predicted she outdid herself in thanking me for the ashtrays. Tomorrow I will mail you a sensational package, having just found the proper packing for the "great voice." Also an added token of my love, a bit of costume jewelry which I hope you will like. A cute book for Roberta is also included. I am very well and quite satisfied with my present lot. I await letters from you with all my love.

Kiss the cherub, Daddy

February 21, 1945 – Somewhere in Belgium [V-Mail]
My Darling:

Life has become so unharried that it is now possible for me to sit down in front of the radio in our spacious and comfortable day room, after chow, and write you a brief though cheerful letter. It occurs to me that this is an excellent habit to cultivate, and I shall do so as long as it's possible. You will gather that my hours in the clinic are reasonable and the whole setup is conducive toward regaining a calm disposition. The job could be a humdrum routine if I was so inclined, but my "scientific" curiosity has been aroused and I find there is much of interest to learn. My first prophylaxis was successful and now my buddies are clamoring for service. Well, even in dentistry one can acquire technique by practicing on long-suffering friends.

Love to all. Kiss the cherub. Love, Daddy

Belgium: Dental Clinic

February 21, 1945 – Somewhere in Belgium
My Darling:

A very busy day has finally come to an end and it would have been a day of accomplishment and pleasure had the mail brought me some recent word from you. As it is, I have to be satisfied with feeling that I've acquitted myself well under pressure. I was the only assistant on duty today (there are three normally) and it meant working at four chairs simultaneously. I am ambidextrous, but the way the instruments were flying around I could have used another pair of hands. The men are so genial, though, that I knock myself out to keep up with them. I really feel "at home" with them although as always I preserve an attitude of dignity and academic interest while working. I think when they learn that I am genuine in this respect I'll go a long way with them.

The movie last night, to which I went instead of writing to you, was a horrible waste of time, considering how little time we have to waste. Serves me right. It was a Bob Hope picture, *The Pirates and the Princess*. Sam Goldwyn ought to have his head examined. What a stinking attempt at sophistication and satire. I hope you didn't strain your eyes in viewing this opus. [*Editors' note: This is a foreshadowing of becoming movie critic after the war.*]

Your letter of the 6th informs me of your cut finger. How I sympathize with you in that. I've come to have a real dread of cans, particularly those mean little ration cans. It's like playing with a dozen razor blades, trying to open one. You remember I wrote you about how I tangled with one on the train when we first came to Belgium. I slashed four fingers that time and believe me it was plenty uncomfortable. I've cut myself several times since and now have quite a reputation. It seems my right hand is nearly always sporting a bandage of some sort. We had quite a laugh over my predicament the other day. I got a slight burn on the middle joint of my first finger recently by accidentally touching a hot stove pipe. Naturally, I ignored it, but by immersing my hands in warm water frequently, to wash instruments, I found that it wasn't healing up. I went to the dispensary for a bit of bandage and tape. When I returned to the clinic the men, upon seeing me, cried out in surprise, "Sam, what happened, when did you injure your hand so badly?" "Hold everything, men," I said, "and I'll show you my wound," whereupon I began to unwind seven yards of gauze. I'm not kidding. My entire hand had been wrapped up to and including the wrist, simply because they wanted me to keep from bending my finger at the burned joint. So remembering my first aid lessons, I made a tiny splint from a tongue depressor and taped it to the underside of my finger. Presto, no bends and no bulky bandage to encourage sympathy. The next day a little mercurochrome finished the job.

My mad pursuit of dental knowledge has led me into a channel of prophylaxis. All my friends are begging for a tooth polishing job. Tonight I shined up Max Neiburg's unusually fine teeth and it pleased me to see them sparkle even more. He's a swell guy and a very good friend. He's one who will remain my friend after this business. I know you'll enjoy him, too. He has golden hands when it comes to foot treatment and is already enjoying quite a reputation in the hospital. Both of us, of course, in our white gowns look more like officers than enlisted men and we are always being "yes sirred" by patients. As Li'l Abner says, "it's amoosin but confoosin." Our "ship" has suddenly come into a very calm sea and we "sail along" without the fear of running afoul of anything. It's a strange calm after the storms we have weathered.

You know that I share your pride and joy to the fullest in the knowledge that our daughter is such a charmer. Through your dear letters I live many moments of heartwarming joy. To see her, to hold her tightly, to talk to her is the great thrill that God cannot deny me much longer. As tiny as she is, she must know that your love is double. Guard her only from angry voices and harshness, but let her know that obedience only leaves happiness for all in its wake. Good night, My Love. It's almost 9 p.m. and again I must go without a bath. My love to all. The "surprise" package is on its way.

Sweet Wife, good night, Daddy

February 22, 1945 – Somewhere in Belgium
My Darling:
Augmenting my letter of this morning, regretfully I must say that there was nothing from you at mail call, but an ever-increasing circle of friends brought me a delightful one from Jean Pierre Bland [the son of the French lady whom he met in December in Paris] and one from the relatives of the little Belgian cobbler of whom I wrote recently. Also, a V-Mail from my folks. Jean Pierre says they haven't received your letter yet, which may be my fault in part. The address I sent you was incorrect in part, but it was the best I could make out of Mme. Bland's writing. On the other hand, I'm inclined to think that the civilian censors have delayed your letter. I believe mail to and from civilians in the liberated countries comes under censorship, and the fact that it was in French makes this seem plausible. At any rate, I have the copy and will endeavor to have it censored and send it on to the Blands. Jean tells me that his class, the class of '43, has been called up, so he's set to shoulder a rifle for his country. They are proud and noble people and the Blands will bear this new burden with pride and dignity.

The letter from the cobbler's relatives is a grateful expression of thanks for my interest in the matter of the cobbler and his little family. I think I can be of some small help in making their life a little easier. The distance, however, to them from where we are now is formidable for an afternoon's trip.

Kiss the cherub. Love to all. To you my love, Daddy

February 23, 1945 – Somewhere in Belgium
My Darling:
I'm sailing high tonight having received two newsy, gossipy, lovely, wonderful letters from you, February 7 and February 9. The story about C. J. Bulliet

[Sam's editor at the *Chicago Daily News*] and how he feels about me fills me with hope and excitement. Our future will be one of success and real prestige if they'll only give me a chance to say what I feel when this is over. I can't write it now because my heart is pierced by the misery around me, but one day this will resolve itself into strong words, well-chosen words. I haven't thought much about writing in the past few months since life was too hectic, but with this new calm which has descended upon us, perhaps I'll again become articulate. Better than the French dictionary, I'd rather have a small, good English dictionary. You know I need only a key word to start a whole flock of words on the way, but I miss my "bible," the dictionary. C. J. uses one constantly too.

Yes, Sophie Tucker sent me a swell box of stuffed fruits and in an earlier letter I asked you to get me her address from Variety or Billboard so I can write a thank-you note.

Darling, there is so much confusion as a result of this erratic mail delivery that I'd appreciate it if you single out a sentence and repeat it from each letter you get so that I'll know which you have received. You see, dates become meaningless after weeks of waiting. I know for instance that both your mother and mine received the small gifts I sent, but I know this only from a brief reference to it in a letter later than the one in which no doubt you actually mention receipt of same. Well, Angel, in the box I have just sent off is a handmade cigarette lighter of unusual workmanship. It was made by one of the monks here and I want your father to have it. It will need fueling but I think he'll know how to fix it up OK. The other things in the box are for you and the baby. Ashtrays similar to those I sent Ruth are also on the way to you. I hope that Mayme got hers OK. Please believe that I am unusually well and cheerful. I really had the grippe and nothing else. I had a wonderful shower tonight and I'm in the pink. That's all for now, Angel. It's bedtime and my bed is soft and warm.

Goodnight, Beloved. Kiss the Love Lettuce. Your Daddy

February 24, 1945 – Somewhere in Belgium
My Darling:

Your letter of February 10 reached me today, and so did one from a guy I met in the long line of sad-sack rookies as we snaked our bare asses before the jaundiced eyes of the Induction Center doctors. It's a real compliment that he remembers me. One evening before I went to [Fort] Sheridan I took him along on the cafe roundup and he was so thrilled and impressed that he pledged me his eternal friendship. He's a nice guy who left a good wife and a couple of kids behind in Chicago and is now in the Glider Infantry. What a deal. He volunteered for the paratroops without telling his wife, so you can imagine how she feels. His name is Sid Rubin.

Well, Angel, the big push is on again. Oh, Merciful God, how much more slaughter must there be before this thing ends? I have just finished wrapping two parcels for you. Small, unimportant things, but the excitement of receiving a parcel lends undue value to the article received. At the moment, I am up to my ears in the clerking end of the clinic, so you see from day to day my life is filled with the strain of learning. But it is a swell job and I hope it lasts. It is good to know that the weather is milder now. We enjoy extraordinary weather and I'll be darned if these Belgiques aren't plowing already. They are early birds. But the temperature justifies such early action. Our nice little camp "city" is like a village built on a huge piss pot. The "profound" odor of generations of pissing—both human and animal—arises to assail the nostrils as the sun's warmth opens the genitals of our cow pasture. It's not bad, though, honey. It's just that Europe generally hasn't adopted modern plumbing. Paris, the city of magnificence, for instance, is the city of perfume and piss. There is no escaping these two distinct odors no matter where you go. Enough about urine, Angel. I am well, have good friends, and am enjoying the dubious pleasure of being a Private First (— — —) Class. At least it's a step in the right direction. Kiss my adorable, brilliant cherub and know that I'm sending you an ambrosial kiss to sustain you in the lean days of loneliness and absence of mail. I need you as much as I love you, which is enormous.

Goodnight, Sweet, Daddy

February 25, 1945 – Somewhere in Belgium
My Darling:
A pleasant, unhurried morning preceded an afternoon of walking through the nearby town, eating a dish of "mistaken identity" Belgian crème de glace, laughing hilariously over nothing with my friend Max and exchanging friendly insults with the kids who flock around for souvenirs, etc. I stepped into a little shop and bought a dozen picture cards for Roberta, the first of which I enclose in this letter. They are so cute and colorful. I thought Love Lettuce would enjoy playing with them. After all, she's getting to be quite a young lady and is entitled to her share of mail from her Daddy. It will be a quiet evening. Our stock of Belgian cola has been exhausted for some days, and our rations for the other stuff have been exhausted, so I'm stuck with my ration card. It's just as well, though, that we don't take too much liquid. The desire to pee overcomes one far too often in this peculiar climate. The last two hours of sleep are usually a battle of survival, survival from drowning in your own flow.

No mail from you today so I can't tell just how far you got towards compiling my letters of January for a more complete picture of what went on. I think, if after you have them all, a rereading in chronological order will tell you far more than you have been able to gather from the erratic manner in which delivery compelled you to piece together the story. It is an interesting story when told in detail and in order of events. I'm sitting in our handsome Day Room, writing this, and the war seems very, very far away, yet tonight the fronts are ablaze again and men are dying. It will end someday and when that moment comes, there is not a heart that will not miss a beat for a long, suffocating moment. What will I do in that moment? What will you do? I'm afraid of that moment and yet I pray for it with every breath. It will come, Beloved, and in that moment we will be reborn, for we will be given back the right to hope, to plan, to build.

There is little else to report. I must try to coax a little fire out of the stove in front of which I sit hopefully. Angel, will you send me 10 bucks? I want to buy a certain thing I've wanted for some time and it will leave me broke for the entire month. Honestly, that's all I want. Please, not a cent more. Send it as a money order which I can cash here. It will be timed just right by the time your reply to this letter reaches me. I hate to ask you, but I sent the excess Francs home before the town was on limits and there was no way to spend it. Now, since we get passes, I find that going to town isn't much fun if you can't spend something.

Love to all. Kiss my cherub, our Love Lettuce. My love, My Angel. Daddy

February 27, 1945 – Somewhere in Belgium

Angel, I have come suddenly to life. I want to write again. I started work on a short article tonight about some of the talented people here. One is Hugh Martin, composer of that delightful tune "Buckle Down Windsocki," from *Best Foot Forward*, and more recently the captivating tune "The Trolley Song." Have you heard it? Please get some reaction to it from the "tunesmiths" we know around town. How widely is it played in Chicago? Martin is the kind of fellow I would back for an Empire Room or Mayfair Room [*Editors' note: Chicago nightclubs in the Palmer House and Blackstone Hotels, respectively*] engagement, a gentle, quiet, good-looking young man who projects his talent and personality with remarkable ease. What's more, he plays excellent piano for his own accompaniments. He's not unknown, of course. He's been a Hollywood and New York personality but for some unaccountable reason has been swallowed up by the infantry in this devastating final push to end this horror. I am forcing an objectivity to all this before I am emotionally ready to do so, but the practice will be good for me. [*Editors' note: Sam will return to the* Chicago Daily News *as a nightclub critic.*] I've taken my cue from what you told me about C. J. Bulliet. I hope he won't let me down. I think now it is in his power to use an occasional item from me even though weeks will pass before I learn about the publication of same. This is the time, Sweetheart. We must push now, too. If I've sent you anything so far that's worthy of printing, use your connections to get it done. I need this now if I am to return to a writing career. The war correspondents have practically knocked themselves out. The public, I think, now wants something in a lighter vein and I have a lot of ideas. I'll take up this theme in another letter. I must close now, Angel.

Love to all. Kiss the cherub. To my love, Daddy

February 28, 1945 – Somewhere in Belgium
My Darling:

Your letter of January 24 has reached me at last. Five weeks for an airmail. To refresh your memory, you wrote at that time that the wooden shoes arrived. I know they are quite impossible to walk in. Some of us had the idea they would be good for shower room shoes, and tried them, with painful results. Actually, I thought you might find some decorative purpose for them. You could even stick little growing plants in them or small cut flowers and use them as a centerpiece on an informal occasion. Your idea to use them one day for Roberta's room is excellent. Until then you can just place them under your bed and let them peek out at you every morning.

You are quite wrong in your guessing, My Darling, and I'm thankful that you didn't know since such knowledge would have burdened you at the time things were happening. That's all been over long ago, so please put it out of your mind. We are safe and happy—well fed, entertained, well clothed and are soon to receive certain decorations for our efficiency during and proximity to danger at the time of the Bulge. Now don't go imagining all sorts of things. This is purely routine military business, but if one has to be a soldier one might as well share in the recognition granted for a job well done.

I await with excitement Roberta's first scribblings to me. All of her pictures are now mounted in a neat little red leather album and it is my pride and joy and constant source of vitamins. I don't remember what I wrote in the "exquisite long last letter of January 3" so I can't make any additions in a similar vein. I just overheard a joke: "the Mama broom and the Papa broom had a little whisk broom and they couldn't understand it because they had never swept together." End of joke. End of letter.

Love to all. Kiss the cherub. To you, my love, Daddy

March 2, 1945
My Darling:

No mail today again but that means that in the next day or so a flock of letters will arrive and I'll have one grand orgy of devouring your beautifully written expressions of love and devotion. We should have learned by this time to expect these painful lapses in mail delivery and not fall into the dreadful habit of imagining all sorts of dire things. There is little to report except that I'm quite well and am daily becoming more a part of the intricate system which governs an Army dental clinic, or any clinic for that matter. It's fun, though, and in moments of leisure I sit back and mentally kick around such whoppers as mandible edentulous, maxillae edentulous, periodontoclasia, and my two favorite terms, abscess parietal and abscess periapical. Two weeks ago these terms had me hanging on the ropes. The abbreviations for these and the formulae for some of the drugs were "classic Greek" to me. But not so anymore. I told you I tried prophylaxis with some success and next I'm going to take a try at dental x-ray, with the hope of learning to read them as well. Thus, the business of learning lessens the daily anxieties and chases the devils of despair and loneliness. If I were doing some dull, routine job I would be psycho by now.

The war news is good, very good. Perhaps the end draws near. The boys who passed before my eyes, borne on litters to various parts of the hospital, are cheerful no matter how serious are their wounds. This is what gets me. This is what tears at my heart. "I'm lucky, I'm lucky, I'm lucky," they keep saying. Each one thinks that he is lucky. How then do we dare to complain to feel that we are not lucky? Oh, My Darling, how merciful and gracious is our God you shall know one day. The sadness of parting with dear friends is upon us again. I can't tell you what a feeling of suffocation seizes one on seeing a buddy move on to more hazardous assignments. The War Department has decreed that those younger than I take their places in the ranks of the fighting men. I am suddenly an old man, but I thank the Almighty God that I can spare you this added burden. My job is here. I do it to the best of my ability. Angel, I tell you this because it is an oath that I have taken. Therefore, I trust that you will read no hidden meaning into it. Undoubtedly, you have or will read about this plan to find eligible men in the rear echelon outfits, and lest you misunderstand my part in this, I tell you the facts. I am well over the age limit and my inclination towards arthritis is a matter of record. So put it out of your mind. To give you even greater assurance, I wasn't even examined. I can get this censored tonight if I hurry, so I say adieu, My Love.

Kiss the cherub. Love to all, Daddy

March 3, 1945 – Somewhere in Belgium
My Darling:

Our social engagements are becoming so pressing that I must beg your indulgence this time if this is short. We have a show scheduled for seven o'clock. It is now six and one has to move fast to get a seat at the GI entertainments. Your happy letters of February 15 and February 20 reached me this afternoon. I'm delighted that a package is on the way. Oh how I want that hairbrush! But Sweetheart, you say you have dispatched more lemons. Angel, I haven't received the first ones yet. I know. The post man is waiting until it gets hot so I can use them for cold lemonade instead of hot tea for the cold weather. I also received a V-Mail from Dave [brother in the service]. He writes with a warm pen and expresses himself eloquently. His reaction to the human wreckage he sees on his photographic assignments is exactly like mine. I, too, wonder how these men can smile as they roll in on their litters. I find myself following each one until he is out of sight. I visit the wards frequently and speak a word here and there. They are grateful for the little attention, but they do not feel sorry for themselves. This is the miracle and the great hope for the future. They will be made well again and as whole as science can contrive to duplicate nature.

Darling, you ask why I don't venture a guess on the end of the war. This whole business has become too personal at this stage. We feel deeply this painful separation and the best way to endure it is to refrain from guesses and predictions which invariably prove ridiculous. That the day will come, we are certain. To say that it will end tomorrow or next week, or even next month is to set oneself above all others since such thinking springs from a selfish urge to be rid of the whole thing. A victory achieved through such weakness on the part of some can lead only to future trouble.

I agree it is no great shakes being only a "Mrs. PFC" but perhaps I can remedy this soon. It would please me no end to become Mr. Lesner again, but until then, I would enjoy sewing on a few stripes. You see, Angel, this thing gets into one to some extent. You can't help it. Knowing you are stuck with the deal, you play as shrewdly as possible. No one enjoys being the lowliest of mortals. The PFC hardly changes this, but it's a promise of something better. Well, you got quite a letter after all.

Love to all. Kiss the cherub. To you my heart, Daddy

March 7, 1945 – Somewhere in Belgium
My Darling:

There must be another PFC Samuel Lesner in Belgium, because I did not broadcast last Friday. Even if I had been so fortunate I would have spoken just two words, "Hello Angel," and then there would have been a long and eloquent silence, for no guy who loves his wife as I do you could possibly find the voice to say so over the radio.

Your letter of the 24th, which relates the startling news that I was to broadcast, reached me today, a day later than usual because a well-meaning friend carried it in his pocket for a day since I was not present to collect my own mail yesterday. Where was I? Shopping, Angel, and I returned with a treasure that will fill our future home with beauty no matter in what corner you place it. You remember the incident of the bronze figure I nearly bought on Maxwell Street one Sunday morning? I was heartbroken after being foolish enough to let a treasure get away from me. Yesterday Max Neiburg and I were having a hilarious time window shopping in a driving rain. Max was looking for some ashtrays similar to what I bought. We staggered into a fairly prosperous-looking house-furnishing store. Displayed on cabinets, etc. were various pieces of pottery. I always look in the out-of-the-way corners, and this time I felt my pulse beat step up. You know how I admire the colors of Cezanne, Monet, Manet. There it was. The rare coloring of these geniuses caught in the delicate curves of a pitcher-shaped vase. "Vase" is such an inadequate word, and I detest the fancy pronunciation "vahz." Well, I've told you what I bought, and I shan't be disappointed if you query, "but Daddy, what the devil are we going to do with all the "vahzes" we have already?" All I can say is, "wait until you see this one." I shall pack it this week and put it in the mail.

Now for the radio broadcasts again. I read the letter to some sundry members of the detachment, and some came up with some wild conjectures, to wit, I'm even the dupe and victim of a Nazi propaganda broadcast. That will give you some idea of how confused I am about the report you heard from my father, who heard it from a lady who heard it on her radio while vacuuming the carpet, no doubt. My own wild guess (and hope) was that possibly one of my letters, which you claim have such literary value, found its way to some enterprising radio program. I await the results of your research in this matter with great interest. Darling, I hope the thing wasn't a complete "washout" for your sake because your letter imparted all of your great excitement and anticipation. You did some fast thinking in checking this business with the radio editors before getting all steamed up about it. If there was any truth to the lady's assertion, there is a record of the announcement somewhere, as such an announcement would be carefully checked. International broadcasts, if that is what it was to be, don't come off casually in wartime. Just in case the thing was a misunderstanding, you won't be entirely disappointed, for in the next couple of weeks you will receive my voice as I promised. It's not a good recording for it's full of breathless pauses, but I can't be glib of tongue where you are concerned. I had my picture taken yesterday and within two weeks I shall have them. I hope I'm afraid they won't be good for I get so stiff in camera range, but I'll send them regardless so you can see the two campaign stars pinned on my chest. Of course, the whole outfit is sporting the same award, but I feel that mine are something special, for who among them dripped more sweat into the concrete than I?

Your letter of February 18 is at hand, too. It came today. Well, it has been determined at last that I am a dental assistant, which makes my prime duty that of assisting a dental officer rather than that of taking orders from the incumbent receptionist who outranks me and is something of a pill. Since I am the only PFC in the clinic I shall have to abide with the rank for a time, but I daresay time will set things right again. In other words, the compassion, the self-effacement that governed my life in the wards has no place in a dental clinic apparently, and I have no choice but to take my cue accordingly. On the surface all is calm and "beautiful" and so I will accept this "skin deep" gentility and let it go at that. I have a plan that will keep me too busy to be concerned with the politics.

Sweetheart, I am writing under a barrage of verbal diarrhea that threatens to get ankle deep any moment, so I flee to choir practice this very moment, but not until I say I love you. Kiss the cherub. How about a picture of her with the new hairdo? Goodnight, Angel. More tomorrow.

Daddy

March 8, 1945 – Somewhere in Belgium
My Darling:

This must be some diabolical game the mailman is playing on us. Today I got your letter of February 27 in which you tell me that your letter of the 26th is a pip since it was a reply to seven of my letters. Well, where the devil is the letter of the 26th? My Sweetheart, your disappointment must have been enormous in the radio program that did not come off. It's the damnedest thing I ever heard. There are no broadcasts from here as far as anybody knows. I only hope that you got the thing straight before that mythical Friday night broadcast. I can only hope that for your sake it was a hoax, but for the life of me I can't figure out the thing. It might have been possible had I figured in a certain incident during the Bulge, but I wasn't here for the incident so I wouldn't be eligible for a radio interview on that score. Well, I must put it out of my mind until I hear from you about the radio program that I didn't appear on.

I had a trying day as assistant to the chief of the prosthetics department. This, I gather, is to be my permanent assignment. For the first time I experienced displeasure in learning, not because I don't like to work, but because personality factors make this department a hodgepodge of unresolved statistics. I guess I don't have the bookkeeper's mind, and heaven knows that absolutely nothing happens in the army without its prelude of involved bookkeeping. I saw red today when my superior, Corporal Schmuck, tried to explain how he "picks them up and drops them." He was talking about new patients, I believe, but it all sounded like caprice rather than common sense. I'm sure I'm wrong, but if I don't get the hang of it in a week I'll do something drastic, such as going back to the wards, which I love.

Well, Honey, I guess this sounds like a gripe letter, but I don't mean it that way. I'm awfully lonely for you and the cherub. We are to have a dance Saturday night, and maybe just seeing some femininity might brighten me up. You are my best gal, though, for all time. Just to be sociable I asked a patient today where he was from. "From Chicago," replied Herzl Halperin. "What part of the city?" "Madison and St. Louis," said Halperin. "You know that little grocery store on the corner of Madison and St. Louis?" "Sure, I used to buy rolls and butter and lox, etc. in that store. That was special butter and the owner used to order it special for us. Boy that was good butter." "Do you mean Daisy Brand butter, Halperin?" "Yeah, that's it!" "That's my father's store, Halperin!" "No kidding! Gee, what a small world!"

Goodnight, My Beloved. Kiss the cherub. Love to the folks. Daddy

March 10, 1945
My Darling:
By this time, you have gathered that your letter of February 28 plus that of February 11 plus that wonderful box of cookies, can of anchovy paste, and lemons arrived today. I tried to read your letter of February 12 to Max, but I choked up and turned away with tear-filled eyes. Laddie was just another guy, a quiet, sickly kid who will really know he's been through hell if he survives. He left the hospital a day or two sooner than I and returned to the Replacement Depot to

await assignment to the Infantry. I haven't heard from him and don't expect to, but when he told me his mother had a heart ailment I knew that I had to tell you to try to relieve her worry. I hope she has had a letter from her boy. We aren't suffering, Angel. We get tough, rough, boisterous. We can let off steam. We get over our body aches, but the heartaches we have, because they are the heartaches of our wives and mothers, are the real pains of war. Facing danger in itself is not too bad. It's the consciousness of the sorrow it might bring to others that withers a man's soul and courage.

I'm glad the mailman has redeemed himself. You also have proof of my constancy in the total number of letters which line up chronologically. As the weather brightens, Angel, I may pass up an occasional letter to enjoy the beauty of the evening, but my joy in writing to you is too real for me to miss more than an occasional letter. I must get shined up now for tonight's party, so I bid you goodnight. Kiss the cookie. In a few weeks you shall have a portrait of me. Also, the "vahz" and other small things will be mailed possibly tomorrow. I still need some suitable packing.

Love to all. To you all my sacred love, Daddy

March 11, 1945 – Somewhere in Belgium
My Darling:

A Sunday of feeling beaucoup tired from last night's indulgences leaves me without inspiration for tonight's letter. Since we don't have regular appointment patients on Sunday, and since there were only a few minor "emergencies," we all are finding time heavy on our hands. I certainly gave my feet a workout last night. Dancing with some of the Belgiques becomes hard labor, and the few who are light of foot enough to jitterbug were mobbed by the young squirts in the outfit. It wears me out just to watch them. You have never seen more uninhibited dancers than a bunch of fun-hungry GIs. They dance with a frenzy that's akin to madness. The band was good, the cement floor sticky and suffocatingly dusty, the mob enormous, the chicken sandwiches, ice cream, and coffee, wonderful. It was 12:30 before we stumbled back to barracks. Fortunately, we can sleep later on Sunday morning, but at that I was on my way by 7:15 a.m. Tonight I shall read for an hour or so (I have the Omnibook condensation of *Caesar and Christ*) [by Will Durant] and then call it a day. The week ahead promises to be a pip if the appointment book is any indication of what lies ahead. While the news is very good, we go easy on predictions. When for hours on end you hear the bombers roaring overhead and still there is no end, you come to the grim realization that it takes much more than these gigantic raids to write the finis to this stark chapter in history. Despite this we are now enjoying the fruits of our toil in this forsaken cow pasture. The whole project has taken on a neatness and comfort that is most satisfactory. Must close now, My Love.

Kiss the cherub. Love to the folks. Your Daddy

March 13, 1945
My Darling:

A very dull movie robbed me of a precious two hours tonight, but, ever hopeful, I continue to go in the hope of catching a memorable film about which to enthuse in my letter.

The day was so glorious—warm and very sunny—and all morning I looked forward to my afternoon off. Well, it didn't come about, but for a good reason. Here's the present setup. I have been chosen to assist the new chief of the dental service here. He's a small human dynamo and I have to push to keep up. But I'm holding my own. It's hard to tell yet whether I'll be a "favored one or a hounded one," but I am trying hard to fulfill expectations. We have a private office and we do all the surveys and examinations and refer the cases to the proper departments. He also does some difficult extractions and I've been "baptized" properly already. Our first day together, yesterday, he let me tap the chisel with a lead-weighted hammer as he excavated a root from a particularly tough spot behind a fixed bridge. I turned cold and green for a few moments but recovered myself and am happy to report that I can take it. It was a rough beginning, but I think I was secretly pleased because he chose me as the least experienced of the clinic personnel and his aim is to teach me his way.

The book work involved is terrific but today, the second day, things went smoothly and before the week is out this thing should be going like a well-oiled machine. One has to be very fast to carry out all the necessary movements, and once in a while my hands cross and I have moments like Zazu Pitts, my hands fluttering in despair and frustration.

About the afternoon off: Well, this morning the boss decided to do some general surveying in a number of the wards and he asked me to accompany him. Thus, the afternoon off went out the window. I don't mind, however. I want very much to succeed in this thing and begin to feel that I have some worth.

I have been so busy these past few weeks that I even forgot to mail the package which is securely wrapped and censored. It goes out in the morning, though, I promise. No mail today, and I'm afraid that what we will get for the next few weeks will be some pre-Xmas stuff that finally reached the continent, according to a story in *Stars and Stripes*. I imagine they'll try to clear this before the new stuff. I suspect that some of the Xmas mail I have never received will turn up now. "C'est la guerre!" as they say. The boys are brewing some tea in the next office. I just sent in a lemon and now I'll go collect a mug of tea.

Love to all. Kiss the cherub. My Darling, I am well, thankful that my lot is not a miserable one and hopeful that the day I take you in my arms again is not too far off.

Yours, Daddy

Belgium: Dental Clinic

March 14, 1945 – Somewhere in Belgium
My Darling:

Guess what the mailman brought me today: your sweet letters of DECEMBER 7–8 and other long-awaited mail. *Stars and Stripes* reported that the unlucky ship which tried to bring this mail to us three months ago finally made the crossing. I don't know what I'll do with so much stuff. I guess we'll pool our stuff and have a party, as has been our custom of late. There is also the morning and afternoon coffee which is served to the clinic personnel at behest of the new boss, and an extra box of goodies disappears quickly in the course of a day.

Another terrific day has come to a close. The weather is magnificent. Even the field jacket felt uncomfortable today. The nights and the mornings are clear and cold, though, and one steps lively once out of the fart sack.

So much has happened since your Dec. 7–8 letters were written that I won't attempt to answer them in kind. Our angel baby is three months older, the war is three months closer to the end, and I'm three months lonelier—yet closer to you.

You have asked me repeatedly to enlighten you on what we think about the war and our chances of getting home soon. Well, Angel, only a sap would make predictions, but if this weather keeps up, there will be no holding back our land and air forces from sweeping over all Germany. That is a certainty. For several days now truckloads of liberated victims of the Nazi monsters have been speeding down the highway. I can't describe just what happens to one as these trucks whirl by and the scarred, dirty, weary faces break into spasms of joy and tears as they shout greetings to us. It hurts inside of you. More concretely, though, is the fact that our unit has become famous on the continent. I think I may quote the C.O., who flatly stated that our record will go far in getting us home sooner than might be expected when this business is over. True, some of us feel pretty useless as individuals, but as a unit we have established a brilliant record.

Enough for now, Angel. Have a few personal tasks to carry out tonight.
Love to the cherub and the folks. Your Daddy.
P.S. The "vahz" was mailed this morning.

March 17, 1945 – Somewhere in Belgium
My Darling:

With some misgivings, I enclose the newest photo of myself. I do look remarkably well, and that's the thing I want to convey to you. Don't show it to anyone who knows about the rules of wearing decorations. I received my campaign ribbon the day I took the photo and in ignorance of the rules, I put the ribbons on in the wrong order. If you look sharply you will make out the two little stars on the first ribbon. They are for the Battle of France and the

Germany–Belgium fracas. Just how we fit into any battle awards is beyond me, but we were around so we are entitled to wear the ribbon. Ho, hum, these campaigns are such a bore!

Angel, my social program is a heavy one this week and in a moment I'll be off for a party, so I must beg off. No mail from you for almost a week. I try not to think of the wrong things, but I am anxious. Love to all. Kiss the Cookie. I wish I could be there in person for our fourth [anniversary, April 6], but a bad picture will have to suffice this time.

Love, Daddy

March 18, 1945 – Somewhere in Belgium
My Darling:

I'm a sad sack today. Too much party and not enough restful sleep has left me weary, stiff-necked, and confused. Actually, it was a very simple party and I shouldn't be so dragged out, but in this country one walks to one's social engagements and our friend and hostess, Gabrielle, lives way out in the hinterlands. It took an hour of fast walking to get there. Since I was C.Q. [Charge of Quarters] the night before and had to sleep in the hospital on a cot, I was already short on rest, but to top it off, today we started our new system of time off, so last night I again drew the canvas cot, and tonight again, after an all-day session of policing the dental clinic. The only nice part about it is that for the next eight Sundays I'll be as free as a lark, and since the day is not too pleasant, I don't mind getting my Sunday duty now.

The party was fun. Max, who is my constant companion, wasn't asked to the party since it was plainly a department affair. This morning I asked Gabrielle if next time I could bring my good friend. "Gaby, mon ami Max, good boy. Next time he come to party, yes?" "Oui, oui, Sam. Excuse me, bad no ask friend, excuse, yes?" They are all delightful people and beg us to visit them often.

You must believe, Sweetheart, that we are experiencing no hardships at the present. One gets accustomed to army routine and I find that even when it's possible, I rarely sleep beyond 7 a.m. We have movies more frequently than it is

Belgium: Dental Clinic

convenient to attend; we have USO shows, and there is always the nightly temptation to go to town, even though we have exhausted the possibilities of entertainment there. Max and I, of course, have our own music lessons, and we get plenty of exercise going and returning.

I sing Wednesday night in chapel, and I am also hard at work on the Easter music. I hope the occasion will be a happier one than was the Xmas Eve for which I studied and vocalized so hard. I'll always regret that the Xmas Program was blitzed. The stirring solo suited me to a tee and I was so excited in anticipation of singing to a jam-packed chapel. Well, maybe the Easter program will compensate somewhat for that. The record of the Xmas hymn which I was to sing doesn't do justice to it at all. We have some splendid voices in our group.

Angel, for an anniversary present, I can only give you my unmeasured love and assurance that I am well. If the package arrives in time you will have my "voice" and a bit of costume jewelry for the occasion. The bracelet isn't much but someday I'll replace it with a diamond one.

I must close now, Sweetheart. To supper and then to the showers before people start shunning me. As I thought, the current mail is being held up somewhere and I'm as nervous as a cat since nothing came all week. Kiss the angel child. I have a private office and desk and on the desk in a handsomely framed picture of the cherub. How about a picture of you with the baby? That would be the best present.

Love, Daddy

March 21, 1945
My Darling:

I have a long and frightfully complicated report staring me in the face, but I also have a painful conscience to live with so I hasten to remove the source of the latter before turning to the report. I haven't written you for two days and I'm troubled indeed. My reason, Pleasure, the kind of pleasure, however, which you would approve, and since I am now under a considerable strain, the relaxation is of particular "therapeutic value." I love my new job. It's terrific, but the energy expended is also terrific. I have literally become the hub of the dental clinic through the system installed by the chief, for whom I work personally. Between the dental surgery, which goes on most of the day and every day, and the numerous and involved reports which must be filled out for each patient, I keep far busier than the proverbial one-armed paper hanger with the seven-year itch. But there is compensation. You may recall that in an earlier letter I expressed some doubt about my part in the clinic and what I expected from sundry personalities around here. That's all over with now. I take orders from the chief and they take orders from me. The surgery room is my private domain and what's more, I shut the door when we are working. Enough said. The chief is a Chicagoan and a brilliant though exacting oral surgeon. I think in time he will be my friend.

Now for my diversions which kept me from writing. First of all, the weather has been magnificent. The long walks to and from the vocal teacher are tiring but beneficial. The singing goes very well. The professor, frankly, was astonished the other day when he took me to a high B-flat in full and bell-like tonality. I was surprised too. If only I could work every day at this! How I'd enjoy singing for your leisure someday. Now, one night was spent viewing a wonderful movie, *Hollywood Canteen*. Have you seen it? Perhaps it's only for GIs to appreciate. It's an odd picture, full of the obvious sentimentality, hope, despair, loneliness that only a soldier far from home can respond to. I howled and I also sobbed uncontrollably for a few moments. The longing to see you and the baby overwhelmed me as the scene of the "Going Home" flashed on the screen. Beyond that, though, there are some wonderful musical and artistic moments. Szegetti, Carmen Cavellero, Rosario and Antonio, and many more.

Last night Max and I were invited to a home that was a rare treat. The entire family (six sisters), the father and the husbands of two sisters gave us an evening of excellent music. Such talent! We drank wonderful wine, ate a delicacy that melted in the mouth, and all sang anything we could think of including a good portion of the standard operatic repertoire. We got home late! Tonight I sing in chapel, then I return to struggle with the report, so again I'll have to be satisfied with about five hours of sleep. I feel grand, though.

Your love letter of March 5th came yesterday. The one with the money order hasn't reached me yet, but I'm not hard-pressed, so don't worry. I pray that you get the package for our anniversary. It isn't much, but I hope you'll enjoy its contents. Perhaps tomorrow the mail will come through. Nothing today for any of us so we are all miserable together. Good night. X for the cherub.

Love, Daddy

March 23, 1945 – Somewhere in Belgium
My Beloved:

It is not yet 7 a.m. but if I'm going to get a letter written at all, it's now. The days have become so full of activity there is literally no time to move one's bowels. All these urgencies, therefore, are performed before 8:30. I must shave, shine the shoes, clean up the surgery room, get the records in order, and a dozen more detailed things in an hour or so. At the end of the day I'm usually stuck with the instrument sterilization, a pile of hastily scribbled notes and records, and a loyal but impatient Max waiting for me to go to chow before the mess sergeant shuts the door. I'm not complaining, Angel. I love this and thrive on such activity. But you are the one to suffer since a daily letter has become almost an impossibility. Sunday, however, is a gloriously free day, and I'll pour out my heart and mind to you, my only love. Each day, I thank the Lord for watching over my little family. Love to all. I may not write tonight. I have a social engagement with some musical people.

Love, Daddy

Belgium: Dental Clinic

March 25, 1945, 9:30 a.m. – Somewhere in Belgium
My Darling:

I'm a no-good, low-down bum, totally unworthy of so good a wife and angelic child. Seven wonderful, magnificent letters I got from you Friday night, and instead of sitting down and writing a worthy answer, I let Friday and then Saturday nights go by without taking pen in hand, and from all indications, there will be no letter for you tonight. The reason: our social activities have become so time devouring that there is literally no chance to take off the necessary hour or two for letter writing. I know this, though, that after today, I'll stick to my resolve to pass up all recreational events except those of a real value. For instance, a French film, *The Blue Danube*, was advertised for showing in the local theater. It was necessary to go early. We went thinking it would be the musical version. About 9:30 p.m. the gypsy cast were still raving about something, but hadn't gotten around to playing any Strauss music. They did play "Poet and Peasant Overture," which had absolutely nothing to do with the story. At 9:30 there was a much-needed intermission, so we escaped, returned to the hospital, had some sandwiches, beer, and cake, and then we bribed the shower room keeper to let us in. Oh, how I needed that bath! I scrubbed and scoured and thus to bed about 11 p.m. Friday night there was another gathering of the clinic personnel, which was excessive in that it robbed me of my evening with you.

One picture of that gathering has stuck in my mind. A great etcher could have caught a wonderful subject for his etching pan. There we were, about eight GIs and a half-dozen girls gathered around Gabrielle's table. The electric power was on the fritz and the darkness descended upon us, the table of food waiting to be eaten up. The only dim light that held off total darkness was dribbling through the window at which I sat, devouring your letters with eyes that could barely make out the words. It was the first chance I had to read them and I could wait no longer. Here are the dates: March 12, 5, 4, 2, and 1, and February 23 and 26—a whole book which I shall read over again and again in chronological order.

This being my day off, I promised Max I'd go gallivanting with him. It's now 10:30 and if we don't start soon we won't get anywhere. The weather is threatening after a week of the most extraordinary warmth and sunshine. Just my luck. How I want to sit in the sun for a few hours. Well, better luck next Sunday. I'll try to write again tonight, Love, and answer all letters. Letters from Mayme, Roy, and the folks also came with yours. The job is wonderful, but very hectic. I'm becoming a brute, too. I watch the teeth being torn out of human heads with nary a tremor. The bloodier the better. Guess I'll go to medical school and get this out of my system.

Love to all. Kiss the angel puss. Love, Daddy

March 27, 1945 – Somewhere in Belgium
My Darling:

It's quiet now. The gang's gone home, and I'm alone to look after the clinic. Here's the setup. The C.Q. sets up a cot in any of several rooms he likes best and makes that his bedroom for the night. It's unique in that for the night one has magnificent privacy. My favorite room is the surgery in which I work. It's full of glistening equipment, all of which is fast becoming a part of me. I have a desk, as I've told you. There's also a very comfortable easy chair. It also allows one an extra hour of sleep since the men don't start drifting in until 7 a.m., whereas in the barracks, one gets up at 5:30.

Our area is fast becoming a showplace. The Heinies are restoring some of the natural beauty of the earth they were so bent on destroying forever. I wish you could see this place. It's really an eyeful. Someday I'll be able to send or bring home some pictures of it. You'll have a hard time believing that I'm showing you pictures of "our place." They are even talking about getting us dressed up like garrison soldiers again. The new style waistline jacket is quite the Pip-Pip, and with all the ribbons and things on it, one looks very dashing. We might as well look sharp, and besides, one will have to watch the hip spread, which isn't a bad idea. For all our griping, Army chow definitely is fattening, and how. You should see some of the "sterns" on some of the once-slim GIs. Believe it or not, I have one strict rule in eating. When there are potatoes, I pass up the bread. Never the twain shall meet in my stomach. I know that I'm holding my own because my much-washed trousers button readily and don't bind. The nightly walks of the past few weeks have helped too.

Now it's very late, Angel, and tomorrow we have a full day, exclusive of the evening's [Passover] seder. So good night, My Love. Kiss the cherub.

Love to all, Daddy

March 27, 1945 Somewhere in Belgium
My Darling:

Two more of your precious letters, March 10, 14, have been added to the stack now piled neatly on my desk awaiting a rereading and a worthy reply. I suppose I should be happy that the days do fly by with exhausting speed since there is no part of any day in this life alone that I would wish to arrest for even a moment, yet I can't help wishing that there might be a few moments during the day for dreaming of one's family. This has become an unbelievable "wartime production" dental factory, and to pause for a moment is to screw up the whole works. One escapes at the end of the day with a mad rush. We plunge into the glorious moonlit nights and are reluctant to return for writing or even sleeping. Max and I have walked miles over the countryside almost every night. It is beautiful. I wish you could see it, feel it with me. Here is a peace and calm that is poignant, inarticulate because of its proximity to mass murder.

Our Sunday off, however, was a memorable day. We went to a city an easy distance from our post and had ourselves a day of laughter and pleasure, such as would sound fantastic to anyone but you who understand so well what pleasure I get from Nature itself. The Meuse River was high and swift so we rented kayaks and had an hour of boyish fun paddling around. Then we sat at a small table on the right bank and drank delicious beer and told each other of home and family. The day was warm, the setting European and definitely beautiful. Out of the destruction had risen a calm and ease to bind the wounds of war. This once lovely city we shall visit together some day, perhaps.

Angel, I am C.Q. tonight again and shall take advantage of the enforced rest to write more about what goes on now. Also I must catch up on a dozen letters. Tomorrow night all the Jewish men will attend a seder in a nearby city. My heart shall beat faster with the love, the longing, the desire I feel for you.

Love to all. Daddy

[Editors' note: In the book *GI Jews*, Deborah Dash Moore quotes one soldier who recalls a GI seder at Passover, 1945.]

> In a clearing in the woods in Germany where the 346th Infantry "had been shunted" temporarily... [he] held a makeshift seder in the morning, two days late. "There were no chairs, benches or tables." Some fifty Jewish GIs "sat on the ground" and formed "a double circle" with [him] in the middle, reading from the lone Haggadah he had brought from the States, "like a tribal story teller." The menu was limited to two hundred pounds of British matzo and some "liberated" wine. The assembled GIs had paused, briefly, in their pursuit of "the soldiers of this latest most malevolent Pharoah." (pp. 141–43)

March 28, 1945 – Somewhere in Belgium
My Darling:
    No letters from you today, but I won't fret since I have something to write about. First, there was the wonderful GI seder last night at which more than five hundred officers and E.M.s sat down at the flower-decked, candle-lit tables to hear the story of Passover, interpret the symbols, and dine sumptuously. It was the most extraordinary affair in that the Army went to great lengths to make it a real seder. The wine, the soup with knaidelach [matzo balls], the chopped liver appetizer, the chicken, the matzos, the tea, all were manna from heaven. It wasn't just soup. It was traditional Jewish soup with all the marvelous aroma and flavor we have known since infancy. The meal was prepared by special cooks and served rapidly by many women who were hired for the event. Men came from many sections to observe the Passover, and indeed it was an inspiring and beautiful scene. Acknowledgments of the day and its meaning, particularly in this day of human bondage and persecution of minorities, were read from all the commanding generals in the ETO. Truly, it was our evening to be proud of our contribution.

Now of a more personal nature. I have been working very hard, but I believe it has been to good advantage. Today, after a trying day, the major said, "Lesner, you and I will go in strictly for surgery starting tomorrow. We'll turn over all the examinations to blank blank." This, of course, gives me real prestige and I dare say a little easier going. I am genuinely interested in the surgery, but I was quite willing to do whatever I was told. I am amused by the major's attempts to make my job easier on one hand while on the other, he gets us involved in a surgical case that keeps us going way beyond suppertime. Tonight, after finishing a very tough case, we had to go foraging in the various hospital kitchens for chow. It was fun in a way. For the immediate future, at least, I have given up hope of catching up on correspondence, so, Darling, be my ambassador of goodwill with various and sundry family members and friends.

Tonight, I got engrossed in the writing of a Survey and Treatment Project for *mon ami* Max. It started when I suggested that he could play an important part in the alleviation of foot troubles on a wider basis than he has been permitted to so far. He is a talented fellow with the temperament conducive to eminent success in the Army, as well as civilian practice. We have many laughs together, and likewise are unashamed to show a tear-dimmed eye to each other upon occasion. It's good to have such a staunch, sensitive friend in this maelstrom of de-civilized humanity, made gross by cheap exhibitionism. Yep, "c'est la guerre."

Love to all. Kiss the cookie for me. To you, My Beloved, your Daddy

March 30, 1945 – Somewhere in Belgium
My Darling:

My luck was good today, and how I needed it to lift my chin off the terrazzo floor, which makes our clinic such a lovely place. I told you in an earlier letter that I was now the hub of the clinic wheel. Well, a couple of the guys are trying to sabotage the wheel and today the hub took a beating. But they haven't got my number. I'll get this thing well greased despite them. Today brought me March letters for the 13th, 16th, 17th, 19th and all had some delightful bits about Love Lettuce. Oh what a happiness fills me as I read these wonderful things.

I'm sorry there are such lapses again in letters to you. I haven't been negligent to such an extent, although I shamefully admit that we were a little "drunk" with our new liberty and freedom in the time off granted us, and consequently we pursue pleasure at the expense of our daily mail output. I'm nice and tired now of gallivanting about and expect to resume my old routine of sobriety and sufficient sleep. Being in excellent health I give little thought to weariness. I promised myself a short walk and an early to bed for tomorrow promises to be a lulu. Love to all. Request: a couple of T-shirts (cotton) if you can get them, size 36. I need them badly. I'm praying you get my gift box in time for our fourth [anniversary April 6].

Kiss the cookie. Love to the folks. Your Daddy

PART 2:
THE CHANGING TIDE OF WAR—WAITING FOR THE END

April 1, 1945
My Angel:

Was I ever delighted with the mailman yesterday! Imagine, a letter dated the 22nd, which actually was postmarked the 23rd, and I had the joy of reading it on the 31st. Yours of the 20th also arrived, and to top it off, I enjoyed the excitement of opening a package from you. The weather has been superb, but today, Easter Sunday, and our day off (Max's and mine) was a stinker. A howling wind and rain greeted us this morning as we awoke ready to "parti." So we turned over and slept through breakfast. We got up just in time to eat a chicken dinner. That for me is a horrible experience. I'm such a slave of the morning canteen cupful of coffee that the chicken and potatoes tasted like straw without this preliminary "gastronomic" treat.

Yesterday was a typical one for me. The activity in the clinic these days is terrific. At a quarter of five, anticipating escape from the nut house, we tackled what seemed to be a simple extraction of an R-12, which is not a difficult one ordinarily. Well, blow me down if the damn thing didn't shatter and produce a major operation for us. Thus, wilted, we prepared to depart, only to be stopped by an emergency jaw fracture, which had become infected. Have you ever smelled one of these things? Wow! Supper, consequently, was out of the question. But about 9:30 p.m. Max and I got some bread and butter and had ourselves some elegant anchovy and caviar sandwiches. That was good timing on the package. The caviar is excellent. Get yourself some of the same brand. It's the best I've had for years in that it is not too salty and happily not fishy. We'll finish it tonight, after the movies.

My major—again I'm involved with a major—tells me he is pleased with the way I'm carrying out my job, and he impressed upon me the responsibility he has placed in my hands. So you see, maybe you won't have to wait a year to become Mrs. T5. It doesn't make a lot of difference to me personally, but as long as it means something in the Army, I'll be quite willing to accept the promotion. It won't happen to me in the Army, but I think we'll manage financially, and our life together will be enriched by my experiences here. I must close, Angel, as suppertime draws near, and we must "rush" to the movies directly after chow in order for "shrimpy" me to get a seat from which I can see.

Love to all. Please ask them to write me beaucoup letters. Kiss our wonderful child. Are you planning to cut her hair in bangs, that is, if she ever sprouts enough hair? I hope so. And please, please, another picture of the angel soon.

To you My Beloved, Daddy

April 2, 1945 – Somewhere in Belgium

My darling: true to form, the mail yesterday produced your letter of the 21st, the day after I got yours of the 22nd. We went on daylight savings time last night and so lost a precious hour of sleep. The result, I can hardly keep my eyes open now, and I still have at least a short one to write to the folks. So, Doll Face, forgive me. The job goes well and hectic as usual. More tomorrow. Keep the chin up. What we shall be denied on our fourth anniversary **we shall be sharing still on our 40th,** I pray God.

Love to all. Kiss the cherub. Daddy

[Editors' note: The 40th anniversary took place on March 28, 1981, at the home of second daughter, Judy Lesner Holstein and her husband, Dr. Robert Holstein, co-hosted by Roberta ("Love Lettuce") and Charles Bernstein. The then grandchildren of Sam and Esther are in foreground, l. to r: Debbie Holstein, Lou and Eddie Bernstein, Aaron Holstein.]

Belgium: Dental Clinic

April 4, 1945 – Somewhere in Belgium
My Darling:

I fear you must think something is amiss in view of my suddenly infrequent letters. I admit that my letter-a-day habit has been shot to hell, and the only excuse I can offer is that I'm very busy. I beg you to be patient for the next week or two inasmuch as I anticipate very busy days and evenings ahead. The clinic, as I have already told you, is under the direction of a new chief whose altruism on behalf of patients can't be questioned. He has reached out far in several new directions, and I am heartily in accord with his plan to save the teeth and health of as many soldiers as it is possible to do. Our daily surveys of incoming patients have revealed some sadly neglected mouths which would continue to be neglected if it wasn't for the major's efforts to get them into the clinic and orally cleaned up a bit. The work, however, is staggering and at the end of the day I am confronted with a pile of records, notes, charts, etc. Slowly, painfully, I have worked out a system which has proven very flexible and satisfactory. It was my idea to keep a master list of all the patients, and divisional lists which break down the master list into various classifications. These classified lists are the guides to the constantly shifting patient population, and each day they are brought up to date so that we can call in the surveyed patients as we need them. It is my duty to juggle all these lists from day to day, besides tending to the surgery office routine, which in itself is a double-duty job. Frankly, Angel, I love it. I thrive on the excitement. I bubble and laugh all day long and refuse to be overwhelmed by it. I make it a point to know the patients and whenever I meet them outside of the clinic they hail me. Most of them address me as "Sir" which is embarrassing. The major, I believe, likes me personally and likes my approach to the job. Courtesy, of course, pays dividends, and I'm courtesy personified. The white gown, of course, dignifies and at the same time glamorizes me. A signal corps photographer took some pictures of me in gown, several weeks ago, but the stinker never sent them as he promised, and by now I think he is in Germany.

An amusing incident occurred today. We were informed that our C.O., a swell guy, was to make an inspection. Naturally, we all buzzed around, dusting here, picking up there, concealing numerous items in drawers, under drawers etc. Things looked pretty good by the time he reached our department. I received him, being the first one he approached, gave him a smart salute and reported for the department and turned him over to the major, who makes the formal inspection with the C.O. They looked in several of the rooms and finally entered the gold technician's laboratory, which is also our meeting room, coffee room, dressing room, and, if one chooses, the C.Q. sleeping room! We examined the scene of action later, but first we had to listen to an excited gold technician spend his ire on our collective heads. It appears the C.O. spotted something on a cabinet and asked, "What is that, Sergeant?" "That, Sir, is baloney," replied the gold technician sergeant, facing the issue squarely, though bitterly. And baloney it was, left there by one of the lab men who fortified himself with baloney sandwiches the night before. Angel, I think you have read enough about GI life to appreciate just what it means to have four thick slices of baloney prominently displayed during an inspection of quarters. It's HORRIBLE, that's what it is. The major was good-natured about it and let it pass. Anyone else would have chewed our hearts out about such a thing. We are becoming very GI again. Once, muddy shoes were an honorable mark of toil in the cow pasture. Today, you get "extra labor" for having dusty shoes under your bunk. Yesterday, for instance, I was hailed into the detention office on an unspecified charge. I quickly cleared myself, though, for the offending shoes belonged to the guy in the lower bunk. The mental anguish, however, before I cleared myself was awful. There is a Gestapo atmosphere about the detention office that strikes terror in the hearts of all of us.

Darling, I must get to my last revising task and numerous other jobs. If I finish in time, I'll do some letter writing to the family. Love to all. Kiss the cherub. I love you with such a depth of feeling that all this intense occupation fails to dim for an instant my longing for you. Oh, to sit quietly again and feel the joy of belonging, of being someone beloved and to love fully, soul satisfyingly. For that day, I pray and pray. Daddy

April 7, 1945
My Darling:

The end of a terrifically busy day finds me contented but utterly without ambition for anything beyond writing this letter and spending the few remaining hours of the evening just lolling in this very comfortable office. Max is here. We are working on the remains of the delicious caviar; we have a "fruit juice" cocktail, some matzos which we brought back from the Passover feast last week, and each other's good company. We can start laughing over anything, and do a lot of laughing when we are together.

How can I begin to tell you just how busy I am from early morning to late-night without giving you facts? Yesterday, for instance, started at 7 a.m. for me and ended at 11:30 p.m. I am not complaining. I enjoy the work tremendously. Again today I put in a few extra hours so that I can enjoy my Sunday without giving a thought to the work left unfinished. Tomorrow, weather permitting, will be a day of royal leisure spent on the banks of the Meuse again, I hope. Did I tell you that I fished out a German Luftwaffe cap from the Meuse? It's in excellent condition. I removed the soiled lining and band and found that it makes a striking tam. I shall send it home. It's a particularly nice shade of blue. See what you can make of it. At any rate, save it as a souvenir.

Our anniversary was snowed under in the rush of work which fell to me on the 6th. I thought of us at odd moments throughout the day, but it wasn't until

just a few minutes ago that I lifted my fruit juice cocktail in a toast to you, My Beloved. Saturday evening has become a time for turning all of one's thoughts and turning all of one's heartstrings on the ever-dominant chords: home, family. Our life here now is not bad. We have even put away the helmets. Soon, we expect to get all dressed up in class A uniforms. The hospital grounds have been transformed by the POWs, the clever bastards, whatever else they may be. I'm in the throes of souvenir collecting again and warn you I'm apt to fall for a "vahz," or something else, now that I have beaucoup francs in my pants again. It's great fun and just about every GI here indulges in the utterly absurd business of souvenir hunting and buying and paying through the nose. I'm neglecting my guests, Angel, so I'll say goodnight. Tea and toast are being served in the "lab" next door. Kiss the cookie. Love to all. The fourth year finds me loving you four times as much as the first.
    Daddy

April 8, 1945 – Somewhere in Belgium
My Darling:
    For no reason at all I started to collect Buddhas and have acquired two already which I will mail home this week. It seems I always settle for a Buddha every time I go on a shopping tour of inspection. We visited the Shangri-La town again which I mentioned in a recent letter, and Max and I had ourselves a rare good time. We did all the things nature lovers like. We climbed the hills, we crossed the river in a crude but picturesque ferry boat, we crawled like spiders all over the great rock formations which have been terraced in layers of breathtaking gardens and nooks, all the more beautiful because they have been left to grow wild since the war came. We sat at our favorite table again and drank beer on the right bank of the Meuse, and, more important than anything, we took two rolls of pictures. If half of them turn out, you will have treasures to gladden your heart for days to come. Darling, how I wish that you were climbing, walking, drinking in the quaint beauty of these crazily winding streets with me. England, France, Belgium. I have seen and responded to the moldy beauty of Europe in the same way. The terrible ruins of war are already being covered by growing things, and soon the scars of war will become the landmarks for tourists to see.
    Love to all. Daddy

April 8, 1945 – Somewhere in Belgium [V-Mail]
Darling:
    Just received your letter of Feb. 21. This is Sunday afternoon. At the moment, no one has a toothache around here so the clinic is quiet and peaceful. We had a nice party last night. Some of the patients, recruited and rehearsed by the talented Hugh Martin, put on a delightful hour of entertainment. Then we had chicken sandwiches, etc. We shall have a dance next week. Our social life is

looking up. I don't think I'll have to sweat out "the next promotion" and the way the news read today we are poised for victory this year.

Love to all, Your Daddy

April 11, 1945
My Darling:

What must you think of me? This habit of missing a night, then two nights of letter writing sends me into a frenzy, yet it seems like almost an impossibility to settle down long enough to get one written. Your sweet letter of March 26 reached me today, and I think you are a queen to accept my non-letter-writing excuse of too much social activity. There hasn't been a social event yet that I wouldn't gladly pass up in favor of letter writing, but not to go out occasionally would produce a lassitude and blue mood that certainly would be reflected in my letters, with dire consequences. The truth is we are enjoying army life to the fullest at the moment. I wish I could tell you in detail about how this place is booming into a vast and lovely garden spot. I wish I could take you with me on the long walks over glorious countryside. The valleys and gently rising hills, checker-boarded with alternating grassy green and freshly plowed yellow fields is something to behold. I have indicated from time to time that we are well out in the open country. Consequently, the warmth of the past month has burst the blossoms on all the trees, plants, hedges, field flowers, and has brought a warmth and joy to my heart that lacks only the excitement of your touch, your love, your marital companionship. Truly, Darling, I am deeply moved by the irony of this Eden-Purgatory. Four months ago we gasped with terror at the nearness of the Moloch of war and his terrible thunder. Today, we lie in the pastures, resting after chow and hear with only passing notice the pop-pop of the boys sharpening up their gun-sight eyes on the rifle range. The horses, the cows, the sheep nary raise their heads from their grazing, and we chew grass as the birds out-sing the chatter of the rifles. This has nothing to do with us, mind you. It so happens we like to rest in a field that happens to be within earshot of the range. I have never gone near there and have no reason to go, so don't misinterpret my rhapsodic ravings. It's just another sound that one learns to accept as one of the post-pangs of war labor.

Angel, I mailed two parcels yesterday. The baby's things I bought, plus the Nazi hat and a small box of assorted Buddhas and a "Manneken Pis" a reproduction of the famous Belgian statue of the little boy pissing in public. It's mighty cute.

The job continues to be enormous, yet interesting. I make much of joshing the patients and helping them over the dental chair nerves, and we all have fun out of it. The constantly ringing telephone got me for a time, but I learned to drop a French word here and there and it breaks the tension. For instance, I get Manny wild with my constant telephoning to various wards. The other day I got

Belgium: Dental Clinic

him nutty with my addition of "s'il vous plait" after each ward number request. After the tenth call, however, I thought I'd give him a break, so I said, "Manny, give me ward 30, "zie azoy gutt." [s'il vous plait in Yiddish]. He howled. It caught him with his plugs down, and he really had a laugh and as a result got rid of his distemper. Now, Angel, its way beyond bedtime.

My love to all. Kiss the cherub. Love, Daddy

April 12, 1945 – Somewhere in Belgium
My Darling:

No letter today to lift my sagging spirit but I can dream, and that's what I'll do tonight as I am beaucoup fatigué but not unhappy. The day, a devilishly busy one, went well and the dreaded report, now completely formulated in my mind, will begin to take shape tomorrow. I'll have to work like the dickens since the thing was thrown in my lap without warning or preparation, but I think I can handle it. The boss is a bit vague himself about it, but I guess we'll manage to come to some agreement on it. He appears to like me enough to listen to what I have to say. He expects a lot of his help, and heaven knows I've given with the energy, but good. This is not a gripe. It's just another period of adjustment to a new phase of my army career, and it leaves me limp at the end of a day. Well, tomorrow promises to be an easy one. We have kept the appointments down to a bare minimum so that all of us can get a breathing spell. The excitement at times is terrific, and I find myself riding on the crest with an abundance of spirit, but the tired feet and eyes at the end of the day tell me I am no kid anymore. Well, Angel, I'm pressing hard to make up a letter. Better, perhaps, that I should get an extra hour's sleep, so forgive me this poor try and know that even a clumsy letter spells the love I feel for you.

Kiss the cherub. Love to all. Daddy

Franklin Roosevelt's Death

Friday, April 13, 1945 –Somewhere in Belgium
My Darling:

I know what you must be feeling in these sorrowful hours. Still half-asleep, I heard it pass between two equally sleepy GIs near my bunk. I didn't quite catch the name. A few moments later the next bunk came to life and we heard the terrible announcement. I can still feel the chilling cold that gripped me from head to foot. Rumor, rumor, damn these guys who are always starting these rumors. But this was one that had never been whispered before. He had come through so many dangers in his tireless efforts to bring a crazy world back to the ways of peace among men. Shortly, though, I was convinced, stunned, numbed into acceptance of the bitter truth. There was the flag at half-mast, furled, wrapped around its sustaining staff like a shroud. The calm of death even embraced the flag which otherwise flutters so brightly in the morning breeze. We say dull, stupid things on such occasions. I said, "Max, it's true!" What now? Who knows? The greatness of our country was not alone in the one man. Other leaders will arise. This is your task at home. Find these leaders who are worthy of the task of pointing out our Destiny. Not a fighting, toiling, sweating, lonely son-of-us wants a compromise with the enemy, but neither do we want to be made a political football now or ever.

The rich will sigh with relief and call their brokers. The poor will remember the Hoover bread lines and in a frenzy try to emulate the rich in amassing wealth. The heartsick soldier will think of his family and wonder how secure are those sweaty little $10 bonds. The war will be won. Great men lead our fighting forces, but what of the man who will direct the forces of peace and prosperity in the postwar period? How much of the Rooseveltian influence went with him to his hallowed grave? May God grant that men will continue to think great thoughts in simple, understandable words rather than small thoughts in grandiose political mumbo-jumbo. I beg you to save the newspapers for this period. I want to read all that is being written about this Moses who has gone up the mount to give account of himself. Were he to return, he would bring back the same stone tablet that once was brought down and so ignobly misinterpreted through the ages. I would have liked to look upon the living man, just once!

My Darling, I must return to my duties. They are many, but engrossing. Perhaps you can send me a few of the best written stories about the president.

Love to all. Kiss the angel. Daddy

Esther's Letter to Sam, Friday, April 13, 1945

My Angel,

I'm sure you'll forgive my failure to write to you last evening. The shock and grief which seized me and all freedom-loving people of the earth with the tragic news of the sudden passing of our beloved president and humanity's greatest friend left me immobile. A pall of profound sadness and bewilderment over our very personal loss grips our land tonight, My Darling. Every home, every decent heart is heavy in mourning and prayer for guidance now that humanity's greatest benefactor and soldier is lost to us. The impact of the tragedy at so crucial a time in the history of the world cannot even be appreciated yet, while a stunned world is in the throes of emotional unbalance. Only when this initial shock abates and the good peoples of the earth recover enough to think will we begin to realize what we have lost. The world is a family without a father. Every man on the street feels his <u>personal</u> loss of the great man whose benevolence, courage, and statesmanship shall be immortal. I have never felt so keenly the death of anyone I have ever known, for our Roberta's world will be a poorer one without his great vision at the peace table, for which he lived and died.

The day has been one of consecration here, Darling. Of sincere tribute to a man whom only time and history can justly measure. The air has carried only sacred music today—nothing commercial, nothing gross. We are a nation mobilized in sadness and homage to our good friend. We are a nation unashamed to show tear-stained faces and very long ones.

I have been unable to get you out of my mind, Beloved, for I know how you loved our president and I know how bitter this day has been for you. As our music, "Panis Angelicus" has been played over and over again throughout the day, I have felt a stricture at my heart, and terrible pangs of loneliness for you.

In the face of such cruel irony, I cannot help asking the question, Where's God in a universe where a Hitler is permitted life, while Roosevelt is denied life? It is this kind of inexplicable injustice, Darling, that tries one's faith and besets a man with doubt. Who indeed are we to ask the reason why. The little man all over the earth has lost his greatest friend. What is there left to say.

But somehow life goes on and we must pray that our new president be given the fortitude and wisdom he will need for the Herculean task confronting him, so that our valiant sons will not have died in vain. The great spirit and power of Roosevelt may still guide the hands of those who make our peace. That it be a firm and abiding peace will be the only monument worthy of our leader who died on the eve of its realization. What a pity!

Angel, the impact of the blow, received with the announcement at five o'clock yesterday, was so great that I couldn't even summon the energy to answer your wonderful letter of April 4, received a couple of hours earlier. The intense and hectic program of your work, My Darling, has me scared and worried. I'm so afraid you'll knock yourself out in your overwhelming will to please and serve. Please, Daddy, please watch yourself and accentuate the minimum. I'm not aspiring to the dubious honor of being Mrs. T5 Lesner. My only goal is the return to just plain noble Mrs. S. J., with a Sammy not worn to a frazzle because of his all-consuming goodness and altruism. Of course, chances are you have nothing to say about the volume of work you turn out, but knowing your penchant for extracurricular activity, I daresay you are giving far more of yourself than honor and duty demand. Just don't let your health suffer, Angel. The toll of shattered nerves and bodies is high enough.

Your story of the inspection characterized by four slices of baloney would be funny if it weren't so symbolic and grim. One can't help reflecting over the typical incident and terror wrought in your innocent hearts by a piece of baloney—in a world gasping for its very life. In my own dumb way, with my lack of perspective, I can't fathom the importance placed on a piece of baloney or pair of unshined shoes in the face of matters of such magnitude as face you in the basic struggle for survival. But undoubtedly there's a reason someplace. Again, who am I to wonder why.

Our radiant, lively, lovely Love Lettuce was able to romp and play today as usual, thanks to her innocence. How glad I am that she can't feel the sadness and mourning that grips a bereaved people.

Goodnight, Good Husband. What I wouldn't do for the comfort and confidence I would feel at the slightest touch of your hand! When our gallant armies join hands with our Russian ally—which will doubtless happen long ere this letter reaches you, you will feel my hand clasp yours—my heart fuse with yours in thanksgiving and renewed hope.
Forever and ever, Your Honey

April 14, 1945 –Somewhere in Belgium
My Darling:

The mailman is a square shooter and his favorite number is five. I too received five wonderful letters yesterday, and today a box of delights: crackers, dates, cookies, all in perfect condition. The cookies this time I shall ration to myself with my mid-morning coffee. The crackers I shall munch at night for the before bedtime snack, and the dates, so beautifully packed, I shall save for some special occasion.

The Horowitz recital must have been stupendous. I'd certainly like to hear him. Speaking of music, I'm going to Liège to hear a special performance of *Rigoletto* on Thursday evening. It's a rough ride, but I'm sure it will be worth it.

A memorial service [for President Roosevelt] was held this morning in front of the hospital. It was a sad yet memorable moment. The "supermen," too, lay down their picks and shovels and stood rigidly at attention as taps sounded and echoed our fast-beating hearts. May he find the peace he sought so valiantly for the troubled world he has left behind. Our children will have their Washington-Lincoln-Great American to read about and revere. Angel, I must spend an hour on the monthly report, so I say goodnight. Kiss the Love Lettuce. My love to all. Give my best to all who still think of me occasionally even though the "letters" never reach me. If the sun shines tomorrow, I shall go into the hills and dream of you.

Daddy

April 18, 1945 – Somewhere in Belgium [V-mail]
Darling:

Don't get excited. Our new APO is now 228. All it means is that the war is running away from us so fast we don't rate the 350 anymore, that being an APO for forward installations, I guess. Well, the mail situation can't get much worse. We have been told to expect no mail until Saturday, this being Wednesday and letter-less. Angel, I'm up to my ears in the job and I can't tell when I'll be able to climb out. I discovered some glaring errors in my monthly report to date and am faced with the awful job of backing up and making corrections—tonight. Got a swell compliment from the chief, however, and a friendly pat on the back, so things aren't too bad. I hope to get an airmail written tonight. I can hope, can't I?

Love, Daddy

Belgium: Dental Clinic

April 20, 1945 – Somewhere in Belgium
My Darling:

It doesn't seem possible that two whole days have passed since last I wrote to you, but that's the truth, and it hurts. Yet almost every moment of the waking day I am scheming how to rob enough time from the tumult of this office to scribble a hasty V-Mail, at least, but to no avail. It is now 11 p.m. but I know I can't go to bed until I get this down at least. First and foremost, I repeat what I have said in an earlier letter, lest you find cause to worry unduly about this. The change of our APO from 350 to 228 doesn't mean a thing, lest it means we are a tiny bit nearer to getting home after this mess is over. The news tonight at last was such as to bring a shout of joy to my throat as I listened in. No more piddling advances here and there. No more mere footholds and precarious beachheads. Now we are smashing on to Berlin and the ultimate destruction of Nazism. May God grant us the strength to bring this about soon. If such news continues to come to us, I shall sing in chapel Sunday morning with an undisguised passion. My solo is to be "Supplication," a stirring piece written in the cantorial style.

Angel, please explain to your folks and mine how pressed I am for time at the moment. Kiss the cherub. To you, my eternal love and devotion. The opera was very good. More tomorrow on that.

Daddy

April 22, 1945 – Somewhere in Belgium
My Darling:

We have just come home from chapel (the service was at 1:30 instead of the usual 10 a.m.), and Max is still shivering with pleasure (so he says) over my singing, which did go well. We also had a visiting chaplain for today's service, a doctor who was formerly a minister and who has the rare talent of bringing about a fusion of science and religion with such telling effect that we [were] all stirred by his sermon. So all in all we combined to give the patients and such of the detachment as ventured into chapel a memorable service. I get a real thrill out of singing in the services. I don't know whether I ever mentioned it before but one of the reasons for my finally making the dental clinic was that my good tenor might be useful to the quartet, the personnel of which is composed largely of clinic men. Well, I tried them once and decided to go my own musical way. That's only a tiny part of the mass stupidity one encounters in the Army.

A lone V-Mail from Mayme yesterday, in praise of our lovely Roberta, filled my working hours with ecstasy but disturbed my sleep, for having read so much joy consciously, I had a bad dream unconsciously. I shook it off, however, in the solid, everlasting faith in God to protect my loved ones.

The opera we heard in Liège last Thursday [*Rigoletto*] was really fine, considering the enormous handicap of a skeleton chorus, no ballet, and not enough good singers for the small but important parts. The baritone, Monsieur Mancel, is a brilliant artist and vocalist. The diva, Clara Clairbert, is famous all over Europe, and even in her advanced age (for a singer) she employs a remarkable technique. Her singing is effortless except when it comes time to hit a high one. Then it's downright bad, vocally. But being an artist, she knows how to draw attention away from the strained high C. By American standards she has some stage faults, but again her vocal skill makes you forget them. The tenor, of course, was a washout. He made much of the pearl earrings he wore in the hope of overcoming the absence of pearls in his throat. "La donn' e mobile" was as strained as the Gerber's squash our little Roberta decorates herself with. Squash just about sums up that poor tenor. We may go to hear *Aida* this week if enough tickets are available. It's only fair to give some of the others a chance to go since both tickets and transportation are limited.

I'll know more about my daily routine tomorrow as again some change in duty is contemplated for me, meaning that things will really work out good for me. I've heard that you shall soon be "Mrs. Corporal" but shall say no more about that until it happens. Darling, more tomorrow, and every day in a resumption of my daily letter to you.

Love to all. Kiss the cookie. Daddy

Possible Transfer to the Pacific

April 23, 1945 – Somewhere in Belgium
My Darling:

I'm sorry the Christmas record broke. I wanted it as the war memento, but I can replace it, I believe. It was a good recording of the beautiful aria I was to sing on that last unhappy Christmas Eve. But God was good to us and led us safely through great danger. Today we talked to a Chicago boy who has just come back from hell. For nine months he was a prisoner of the Nazis in East Prussia. The horror he has endured and seen left us in a helpless rage all day. The major, you know, is a Chicagoan, so the three of us sat down and talked. If I can get permission to use his name I shall write it to you. That's one name that should make the news columns.

Please don't swallow all you hear on the radio. Undoubtedly, many veteran troops will be shipped to the Pacific theater after this show is over, but at present we are not a very "shippable" unit. I can't say much more on this subject because I'm sure to convey the wrong impression. I beg you to believe that my chances of returning home are greater than my chances of going to the Pacific theater. We are being "educated," though, to a program of useful waiting for the necessary transportation when that time comes. Anyone who thinks he's going to hop right on a boat and scoot home at the termination of hostilities here is plain nuts. The sick and wounded will come first. I can wait, Angel, just so I walk down a gang plank a whole, healthy, sane person. That's the way I want to come back to you. I wish I could tell you how one of our boys recently went home.

I've sent C.J. Bulliet a little souvenir so you should be getting a phone call from him shortly. Just so they hold that music desk for me—that's all I want.

Love to all. I kiss you, My Darling. Daddy

April 25, 1945 – Somewhere in Belgium
My Darling:

Max and I visited some civilian friends last night. We became acquainted with them before the Bulge and have been able to renew that friendship only now. They are people of more than average intelligence and are stimulating to boot. I am still a hopeless dummy when it comes to speaking French (and they know no English), but I am surprised and delighted to discover that I understand quite a bit of what is said. Last night, however, after a particularly delicious supper, I took a deep breath and said, "Madame, pour cette recipé de la salade vous recevoir in Amerique un grand réputation." Honest, Honey, I said all that in one breath and then was so overcome by my linguistic ability, I couldn't utter another word. I don't know what it is that keeps me from diving in like most of the guys do, but I have a horror of speaking a foreign language without verbs and adjectives. I am learning, though, through concentrated listening. Mine is the slow method, but I think I'll get more out of it that way. Max is nonplussed when I tell him what our friends are saying when he fails to understand. I realize at such times that the hours I spent building a vocabulary as I wrote my articles have come in very handy. Many good French words are the same in English. For instance, our hostess, while reading our fortunes with cards (and I had a swell fortune—three kids, lots of money, prestige, and a long voyage soon), had occasion to use the phrase "light character," which Max didn't quite catch. I added, "frivolité," just giving the good English word a twist. Well, they were surprised and began to disbelieve my assertion that I don't speak French. This has happened numerous times. I have thought that I could settle down to a daily short period of French study, but somehow the days slip by, and the incentive to concentration and study is too often absent. We do have delightful times in these visits, though, and trying to make myself understood, I have become a vivid and utterly unselfconscious pantomimist.

The weather has turned fair again after some days of dreary damp—and how my bones creaked—so our evening walks will be resumed. More later, perhaps, Angel. Love to all. Kiss the gorgeous cherub. Please, Darling, get me a picture of her. I can't stand it much longer, hearing about her, and not seeing her, even if it's only a picture.

Love, Daddy

April 27, 1945 – Somewhere in Belgium
My Darling:

Your letter of the 7th was based on the depressing news that we were to be shipped, lock, stock, and barrel, to the Pacific. Darling, I've warned you about swallowing all this guff those miserable newscasters dish out. These announcements are all feelers and are undoubtedly far removed from what might really happen. Certainly, men of 42 or over ought to go home. That's starting this thing from the right end at least. And it's reasonable to expect that most family men over 35 will be mustered out. Months must pass before anything is done about us, and as long as we have to stay, this Belgian countryside isn't the worst place in the world. Please don't fret over those damned radio newscasts. When we have finally polished off the Nazi monster, we ought to go after the newscasters, more aptly name "blues-casters." That's all for now, Sweetheart.

Love to all. Kiss the beautiful Love Lettuce.

April 30, 1945 – Somewhere in Belgium
Sweetheart:

Having just come from a funny movie, *The Dough Girls*, an oldie but yet entertaining one despite the now un-humorous clips about the president, I find that I have been able to shake off some of the pall that descended upon me over the weekend. I guess you, too, and most of the world's civilized people are feeling the bitter disappointment following the exhilaration of thinking for a glorious few hours that the war had finished. How we tried to talk ourselves into it, even after the reports over the air cautioned repeatedly against accepting rumor for fact. For the first time in my life, Angel, I wanted to get drunk.

Please don't entertain any foolish fears about me in relation to my job. The Army teaches one to be selfish. I do what is necessary, but I do it with a flourish, which adds the desired realism of extraordinary diligence. I happen to like what I'm doing and I happen to have earned the respect and courtesy of my superiors, which is all that matters after all. That alone makes things easier. I intend to retain that even at the cost of expending a little extra energy during my so-called free time. As a husband and parent I have a purpose in life—to provide amply for my family. Learning to get along under such trying circumstances is not a bad habit to cultivate.

There is little else to report at the moment. The weather has been foul so even an evening walk is out of the question. When the sun returns to the sky my spirits undoubtedly will brighten too. We just got a new piano for our Day Room and I have a mind to do a little practicing tonight. Perhaps we can play pieces for four hands, but I can't guarantee that my hands will stay on the keys. Good night, My Wife.

Kiss the cherub and give my love to folks. Daddy

Belgium: Dental Clinic

May 2, 1945 – Somewhere in Belgium
My Darling:

I have just read through about a dozen of your letters, ending with the exciting one of April 23, which I received today. I insist, though, that if I am good, you are my literary equal. Your Roosevelt letter was very well done, my angel. I can honestly say that literary style was far from my mind in those terrible early hours of our president's death. I, too, knew at that time the paralysis of despair and loneliness creeping through my mind and body. Then the short-lived joy of the premature peace, and I was licked, for the first time. Even that terrible first night in this once-forsaken pasture didn't beat me down the way the events of the past two weeks have.

I should apologize for my "jealousy letter" at this point. I know it gave you small comfort, but I can't. It wasn't anger or prejudice or any of the superficial emotions which prompted it. It was the honest, unbearable, uncontrollable outpouring of an accumulated longing, hunger, and overpowering homesickness which all but swept me into the abyss of dark despair. There are those who win favor through cheap flattery while the others sweat and die. What right have they to come home on a furlough while many, many hundreds of thousands have tortured their minds and bodies in hellholes for two to three years yet dare not hope for a trip home? No, I'll await my turn, after the real heroes have washed the blood from their weary hands. What are their small ailments, their discomforts, yes even their losses compared to the stark tragedy which is daily being uncovered in the wake of the retreating hounds of Nazism? Well, I've had my say. I feel better for it.

I'm sorry Love Lettuce can't get into the dress. Heavens, just how big is a two-year-old? I had visions of you taking it in a bit. It looked so big. Angel, can you see me in the store debating, questioning, being doubtful one moment, reassured the next, for two hours or more? I really don't know how big our baby is. What a theme for a play: "G.I. Daddy Goes Shopping." Please take the measurements from stem to stern and roundabout. I'll buy her a dress if it's the last thing I do. What a kid! Toast and peaches and cream, what a morsel! On this joyous note, My Love, good night. Did you really get the "vasz" in one piece, or are you sparing me the shock?

Love to all. To you, all my love, Daddy

May 3, 1945 – Somewhere in Belgium
My Darling:

This will be a short one for tonight we go again to Liège to hear the opera, and I'm afraid I'll not get a letter written. The days fly by so quickly that I hardly realize now how many are the days that have lengthened into months since I saw you last. This may well be the weekend for which the world has waited in such sorrow and pain. With Hitler and Mussolini dead, it can be expected that the lesser fry will turn "chicken" after a brief grandstand play and bring this horror to an end. Strangely, the news of Hitler's death fell upon deaf ears as far as we are concerned. A dog died and the Army held its nose until the stench floated away.

We are to hear *Count of Luxembourg* tonight instead of a regular grand opera. There was some misunderstanding about *Carmen*, which we thought we were to hear, but it doesn't really matter. Just getting away from camp for an evening is fun. Angel, I must go into the surgery room now and prepare for the day's extractions which are already scheduled. Until tomorrow, Beloved, your faithful, worshipful, "jealous" husband.

Love to all. Kiss the cherub. Daddy

May 4, 1945 – Somewhere in Belgium
My Darling:

Today the mail brought me your letter of April 15, a sensitive, poignant expression of your feelings and the nation's at large over the death of the president. Our great loss, however, has become our great gain, our salvation, for the events which are following the complete destruction of Nazism, which should be cause for a Roman holiday—these events, because of our great loss, are being viewed seriously, quietly, as they should be. Far better that we are bowing our heads in prayerful thanksgiving instead of making a mockery of the death cries of our brothers. There has been no attempt here to start a "celebration" of the great victories which are being announced hourly. Just a few minutes ago we heard the news of the millions of "mighty supermen" surrendering unconditionally. Perhaps the weekend will bring the last and final chapter to their horror. I don't think anyone will feel very gay. Our feelings about this are so deep and so intermingled with the loneliness that pursues us at all times that we are more likely to utter a profound "thank God" and let it go at that.

Your sweet and enthusiastic letter of April 21 reached me yesterday. I am so glad the "vasz" arrived OK. I really sweated that one out after hearing about the ill-fated ashtrays. Darling, while in Liège, yesterday, I've priced some perfume. Honey, I guess you'll just have to get along without the sweet-smelling stuff. Christmas Night is 1800 francs (almost $40). Indiscreet and Scandal are priced at 1200 francs. I guess I got a bargain after all in Paris. Maybe on the way home I can get some.

The operetta was delightful. The Lehár score is warm and tuneful and the singers were in good form. I am soloist again this Sunday in chapel. I do enjoy and welcome these opportunities to keep in form. Good night, My Love. I feel fine and in much better spirits. I expect we will be allowed to see something of Europe in the near future as the pass system is being worked out for us.

Incidentally, I'm going to enroll in the GI school for a refresher in journalism while we wait our turn to go home. This is a sort of self-teaching plan to keep troops occupied after the fighting ceases. It's a good idea. I talked it over with an officer and it is in the realm of possibility that I may be allowed to go to one of the capital cities for some research work, too. Brussels would be nice and Paris would be wonderful. Love to all. Kiss the cherub. It's far beyond bedtime for this GI.
    Daddy

CHAPTER ELEVEN

Peace in Europe

VE DAY May 7, 1945 – Somewhere in Belgium
My Darling:
It was about 5 p.m. today when we heard the official news. We were at chow. There was absolutely no demonstration because every man of us at that instant thought only of home. What are our wives doing? What are our folks doing? What are our sweethearts and friends doing? There was some handshaking and then we returned to the barracks and sat on each other's bunks. "Gee, I wonder how our families feel?" It was repeated over and over and none of us had an answer. But I know what you are feeling, My Beloved. Because I am suddenly frightfully lonely, I will follow the crowd tonight. We will simply move in a crowd toward the town and the thing will gain momentum as we go along. I don't know what I'll do or what I'll say. I know, though, that I must move and with each step I'll hear the beat of my heart. It keeps saying, Esther, Esther, the worst of this is over. My Darling, there is hope now, a real, joyous hope. I must go now, beloved. The day is glorious. Last night I smelled the fertile earth for the first time, and I remarked on it to Max. It was a strange sensation, suddenly being so aware of the fruitful earth. "This is spring at last," I said, little realizing the morrow would be truly spring again for the world. This day then, May 7, 1945, is the beginning. While much of the world's war-weary bow their heads, we raise ours high and say "Thank God" for His safe guidance and protection. Tomorrow, My Darling, perhaps I can tell you just how it feels. For tonight and every night, My Love, undivided, and my thanks for the child you gave me. Even on the bad pictures I received yesterday she is the cherub I know her to be. My love to all the folks. I know that you must have had a real session with my mother over this great May 7, 1945.
Good night, Beloved, Daddy. Belgium, May 7, 1945, 6:00 p.m.

May 9, 1945 – Somewhere in Belgium
My Darling:
Well, here it is, the second day of peace in Europe, and except for the lights which now shine unheeded by the guards, there is little change. So you see, for some time now we have lived in comparative safety. Even the celebrating Monday night wouldn't have disturbed a light sleeper. Actually, Max and I and two other guys, making up a gruesome foursome, made more noise than all the rest

together. Maybe I did act a little foolish, but I had long ago made up my mind that the death of Nazism was an occasion for a good drunk, and that's exactly what we did. It was glorious. We four, all of the same imaginative stripe, stopped a jeep, climbed in, and rode to the town shouting, singing, laughing for all we were worth. The whole town, apparently, saw and heard us and practically everyone in the hospital heard about it because yesterday we were the topic of considerable discussion. One of the fellows knows some swell people in town. Recently he warned them that the moment VE Day was officially announced, he and company would arrive for a celebration, and that's exactly what we did. We brought our own champagne, sardines, caviar, and anchovies, and it is still a mystery to me how I managed to make the little sandwiches. I didn't know my left hand from my right. Later, the townsfolk came to life, and there were some fireworks, singing and general merriment. But over all, there predominated the seriousness of the occasion, further heightened by the fact that on the same evening some of the town's war prisoners returned from Buchenwald and other equally "lovely" German "rest havens." One look at these unfortunates and the desire for celebration fled. That was Monday night. Yesterday we declared a holiday in the dental clinic, at least, and spent the day recuperating from the night before, only to resume the eating and drinking last night. I should be quite satisfied to go to bed after finishing this and one or two other letters.

Again, My Darling, we are all asking, "What now?" You know as much about it as I do. Age alone seems to be the important factor at the moment. I am safely beyond the age limit for the CBI [China Burma India] theater at the moment. I have a family and the few other points. Need I say that I am ready to come home! I have had butterflies in my stomach all day just thinking about it. Things may happen fast here, or it may be months before any of us can even dare hope. This will be our real "trial by fire," My Beloved. You and I must remember that despite the fact that many don't even know what an Army barracks looks like, there are still several million who know a foxhole intimately. They should and must come first. We have made this camp very beautiful in the past few months, but it is still not home. Thus, it makes little difference where a soldier must "live."

Each day from here out will be a challenge, but one we must meet. I shall not hide anything from you if I am permitted to mention it. I do beg you to cling to your hope no matter what is reported via radio and newspapers. Your hope is based on a very sound principle of postwar adjustment. No great armies can be kept here because supplying them will cut deeply into the far more urgent Pacific theater supplies. Likewise, there is no room for all of us in the Pacific theater. Our hope is that our type of hospital will be far more useful at home now. If I must stay in uniform for months yet, I won't complain if it is spent somewhere at home. Whatever happens, My Beloved, you and I and our courageous parents will find the strength to see it through. Bear this in mind, Sweetheart, that for countless parents there can be no peace and forgetting in our

time. This Belgian countryside is lush and promising in the warmth of the May sun. Tomorrow, new rumors will make some of us pale and others will be flushed with hope. Until tomorrow, then, when, God willing, I can say, "I'm coming home, Darling." For that's the way I shall say it when that glorious day comes.
Daddy

May 10, 1945
My Darling:
A busy day has left little time for thinking. There is nothing new to report, and, as far as I can determine, I shall not be called for any examinations, which is a most encouraging sign that neither the infantry nor the CBI theater wants me. I wrote you some time ago that many of our boys were examined and a good number transferred to the infantry. They didn't even bother to call me in, and I feel perfectly safe in saying the same situation prevails now. I am an optimist, My Angel. It is conceivable that we shall celebrate Roberta's second birthday together. For this I pray.

The dental clinic continues to be busy, and I'm glad it is so. Things will slow down considerably no doubt before long, and then we will be able to get some personal attention. I have a couple devitalized teeth which have become annoying, and at the same time I have noticed an increase in the arthritic symptoms in my left knee and arm. If, after a consultation, I find there is some connection, I shall have them out. I'm sure the major will restore them by some artificial means since the bothersome teeth are on my chewing side. We have excellent technicians and as long as I must have it done, I'll let the Army do it for free.

Middle age, Darling, is bringing its complications on. My eyes need checking again. My feet hurt, my teeth are touchy. These are small annoyances, but bothersome just the same. I've also discovered that the sun makes me dizzy. Imagine that! Lesner, the sun worshiper, now prefers a cool shady spot. That's what we shall do at the very first opportunity. We shall find a cool, shady spot. I shall stretch out on my back, and you shall drop "grapes" in my mouth one at a time while little Roberta howls with delight at our strange behavior.

Until tomorrow, My Love, Daddy. Kiss the cherub.

May 11, 1945 – Belgium
My Darling:
I got the big needle a couple of times today. My luck, every time I want to do a noble deed, the machinery breaks down. At any rate, here's the tale. I was right in the middle of giving 500 cc of blood for a poor lad here when the apparatus clogged up, and for almost an hour I sweated it out. Mine was exactly the type blood needed to help stem the hemorrhages which afflict the poor fellow, and I was glad to be of some small help. Gosh, Honey, I have such rich, red

blood. A real he-man, I am. I felt fine after the operation, but they decided I needed a shot of "schnapps." The damn stuff made me drunker than a loon for several hours. I've just recovered my equilibrium.

Darling, you can well imagine that we are having a Roman holiday currently, and with the announcement of a point system last night, we are really up in the air. The wave of disappointment which swept over nearly all of us at first passed quickly, and already the corniest humor on the books is now being exchanged between all of us, re: the point system. My own contribution to the business was: "Look, dope, you are advancing the most 'pointless argument' for going home I ever heard." We have set up a sort of Stock Exchange and barter points all day long. One poor devil added up to 84, a couple of guys squeezed out 80s, but they're no better off than the 11s, 20s, or 45s, of which I am one. We'll just sweat this thing out, I guess. But I am convinced that once the battle veterans who are the only ones who can muster 85 points are skimmed off, age and parentage will take precedence over other qualifications. The rumor, however, that this unit will come home intact, persists. It's a delightful rumor.

Now, about mail. Angel, I haven't been lax to the extent of creating a three weeks void, but I have missed a few nights, to my regret. Please don't worry. Actually, there is so little to write about now. The surroundings have become boring and the people even more so. Surely, we will get some sort of pass before long so we can get out of this cow pasture for a few days. Then again, I shall fill my letters with interesting detail, I hope. Remember, Beloved, that the danger here is over. We are perfectly safe, no matter what we do or where we go. It is possible that some of us may even go up front for detached service. There is so much work necessary to be done to restore order that I wouldn't be surprised if we are called for a few weeks' duty. The dental personnel will be busy for some time to come, and I, in particular, but should opportunity present itself, I think I would enjoy seeing just what happened up front. It looks like we are stuck here for the next couple of months anyhow, so I welcome the change of pace and scenery. I assure you, however, that I'm not intimating anything. The first thing you learn in the Army is not to volunteer for anything. They get to you soon enough.

The women of America could start a movement to get the papas home if they really bent to the task. I agree that young children need both parents, and there are plenty of papas who would welcome the chance to take over the kids and give the mamas a rest. How about it? Are you a crusader? I'm just itching to get home, Darling. Well, Sweet, the bed has to be made yet and order restored in general. On Fridays the barracks are scrubbed down by the Heinies and our duffels are piled in small mountains on our beds.

Love to all. Kiss the cherub. To you, my heart overflowing with love and longing, Daddy

May 13, 1945 – Ciney, Belgium
My Darling:

It frightens one to know that now one can say so many things which were well guarded secrets for so long. We are slow to realize just what has happened, having become accustomed to endless restrictions. Well, Darling, this is the little town in the middle of nowhere that stemmed the tide of the Nazi might in that eventful Christmas week of 1944. It appeared on the daily maps only once and then only because it was where the Nazis knew they had spent their force. There was no large-scale fighting here since the actual battle was fought in the Ardennes and at Bastogne, as all the world knew, but we know that had the Nazi spearhead been able to sweep over this immediate vicinity, all of Belgium would have been lost, and possibly much of France again. We were the last ones out speeding through the bitter cold and dark over roads that were already heavily mined and blocked to stem the enemy. I'll never forget those hours. I couldn't believe it. Were we then to be beaten after all? Were we really the disorganized, unwilling mob we appeared to be? Those were hours in which to regret one's own laxity and indifference to the months of basic training. One felt terribly bitter about the home front, where pleasure was the only concern of so many. One felt a terrible desire to get behind a big gun and blast away. This running away was humiliating.

[*Editors' note: In the 1986 interview with his grandson, Sam reflects more on the period just described in his May 13 letter.*]

[*From Oral History interview with grandson, Edward C. Bernstein, in 1986*]:

The Ardennes forest and the Battle of the Bulge had taken place in that particular part of Belgium. For some strange reason, we got way up ahead of that, so we were getting combat casualties directly into our hospital even though we were not prepared to deal with that. We were dealing more with combat fatigue and that sort of thing. I really witnessed some bloody messes, but you develop a strange protective covering in these situations and I know that I was heartsick when I saw the condition of some of these people that were brought in on stretchers on the top of a jeep. There were many instances in the course of the stay in Belgium. The war turned around and Belgium again was threatened with a second invasion by the Germans. That period of the Battle of the Bulge, which was Christmas season of 1944, was a very, very critical period for the Allies. The Germans were moving in all directions. We didn't know it until later that much of it was a bluff. They were in desperate straits. They had very little ammunition to back up their threats. Their uniforms were in terrible condition, their supply lines were shattered, but those madmen in Berlin decided they were going to make one more try and they started to push back and both Paris and all of Belgium were threatened again with a second invasion. But it didn't hold. The Battle of the Bulge determined that. Finally the Americans pushed the Germans back.

It all happened on the eve of my return from Paris. I had been given a pass to go to Paris as a reward. In the course of walking around Paris, I walked into a record shop that made souvenir recordings for soldiers to send home. Another soldier, a corporal, and I—we always traveled in pairs; that was the rule—went in and we negotiated in very bad, limited French and limited English as far as the proprietor was concerned, and we were struggling with this thing. Madame Bland, a typical French beautiful lady, stepped up said, "Young man, are you having trouble with the language?" She negotiated for us. We got into a long conversation. I told her who I was, that I was so interested in ballet and theater. She said her daughter was making her debut at the Paris Opera the next night [December 22] and she asked if we would like to come. Well, we were so excited about this. She had two box seats for us. She was there when we arrived. They were doing Otello, the first time that an opera had been presented since the war started because the Opera House had been closed during the invasion. Now they had reopened the Paris Opera and were doing this marvelous performance. Before the second act, a high-ranking American officer came on stage and said that all American and Allied troops must leave the city as quickly as possible and go back to their units. He didn't say why. (We later learned it was because our hospital had to evacuate from Ciney to Namur.) My friend and I said, "So what do we do?" Transportation offices were set up all over Paris, wherever the army was, to help in this thing. We went to the transportation office and they said there was a troop train going back to Belgium, to the area of Ciney, tomorrow [December 23], and we had better get on it. It was a train that had come from the front to deliver wounded soldiers to hospitals in Paris and now was returning.

I was terribly frightened but I was also concerned about what I should do about our hostess. She was so kind, so gracious. It was customary for soldiers on furlough anywhere to carry chocolate bars, bars of soap, whatever you had that was impossible to get in Europe you took as presents to your hosts. I had this bar of Palmolive soap in my little kit. Just before we said goodbye to Madame Bland, I took her hand and put the bar of soap in it and said "You must forgive me, this may not be the thing to give to a lady, but it's the only thing I have with me." She started to cry and said, "My God, it is the first piece of decent soap we've seen since the war began." She was overwhelmed to get a bar of perfumed Palmolive soap.

It was December and bitter cold. We climbed into this train and it was like a refrigerator made ourselves as comfortable as possible and proceeded to roll back to Belgium. The trip took about thirty-six hours. The problem was that since it was an empty train, every time a full train was approaching, we had to pull off tracks to let it pass. It took forever to get back to Ciney, Belgium. What I had started to say is that we were ordered out of the Opera House because we were told that the Germans had attempted to come back and recapture Paris and it was very dangerous for American soldiers to be on the streets. The Germans had gotten hold of American uniforms, trained special groups who spoke English and knew about American baseball and such, and were told to mingle with the American troops and knock them off.

When the Germans tried to push back and recapture France, the hospital got caught in the middle of it. I was ordered to come back from Paris to rejoin my outfit because the outfit was going to be evacuated because of the threat. As I walked down the Main Street of Ciney to where the hospital was, I saw these huge German tanks lined up in various positions and the tank corps men who were sitting on top of the tanks with their arms folded—they had no ammunition, no cannons to fire—they just sat there and paid no attention. I got down to my barracks. There was a message to take just personal items, leave all souvenirs as they will be burned, and get out and go to Namur [northwest of Ciney on the Meuse River away from the red line marking the advance of the Germans back into Belgium] where the outfit had evacuated before I got back.

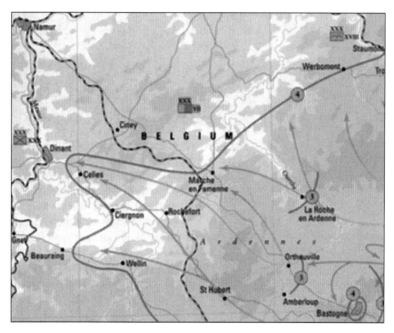

Reprinted with permission from John Ray, *The Illustrated History of WWII* (London: Weidenfeld and Nicolson, 2003), p. 181.

May 13th letter continues:

[Arriving in Ciney] I had just jumped out of a Jeep, startled by the peculiar air of abandonment of the camp. A moment later, a nervous sergeant barked at me, "Hey, run to your barracks, grab two blankets and that's all, and get the hell over to the basement of the hospital. The scene of utter disorder which I saw upon entering the deserted barracks frightened me beyond description. At that moment, the big guns a short distance away went off, shaking the tinderbox structure. I made some attempt to put my possessions in order, still unwilling to accept the order to abandon everything. I remember with a terrible pang placing the record carefully on my bed. Scattered about me were the many little things I had accumulated to send to you and Ruth and Mayme. I couldn't take them. I put the little Parisian dancing figures in my pocket, made a hasty and clumsy bundle of my blankets and toilet articles, and fled to the hospital. As I searched for a place to sit down somewhere, I can't remember who remarked that there was a package for me up in an office at the very top of the huge building which is our hospital. I knew it was from you, and no power on earth could have stopped me from going up there even though the building trembled from the concussion of the shelling nearby. I found the scarf you knitted with such care and a box of goodies—from Mayme, I think. I don't seem to remember. Also in your box were the steel wool, silver polish, I think, and some other things which spelled order and neatness—in this scene of confusion. It turned out that I could have taken many personal things along, since those men who had time, packed some pretty complete duffel bags. Well, we made an orderly retreat after some painful delay. I can't give you the facts surrounding that retreat, but the story will be told and it won't be a pleasant one. With your scarf warming me, I regained confidence. Before long Len Goldhammer and I, delighted to do some sort of job or other, were laughing hysterically and damning the whole miserable lot of exasperatingly stupid GIs.

[From Oral History interview with grandson, Edward C. Bernstein, in 1986]:

When we were chased out of Ciney, with our little packs hanging over our shoulders like refugees, and we were dumped into trucks and taken to Namur, we were taken to a place where there was a huge building that apparently had been a school and behind it there was a huge stadium. I was assigned to guard duty. Up until this point, I had never handled a gun in the Army. They gave me a carbine and showed me which shoulder to carry it on and I was told to walk back and forth until I was relieved. Leonard Goldhammer from Cleveland, a wonderful guy but as innocent as I was about guns, walked in the opposite direction. As we passed each other in the middle of the night, about 2 am, we heard shots. We both hit the ground. I said, "Stay down." I went to the main building and found the guard and told him "call the corporal of the guard who's in charge and tell him that we want to be relieved, someone is firing weapons out here." So he came down in his underpants—he had been sound asleep—and said, "What's the matter, waking me up?" "Dammit," I said, "if you want me to be on guard duty you'd better tell me how to fire this thing. I don't want to be on guard duty any more." Oh, I was so mad. So we were relieved right then and there. They took the weapons away and we went in and went to sleep I guess. The next morning we found out what happened. The stadium had been turned into a POW camp. During the night a prisoner had attempted to escape. Our guard saw it and fired at him. That was my last time on guard duty.

May 13th letter continues:

A Heinie [German bomber] came after us one night with his bomb sight aimed at us. He dumped two loads and we hit the sidewalk and pulled our steel helmets over our ears. That was really exciting, believe it or not. We had heard so much about this sort of thing but had never experienced any of it. I had learned my basic training lessons well, apparently. I hit the ground so fast, so flat, I just fused right into the concrete. "Bed Check Charley," as we had named that bastard came over several times but never got a chance to drop anything after that first time, and eventually he was checked right into hell. In all the months that we have been in the European Theater of Operations, I swear these two instances were the only ones of danger. They had a sobering effect on all of us, you can be sure, and perhaps, the Belgian Bulge near-disaster was the real turning point for us, in that we really all bore down and brought this agony to an earlier end than we dared hope for. Germany's losses in that Bulge were enormous and broke her back.

[Editors' note: When it was safe, by mid-January, the unit returned to their hospital in Ciney for the remainder of the European assignment.]

The day is glorious, but we are restricted to the area today in order to see the government film which tells us why we aren't going home yet. It's a shame it has to be on my day off, but "orders is orders" and you don't ask why. Well, Sweetheart, on this Mother's Day, a happy one for many, a tragic one for most. I hadn't intended writing a hair-raising tale. I know your good sense and balance have allowed you to accept the fact that war is dangerous, and that the end of danger is time for thanksgiving, rather than reliving the moments of danger and anxiety of the past. The months to come will fill us alternately with hope and despair, but even this must end one day, and our reunion will be everlasting and filled with love and devotion. On this glorious Mother's Day tell our baby that her mother is my only beloved.

Daddy.

May 15, 1945 – Ciney, Belgium
My Darling:

Lest another day passes without a letter to you, I hastily assure you via V-Mail that all is well despite the "paralysis of analysis" which is creeping over us from trying to figure out where we stand. The rumors are devastating as usual, and the news accounts of how long it must be yet before Japan is licked is most discouraging. All we get are promises of more decorations. It is said we have merited the Presidential Citation, and another star for the Ardennes affair. Well, the extra points won't get me home in the immediate future, so they are empty honors. I am writing this very early in the morning as Max and I are going to a very nice dinner party tonight, and I may not have a chance to write tonight.

My love to all. Kiss the flowering cherub. All my love. Daddy

May 15, 1945 – Ciney, Belgium
My Darling:

Having received three pleasant oldies from you today—April 9, 11, 17—I am inspired to write a chatty letter but hardly know where to begin. The clipping enclosed, showing the poor GI husband trying to get a spark of recognition out of the baby got a laugh out of the men. There are so many of us in the clinic in the same boat. No matter how much you tell Roberta about me, she's going to give me the critical onceover, but good, when she sees me. I'll forgive her, though, and if love and devotion mean anything to a child, she'll be squealing with glee five minutes after I bundle her into my arms. What's more, I urge you to preserve her "lellah to dadee" which she engraved upon the dining room wall. Woe unto the decorator who removes that spot!

Tomorrow I am going to help one of our intelligent sergeants to compose the story of the 130th General Hospital since we came to the sea of mud and cow flops and transferred it into an amazing community of medical activity. It is a great story. I may even be inspired to expand and submit it for magazine consumption. I thought some weeks ago that the urge to write had returned, but I wasn't ready. I am too keyed up emotionally yet and the sparkle isn't there. But this time, I'll try. From everywhere have come commendations and praise for the 130th since the magnificent part we played during and following the breakthrough. Despite the many disappointments and heartaches, I have the right to feel that I made a real contribution personally. I need never feel ashamed. What I should do now is begin at the beginning and tell you the whole story of my life in the Army. In so doing, I may recall many things that might otherwise be lost if I let them go.

I'll compile a chronological list of dates and events and start the project this week, I hope. In a sense, I will have my own project —a writer's project— during the time we must stay here. There is some talk of sending some GIs to Oxford and other great centers of learning here. I'm excited by the prospect and will make further inquiry. We have been told that such enrollment will not in any way hold a man from returning home when his time comes. But today, my final tally was 47, so figure it out yourself. There are months of waiting in store for most of us.

Max is a true and consoling friend. When things go badly, I unburden myself on his broad shoulders and he helps to clear my dark perspective enormously. Likewise, I have been of some help to Max in undoing some very knotty problems. In this cockeyed, distorted and distorting world at war, he is a welcome contact with the civilized human relationships we once knew.

– Interruption – Resumed the following night at 10:30 p.m.

Last night's dinner party was a delightful affair. The food was marvelous. We returned to camp very late. The five hours of sleep were as only five minutes. Oh, I'm so tired, but excited. A long talk about the 130th G.H. story has set me in a whirl. Sergeant Launton, my collaborator, is a swell guy. It appears that I'm elected to do the whole creative job. Swell, it's a challenge. Angel, for the next few nights, I'll scribble hasty letters, but I hope the "story" which you shall receive will justify the sacrifice. No mail from you today and already I have butterflies in my stomach.

Goodnight, Love. Kiss the cherub. Daddy

May 17, 1945 – Ciney, Belgium
My Darling:

Again, I must ask you to be contented with a brief V-Mail. I am rushing this in the interval between lunch and resumption of activities. The afternoon promises to be a lulu since we must rush through a number of cases today for disposition. My appointment book, already solidly booked, will have to be juggled to accommodate and reappoint all who are due this afternoon. I am developing severe writer's cramp and must rest my hand as much as possible. The weather is magnificent, the rumors most encouraging. I feel fine and continue to startle everyone who discovers my advanced age. The gray hairs, however, are appearing in greater number.

Love to all. Kiss the cherub. All my love, Daddy

May 18, 1945 – Ciney, Belgium
My Darling:

No mail from you for several days now. I await breathlessly your letter on "Victory Day." I am so anxious to learn just what reactions were in the final declaration that peace had come to Europe. In typical Army fashion, I was told yesterday that the story of the 130th G.H. had to be submitted to Headquarters almost immediately. I had hoped to get at least forty-eight hours to gather statistics. Instead, I had to plow right into the thing yesterday, after a real bitch of the day in the clinic. I can write only in the few hours between supper and bedtime. I'm happy to say it went very well last night. Tonight I shall incorporate some of the statistics which "scouts" will gather for me today, and by tomorrow I shall be able to turn it over to the typist. This, I am sure, will be the parent of a more skillfully written, more entertaining magazine article upon which I shall start work immediately.

Now that the fighting in Europe has ceased, the parts played in this show by the service forces should have a real chance to grab some newspaper and magazine space. At any rate, I needed just this incentive to get going again. When I finish this piece, I'll take time out to mail you the perfume I've been carrying in my pocket for days. It's called "Kobako," by a Parisian maker. Do you know the brand, Honey? It smells pretty good. I've been promised some Worth, but Angel, I'm only a Private First F..... Class, and it takes beaucoup francs to buy smelly stuff. The "Kobako" was 445 francs. See what I mean? It's tough being a PFC. Now that we have privileges, prices may come down with the resumption of industry here, but the really fine things are rare and very, very expensive. That's all for now, Sweetheart. I'm only half awake. In a few moments the first patients will begin to arrive and I'll be off again for the day.

Love to all. Kiss the cherub. Daddy

May 20, 1945 – Ciney, Belgium
My Darling:
    I have come to an impasse. I am confused. First, over the business of my promotion. Naturally I wouldn't write such a thing until it actually occurred. That's why you have no letter to that effect. What I wrote Mayme and the folks was that I hope to have the promotion soon. The boss had told me that he had put in for it, but that's a far cry from actually getting it. Naturally, I am painfully disappointed that there should have been any delay in it at all. His recommendation should have been sufficient to induce prompt action. Unfortunately, things don't work that way in the Army. When the C.O. wants to do it, everything is possible. When he doesn't want to take action, there are always some handy regulations to hide behind. I refuse to change my attitudes about this, however. I have worked and continue to work like a slave in this job of mine. Often the day ends with everybody being irritated because it has fallen on my unhappy lot to push them all day long. The past three nights have refreshed me, however. Last night, I completed my eight-page "Review of the 130th General Hospital's Activities for the Period October 16 to December 23, 1944," and it reads expertly and entertainingly. I told you that it was a project thrown in my lap by a sergeant who frankly wished me to be his ghost writer. He can think what he likes. The story is wholly mine. It's a part of me for it is the final articulation of all I thought and felt in that period. It is not me only in the sense that it is necessarily "doctored" up for the particular reason for its writing—namely, to establish the basis for the "Meritorious Service Award" which the unit is to receive—we hope.
    Well, I face this beautiful Sunday lonelier than usual. Since I was stuck with the writing project last night, I urged Max to go to Brussels with a group which I had hoped to join too. I don't regret it, though I'm pleased as punch with the story, and heaven knows I needed the practice. I am mailing you a copy this week. Had I gone to Brussels and neglected my difficult job at hand, I would've had only vicarious pleasure and no peace of mind. Thus, My Beloved, I end with a bit of philosophy that I could adopt to good advantage myself.
    Kiss our cherub and know that she is the fulfillment of our love. Daddy

May 21, 1945 – Ciney, Belgium
My Darling:

This evening I did the wisest thing possible considering it was raining. I took a nap after chow and actually felt the weariness of months roll off of me. About 8 p.m. I came back to the hospital, wrapped up your perfume and a box of picture cards and souvenir programs, etc. Since the censorship has been lifted, we can send these things home for safekeeping. I lost so many things during the Bulge, I won't take the chance of losing these. Now I'm not hinting at anything. It's just that I want to keep them and the duffel bag is full to capacity already. What with the daily inspections, the smart thing is to send them home now that we can. In the box you will see places we have been, starting with Meaford Hall, Stone, England, where I spent so much time smelling huge roses. [*Editors' note: This estate was founded in the eighth century in Stone, Staffordshire. In the seventeenth century it was a country house. The river Trent runs through the estate's meadow. The Hall was modernized in the late nineteenth century. During World War II the U.S. forces occupied Meaford Hall.*]

There is little else to report. Max had an elegant time in Brussels and promises to go again next week for my benefit. I wouldn't venture it without him since I rely on his glib French for all negotiations. I'm hopeless as a linguist. I think there is some Worth perfume in town. If I can snag some tomorrow I will if I can make a loan. Oh the life of a PFC! Do you wonder that I wish so much for that T/5 rating? The extra francs would make shopping so much more interesting. And so to bed to prepare for a busy tomorrow.

Love to all. Here's my longing heart. Daddy

May 22, 1945 – Ciney, Belgium
My Darling:

A ray of hope has broken through the dark curtain which screens our immediate future. Today, *Stars and Stripes* announces that the age limit has been scaled down to 40 and that more reductions may be expected. It is the thing which I felt would happen since despite all of the bilge that emanates from Washington, there must be some few with some common sense. Men over 35, whether rich or poor, educated or uneducated, are the hardest hit in this terrible thing called war. Economically, socially, they are the hardest hit. On the threshold of some small success, at the very moment when their young children need guidance, at the very moment when they are making their greatest effort to make the future certain for their families, which in the final and most important analyses are the structure of society, in that moment, they have been torn away from their greatest responsibility. We, the 35s and over, are the real sad sacks. The young have the future. The young have the world. The young have the years in which to forget. We have neither the years nor the unwanted independence. We know only that there can be no "periods of adjustment." We know that to survive, one must plunge right into a job and shed the war and the influences with the shedding of the uniform. If our government can't see this, then they will see many, many middle-aged men, desolate, lost in a young man's world if we are dragged through this thing for another year, possibly two. The young are the brave. They have won the battles, but they haven't begun the real battle yet. A postwar world will be tailor-made for the young heroes. We middle-aged will have to be satisfied with crumbs unless we are given some slight advantage over youth. I sound like an old man. I'm not physically or mentally, but what of the shortened horizon? What of the children to whom we will be strangers? What of the wives crushed with the accumulating agonies of waiting? Thus, I hope, and I feel my hope shall be realized before too long, My Angel.

Kiss the cookie. Love to all, Daddy

May 23, 1945 – Ciney, Belgium
My Darling:

There is little to report that is new. Attempts are being made to keep up our morale. They even found a German Focke-Wolfe plane somewhere and dragged it home. It has been assembled and set up in our detachment area. It looks very zippy, but what? A plane is no novelty here. I suspect that one of these days we'll be summoned out to sit around the plane and listen to a lecture on it. All through basic, we were dogged with aircraft identification lectures. I never could tell one tail from another, and that's where one looks for the most characteristic identifying marks, apparently. I flunked that course something awful.

We are to have a dance this Thursday night and beaucoup girls are promised us. So far, I have yet to see an American girl at our dances. It's incredible. Nary an American girl in all these long months. The nurses, of course, don't come near us. Well, I've made up my mind that when I get home, the first thing you are going to do is teach me to rumba, and Cookie, I will really rumba. You won't have to coax me onto a dance floor. It takes this sort of isolation to make you realize what you miss the most, and dancing is one of them. I might get to Brussels or even Antwerp Saturday as we have been given an extra half day off. That means I'm free from Saturday afternoon to Monday morning, and I'm broke! Oh well, I can always become a gigolo. The rains have come again, apparently, and I have to hang on to keep from exploding. Gosh, how I hate rain. It's a regular phobia with me.

Yesterday, I witnessed a sight that filled my eyes and my heart with tears. For some days now, prisoners of war and political prisoners have been returning to their Belgian homes. The small, shabby Ciney is ludicrously decorated with the "palm of welcome" which are small uprooted trees, stuck in the cobblestones in front of the returning man's home. Max and I, walking to town, drifted toward the railroad station where a crowd had gathered. We knew then that a trainload of victims was due. Children, their arms loaded with makeshift bouquets of field flowers, dashed about excitedly. Finally, the train pulled in and stopped. The few who were returning to Ciney jumped off as many others stood in the doorways of the long train of boxcars. There was a rush as fathers grabbed up their kids, crushing them and their flowers. I shall never forget one little girl who was too young to know such emotion, clinging to her "hero" Daddy as he held her high in his arms. That child was sobbing with the suddenly released emotion that was far too mature for a child. Will men remember those moments of reunion with their children and direct their lives toward a world of peace? Or will they forget again and start fighting each other with the hatred and savagery of wild beasts? Even in this small community, already the seeds of future wars and disturbances are being planted. It is a bitter thing to watch. May God grant them the wisdom to settle their differences without violence.

So, until tomorrow, my love, Daddy

May 25, 1945 – Ciney, Belgium
My Darling:

Every time you write that "she talks, laughs, runs," I get a tingling in my spine and an awful emptiness in my stomach. I can't quite believe this thing that happens to a parent, Angel. Here I am so far away. I haven't seen her for so many months, and when last I did, there was literally no intelligent communication between us. Yet with each passing day, she has become so much a part of me, physically, mentally, spiritually, that I'm overwhelmed when I allow myself to dwell on the day when I'll catch her up in my arms. You must promise me, Angel, that when the day comes, you will do it the way I dream of it all the time. Roberta will come to me first. She will take my hand and lead me to where you will be waiting and where I will again find life.

We had a very nice dance last night. An excellent band and some better than average dancers. Even a few American WACs from Namur, but the cutting in was so constant that one couldn't take three complete steps without losing one's partner. Oh well, my feet hurt, anyhow, and I was content to watch! The sight is something. GIs can certainly cut up. To bed very late, as a consequence, and this morning (it's not yet 8 a.m.) I'm very sleepy eyed and a big day is ahead. So I'll close for now, Love. I must sneak one in for the folks and Mayme sometime during the day (I'm an optimist, you see.) Love to all. I sent off the perfume. I hope it's the right smell.

Kiss the cherub. To you, my heart, Daddy.
P.S. Angel, if my watch is fixed, send it first class. It should reach me in ten days. I am totally lost without a watch.

May 30, 1945 – Ciney, Belgium
My Darling:

My letter writing has of necessity become so sporadic, that I'm terribly mixed up. I'll just comment on the letters I have at hand so that at least you will know that I'm getting all of them. The package arrived in excellent condition. Was I delighted to see the hairbrush and the wonderful T-shirts!

It stands to reason that a month's furlough will be in order once we get home, whether it's the end of war for us or the prelude to more. In *Stars and Stripes* today I see where a strong movement is under way to release men over 35. My good friend Max is far from this age and will undoubtedly have to see this through, but a friendship has been established which I hope will endure.

I enclose a sweet letter from Sophie Tucker. Why don't you continue to visit the Chez Paree [famous Chicago nightclub, 1932–1960] and greet her for me. I shall write, myself, of course. We're hoping to get to Brussels again this weekend. We have been awarded our third Bronze Star. What a tinhorn hero I am.

Love to all. Kiss the cookie. Love, Dad

June 2, 1945 – Ciney, Belgium
My Darling:

Lest this weekend pass without a letter to you, a thing I dread more than anything, I scribble this hasty reply to your letters of May 22, 24. I'm glad you had an easy trip both ways and because our baby was such a good child I have a special picture book for her which I am making up myself. Gosh, if I could only hold her for a few minutes, the aches and pains, physical and mental, would flee from me.

My haste today, Angel, is brought on by the fact that in an hour we take off for Brussels. The day started out promisingly but is already dark and ominous. "The rains," as the Belgians say, have come again so we pretend not to notice it. How I crave some sunshine! Monday night you should have an opus, again, on the weekend's activities. Give my love to all. Kiss the cherub. To you, My Love, all that I am and all that I live to be to you. Soon, soon, Beloved, the Good Lord shall bring us together again. This I believe with all my heart.

Daddy

June 3, 1945 – Namur, Belgium
My Darling:

I'm attempting the impossible—to write a letter with a Red Cross pen. We have just pulled in from Brussels and have a two-hour wait for our transportation back to camp, and this isn't a bad place to wait in. Formerly one of the finest gambling casinos in Belgium, this magnificent place is now a Red Cross club, vying with the finest anywhere. The casino is on the Meuse and at the moment we are sitting on a terrace overlooking the water. It has been a wonderful day. Restful, leisurely, entertaining.

Our hosts, the Chananias, continue to overwhelm us with their hospitality.

La Meuse River, in Namur, Belgium

[From Oral History interview with grandson, Edward C. Bernstein, in 1986]:

We spent the greatest part of two years in Belgium. Every time we would get a weekend pass or a furlough, a couple of the Jewish boys in the outfit would take off for Brussels. We had heard that in this city there was a Jewish serviceman's club. It was so wonderful. It was in a beautiful building. The food was marvelous and the Jewish soldiers were treated so well. Some of the non-Jewish soldiers got wind of it and they wanted to go too. They even offered to be Jewish just to go to this club. We met the woman who was directing the activity, Mrs. Chanania. Before the war she had been the Belgian Correspondent for the New York Jewish News Agency. But of course, during the war this job had been disbanded. She was such a gracious host. She would always invite two of us to come to her home, a lovely flat. They were somehow able during the war to maintain some semblance of civilization, and they were very active also in helping other Jews. The husband, Mr. Chanania, had been a very respected diamond merchant and cutter in Belgium, which is a seat of the diamond-cutting industry. When the Germans came in and grabbed him, they threw him in one concentration camp and they threw Mrs. Chanania in another one. But word came out that she had been a recognized world correspondent, so for some reason they didn't get too rough with her. But the children—the young boy, 13 or 14, died of a ruptured appendix because the Nazis would not allow a doctor to come to a Jewish home. The young daughter, age 14 or 15, was spirited away to a nunnery where she was protected by the nuns. At any rate, now Belgium had been liberated more or less so they were back in their home and able to retain some of their things, lovely furniture and so on, and they were very kind to us. In time I learned that Mr. Chanania had a brother who lived in Chicago [In Englewood, a little south and west of Hyde Park] near where I lived just before taking off for the war. When I found out about this, I wrote home and asked the folks to go over and get acquainted with the Chananias' relatives, who were called Channon in America. Dr. Benjamin Channon was the brother of Mr.

Chanania. I acted as an intermediary because they, as Belgian citizens, could not receive any property from America, so the packages would be sent to me and I would deliver them to the Chananias. I've never forgotten that gorgeous hospitality. They were so kind.

June 3 letter continues:

Last night Max and I erred for the first time by selecting *Chocolate Soldier* for our evening's diversion. While it was brilliantly staged, the language barrier was too great, and even quick-witted Max had difficulty in following the lines. The singing was mediocre so my pleasure in *Chocolate Soldier* was negligible. Well, we can't pick a winner every time, and next time we go, we'll be a bit more discerning.

Darling, I am enclosing a letter written by Mme. Chanania to her brother-in-law, Dr. Channon. Please put it in an envelope and forward it at once. This will bring the letter to them much quicker than through civilian mail channels here. They are so gracious I asked them to let me do this small favor. Dr. Channon's address is enclosed. We were given a key to the house and when we returned at a late hour we found two beds made up with the most beautiful bed linens I have ever seen. We were like a couple of princes in royal beds, even though Max's long legs dangle over the end of his "couch." I sleep curled up, as you know, so didn't have any difficulty. Well, there was a leisurely breakfast, a sightseeing tour which brought us to a street carnival, a hectic few moments on the "auto scooters," a visit to the "Manneken Pis," which was a great disappointment, a turn around the Grand Place where are grouped the famous Guild Halls, and then we ran smack into a religious pageant that was truly spectacular. It seemed that half of Brussels donned garb of ancient biblical characters to parade throughout the city. It was a festival of one sort or another, and very colorful despite its frightful implication of people still living in the Dark Ages of religious superstition and fear. We returned "home" for an excellent dinner and then retired to the garden for sunning and eating of cherries. I stretched out on my back and entertained our hostess with a version of our private "grapes" eating ritual. They thought it was funny. So train time overtook us too quickly, and here we are, ready to go back to the Army from which we escape periodically. I must close now. Hope I find some mail when we get back.

Love to all. Kiss our cherub. Love, Daddy

[Editors' note: Since 1984, Roberta and her husband Charles Bernstein have been friends and neighbors in Hyde Park of Dr. Robert Channon and his wife, Leslie Jellinek. Their respective children have attended the same schools and social events. When Roberta read this letter, she immediately told her friend Bob Channon about it and he said that the Dr. Channon mentioned in the letter was his grandfather, whose brother and sister-in-law, Elias and Rose Chanania, lived in Brussels and *struggled through but survived the war. He was thrilled to know of this connection and to read Sam's loving descriptions of his relatives.]*

June 4, 1945 – Ciney, Belgium
My Darling:

Your letter of May 25 awaited me and even though I expected a half dozen, I took the one lone letter to my heart like a long-lost friend. It's funny how being away from camp for twenty-four hours fills you with all sorts of anticipations and expectations. Even an Army camp becomes "home" in all its aspects. Eating, bathing, sleeping habits, one discovers, are suddenly disturbed on a vacation and it's with a certain sense of relief that one drops back into familiar surroundings and routines. Rumors fly thick and fast and I listen with a fast-beating heart.

Well, Honey, the "circus" is starting and I must close this and open the appointment book for today. These "children" don't get going until I seat the patients and put the drills in their hands. Love to all. More tonight. Kiss the angel.

June 4, 1945 – Ciney, Belgium
My Darling:

Our solemn promise to tell each other all urges me to write of the ray of hope which dawned for us today. It is still nothing very factual, but it is a verification of a rumor we heard and it was good to hear. What I said about being present for Roberta's second birthday now comes within the realm of possibility. Let me put it this way. For the present and, possibly, future, the CBI theater is not in the cards for this unit. Looking at it realistically, certain new arrivals who have very low scores and a few who meet the critical score will be detached. The nucleus, with an average of about 60 points, by all sound reasoning should hang together, thus bringing this unit home for other duties there. That is our great hope and prayer, based on fairly logical reasoning. It is a small thing to pin one's hopes on, My Darling, but today when our C.O. talked to us, giving us certain information that I can't divulge, my heart leapt with a suffocating surge of joy. The same divine power which guided us through great danger will bring this second miracle about. In Max's Jewish letter from his mother today was this line: "Wus is schwer far dem mensch is gring fur Gott." [What is difficult for man is easy for God.] We repeated that phrase as we left the meeting this afternoon. I must stop, Angel, before I lose control of myself.

With all my love, Daddy.

June 5, 1945 – Somewhere in Belgium
My Darling:

With the inauguration of a new routine, it should be possible for me to write every morning before the day's work starts, and thus assuring you a daily letter.

Until yesterday, we had breakfast in our own mess hall. We usually went to breakfast, then lolled around the area for an hour, shaving and generally putting things in order. As of yesterday, we started to eat all our meals in the hospital which means that once over here, we stay. It also means that the hour before work starts is spent here in the hospital and so I'll use it to write my daily letter. The new arrangement has its good points in that it eliminates the messy mess kits. Trays are used at the hospital.

The patients are becoming fewer and fewer in number and soon we'll have to start boon-doggling to keep from going goofy. A small jazz band gave an hour's show last night and believe it or not I had to fight from falling asleep. I didn't realize that I was utterly fatigued until I dragged myself to bed at 8 p.m. In the middle of the night, I awoke with a terrific headache, the result of having slept in an uncomfortable position. But sleep, being the greatest of all medicines, restored me to normalcy. I'm myself again this morning. Kiss the cherub.

Love, Daddy.

June 7, 1945 – Ciney, Belgium
My Darling:

The post-holiday weariness has me in a tight grip this morning. Yesterday being June 6, the anniversary of D-Day, we declared a holiday. Max and I took off for Dinant [sixteen kilometers west-southwest of Ciney] where we proceeded to have ourselves an orgy of eating and drinking. We were there Tuesday night and Max met a fellow Philadelphian who had come back from Germany to rest for three days in quiet, picturesque Dinant where the 15th Army maintains a rest center. Ordinarily these centers are off limits to all other troops except those on rest passes. Since these centers control all the entertainment in the town, Max and I found ourselves enjoying all the privileges of the "restees" through the influence of the Philadelphian. Generosity, however, goes too far at times, and our total consumption of real "cokes," cognac, beer, strawberry shortcake, ice cream, peanuts, dinner at the Hotel Herman, more "cakes," and two kippered sardine sandwiches at 11 p.m. when we returned to camp, has both of us suffering from the "pip" this morning. Dinant is a nice place, that is if you avoid looking at the war ruins. In a few weeks they'll have the riverboats going again and I shall have my fill of boating, perhaps a delightful conditioning for that long ride home.

This is to be a short week. Saturday afternoon we knock off again until the following Monday. But we are resolved to "sit this weekend out." My goodness, even pleasure gets one down. Achieving pleasure, of course, means traveling great distances since we are miles from everything. And hopping in and out of Army trucks is anything but soothing. We do take a train occasionally, but even these are painful journeys.

No mail from you for several days and the "butterflies" are beginning to flutter again in the "coke" filled tummy. My brain refuses to dictate anymore this morning, Angel, so with beaucoup love I sign off this morning of June 7. It's going to be a gorgeous day. X for the cherub.

Love, Daddy.

June 8, 1945 – Ciney, Belgium
My Darling:

Just came from a swell USO show and feel refreshed and "important" again since one of the gals, Patti Long, a singer, remembered me quite well. She's an Oak Park girl who did pretty well in Chicago with various bands, etc. Ever-faithful Manny Levin is my constant publicist. He has a finger in the Special Service pie here and insists that I meet all the entertainers, even though I shy away from this sort of thing. I was glad, though, to go backstage to meet Patti. She was genuinely cordial, a trait many of these "patriotic entertainers" don't even have a bowing acquaintanceship with. But I guess they get pretty tired of the rough life, too.

Again, no mail today and I'm most anxious even though I know that all the ships are going home and few are returning here. There is a movie on tonight too, but while I was out talking to the entertainers, the theater jammed up to capacity and there was nary a seat. So I'll just sit here for a while and think of home, family, friends, and the good life that is to be ours.

So, Darling, with a whispered prayer that tomorrow will bring me a letter from you, I say good night. I am powerless to fill the aching void in your heart with my physical presence, but all that I am surges out to you with the message of my devotion and love. To the cherub and her good mama, then, a thankful daddy and husband.

Daddy.

June 9, 1945 – Ciney, Belgium
My Darling:

Well, it looks like I'll get a good deal of rest this weekend. "No passes," says the 1st Sgt, because King Leopold III is coming back to his troubled throne and the populace is divided and very touchy. [*Editors' note: According to Wikipedia, after King Leopold III of Belgium surrendered to the Germans on May 27, 1940, he was denounced as "Traitor King" by his own government and the British press. His brother, Prince Charles, was asked to serve as Regent.*] Little GIs have to stay off the streets so they don't get hurt. It's strictly a lot of bull, but that's the way it is. Well, I hope he gets settled before the next weekend because I'm going to be a very sore guy if some little tin king keeps me cooped up for another week.

I am enclosing a few snapshots made in Brussels. Max and I divided the set, and as soon as a second set is printed, I'll send the ones he got out of the first batch. There's one of me reclining in a deck chair that's a "lulu." I will get to Dinant tomorrow morning, though, as I promised to sing there for a morning service. It's a nice ride and the scenery is lovely. Max and I hope to get to Luxembourg, too. It is a fabulously beautiful place, they say! So, Angel, I'll say adieu for today.

Love to all. Kiss the cherub. To you, my love, Daddy.

June 11, 1945, 7:30 a.m. – Ciney, Belgium
My Darling:

This is the hour of charm in which I reread and compose a reply to your letters of which I have at hand those of May 26, 28, 29, and 31. Now for the weekend activities which always are so variable and interesting. It wasn't the king's rumored return to the throne which temporarily restricted us. It was something more exciting. Somebody hollered "rape," it seems, and the Army wanted to clean up the mess before any more GIs got "caught." The restriction, however, was lifted Saturday morning and Max and I took off for Liège pronto. It was a pleasant excursion in that being with Max is always a pleasant experience, but Liège stinks. The war scars are still too prominent. It's depressing. The Meuse cuts the city in half and one must walk to get to places. European hotels are the last word in inconvenience. Washington slept in a lot of American beds, history tell us, but historians ought to add a chapter on the beds I've slept in. It takes a terrific sense of humor, Darling, to put up with it, so I guess I'm a pretty rugged guy at that. One week it's French embroidered sheets, the next it's a bed of spikes and broken glass. Oh, my aching back! But it's fun and adventure. We spent most of our time in a swell GI movie house; saw the film *Wilson*, a four-bell movie, for my money. We paid an enormous price for a meager dinner, got just a tiny bit tipsy and laughed about nothing like a pair of idiots. That, Darling, is the norm. That's all for now, Sweetheart.

Love to all. Kiss the cherub. Daddy.

June 11, 1945 – Ciney, Belgium
My Darling:

Without another moment's delay, please find the copy of Col. Knox's [publisher of the *Chicago Daily News*] letter commending me for my work and mail it to me. Also, select one or two Saturday pages that are outstanding as to makeup and include them. I should have had these long ago. I had some clippings and promotion ads but I lost them during the Bulge. It's very important that I have these things immediately. I also want a copy of *Music News* in which all the fine ads about me appeared. Please, Honey, don't fail to do this at once. Perhaps one or two music clippings will be useful, too. I have a plan. It's time that I started to let people know who I am. [*Editors' note: Here Sam is preparing to continue his journalism career at the* Chicago Daily News *after the war.*] Please, Angel, act quickly.

Love, Daddy.

June 12, 1945, 12:30 p.m. – Ciney, Belgium
Darling:

Just finished a pretty good lunch and being momentarily satisfied with the world, I am weak enough to indulge in the desire for some luxury, so I am bold (perhaps crass is a better word), I am bold enough to ask for some money. I need not less than $25 with which to buy a pair of binoculars I have negotiated for. I've always wanted these damn things and I'm weak enough now to spend that kind of money for them. Actually, this is my first extravagance. A PFC's pay leaves me broke long before the month is over. For instance, it cost 500 francs for an ordinary weekend in Brussels and that included free lodging with the Chananias. So you see what I mean. I'm so furious with these bastards for holding up my promotion. To hell with the honors. I want the extra pay so that I don't have to pinch a franc twice before spending. This weekend is to be fairly inexpensive, and then I'll dig in for a couple of weeks to make up for the binoculars. Sweetheart, if you need the money for any reason whatsoever, don't send it. But if you think we can spare it, OK. <u>But no more than what I asked for</u>. Please. Don't forget the clippings. I'm sending another box of odds and ends home tonight. Don't forget the newspaper tear sheets and clippings.

Last night we held an impromptu banquet on the bed below mine and the marinated herring and caviar were devoured. Oh, Sweetheart, that caviar is out of this world. Where do you get it? It's Smith Bros. from Port Washington, Wisconsin, according to the label. Stock up on it for our future evenings at home. It's really excellent stuff. Do you remember Port Washington, where we ate that wonderful bass? Do you remember our big limousine that took us there?

Hold on to your hat, my Angel. According to the Army profile which has been filled out on me, <u>I AM UNFIT FOR ANY OTHER THEATER OF OPERATIONS</u>. I have every reason to believe that homeward bound is to be the direction of my next journey. When that will be is in the hands of our gracious Almighty God.

Love to all, Daddy.

June 14, 1945 – Ciney, Belgium
My Darling:

The "hour of charm" will probably be of morning's duration today as the Heinies are painting the clinic and it's impossible to do any work. You'd think we were here for good with the way they are working on this place. The entire vast building is being decorated inside and the landscaping around it goes on without end. It's really one elegant sight now as compared to the mud hole we found. Actually, all this activity doesn't mean much. The general consensus of opinion is that we will be here for several months yet. That is the unit. The personnel is subject to change as individuals are deployed and discharged. This is inevitable and it's not pleasant to contemplate since some will be going home while others will be Pacific bound. As I told you earlier, if the records are worth anything, I personally will not have to worry about the Pacific. I'm a class III with a D and a B classification which means "no other theater of operations." Max, however, being much younger, and quite sound physically, is destined for the Pacific, I am afraid. I dare not think of the day I will bid him au revoir. I pray that we can come home together before the Pacific adventure. I can tell you this, Honey, that a few weeks ago I had my leg and back x-rayed again and the findings were definitely arthritic symptoms, a fact which is entered in my record. While this cannot get me home before the outfit moves, it's certainly classes me as physically unfit for any more hardship. The prolonged damp weather currently plays havoc with my leg but I manage to go along. I feel perfectly swell otherwise and certainly look better than I have in a long time. Angel, please don't worry about me. Even my working day has suddenly become a very easy one. Here's the story.

The colonel, who was formerly boss of this department, has returned to his job here, displacing the cocky little major, who is now just another dentist. The colonel also threw all the bookkeeping into the ash can. Thus, one moment I was up to my ears in work, and the next I was out of a job. Said the colonel to me, "Guess you're out of a job, Lesner." Said I to the colonel, "Looks that way, Sir, doesn't it?" "Well," said the colonel, "You can help me." So Private First Class Lesner now assists a colonel who is a gentleman, balm to the nerves, and easy on the assistant since he works about one hour out of the day, just to amuse himself. I can either sit and read or putter around in the laboratory if I choose. I told him, though, that I flatly refused to learn any more "trades" in the Army. Love to all. Kiss our cherubic Love Lettuce. And take a big one for yourself, Madame.

Love, love, love, Daddy

June 14, 1945, 4:45 p.m. – Ciney, Belgium
Darling:

Your letters of May 30 and June 2–3 came an hour ago. The pictures of you are stunning. I'm pleased to have them since everyone asks me if I carry a picture of you. But the baby—Darling—where is that tiny little bundle I left behind? I simply can't believe it. She looks like a child of 3 or 4. So grown-up. God, she's cute, but I don't know her. I'm terrified. How will I ever bridge the gap of a year or more? If you want to make me happy, take her to a photographer and have a real portrait made of her. Her eyes are magnificent. But, Honey, where is the curly hair you speak of? Her hair, thank God, is long and lovely like yours, but it's awfully straight.

I'm miserable over the slowness of my mail to you. I await answers on several urgent questions and you don't even have the letters yet after three weeks or more. Yours invariably reach me in ten days. It's maddening! I must close now. This is the second letter today. I hope one of them reaches you this month.

Love to all. Kiss the cherub. Love, Daddy

June 15, 1945 – Ciney, Belgium
Darling:

An uneventful day is drawing to a close. Rumors fly thick and fast. We have ceased accepting patients as of tomorrow and a time limit has been set for termination of our activities here. But rumor and fact are so hopelessly intertwined that it's agony to try to figure it out. It's also depressing because invariably you wind up with a discouraging note. Only one thing is left us, the right to pray that our hearts will be united soon. More optimistically, I can say that the facts are facts and the CBI is not for me. I can't say any more since I know nothing more. The hardest thing in the world to do, I have discovered, is to do nothing, to be idle. It was a day of complete idleness for me today. I wrote letters, read, and wandered around. The colonel apparently doesn't care and when he does cross my path, he looks at me in what I think is astonishment. He got me into the clinic before he left some months ago, and now that he has returned he has discovered that he still hasn't made up his mind what to do with me. That's the feeling I have. The noncom in charge of the E.M.s in the clinic tells me I'm nuts to fret about it. "For Pete's sake, relax and enjoy your leisure," he said today. "The colonel doesn't care." He is a swell guy, a prince among officers, but I feel like such an idiot just standing around jiggling the coins in my pockets. Well, it's shit and shower time, so I'll close this one. Going to Brussels tomorrow. Love to all. Kiss the cherub. Honey, give my Ma and Mayme a snapshot. I'll have more made later.

Love, Daddy

June 16, 1945, 4:45 p.m. – Ciney, Belgium
Darling:

Keeping up a cheerful front on this miserable Saturday morning is difficult. The weather is awful. Where does all the rain and mist come from? It's worse than England. Well, it's a short day and at noon we'll prepare to take off for Brussels. Then our spirits rise. Now we can take a convenient afternoon train at 2:30 p.m. Up to now we had to depend on our thumbs or wait until the end of the day for a painfully slow pre-First World War choo-choo. European trains are funny. They're just like you see in the movies. All cut up into compartments and you enter directly from the platform into the compartment instead of climbing aboard at one end of the car and working your way through. They are the last word in discomfort, for we ride first or second class, depending on what is available at the time. Being Allied soldiers, we just get on, take possession of a seat and settle down. We don't pay. Max and I play a little game, however. When the conductor starts through, we pretend to be sound asleep, a challenge to him to dare and wake us. We had a well-rehearsed "Speech of Indignance" all ready to turn loose on the hapless creature who dares to wake us. After he's gone we open one eye apiece and laugh like hell. The other occupants of the

Peace in Europe 281

compartment not knowing what's what, laugh too, and probably say to themselves, "those crazy American soldats." See, just thinking about this I feel better already.

I had hoped to have your letters in reply to the request to call the Channons in time to take them with me to Brussels today since we are to be guests of the Chananias. But we leave before mail call and even if there is a letter from you today I shall not have it until Sunday night when we return. Angel, I hope you are keeping the snapshots etc. We will make up a scrapbook of the stuff and keep it for Roberta. Certainly it will be of interest to her someday. I dare to dream about bringing you and her back to a peaceful, beautiful Europe someday. We might even visit this part of Belgium, in May when the strawberries are as big as eggs. I've never seen anything like it. With so little sunshine, it beats me how anything grows so lush here. The roses are like peonies, and, Angel, I wish you could see the fields of poppies. I always thought the "Flanders Fields where poppies grow" was a poet's pipe dream. But it's true. They bloom for only a short time and appear quite suddenly apparently. On seeing a field sprinkled with blood red poppies, your heart stops for a moment. Association of ideas, I guess. They are the most dramatically tragic flowers I have ever seen. I guess they are almost sacred here for they are seldom picked. They look best in the field where they bloom so suddenly and as quickly fade away. Love to all, Angel. Kiss the Love Lettuce. When there is news, you shall be the first to know, My Beloved.

Daddy

June 18, 1945, 4:45 p.m. – Ciney, Belgium
Darling:

The good old Monday blues just smacked me right between the eyes. No mail! I wait for three o'clock in agony and then I get nothing. This on top of the disappointment of having netted nothing in the Saturday-Sunday mail. It's awful.

We had a swell time in Brussels despite a difficult trek to that fair city. The 2:30 train was only a rumor, and we hitchhiked via a mad jeep and a monster truck. We arrived numb and hungry. But the gentle Chananias soon revived us and we spent a delightful evening in the theater and an altogether pleasant morning and afternoon eating and sunning ourselves in the garden. Although I still have no word as to whether you were able to call Dr. Channon, I have confidence that you did so and that you also forwarded the letter to Dr. Channon. I enclose another, plus two snapshots for them. Please forward the same. The address is: Dr. B.Z. Channon, 6509 S. Ashland Avenue, Chicago 36, Ill. Marvin's new address is: Marvin Channon, 2106 Cuyler Street, Berwyn, Ill. You might also call Dr. A. Olbermann. They are also relatives of the Chananias. I can't begin to tell you how nice these people are. Max and I call them Aunt Rose and Uncle Elias and they refer to us as their American nephews.

Brussels, as of today, is off limits, but we'll find a way to get there as we have a date for next week. That's all for now, Honey. I'm too disappointed in the mailman to think of anything pleasant to write about. Maybe I'll have luck tomorrow.

Love to all. Kiss the cherub. Daddy

June 19, 1945, 4:45 p.m. – Ciney, Belgium
Darling:

Lest the disappointment of no mail overtake me again, I write this in the pleasant interlude after lunch. Then I can go back to hoping for a letter at three o'clock. All is quiet here. The usual rumors continue to weave a net of hope, despair, and half-truths into which to become enmeshed. Even the date for sailing has been "established" and of course this preposterous rumor is bandied about with devastating results. Only one thing is sure. Someday we'll leave this place, which tells you all and nothing at the same time and which neatly sums up just how much any of us knows about what's to happen. I did tell you that patients are not arriving anymore. Only emergencies, and I've just seen one that made me very shaky for a few moments. A poor devil, with both feet severed at the ankles, was just brought in. What was regarded as routine in war is now suddenly awful. I have "joined forces" with the major again for a few days, while one of the other men is on D.S. [Dental Service] in Paris. The major is a different person under these changed circumstances. Our morning was delightful. We did some work (as little as possible) and much discussing about fishing and relaxing in that postwar period to come. We also complimented each other on the pleasure of enjoying a typical Chicago summer day, today. It is beautiful. A light haze, a bright sun and a warm, scented breeze. The afternoon should be equally restful. I don't mind sitting around when I have someplace to sit. Last week I was so uneasy because I had no specific duty and consequently felt that I was in the way wherever I stood or sat. I'm back in surgery and this nice room is conducive to relaxation.

That's all for now, Angel. Kiss the cherub Love Lettuce. I can't quite get used to the idea that she is no longer just a baby, but now a little girl with a distinct personality. I guess we'll make Brussels again this weekend, perhaps for the last time.

Love, Daddy

June 20, 1945, 4:45 p.m. – Ciney, Belgium
Darling:

I'm very, very lazy this morning. For the third day the sun has greeted us upon our awakening and it's a very pleasant feeling, although it kills ambition. This promises to be a busy day too as half the staff are either on pass or D.S. But I guess I'd rather be busy than just sit around wishing I were free to go outdoors. No mail yesterday again. I guess the government doesn't think the state of our morale is very important now. How wrong that is. If ever a guy needed this daily contact with his family, it is now.

Some time ago I sent Mr. Bulliet a little souvenir. I wonder if he received it. What goes on at the *Daily News*? Please let me know how things are going.

Of the news there is little except that I have started to smoke cigarettes, mainly because we found some attractive cigarette holders in Brussels. But I really don't like them and shall probably stop again after the novelty of the holder wears off. There seems to be some doubt about our getting to Brussels again without a special pass. So we'll have to look for another spot, although I doubt whether we'll find silk sheets to sleep on anywhere else. The outfit is offering a three-day holiday at Reser, our rehabilitation center which we maintain about three miles from the hospital. Reser is in a cow pasture even more isolated than the hospital. There is a swimming pool, golf course, and tennis courts, but all sport activity is regimented and one must take calisthenics in the morning. I signed up for a pass to Reser mainly because I want to sunbathe for a couple of days. It will be awfully dull since I doubt if Max can go at the same time, but perhaps the complete rest will be good. That's all for now, Angel. Perhaps your letters will reach me today. Love to all. Kiss the Junior Miss. Wouldn't you know it? It just started to rain. That knee of mine never fails me.

Love, Daddy

June 21, 1945, 4:45 p.m. – Ciney, Belgium
Darling:

At last a letter arrived. Yours of June 8 came this afternoon, but it was only a meager appetizer. How hungry I am for all the missing letters, and how anxious I am that mine reach you. I have boldly asked for some money in several letters and apparently you haven't received them for you keep asking me about my need for finances. It is rumored that this month's pay will be the last in Belgian francs. What that means I can't possibly say, but perhaps you had better not send any after this letter. I assume that you have filled my requests made in earlier letters. No doubt the mail situation will become very precarious once we are under way.

About Brussels and beds! The first time we were there we stayed in a hotel, but on all other visits we stayed at the Chananias'. I described the elegant silk sheets etc. in an earlier letter. They have since fixed up a very small room for us and we enjoy all the comfort and privacy of our own homes. They are such good people

Mid-morning. Nothing new to report I won't even repeat the idiotic rumors that have been set in motion since yesterday. We should be enjoying this period of leisure but it is impossible to relax in the atmosphere of uncertainty. The curtain hanging over the future is so thick and so opaque, we are left only the avenue of prayer and faith to sustain us through the aching void that is this living apart from each other. There is nothing, absolutely nothing, here to brighten even a corner of that dark abyss. Even loyal, affectionate Max upon whom I lean heavily can at best only distract me from the moment. I allow him to usurp all my free time because I can't bear to be alone. My need for the kind of communication that existed between us; my need for the deeply satisfying love and affection which you always had ready for me is great. Anything else in comparison is trivial, undefined, and elusive. I'm reading *The Razor's Edge* but may cast it aside. It's a disturbing book at such a time.

Love to all. Kiss the Junior Miss. Love, Daddy

June 21, 1945, 4:45 p.m. – Ciney, Belgium
Darling:

The rumors continue to excite and distress. I'm still hoping to be on hand for Roberta's second birthday, although if the latest rumor materializes we'll have to celebrate at the end of the month instead of the middle of the month. Pray for that miracle to happen, Angel. What a birthday party that will be! I just finished a mass of extractions. I must clean up the tray and get ready for lunch.

Until tomorrow, My Love, Daddy

June 23, 1945 – Ciney, Belgium
Sweetheart:

The day was brightened yesterday by the arrival of two letters, June 4, 6. Eight dollars a day isn't bad pay, Honey. I guess I'll let you do the breadwinning and I'll stay home and get acquainted with my daughter. You might as well save yourself a lot of trouble and accept the new arrangement because you are going to have a hell of a time making me go to work in the morning. Roberta and I will read the French picture books in the morning, play games, have lunch, and then spend the afternoons at the beach. Then, when Mama comes home from the office, hot and tired, we'll kiss her a whole lot, make her feel good again, and then we'll go for long auto rides to cool off.

Gosh, Honey, I didn't realize how tired I was until this week when we just decided to slow down and stay in camp. Going to bed at a reasonable hour for several nights now has released the tension. You can just feel the weariness rolling off of you. I know I'm getting rested again because I woke up refreshed long before the bugle, a thing I hadn't done for many months. Getting up has usually been a business of terrible effort. The weather is so beautiful I think Max and I will stay in camp this weekend and just sunbathe. While visiting Brussels is always an exciting adventure it is awfully exhausting due to the uncertain transportation.

Love to all. Kiss the cherub. To you, My Darling, Daddy

June 25, 1945 – Ciney, Belgium
My Darling:

The weekend produced no mail from you, but the pleasure of having yours of June 8 in which you tell me of the contact with Dr. Channon sustained me. Perhaps today mail will come. We did not go to Brussels, having changed our minds at the last moment. Frankly, it was too hot to struggle with the transportation problem. So Saturday afternoon Max and I went into one of the nearby grain fields and soaked up sunshine.

About 7 a.m. we were told we'd have to move to another barracks that morning: of all the goddamn nerve, on a Sunday morning. Well, we've learned to do what we are told without too much mental resistance, so we gathered up our mountains of stuff and our mattresses and moved. The new arrangement isn't as nice as the one we left but apparently it won't be for long. We have learned that two other units are moving into our area. We have created such a livable, spacious area that someone decided it would be good for a sort of marshaling area. No doubt, some shifting of personnel will take place. The high pointers being grouped together, and likewise the low pointers, I don't know where I stand with my 50-odd points. I am prepared for the worst as well as for the best which "at best" would mean duty in the States since release is apparently for the 40 and older veterans only. But at the rate Japan is disappearing under the deluge of bombs, it won't be too long before we can all say, "it's over." I don't believe all this nonsense about taking a year for all the troops to get out of here. I've never read and heard so much bullshit in all my life as appears now in the press, including *Stars and Stripes*. The confusion and the glaring contradictions are laughable and disgusting. We are a mighty nation, indeed. If we can lick such a formidable enemy and yet remain so divided in opinion, effort, and intention, no wonder Europeans think we are all crazy. But they can't resist us. Once you break down their reserve they do handsprings to please you.

We have two parties on our social calendar for this week. Getting back to the weekend activities: After a good Sunday dinner Max and I took two Red Cross bicycles and rode through this magnificent countryside for four hours, winding up at Reser, our hospital rest center which can be truly described as Shangri-La. We swam in the outdoor pool, ate supper there, and then rested under a gigantic elm tree. The landscaped gardens at Reser are beautiful. Sweetheart, I'm afraid I can't quite convey to you just what a European château really is. In America we would readily think of it as a palace. No wonder there are wars here constantly. One man will control vast areas of the fertile farmland and use it solely for a park for his own pleasure. In a country as vast as ours such a thing possibly can be condoned, but in little Belgium such a thing is criminal. Europe need never know a food shortage if the châteaux and the barons were busted down to a normal size. It's all very glorious to look at, but there is some terrible poverty to look at too.

The chiefs are all away on various official and unofficial duties. I have absolutely nothing to do but sit still, which is what I intend to do. By the end of this week we shall know our "fate." I believe we will spend a few weeks here getting back into physical condition. I don't mind that. An hour of drill and exercise is good. I'm getting fat from the beer and French fries. If it's no worse than it was in France, we are due for a delightful vacation and then, My Darling, I look to a gracious God to bring me home, at least for a while, so that I can drink in your love again and get acquainted with our child.

Love to all, Daddy

June 26, 1945 – Ciney, Belgium
My Darling:

He keeps me in such good humor just watching him discover his own latent talents as a "creative artist." I turned his last fine poem over to our talented chapel organist who will give it a musical setting. I hope to sing it before we leave here. I must warn you again, Darling, that with the end of activities in our hospital I may be sent to some other place for seven days to two weeks. I dread this sort of thing but the Army thinks we must keep busy to keep out of trouble. If it's Antwerp or someplace like that it won't be bad. I suppose I can assume that such a trip will have some relation to one of the professional services of a hospital but I won't be too surprised if it is something like that "gotsa dooty" we endured during the breakthrough. Although this time there won't be any Heinies to shoot at.

Well, wouldn't you know it! Just this moment I've been told I'm going on guard duty here on the post. Of all the stinking deals. Well, maybe it's better than to go doing some filthy job somewhere else. More about it when I get the details.

Love to all. Kiss the cherub, Daddy

June 28, 1945 – Ciney, Belgium
My Darling:

Your letter of June 11 which reached me yesterday has buoyed me up immensely. I wish I could comply with your wish to see my 130th story in print, but first, I don't think I could get permission since for some strange reason the document is on the restricted list, and secondly, I don't think this bunch of goons is worthy of what I wrote. I have a very personal feud with the Army and the sooner I can leave it all behind the happier I'll be. I did try very hard. I knew that you would understand the style in which it was written and countless thoughts that were conveyed by suggestion rather than long drawn-out passages. But this very thing was completely overlooked by the idiots. One "brainstorm" said to me, "Why were you in such a hurry? It reads like you didn't know how to end it." I thought at first to tell this moron that only God knew how it would end. I thought to tell him that there was no time for words with the Nazi tanks and guns at our heads. I thought that they would understand all this. I wrote as I felt in those last critical days of December, but it was in vain, I see now. I not only didn't get my T/5, I didn't even get a "thank you." And on top of that I got this painful guard detail for all my "genius." The detail in itself is not bad. It's the humiliation. It leaves me little free time in that you are so weary after a four-hour guard tour that the eight hours following are spent largely in sleeping. My weekend holiday is a thing of the past for the present. I could have gone on D.S. to Antwerp or Ghent, but I have no more faith in other units than I have in my own. They'd find some shitty detail for me too. So I decided, since I had a choice of two evils, I would stay here and guard. I don't know what will happen to Max after the hospital closes down at the end of this week. My mazel, [Yiddish for "luck"] he'll be packed off somewhere for D.S. or something and I'll crawl back into my shell. Oh, if this thing were only over and done with for good. Every day the Army hacks another piece out of your heart.

I'm enormously pleased that you called Sophie Tucker. I sure wish I could get home for such a party as she promised to throw for me. How I need just such a demonstration to restore my confidence. The third Bronze Star is now official. My total points number 52 which is neither here nor there. Unless we get a pass, it's quite unlikely that I will see the Chananias again, a thing which distresses me very much. I think I can telephone them, at least. I have asked for a three-day pass, but I doubt if it will be granted. But until it is turned down, there is always the hope.

Don't mind this letter too much, Angel. It's just a reaction to the tension and uncertainty which surrounds every soldier in these trying days of "sweating out" your fate. There are those who get the breaks and there are those who get hell. This time I sincerely believe I'll get a break.

Love to all. Kiss the cherub, Your Daddy

June 30, 1945 – ANTWERP, Belgium
My Darling:

If my last letter reaches you before this one you will have a fairly good idea of what happens to your Daddy who really gets around in this crazy Army. At 6 p.m. Thursday I learned via the grapevine that I was to go on D.S. the following morning. So I went to a birthday party, had a hell of a good time, and Friday morning, sure enough, I and five other guys were on our way to Antwerp. Naturally we worried and speculated about the "deal" we were getting. But after twenty-four hours here I'd be glad to give the cow pasture and all its rural beauty right back to the shitty cows. How wonderful is the big city, and what an alive city is Antwerp! Max isn't on this "detail," much to my regret (and already intense loneliness for him) but two of the lads who also have relatives in Brussels and who happen to be particular buddies of ours are here, too, so at least

I have them to pal around with. Darling, this is a great place. I don't know how long we will be here, but if it's until the day we take off for home, I won't be sorry. The only terrible aspect of this deal is that I'll have to wait days and days for your letters. I shall continue to write every day, though, and keep you informed. We haven't been paid either and it's getting uncomfortable. But the officer in charge of us is trying to get our money sent here.

Here's the deal: Antwerp is a port city and there are considerable troops passing through and stationed for varying lengths of time. So a group of us from the 130th General Hospital set up a dispensary here to take care of the emergency work. At the moment the boys are patching up a few guys with busted heads. They say they were attacked. They didn't do anything. They pled innocence. Unlikely story! But that's neither here nor there. They have to be fixed up. Also, the "clapped" up and the VDs drop in for treatment. I, however, have no traffic with this. In the back room, under a skylight, we have a tiny, ridiculously crude dental clinic where I act as dental assistant for one of the two dental officers. They don't like to work, fortunately, and take frequent and prolonged breaks. This, Honey, is a very good deal for me. How did this ever happen to me? Our quarters are in a private home not far from the dispensary. It's not too clean but it's very comfortable. We don't make beds, we don't sweep, and there are no sergeants around to change our disinclinations. My goodness, is this the Army? What's more, we sleep until 7 a.m. An ambulance picks us up, takes us to chow and then to the dispensary where we shave and clean up in a modern washroom. The day starts about 8:30 and for me apparently ends at 4 p.m., or earlier. I told you these dentists hate to work. A vehicle is available at all times for going to meals, but I love to ride the train. This is an experience. They are always jammed and crawl along so one can get off and on at any point. The shops here are fascinating but I am practicing the greatest restraint.

Angel, the rumors continue to buzz to the effect that we are coming home. Some say a month. Some say six weeks. Some say twenty days. Well, Angel, we're going to do the town tonight by visiting all the free places. There are theaters, dances, canteens galore. I've never heard such wonderful bands as they have in these GI hotspots. This was a great nightlife city once and there are several magnificent ballrooms which have been taken over for GI hotspots. It's all very elegant. Gosh if you could only be with me to do these famous cities. Here is where history was made. Right around the corner is Rubens Straat, named for the painter Rubens. His house still stands. The waterfront is fast and colorful and a sixteenth-century cathedral towers over all. The buzz bombs raised hell with this city but the pulse of this famous city still beats strongly. There is an outside exhibit of war machinery, among which sit two V-bombers captured intact. What horror. What terror they evoke even as they sit there with their fuses removed. The V-2 [bomb], many of which rained upon this city, is the most horrible thing I've seen so far. Just to look at it leaves you in a futile rage.

Our dispensary is in a modern building, formerly a first-class art gallery, but to my way of thinking, totally unsuited for a dispensary. There's so much equipment piled up in the dump and these rum-heads are using the crudest sort of homemade junk. I must say the 130th is great on this score alone. We went out and got the finest stuff available. I'm glad I'm not there to see it being dismantled. The 130th closed down today officially. Well, Cookie, I've told you beaucoup news this time. Tomorrow I shall have more stories.

Love to all. Kiss the cherub, Your Daddy

July 2, 1945
My Darling:

Antwerp continues to intrigue me. I am as happy as a bird here. The day passes swiftly and there is so much activity at night that one has little time to move around. This evening, for instance, I am calling on some people who struck up a conversation quite casually on the train to Brussels Sunday morning. It turns out that they have a daughter who is an opera singer of some vocal distinction. When they learned of my real interest in music they invited me to call on them and meet the daughter (who is 30, so they say). I telephoned them this afternoon to confirm the invitation and Mlle De Wein answered and assured me that her mama had told her all about me and that she would be most pleased to meet me. Well, I shall have to listen to Papa and Mama extol the great virtues and talents of their daughter, but it will be pleasant to visit and talk with people of refinement. Tomorrow I shall give you a report. Tomorrow evening I am going to hear *Faust*, if I can still get a ticket. I shall enlist Mlle De Wein to help me if I fail on my own.

My visit to Brussels and the Chananias yesterday was pleasant as usual. I read them your letter regarding the Channons and I'm looking forward to be able to give them more reports soon. Uncle Elias developed a nervous toothache and retired for the better part of the day but Aunt Rose [Chanania] is a wonderful conversationalist. Also present was a young Viennese Jew who fled from Vienna at 16 (1939), wound up in Palestine, where he enlisted in the British Army and went through all of the bitter African campaign. His unit is now in Italy, but Joseph, anxious to know what became of some of his relatives, came to Brussels where they last were heard from. He learned that they were "taken away" by the Nazis. Fortunately, all of Joseph's immediate family escaped from Austria and are now living in Brooklyn, New York. One brother is in the American Army.

Incidentally, Aunt Rose learned today that her only brother and one child of the family who were in the concentration camp in Holland died on the train that was carrying them to freedom. Aunt Rose is trying desperately to get to Amsterdam to help the widow and the surviving children. But red tape is such that I'm afraid she's doomed to disappointment. You see, Angel, the war isn't over for these people. Now the searching for loved ones begins only to end in the utter despair of finding unmarked graves. Joseph told the story of one boy in his unit, which incidentally is the famous "Jewish Brigade" of Palestine, who upon reaching Italy went to one of the refugee camps on the chance of finding his parents. He went to a certain hovel, knocked on the door, and an old man answered. The broken man did not recognize his son, whom he saw last six years before. The lad of then was now a grown man in a strange uniform. This story is not unusual. Thousands have the same tale to relay.

Max has promised to telephone me and keep me posted on the news about our outfit. He did not come to Brussels as he was held for possible D.S. in Luxembourg, but the deal was called off. He telephoned me at the Chananias yesterday. I miss the rascal. How we would enjoy Antwerp and its many possibilities for social contacts. Fortunately, almost everyone speaks English here, else I'd be lost without him. I find I understand much of the Flemish which is spoken here. Until tomorrow, then, My Love. Adieu.

Love to all. Kiss the cherub. Daddy

July 3, 1945 – Antwerp, Belgium
My Darling:

I shall be brief as it is quite late already. I have just returned from the opera, where I heard *Faust* as Gounod wrote it—all of it. These Europeans won't tolerate any cuts. In fact, I suspect they add a few licks of their own. Despite this it was a good performance with an unusually fine ballet just before the final act. In all the years of opera going in America I had never seen some of the scenes included in tonight's version, and, I might add, the American public is being cheated. But labor would never stand for so much scene shifting at home. It was a gala performance for something or other and the prices were high. I had an orchestra seat and don't regret it. My only great and constant regret is that I am not sharing this part of my life with you. Imagine if we could be together in these historic cities of Europe.

It's a small world, though. Sitting a few seats away was a guy who used to study with Baroness von Turk Rohn some twelve years ago. We used to sing together in the Baroness's ensemble. He's the only guy I've met from home in all these months overseas. But he's a first lieutenant now. How he did it I can't imagine. He's been in since 1941, so he's welcome to the distinction. Max is trying desperately to come. He'd certainly strut in this city and I'd be less lonely for a day or two, at least.

Well, Sweetheart, there's no telling when your mail will reach me. I threatened to go AWOL and go back to Ciney to pick up the mail if they don't send it down here. Remember the people I mentioned in an earlier letter—the ones with the opera singer daughter who has a brilliant voice—well, her parents took me over like a son. Papa before the war was a diamond polisher. My goodness, everyone in Belgium seems to be involved with diamonds. But Mr. De Wein is a nice guy and Mama De Wein is warm and hospitable. I'm going to the horse races with them in Brussels on Sunday. They are racing fans. I'll know half of Europe's diamond men if this sort of thing keeps up.

Love to all. Kiss the Angel Child. To you my love, Daddy

July 4, 1945 – Antwerp, Belgium
My Darling:

My enthusiasm for Antwerp is only slightly lessened by the persistently bad weather. The sun hasn't shown for more than five minutes since we arrived last Friday. It is getting warmer, however, so maybe summer is really just around the corner. There is absolutely nothing doing this afternoon so I think I'll take off soon and explore the city a bit. There is a fine zoo here, and of course the waterfront is always interesting and colorful. One of the two dentists who were on D.S. duty here left with his unit for Germany today, taking along his dental assistant, who also belonged to the same outfit. That leaves me and my captain, a Captain Smith from another unit, to run the clinic until headquarters assigns us some help, but with only five patients scheduled per day, I don't think we'll overwork. The captain just told me I can take the rest of the day off. I'm going to the zoo. Maybe I'll spend an hour in a very interesting bookshop just around the corner. More tomorrow, Angel.

Love, Daddy

July 6, 1945 – Antwerp, Belgium
My Darling:

It is a week now that I have been away from camp and I dare say I've all but forgotten the place. This city living is so engrossing, so full of interest, so full of pleasant human contact as to almost lull one into a false sense of well-being, that is as far as the Army is concerned. As I told you in an earlier letter, there are twelve of us billeted in a private home which is not too old. At least there are signs of excellent modernizing having been done in recent years. Most of the houses are grim by our standards on the outside, although one sees magnificent modern houses throughout Belgium, but the interiors always prove interesting. One thing gets me, though. The toilet is always in a separate closet. It's never in the bathroom. Anyhoo! I'm sitting in my semiprivate room which has a fireplace, a delightful balcony with a French door opening onto it, a beautiful hardwood floor, a checked cloth on the small writing table, several good chairs, and most important, peace, quiet and privacy. I took over the room from the two T/5s who departed this week, and even though I might have had the room all to myself, I invited one of the quieter fellows to share it with me. He's seldom here since he's on night call frequently and sleeps in the dispensary. Some of the rooms are more elaborately furnished but they are all on the street. Mine is to the rear of the house. The lady of the house, sensing that the room had new occupants, came up to see what we were like. I was here alone at the time. She saw what I had done in the few moments, such as arranging a few knick-knacks on the mantel. It made a hit with her and immediately she promised new clean curtains, a checked cloth, etc. She kept her promise. A bar of chocolate and a package of cigarettes and presto I have a friend. She speaks to me in Flemish which I understand fairly well.

Tomorrow, perhaps, we shall have some mail, having taken the matter in our own hands. We sent an emissary to Ciney today and he will bring it to us Saturday (tomorrow). I also hope he will bring the ETO jacket which was being altered when I left last week. If he does I shall get all dressed up and take new pictures for you, My Beloved.

There is so much one can do in the pursuit of pleasure that I hardly know where to begin. I'll go to the opera tomorrow, mainly because even if it's bad it's a better investment than buying rotten beer in the dives. Sunday I'll go to the races in Brussels if my friends will take me and I don't see how they can refuse. My mazel [luck], it looks like I'm going to earn my money here. The clinic, for some odd reason, has suddenly become known to every seaman and merchant marine hitting this port. This, in addition to the thousands of troops stationed here whom we are supposed to look after, dentally speaking. But Captain Smith is a swell egg and leaves it in my hands, with the admonition that several afternoons a week should be left open so we can take off. That plus Sunday which is free after 8:30 a.m. sick call. We'll be here at least another week, I believe. Then return to Ciney for our departure from this interesting country. I'm still hoping for that September date at home with my beloved ones.

Until tomorrow, My Angel, love to all, Daddy

July 9, 1945 – Antwerp, Belgium
My Darling:

Too much of a good thing can even apply to your letters, it seems, for since yesterday I've been hollering "help, murder, I'll never be able to answer all those letters." On Saturday morning one batch reached me from Ciney and on Sunday morning I made the trip back to Ciney to pick up mail and here's what I've got before me as I sit on my balcony composing this all-inclusive reply, I hope. Fourteen letters, June 13 to 30. Some short, some long, but all wonderful.

This week I'm going to the opera on Thursday and Saturday and possibly Sunday. Thursday I shall hear *Hérodiade* (Massenet) which I have never seen staged even though I know the score which I studied some years ago with Baroness von Turk Rohn. But even if it was in Chinese I'd go just to hear the tenor who has the lead, Bricoult. I heard him Saturday night in *Pagliacci* ["Paljas" in Flemish], and, Angel, I wept and shouted in near hysteria over his performance. I don't know why America hasn't discovered this man. A glorious, free,

Antwerp Belgium
July 7, 1945

KONINKLIJKE VLAAMSCHE OPERA

ZATERDAG 7 JULI 1945, te 19 uur

Cavalleria Rusticana

Opera in 1 bedrijf van Pietro Mascagni. Tekst van G. Targioni-Tozzetti en G. Menasci.

Dirigent : Daan Sternefeld
Regisseur : Karel Schmitz

Santuzza	Germaine de Jonghe
Lola	Godelieve van den Broeck
Lucia	Irène Raymakers
Turiddu	Jean Villard
Alfio	Herman de Rydt

PALJAS

Opera in 2 bedrijven van Ruggiero Leoncavallo

Dirigent : Daan Sternefeld
Regisseur : Karel Schmitz

Canio	Simon Bricoult
Nedda	Antoinette Bauters
Tonio	Alfons de Quick
Beppo	Frans Meesters
Silvio	Herman de Rydt
Een boer	Jos Augusteyns

Tooneeldirigent : Hendrik Claessens

An extraordinary singer and actor.

full-bodied, bejeweled voice in a man who has the finest in stagecraft at his fingertips. His "Pagliacci" is not the fleshy Italian heartbroken clown most singers make of the role. His "Pagliacci" is that of an animated puppet turned into a human being for the moment. In his brief hour the puppet lives the whole gamut of human emotions. He cavorts, he's staggered by infidelity, he gives himself to mad rage and in that the final moment he wrecks the mechanism which allows him to move like a human and he burns out the borrowed soul. Exactly like a mechanical toy, Bricoult is one moment a man and the next a broken toy. Bricoult doesn't sing the final line with the bel canto grandeur that most Pagliaccis do. "La comedia e fine," Bricoult articulates with the last gasp, much like a broken man sprung of the toy giving its last feeble whir. I'm afraid I haven't given you the real picture of this man and his performance. But all through the performance, from the very moment of his electric entrance, I was sitting at the edge of my seat, ah-ing and tsk-ing and exploding with ecstasy. I'm afraid the pie-faced Englishman sitting next to me thought I was "quite mad you know". He was so bored and I think annoyed that I was enjoying it so much.

On Sunday when I told Max about it, he wept with disappointment that he couldn't get away. He too became the guard and drew a Saturday-Sunday detail. I think he's going AWOL next week, though, and come in for the opera. I missed him very much since his enjoyment of music has given me so much added pleasure. We had a brief but pleasant reunion. We sat in the sun and read our letters from home to each other.

The trip to Ciney was brutal, and the return was barbaric, but all the wonderful letters I found would have justified my crawling on hands and knees both ways. I had to get up at 4 a.m. to get an Antwerp train to Brussels in order to make the 7 a.m. to Ciney which reaches there at 9:20 a.m. and it's well under one hundred miles only. I took the 6:20 p.m. train from Ciney and reached Antwerp at 10:30, having stood in a jam-packed coach all the way. These Belgiques are the rudest, crudest bunch of animals I have ever encountered on a train. On a tram or a train they become savages, for some strange reason.

Now for the mail. Regarding your reaction to the news that we may be coming home in August, at this very moment there is substantial evidence that a sailing date has been established for early in August. Angel, I will continue to believe this and pray for this until the very moment we go up the gangplank, but I beg you to hold yourself in check. The Army, My Darling, the Army moves in "strange ways." In a flash, joy turns to sorrow and sadness to gladness. One moment I was a miserable guy with a silly gun. The next I was headed for this Antwerp adventure. That is typical of the Army. I am cautious about arousing your hopes only because I know how devastating is the terrible changeability of Army living and planning.

Love to all. To you, all my heart, Daddy

July 10, 1945 – Antwerp, Belgium
My Darling:

I have just come from an altogether delightful visit with Isadore Milner, brother of Leo, and I could kick myself for having delayed it so long since I've had his address almost a week. By a happy coincidence he lives on the very next street from where we are quartered, literally just around the corner. With a show of great pride, he showed me the pictures of Leo's and Dora's sons, and of course was excited and happy over the contact I established with the Chicago relatives by virtue of my visit. Isadore is indomitable. An entertaining conversationalist, he told me briefly but intelligently all about their days under the Nazi hell. He was imprisoned three times. Of the thousands of Antwerp Jews only a mere thousand or so have survived and returned here. His Aryan wife speaks no English so she didn't join us. I could form only a hasty opinion of her. She's a tall, attractive woman who is obviously devoted to her husband. Isadore is a little, wiry, forceful person and a delightful actor. His unself-conscious impersonations of the Superman sons-of bitches, as he related his story, was subtle satire and indicative of the man's sharp perception. I enjoyed the hour and a half immensely. He urged me to visit them again which I shall do, Saturday if possible. Max is coming in for the opera Saturday but I'll run over and say hello again. They do live in rather ordinary surroundings. That doesn't matter, however. He's a most cordial person and I'm glad to report that he appears quite well and high in spirit.

This noon, while taking our after-lunch walk, a little gentleman rushed from a door and hailed me. It was lovable Uncle Elias who had come to Antwerp on business and was dining in a restaurant which I passed in my walk. I have a genuine affection for this cheerful little man. We hope to see them on Sunday, perhaps for the last time, if what we hear comes to pass. By the 20th, it is said we must be on the move. This is a good thing. Antwerp is taking too strong a grip on me.

Well, Angel, I went and "done" it again. I bought a couple of *objets d'art* for our growing collection. I felt they were ridiculously cheap and I made a little deal with the aid of some "smokes." The items are small silver boxes of unusual design. I'm a sucker for these things but I couldn't resist. They were in the shop which is next door to our quarters, and I looked at them a thousand times. They can be classed as miniatures and should look artistic in our curio cabinet. Gosh, if I had about 10,000 francs I'd go crazy here. The things I see! But, of course, the prices on most things I like are outrageous and only a fool would indulge these rapacious shopkeepers. They think we are all millionaires and refuse to believe otherwise. The little things I bought come to no more than the expenditure for an evening of beer drinking, so I felt justified in doing so and staying home one evening to dream about the house they will adorn. I'll get them tomorrow and pack them for shipping. It's almost midnight so I'll call it a day. I'm off Thursday afternoon and will explore the city again. It's fascinating.

Love to all. Love, Daddy

July 13, 1945 – Antwerp, Belgium
My Darling:

This, I suppose, will be the last letter from Antwerp, and possibly the last from Belgium. We leave this wonderful city tomorrow to rejoin the unit and then to a port. Where, I don't know. We had hoped it would be from this port and that we might remain until the very last moment. So fascinating is this place that I can leave it only with regret that I didn't have six months here, at least. To think that we spent so much time in a cow pasture! Thursday night I went to the opera for the last time to hear *Hérodiade*. I took a young lady, an Edith Seifert, a Belgian Jewess who works in the dispensary. She is a highly learned girl. She speaks Yiddish, French, Greek, Spanish, Flemish, and extraordinarily American English. Having worked with her almost two weeks, it was only Thursday morning that I discovered she is a Jewess. Since Max was not allowed to leave the camp, and I had already bought tickets, I asked her to go. It proved to be a very pleasant evening. I met her parents and spoke Yiddish to them, although the mother is as linguistic as the daughter. They, too, had a terrible time during the Nazi occupation. They were hidden for two full years. The father is also a diamond man. Good heavens, everyone is! Apparently, they managed to save some wealth. They live quite comfortably, from what I could observe. Tonight I did a fond farewell to Antwerp in my own way. I took a small steamer for a ride up the Scheldt for half an hour. I sat on the beach for a time and then returned and walked slowly through the old section of the city, fixing pictures in my mind. You alone, Darling, could see the ancient beauty of this place with me. One day we will return and we will walk over the same cobbled streets together. Paris, for me, is like a beautiful lady. Antwerp is like a wrinkled, lovable old grandmother.

My Darling, I have walked my feet off to find you some pretty bauble but there is nothing here under 3000 francs. You will have to wait until we are rich. I will not attempt to write again until we get wherever we are going. Everyone says it's home. But there have been no official announcements and I dare not say that it is so. But I pray to God with all my strength that it is so. Within the next two or three days we shall know. The next few days will be full of tension and discomfort. How I dread these mass movements of soldiers, but any discomfort will be nothing if the compass points to home. Keep this thought in your heart: I love you.

Kiss the cherub, Daddy

July 16, 1945 – Ciney, Belgium
My Darling:

With my last letter from Antwerp I thought that I would not write again until we were "on the way." But at the moment we are "hanging fire" and sweating it out with drops of blood. Here's the situation. This outfit IS going home in the next ten days. It is an outfit that is slated for the Pacific. Now, Darling, as I told you, I have a D profile, which according to the regulations means I'm not going to the Pacific. But, Angel, it can also mean that I can be left behind here for a few months yet. This, then, is the one great decision I am sweating out. If God is with us, I and a few other fellows in my category will sail with the unit and then be redeployed in the States. This one factor alone now stands as a barrier to our reunion in August. You must be prepared, My Angel, if the decision goes against us. How I shall muddle through more months of waiting, I don't know, but I am not alone in this terrible fear and doubt. This whole redeployment plan is causing untold heartache in the same ratio that it is bringing joy to others. Max and Manny and I have spent hours debating whether it is better to come home now for a month's furlough or whether it's better to stick it out here and then be rid of all this for good in the next six to eight months. Well, you know how the debate always ends. No, one month at home would be better than waiting more months for freedom. I keep thinking that it would be sensible to wait and then know that I am free, but my heart, my arms, my guts keep screaming NO. I can draw new strength and courage to face the future only from my immediate physical and spiritual contact with you and Roberta. I can say that we are packed and ready to go at a moment's notice. God Almighty, put me on the ship for home!

Daddy

CHAPTER TWELVE

Camp Twenty Grand: Waiting to Go Home

[From Oral History interview with grandson, Edward C. Bernstein, in 1986]:

As the war was winding down, after the second Hitler invasion of Europe was stopped, they began to unwind some of the troops. Our unit suddenly found itself without a base of operation because it was the kind of hospital that they figured could be used more in the Pacific now. So we were sent to a camp in France, Camp Twenty Grand (all the camps were named after cigarette brands) on the Meuse River. We were stationed there about six weeks waiting for new regrouping and new orders. Meanwhile the outfit had been torn apart. Some were sent to Ireland, a group was sent to England, and our group was being prepared to go back to America to be regrouped and re-outfitted for Pacific duty because our term had been less than two years so we still had some time left to serve.

[The following is reprinted with permission from "The Skylighters—The Web Site of the 225th AAA Searchlight Battalion." With gratitude to Larry Belmont, webmaster: http://www.skylighters.org/special/cigcamps/cigintro.html]

Camp Twenty Grand
Henouville/Duclair, France

A portion of the tent city that was Camp Twenty Grand.

Redeployment Information Center at Camp Twenty Grand. The bulletin board listed all units in camp (left-hand side) and both ships that had arrived at the port of Le Havre and ships that were due (right-hand side). The men looked at this board every day waiting "for their ship to come in" (December 1945).

July 21, 1945 – Camp Twenty Grand, Duclair, France
My Darling:

Take a look at the above and you'll know all, for location is all I can tell you about. That we are coming home is certain, but when we will leave this blazing hot plateau on the very top of a mountain range is most difficult to say. I can recommend the food but that's all. Absolutely nothing to do. No recreation, no amusement, no facilities to speak of, just a huge platter of burning gravel and rock spread mercilessly over the ferns and shrubs which make any other mountaintop heaven. I am black already without even trying to acquire the tan. But I have no right to complain. Your letters, as recent as July 12, have reached me here to my utter astonishment. I have your letters of July 8, 9, 11, 12, and June 22. Also, the magazines and newspapers reached me just before we left Ciney. Angel, why didn't you tell me I wrote so well? What a tonic. What a satisfaction. Max read every word out loud to me as I lay on my back in the sun and mentally patted myself on the head. Max was so impressed, so genuinely proud of me. It was a strange feeling hearing the stories read to me since I have literally forgotten every word of them. They are well written. Darling, I'm bubbling with confidence again! Gosh! I'm really quite good.

Well, Cookie, the Ciney departure was a Cecil B. DeMille tearjerker. It was a poignant pageant. The town's female population, well fortified with handkerchiefs, lined the tracks as the train slowly pulled out of our siding, severing forever the ties that were bound, illicit and otherwise. I shall tell you this story in detail soon. Max is waiting. We are going down to look at the Seine which winds its way majestically below us, and also to seek a breath of cool air. If this reaches you within the next two weeks you will hear by telephone from one of our advance party. He should be able to tell you approximately when we might arrive, God willing. May our gracious God grant that the war department does not change its altogether too confused mind before we board ship. This agony of uncertainty is never ending and each of us is subject to some sudden and unexplainable change of orders and regulations. I have all the snapshots.

Love, Daddy

July 24, 1945 – Camp Twenty Grand
My Darling:

The same old crap prevails as of this afternoon. Nobody knows nothing about anything. Here we sit, speculating, hoping, despairing, praying. The only thing to be said for this sudden and stupid inactivity is that each passing day is one day less to worry about the Japs. We have been inspected, accepted, rejected and alerted seven times over in one hour and at the present we are in that insufferable category of not up to T.O. [Technical Order], which means we have to have a few more replacements before we can "partir." The replacements are on the way, say Paris headquarters. Fortunately, we have a fighting C.O. and he'll pull us out of this hole (literally) if anyone can. Some of these outfits have been here for weeks and are beginning to look like haunted men. I think *Stars & Stripes* wrote up this place once as being a mountain paradise. All those liars! The food is extraordinary. Cooked by German POWs, but already we are sick of eating, sleeping and shitting in the crudest and cruelest quartermaster boxes in the ETO. I'd take a straddle trench any day to the brutal cutting edges of these boxes some sadist designed. We miss our fine mattresses too in our nightly writhings and wigglings on GI cots. But all passes in the indescribable anticipatory joy of seeing home and family soon. If all goes well here we should make it by the middle of August. All our papers are in order, including furlough orders. We need only the order to move to Le Havre and home. "Dear God, don't fail us in this. In utter humility, we employ Thee to endow the War Department with wisdom and a little energy in our behalf." Soon. Soon, My Angel.

Love to all, Daddy

July 27, 1945 – Camp Twenty Grand
My Darling:

I had hoped that by this time I would be heading my letters "on board ship," but here we are, still waiting for some word to move toward a port. How much longer we'll be here no one knows. They have finally broken us down to a complete state of inertia and we don't care anymore. They must have something in mind, though. After a week of terrific sunshine and heat, the skies opened up last night and all but washed us into the Seine below. What a downpour! Yet it was so funny, somehow, because it was a change, I guess. A bunch of us had gone over to the Red Cross tent for doughnuts and coffee when the storm broke. We walked to the movie tent only to run smack into a milling throng shifting hither and yon in an effort to avoid the geysers in reverse shooting through the rotten canvas of what was once a circus tent, I believe. The terrific beating of the rain against the canvas completely drowned out the soundtrack of the movie which was utterly ridiculous, but since Max and I had a few inches of good canvas over our heads, we just huddled together and sweated out the storm. To illustrate just how indifferent one becomes, it occurred to me that all our duffels possibly might get soaked. Once, I would have been in a stew about this and would have "hauled ass" back to camp to protect my precious stuff. Last night, however, the only reaction was one of amusement at having to hang all the junk on the guy ropes of the tent, today. I did a good-sized wash yesterday and left it hanging out. But one of the lads hauled it in as the storm broke. When I said "this camp is crude" I wasn't saying half enough. There are no ablution huts. We wash from marmalade cans snatched from the mess dump. We eat and sleep too much. The food is good and my tent happens to be rain proof so I guess I have little to complain about.

I know what an agony of suspense you must be enduring, Angel, but I can't tell you anything that might ease your mind. We started out with a rush. We should have been on a ship by now if the original orders had gone through, but here we are. I dare not think that the whole thing might be scuttled. It simply can't happen. Just keep hoping and praying, My Love. Max is taking this delay badly since he is hoping to catch his brother who should be on the way home from Italy. He sends his best to you, My Darling.

Love, Daddy

July 27, 1945 – Camp Twenty Grand
My Darling:

This is the second letter today, but I am anxious to inform you that mail is coming through. Here we were, prepared to be cut off from all communication and what do you know? We have had a mail call almost every day. This evening I got yours of July 13, 16, 17 and am relieved to know that at last you had some of my Antwerp letters, all of which should be up-to-date now. You should, therefore, have a fairly complete picture of my two weeks in Antwerp. The balcony, I hasten to add, was completely wasted on me. I have only one Juliet and she awaits me at 5131 South Greenwood. And don't give me that routine—"Mi Lord, me thinkest thou protesteth too much."

As for your reaction to the morons who were privileged to read the "Tale of the 130th," honestly, Angel, I'm not disappointed. I knew it would be so. The thing was done for my own benefit more than for these morons. I was anxious to prove to myself that my small talent hadn't been extinguished entirely.

There is another dull movie tonight, but it's better than sitting all evening in a dark, damp tent, so I guess I'll go pick up Max and go view the movie. If we had umbrellas and a rowboat we'd take them along because it looks like it's getting set to pour again and the movie tent is one helluva place to go to get out of the rain. Oh well! About the tents, honey: relax. We aren't in pup tents. These are six-man pyramidal creations, but at least you can walk in upright instead of crawling on all fours.

Goodnight, Beloved. Kiss the cherub, Daddy

July 30, 1945 – Camp Twenty Grand
Darling:

Lest the day pass, as did yesterday, without a short letter at least to you, I hasten to say that we are still here and no news as to the time of our departure is available. It's a distressing situation but the whole setting of this monstrous camp is so conducive to going stark mad, we have pledged ourselves not to think of it any more than we can help doing. Surprisingly, the days pass swiftly since a good portion of the day is used up in the chow lines and mess kit laundry lines. The food is good, however, and it would be silly to allow one's inertia to deprive the stomach of the very good victuals. But my middle is bulging alarmingly as a result. Sunbathing, washing, reading and napping fill the day. What the cause of the delay may be we don't quite know except that we are a few men under strength according to some mystic calculation known as T.O. Ordinarily a man isn't worth the toilet paper he uses in this Army, but when it comes to letting a whole organization get dry rot from inactivity, a few critters, more or less, suddenly assume gigantic importance. The T.O must be filled! We have no right to complain. Actually, many men are more entitled to passage home than we are but this crazy system has trapped them too. Any day now we should start a private landscaping project here, if we live up to our reputation.

I had no letter from you yesterday, but my latest from you is dated July 19, so I can't complain. Tonight, perhaps, there will be more from you. I beg you, Darling, not to get so frantic if the mailman skips you for a couple of days. I'm not writing every day, for one thing, and if anything goes wrong you will know about it soon enough. So far we have nothing to fear. The orders may come in the next day or two. While I'm impatient to get home, I'm glad it will mean that I'll be there nearer to Roberta's birthday [September 15] than might have been possible had we sailed on an earlier date. Darling, I can't deny you the great joy of thinking and talking about my homecoming, but I beg you to go easy on any public announcement of same until it is an ascertained fact. Then I shall give you the go sign on accepting all invitations. We are going to have one helluva good time. The Jap picture is very good. Who knows? Perhaps we'll say "finis" to that too before anymore sad adieux. My love to all. Be brave, be thankful for the goodness of our God who has spared us the greater sorrow that war has brought to countless hearts. Don't be envious of those who have returned already. Perhaps they had a harder task than mine has been.

Kiss the cherub. Love, Daddy

August 1, 1945 – Camp Twenty Grand
Sweetheart:

It's the same old thing. We're still here, ad infinitum. Don't know what to say. No news as to our movement. Some outfits stay here for weeks and I guess we are to be one of those unfortunate units for which there is no priority available. Well, they should only be in such a hurry to send this unit to the Pacific as they are in getting it home, I'll be satisfied. The day is wet and depressing so I'm going to sleep it out. Going to take a shower, air out my blankets and then retire for the day. We got paid in American money yesterday and the card games raged all night. This morning there are a number of poorer but none the wiser GIs. It's appalling how dumb some of these guys are. All month they wait for the measly army pay and in one hour they shoot it away. Well, I've got this morning just what the paycheck gave me yesterday and I'm a lot richer than the sergeants are this morning. Your anxious letter of July 22 reached me yesterday. I'm not writing to anyone but you, Angel, so pass the news around that I'm well but very anxious to get home.

Love to all, Daddy

August 2, 1945 – Camp Twenty Grand
Darling:
    Two weeks ago today, we moved into this desolate place called 20 Grand but we haven't given up hope. I think we'll make it yet. Little else to report. In desperation, Max, Manny, Bill Blumenthal (a dear friend of ours) and I organized a poker game. I lost $1.50. Please forgive me for being so careless, but it was fun for a change, and I didn't mind losing to my pals. I play badly and know it and beyond a little diversion with my intimates, I have absolutely no tolerance for poker nor any of the other games. I'm still hoping that the 15th will find us home, so keep praying and hoping.
    Love to all. Kiss the wonderful cherub. Love, Daddy

August 4, 1945 – Camp Twenty Grand
Darling:
    Yep! We're still here. It's maddening. We should have been pulling into New York harbor about now. Well, at least we know we are on the shipping list at last. So, from here on, we'll move fast once the order comes. But that order may take another week for all we know. Your wonderful letter of July 25 came yesterday. I'm glad you have some idea of what the Antwerp business was about. I'm pleased, also, that you like my review of Bricoult's performance. I think that I mentioned his subsequent performance as John the Baptist in *Hérodiade*, calling for an entirely different approach. He was equally as stirring as John as he was as Pagliacci, a truly versatile artist and a magnificent singer.
    Honey, I'm writing only to you since I don't trust myself at the moment to indulge in too many letters. It's so easy to get bitter about the stupid waiting. So please explain to my folks that these letters are meant for them too. I received a package from them yesterday, cookies, caviar, sardines and all kinds of things, and I needed it like a hole in the head. Tonight, however, I will try to eat it up. We have some beer and this being Saturday, will have a buffet tonight. It will be a sort of "Smorgasbord under dirty canvas." These Army cots of ours certainly get a workout. We sleep, eat, wash, gamble and sunbathe from them. It reminds me of the ship we took across the English Channel almost a year ago. For two days we didn't emerge from those horrible hammocks where we ate, slept, farted, shaved and indulged in filthy talk. What a cockroach farm that ship was. It had a tragic end. Several months after we crossed, it hit a channel mine and sank with all hands onboard. It was one of the major disasters of the European campaign. Well, My Love, this is the siesta hour, in the sun.
    Kiss the cherub. Love to all the family. Daddy

August 6, 1945 – Camp Twenty Grand
My Darling:
    Like the lost, unhappy tribes of Israel, we wander around looking for our Moses who will lead us out of this wilderness. But the Messiah doesn't come.

Soon we shall set up a golden calf and invoke the deity to get us out of here. Oh, to see the Promised Land! In despair, I turned to literature. I lost myself for the past two days in the most engrossing tale I've read in years, *The Robe,* by Lloyd Douglas. I believe you read it. It's magnificent. It's stirring. It's frightening. I dare not open another book now until the spell wears off a bit. Angel, forgive me. There is nothing to write about. This is the third week here. Maybe tomorrow will bring us the reprieve from the state of suspended animation.

Love to all, Daddy

August 7, 1945 – Camp Twenty Grand
My Darling:

Things have come to a pretty pass. On Friday, we start a training program here which means they expect us to be around for a while, or may not mean anything more than that we are getting sluggish and need some exercise. It is true that unless we are pushed into some activity we sleep all day. It's beginning to tell on all of us and my belly is bulging more and more. I vow to leave the potatoes and puddings alone but my resolve melts as I go through the chow line. It is good food and enthusing over it is about the only pleasure we have. What a situation! Just keep hoping, Angel. We'll get home one of these days.

Love to all. Kiss the gorgeous Roberta. Daddy

August 10, 1945 – Camp Twenty Grand
My Darling:

This may be the day we have prayed for. After twelve hours of steady downpour the sun has suddenly broken through and the radio has just informed us that Japan is ready to accept the terms of unconditional surrender. There is great suppressed excitement in this huge Red Cross tent where several thousand men are preoccupied with card playing, doughnut eating, reading, restless moving back and forth, and each ear is cocked for the news which may come over the radio. My stomach aches with the excitement of this. The radio says it will be Monday before Japan finely capitulates, but as in the case of Germany, it may come sooner. These things can't be stopped once the tremendous force of willing it is set in motion. I'm sad that we have been denied the great joy of celebrating the victory at home with our loved ones as would have been the case if we had departed on our original day. Now we have been put off the shipping list again and it may be weeks before a new day is available. But, My Angel, our celebration will be whenever our hearts are reunited and again I dare hope that family men will come first in the new redeployment which must follow the surrender of Japan.

Continue to write, Sweetheart. I am quite lost when there is no mail from you. You may use the new APO number 562, which has been official since we left Ciney. Don't worry. I am well. I'm gaining weight rapidly and with the weight of this Japanese menace lifted from our hearts and minds, this leisurely waiting without any responsibilities is not unbearable, for ever present is the thought that after it there will be no more farewells. I can tell you now that I wasn't too sure that I wouldn't be caught in the Pacific movement after all. God moves in strange ways, My Darling. When that moment of final victory comes, I know that I will thank Him first. I think you sense the terror I have known as I've been swept hither and yon in this mass of helpless, inarticulate humanity. Each one is hiding his own fears under a thin veneer of blistering crudeness and false bravado. How good it will be to leave all this behind. Soon, soon, perhaps. I'm on guard duty today so in the four-hour intervals between watches, I'll have time to dream of you and Roberta and the life that is to be ours.

Love to all. To you my love, Daddy

August 11, 1945 – Camp Twenty Grand
Darling:

Just a few words to inform you that we are still here and likely to stay for another week or ten days. It is distressing beyond words. We "missed the boat" three times so far but we are praying that we will make the next one. I know what such news must be doing to you, but not to write at all would be worse. This whole thing may break down into an individual rather than unit movement and if a grain of common sense still prevails in our government, I should rate a priority over the single men. I don't know what to think. If the Japanese accept their fate this week, it is expected that great confusion will prevail for a short time as regards the disposal of troops already jamming ports and processing areas. Since we are already here, it would seem sensible to get us out of the way as soon as possible, but anyone who expects the army to be governed by common sense is stark mad. Our poor C.O., a gentleman if ever I saw one, is beside himself with disgust and chagrin. Our record, as a hospital, has moved many high-ranking army officials to heap glowing praise on us, but that was when we were needed. Now we are those "pill pushers" who are always looking for a soft spot. I guess I'm slightly bitter but even this distressing waiting must end one day, and it is even conceivable that one will get out of this miserable "profession." The chicken shit is becoming painfully evident all over the place. Nuts! I'm going to the movies. More tomorrow, in a lighter vein.

Love to all. Kiss the cherub, Daddy

August 12 1945 – Camp Twenty Grand
Darling:

Same old place, same old crap, same old push around. Nothing is said about departure, but we have tapped the grapevine and the 18th seems to be the favored date. You must be frantic by now. I wish I knew whether my friend on the advance party has telephoned you from Philly. He must've told you that we were to leave within a few days of their departure. That was the plan, until some guy with clout did us out of our priority. The Jap thing has cooled off and I think even if the announcement comes that the war is over, the guys here, at least, will pass it off with, "So what, when do we go home?"

I got a letter from the folks today, August 4 date, and I'm certainly surprised at the quick delivery. Honey, I guess you stopped writing! I hope you didn't because the letters are coming through pretty good, and if we should leave here, those not yet received would follow us almost immediately.

Well, I did a terrific washing today and even though it's Sunday: a pair of O.D.s, a fatigue suit, a woolen undershirt, bath towel, socks, handkerchief, etc. All this is done in cold water. Each piece is laid out flat and scrubbed with a big brush and GI soap. They come out clean and fresh smelling. The sun dries it all in a couple of hours. The weather is wonderful. Hot in the daytime, cold at night. We got our sleeping bags back this week and we are all as snug as can be. Those bags (sleeping) are wonderful. I'm going to bring mine home.

Passes are being issued and Max and I are trying to snag one for Paris this week. The passes are only for the day. You leave at six in the morning and return late at night. It's gruesome but I think worth it. I want to see Paris in the summer and I certainly want Max to see it since he has never been there. He's so excited by the prospect of going he can't talk straight. I have decided that if I get a pass and he doesn't, since the whole thing is based on the mood of our respective platoon sergeant at the moment, I'll give him mine so that he can satisfy this burning desire to see Paris. Well, Angel, there's a GI show tonight, and if one wants to see it, one has to shake one's ass.

Love to all. Kiss the cherub. Your Daddy XXXXXXXXXXXXX

August 13, 1945 – Camp Twenty Grand
Darling:

The same old place, the same old routine, the same old shit. I'm disgusted. Rumor has it that the 18th sailing date has gone by the boards too. What a day. Max and I weren't lucky enough to draw a Paris pass out of the first sergeant's hat. We might have known it. When I saw Max's face, twisted with disappointment, I felt sick. He had prayed that he would get one. Then a little later we tried for passes to nearby Rouen. He got one, I didn't, due entirely to the stupidity of my platoon sergeant. So, Max told them to shove his up their expanding behinds. He refused to go without me. We'll try again tomorrow, though I have no appetite for bovine Rouen. I've had enough of Belgian and French rural life. Also, hot on the grapevine is a rumor that there will be numerous passes to Paris, suggesting that we are to be around here for a time. I hope this one dies like all latrine rumors usually do. If I could indulge in the athletic program here I'd be more tolerant, but my feet flatly refuse to do more than carry me through the necessary movements. I have developed a large wart at the back of my right heel and surgery is the only thing left to effect a cure. Max has done his best over a period of months but chiropody in this case must give way to surgery. Our plan is to wait until after the furlough (if we ever get it) and then be admitted to a hospital and have it removed. Since it is always painful, I have shifted my weight off-balance, which naturally has disorganized all the muscles and nerves governing locomotion. I can thank Uncle Sam for this. Army shoes have completely wrecked my feet. Don't fret about this, Angel. Once I get rid of Army shoes I'll regain some pedal comfort. I also believe that my recent inclination to warts is due to the growing nervous tension of being away from you so long. I find that several warts are developing on my left hand for no accountable reason. These are all small complaints however because no one believes my advanced age. I continue to look like 20 in my deep tan and short haircut.

So, goodnight, Beloved. Kiss the cherub. Daddy

[Editors' note: This is the last letter that was found in the collection. The 130th General Hospital departed for the United States on the SS Aquitania in mid-August. The ship arrived in New York on August 31.]

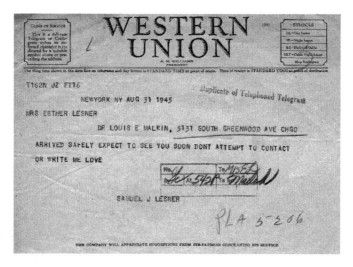

[Editors' note: He describes his arrival home in his interview with his grandson in 1986.]

[From Oral History interview with grandson, Edward C. Bernstein, in 1986]:

We finally got on a ship [in mid-August] and were in the Atlantic Ocean, sailing merrily along, enjoying the fresh air. On the way to Europe in August 1944, we weren't allowed on deck at all for fear of being spotted, but now, in August 1945, it's wonderful. We were all on deck, stripped down to our undies, enjoying the ocean breezes. I was assigned to do a mimeographed newsletter for the troops every day, along with Jack Garber. We'd get out this paper every day and I'd run around on deck and give each guy a sheet to read. We'd get the news from the radio shack on the boat.

One day we had just finished the mimeographed sheet and word came that the Japanese had finally surrendered. [The surrender followed the U.S. dropping of the atomic bomb on Hiroshima and Nagasaki on August 6–9, 1945, about a week before boarding ship.] So we pulled back the paper and we rewrote it to announce that this is what had happened and it looked like the end of the war as a the result of the atomic bomb and surrender. But we were still not sure whether this had actually taken place. [The surrender was announced on August 15th, but the official surrender papers weren't finalized until Sept. 2, after they had arrived back in the U.S.] Still, the feeling on that ship when this was announced, that this atomic bomb had wiped out 60,000 people in one sweep—it wasn't a pleasant thing to watch. The officers, when they realized what had happened, were sickened by it. But we continued on our way home. We were like a ship just sailing into nowhere. When we got back to New York harbor [August 31] and saw the Statue of Liberty, all the boats were out whistling and the flags were flying. We were going to be dismantled. They didn't need us because the war was over. So that's it. We came home on that happy note. There was no more war for us.

[Editors' note: Tom Brokaw reflected that the soldiers came home and went on with life, as Sam did. Brokaw wrote, "They had survived an extraordinary ordeal, but now they were eager to reclaim their ordinary lives of work, family, church and community. The war had taught them what mattered most in the lives they wanted now to settle down and live." (The Greatest Generation, p. 18).]

Epilogue

[From Oral History interview with grandson, Edward C. Bernstein, in 1986]:

ECB: *Do you remember the day you actually returned to Chicago?*

SL: *Yes I do. We were sent from Camp Kilmer, New Jersey, to Camp Grant in Rockford, Illinois, to be mustered out of the Army. There was an awful lot of paper work involved—insurance and hospital and everything—and it takes a couple of weeks to do that. So, we got back there and I remember I was sitting in one of the big rooms being instructed on coming back to civilian life. Suddenly one of the soldiers tapped me on the head and said somebody out there was trying to get my attention. I looked out and it was my wife. She had heard that the unit had been sent to Camp Grant and she got in a car and came out there just to see me. I was sitting there and I was so completely stunned by it that I just sort of waved and said "Hi." And then after I regained my senses, I went out and greeted her. She went back to Chicago. And then on September 15th, I was discharged and sent home and I came back to the family on Greenwood Avenue. Roberta was two years old on that date. When I came into the house she was asleep, the poor child, and they woke her up to come greet her soldier daddy. When she came out, she didn't know what was going on. She just stood there in a daze. She didn't know me—and, in the excitement, the poor thing, she wet the floor. I kissed her and put her back to bed.*

[Editors' note: This is not how Sam had envisioned his reunion with his daughter. In his letter of January 29, 1945, he wrote: "Our sweet child. How your letters about her fill me with a warmth, an unspeakable pride, a tranquility! I'm afraid to think of the moment when I will catch her up in my arms. Darling, we must not let this moment escape us when it comes. It must be so. First, she will come towards me, alone, and then she will take my hand and lead me back to you, forever, forever." Alas, the best laid plans of mice and men often go awry (attributed to Robert Burns in "To a Mouse").]

ECB: *When did you go back to work at the Chicago Daily News?*

SL: *Well soon after that I came back to the paper. I had in hand a very warm letter from the boss saying welcome home, we hear you're back. I saw the managing editor and greeted him very warmly. He said, "What do you want to do?" I said "I want my old job back as night club critic." He said, you can't have it; we put somebody else on it, a very sick man; if he dies, we'll give it back to you." So, he said, "You want to be the film critic?" and I said. "Okay." It took until October before I was finally released from the Army and I came back. The very first film I reviewed in my new*

Epilogue

Kup's column

CHICAGO TIMES, THURSDAY, NOVEMBER 15, 1945

HOLLYWOOD.—A group of movie stars, including Pat O'Brien, Lauren Bacall and Humphrey Bogart, recently appeared at a bond rally here, which was featured by the presence of Gen. A. A. Vandegrift, commandant of the U. S. Marine Corps. . . . O'Brien arrived early and sat next to Gen. Vandegrift. Shortly thereafter, a roar from the audience indicated the arrival of other movie stars. O'Brien nudged the general and whispered, "This must be Baby and Bogie now." . . . Gen. Vandegrift looked puzzled for a second and then asked: "And who are Baby and Bogie?"

Irv Kupcinet

* * *

WEST Coast aviation leaders report Mayor Kelly and Gov. Green will be aboard Pan-American's inaugural Chicago-to-London flight next week. . . . The amazing number of recent military plane accidents has Washington upset. Army and Navy leaders believe the reason is due to the wholesale discharges of expert mechanics and engineers, who are being supplanted by inexperienced replacements. . . . Paul Small, who lost $25,000 when his "Merry-Go-Round," starring Jack Pearl and Jay C. Flippen, folded last week-end, has purchased the West Coast rights to "Anna Lucasta." He plans to confer with Producer John Wildberg in Chicago next week.

* * *

UNUSUAL Hollywood scene: Orson Welles, who brought down the wrath of William Randolph Hearst when he directed and starred in "Citizen Kane," sitting at the same table with young Bill Hearst at Ciro's two nights ago. . . . Sam Lesner, recently discharged from the Army, returns to the Chicago Daily News as movie critic. He formerly was the paper's night club editor. . . . When Gen. Eisenhower appears at the American Legion convention in Chicago next week, he'll be accompanied by Adms. Nimitz and King and Gen. Vandegrift of the Marines, as well as a group of cabinet members.

Orson Welles

* * *

JOAN CRAWFORD returned home the other day after a long stay in New York, where she made a number of personal appearances in connection with her latest movie, "Mildred Pierce," which has been the subject of a high-powered publicity campaign by Warner Bros. When Miss Crawford arrived here, she was greeted by her adopted daughter. The station was crowded with military police, wearing their "MP" badges. When the daughter spotted the military police, she turned to her mother and asked: "Mom, don't you think they're carrying this publicity too far—having soldiers walk around with Mildred Pierce's initials on their arms?"

status as film critic was a British film called On Approval. That was another ironic twist. And, of course, that developed into a major career as the film critic for the Daily News, which went on for thirty years, from 1945 to 1975.

ECB: When were you asked at the Daily News to retire?

SL: They wanted me to retire when I was 65 years old, i.e., in 1974. But I decided I didn't want to retire and I told them I wasn't ready. I managed to wiggle another two years out of them. After that, I demanded they give me a contract for a year. The year stretched into two years. An editor at the paper said, "Don't worry, we'll use you as a special writer." For the next two years I was a special features writer. I did all sorts of beautiful interviews and features, and that lasted until March 1978, when the paper closed officially. I started on April 9, 1928, and the paper closed on March 9, 1978. By one month I missed fifty years.

ECB: *Why did the paper close?*

SL: *In my opinion, the Field family who owned the paper saw opportunities to make more money in other fields and they wanted to get their money out of it.*

ECB: *Once that was it with the* Daily News, *how did you like retirement?*

SL: *My first reaction was one of great relief. I thought it was wonderful not to have to get up in the morning, and be preoccupied with what I'm going to write that day. A writer constantly fears that he will dry up and not be able to come up with another five words to put down on the typewriter. Every morning I'd say, "Oh boy, how am I going to start the column today?" So knowing that I didn't have to do that anymore, was a great relief to me. But the relief lasted only two years. After that I became very*

---

* Larger, more legible reprints of these newspapers clippings can be found at the end of this Epilogue.

Epilogue

restless. *I read about an organization called Operation SCOPE in Hyde Park. I called them up and they sent me to the* Hyde Park Herald *and they hired me right away. That was March 1980.*

ECB: *What were you doing at first when you came to the* Hyde Park Herald?

SL: *I started out in the classified ads department, taking ads over the telephone. That was a lot of fun because I identified myself saying, "Good morning, this is Sam Lesner at the Hyde Park Herald." "What?, the Sam Lesner?" And then I'd tell them what it was all about and that would establish a friendly relationship right off. They'd wait for me to call them every Monday morning to renew their ads. I got to know a great many people that way.*

the herald, wednesday, march 17, 1982 page 3

Lesner wins award

Sam Lesner, 73-year-old ad salesman and columnist for the Hyde Park Herald, received one of six Claude D. Pepper Distinguished Service Awards this week as an outstanding older worker.

A veteran film and nightclub columnist for the old Chicago Daily News, Lesner was honored with five others at a luncheon held Monday to observe Employ the Older Worker Week in Chicago.

Congressman Claude Pepper (D-Fla.), 81, was keynote speaker for the second year at the event, sponsored by Operation ABLE and the Private Industry Council of Suburban Cook County. The awards were presented by Buster Crabbe, 74, former Olympic swimmer and star of "Tarzan" and "Flash Gordon" films.

Among the 72 people who received "Senior Achievement Awards" were two Hyde Parkers. Annie Brown, 68, is a public relations clerk at Encyclopedia Brittanica and Maxines Laves, 72, is director of Operation SCOPE, the senior citizens' placement service at the Hyde Park Neighborhood Club.

Sam Lesner

ECB: *How and when did you start your column?*

SL: *The column started in March 1981. I never dreamed of starting a new writing career. But one day, Barbara Tieman, the general manager, said, "We've been trying to get a columnist on this paper for years and it never works out. Do you want to try?" I said, "Sure." Hyde Park is a community with wonderful people who have stories to tell. So I started out with: "Doctor-lawyer-merchant-chief-farmer-policeman" and said all of these people are represented in Hyde Park. I gave a little history of Hyde Park. It caught on right away. The first week people said, "Oh that's a fun column; it tells so much about Hyde Park. The first few months it was twice a month and soon after that I began a weekly column.*

[*Editors' note: Here is a sample of his weekly column, which ran from 1981 to 1990.*]

the herald, wednesday, march 17, 1982 page 25

HYDE PARKERS, ALL!

"Our mom, the banker!"

By Sam Lesner

After 40 years of dedicated service in the same job—banking in this instance—Annetta K. Purka understandably could call it a day and settle back for a steady round of library visits and in season, boating with her husband, Joseph, also a retired banker, at Cedar Lake where they have a summer home.

But Annetta Purka, senior vice president and a director of the University National Bank, 1354 E. 55th Street, called it "a new beginning" Tuesday when the bank's officers, many of her long-time customers and invited guests, celebrated her 40th year at the bank, with a late afternoon party in the bank's main banking quarters. (The bank has a second facility at 55th & Lake Park which was opened in 1973 for the added convenience of Hyde Parkers.)

In May of this year University National Bank will have completed 63 years of continuous service to the Hyde Park community.

But this is Annetta K. Purka's story as a banker who has been honored numerous times as much for her "human relations" as for her banking skills.

Tuesday she recalled that one of the proudest days of her life was when she received a Citation of Merit, July 19, 1972.

"I was selected 'Woman of the Day' by radio station WAIT." It was in recognition of her "outstanding contribution to her community in the field of human relations." She recalls that she was honored twice during the day in the station's broadcasts.

Mrs. Purka, however, has adjusted easily to the vast changes in both society and the banking business in the past 40 years.

"When one looks ahead, 40 years seems an eternity. However, when one looks back its just a flash in time—one event, one time space, to be followed quickly by other events, in the creativity of which Hyde Parkers will be instrumental."

"Many Hyde Parkers of years ago have had to leave the community for a variety of reasons. But these good business people continue to remain loyal customers of the University National Bank and it is this continuity that has made my 40 years the keystone of my career at the bank."

Mrs. Purka says that her only daughter and her two grandchildren, now young adults, are not given to teasing her about being "my grandma the banker." But she chuckles when she recalls that they say they expect her to keep going to the bank until she's "93 and clicking a cane along the pavement."

Annetta K. Purka should make her 50th year at University National easily. I had forgotten some papers I had placed on her desk during the interview. I was almost half a block away when I heard her calling me back. She hadn't even bothered to put on a coat.

She regrets that the young people going into banking jobs today appear to be "humorless creatures stamped out by a machine."

"They seem to lack warmth, personality, real interest in the people they serve. After all, service is what we really sell. But I guess that's progress and you learn to accept these changes that apparently are dictated by the increasing computerization of society."

Annetta wasn't thinking seriously about a steady job, either, when she graduated from high school. She was living in Hyde Park with her family and travelling to the loop every day to work at two jobs—one in the Chicago Public Library and the other "in a printing concern."

Her father saw an ad in the newspaper advertising a job at the Hyde Park Bank.

"It was a weekend. I had had a Saturday night date, and I was in no mood to think about a new job. But my dad (Jack Armstrong) insisted that I sit down right then and there and write a letter of application to the bank.

"In those days the mail was delivered promptly. It seemed like the very next day I got a reply telling me to come in. I was hired."

Annetta, however, did leave the banking business for a few years before March, 17, 1942, when she joined the University State Bank as a collection teller.

In May, 1943, University State Bank became University National and through the years Annetta served as assistant cashier, assistant vice president, vice president and in 1972, she was elevated to senior vice president. In 1978, she was elected to the bank's Board of Directors.

She has a graduate certificate from the American Institute of Banking and currently is a member of the Chicago Association for Bank Women and the National Association of Bank Women. Her husband still gives one day a month as advisor to the board of the Eastside Bank & Trust Company while Annetta gives two days a week to her bank job.

She didn't get a wristwatch Tuesday. She got that on the occasion of her 35th year. But University National Bank's Vice President, Kenneth Sticken, and the bank's public relations director, Susan Westfall, did give Annetta K. Purka "one grand party" for her 40th.

PEOPLE PLUS:

It's always open season on Gilbert & Sullivan and Hyde Park has its G.& S. tradition, too. Since Hyde Park itself drew its very name from London's famous Hyde Park, its appropriate that our local Savoyadians should excel in the beloved ear-catching, tongue—tripping tunes and lyrics of Gilbert & Sullivan's "The Gondoliers" which was presented last week at Mandel Hall by the Gilbert & Sullivan Opera Company of Hyde Park.

A Hyde Parker known for his Savoyardian skill in this G. & S. company is Ray Lubway who this year created one of his favorite roles, that of the Duke of Plaza Toro, in "The Gondoliers."

Lubway, with the company since its inception, also teaches at the Lab School where he has introduced G. & S. into his classroom. Other Hyde Parkers active in the Hyde Park G. & S. Company are Roland and Helen Baily, Robert Ashenhurst and Rafaello La Mantia.

NOTES:

There still is time to learn how to cook Chinese from an expert, Ruth Law who will be conducting her final cooking classes, Tuesday and Wednesday, March 23, 24, at Mr. G's Finer Foods, 1226 E. 53rd St. These last two sessions are devoted to shrimp stuffed black mushrooms, barbecued pork buns and other Chinese delicacies. The fee is $18, plus a $3 lab fee. But what a maven you'll be after Ruth Law's instruction. For more information call 986-1595.

ONE GOOD TURN DESERVES ANOTHER: Helen Wong Jean, who recently kindly supplied me with the information that the new Chinese New Year (Year of the Dog) is 4680, expressed her pleasure at being given credit for that information in a recent column of *Hyde Parkers, All!* Helen Wong Jean who belongs to the Chinese American Civic Council of Chicago, says she is Director of the Oak Leaf Singers, an intergrated group of 12 residents of Dearborn Park.

"They are all senior citizens who love to sing at the drop of a hat and would love to sing for any organization in Hyde Park for a fee of only $25, to cover transportation," wrote Helen Wong Jean whose address is 820 S. Park Terrace, Nu. 508, The Oaks, Dearborn Park, Chicago, IL 60605. Tel. 663-9037.

After reading this column, which I hope you enjoy, don't throw the Hyde Park Herald into the refuse box. It can help beautify your garden. Shred the paper into half-inch strips and place on the compost pile. The paper will turn into a mulch that will conserve moisture, shelter young seedlings from the damaging effects of sun, wind and rain on exposed soil. The paper gradually decomposes into soil-enriching humus by the end of the season.

Hyde Parkers, All! We would like to hear from you about your own business, backgrounds, ventures and happenings in the Hyde Park Herald, 5240 S. Harper, 60615

Feature of the Hyde Park Herald Advertising Department.

[*Editors' note: On the occasion of his seventy-fifth birthday, he used his column to reflect on his life.*]

HYDE PARKERS, ALL!

How old is "old"?

By Sam Lesner

Three score and fifteen years ago tomorrow, I was born "in humble circumstances," as the novelists like to say. But I have no memory of lying in the buggy in front of my parent's neighborhood grocery store, nor of friendly neighbors and customers shooing the summer flies off of me while I suffered from various infant rashes and fevers.

I learned that much later. The earliest childhood memory I can still vividly recall was being frightened by the prairie weeds which were taller than I and which abscured my view as I waited in an overgrown yard for my parents to negotiate a lease on a far northwest side country store and house where I grew to boyhood before we moved back to the city "to become civilized," my father explained.

I remember also that at the age of six or seven, having been taken to the Lincoln Park Zoo by a friendly neighbor, upon returning home I excitedly exclaimed: "elephants lay eggs in trees!" Everybody laughed, of course, and after my humiliation subsided I figured out that they were ostrich eggs that were laid in elevated nests in the elephant compound so that the pachyderms wouldn't stomp on them, I guess.

Adult relatives visiting us for a day in the country, began to call me "Der Alter Kopf" (the wise old head) because I was always eavesdropping on adult conversations in order to become wise.

The only other traumatic childhood experience I can recall was smoking 16 corn silk, toilet paper—wrapped cigarettes after being peppered by a farmer's buck shot gun for pulling the silk tassles from the still maturing corn.

More pleasantly "fearful" experiences were involved with riding the streetcar up that looping ramp to the upper level of Municipal Pier, now called Navy Pier, where on a warm summer's day the whole "mishpocha" (family) gathered to claim big wooden reclining chairs in invasion—secure locations on the boardwalk, all according to various social organization, largely dictated by the European shtetls from which our respective elders came.

To this day, nobody believes me. But the highlight of those Sunday's at Municipal Pier came at nightfall when a man in fisherman's oil skins dived from a tower on the pier. When he emerged from the water he would predict the weather for the following day. The steel tower, I believe, is still there.

Another "fearful" joy, at age 13, was riding the swift elevated train to the loop, (for the first time) to get off at Congress and Wabash for a visit to the top gallery of the Auditorium Theater to hear my first grand opera. I remember, it was the stupendous "Aida," (with elephants) and with Charles Marshall and Eve Turner singing the leading roles. Now why would I remember that? Were these childhood experiences preparation for the half-century of newspapering at the **Chicago Daily News**, followed by this happy encore at the **Hyde Park Herald**? I confess I never had a burning desire to be a newspaper columnist. Yet I have a record of columnizing in my high school newspaper. It was called S-Ays." How about that for journalistic corn? I really wanted to be an opera singer.

And in the U.S. Army (1944-45) lo and behold, in basic training camp (South Carolina and North Carolina) I was "drafted" to write a column in the camp's mimeographed paper, called "Hot Com-Press." And on the troopship S.S. Lamy returing home from France (August, 1945) again I was drafted to write a column in the daily mimeographed ship's paper and on one sunny unforgettable day at sea, I had to re-do the day's edition to report the dropping of the atomic bomb on Hiroshima, as reported over the ship's wireless.

Incidentally, in the army, the classification officer, after my completion of basic training, snootily informed me that "the army doesn't need a nightclub columnist, so what else can you do?" Just as snootily, what did I have to lose, I was only a basic trainee?) I told him he could put me in the army dental clinic because I had married the daughter of a veteran Chicago dentist. (The late Dr. Louis Malkin).

Incidentally, in my barracks bag was a fine letter of recommendation from the late Col. Frank Knox who was then publisher of the **Chicago Daily News** and Secretary of the Navy in the Roosevelt war cabinet.

But the army, in its wisdom, had assigned me to a medical outfit, the 130th General Hospital, which service eventually earned me two Overseas Service Bars, European, African, Middle Eastern Theater Ribbons with three Bronze Battle Stars, the Good Conduct Medal and the World War II Victory Medal, all for being a conscientious "bed commando," as the heroes referred to us while they were still full of battlefield braggadagio.

But when we hauled them in, shell-shocked and bleeding, and restored them to sanity, they said we were fine fellows, and in my case, voted me "Medico Numero Uno" of the 130th.

When I returned to the **Chicago Daily News** in December, 1945, the managing editor said: "How would you like to be our movie critic?" A new war of words, lasting 25 years, had begun for me. As a civilian movie and nightlife critic, I revisited Europe and Asia too, numerous times in the cause of world wide cinema production with many side-trips to Las Vegas—for the shows, not the gambling casinos.

Incidentally, I was 16 years old before I discovered my true birth date, February 16. My parents and some aged relatives "remembered" that it was warm when I was born, possibly in September because they recalled a religous holday, probably, Rosh Hashanah.

So all through grade school I observed September 15, as my birthday, but strangely, I never was comfortable with that date. At 16, I visited the Bureau of Vital Statistics in the County Building, and starting with 1909, I soon found my registered birth as February 16. My parents never disputed it. Ma said she was awfully busy the day I was born, "virtually behind the grocery counter," and nobody else thought to record it in the family Bible, as were the birth dates of the other three children born to Jacob and Syma Lesner. May they rest in enternal peace. I forgave them.

Ironically, my first child, Roberta, was born on September 15, 1943, and since a wartime provision extended the income tax deadline from April 15, to September 15, my tax form, already completed for mailing that day, was torn up and made over. It gave me an extra $500 deduction. How can you forget that birth date?

The three years since I began this column, *Hyde Parkers, All,*" in the **Hyde Park Herald**, (March 3, 1981) have been some of the happiest years of my journalistic life.

I have given you a few "insides" into my personal life and I would enjoy sharing some of yours with readers of *Hyde Parkers, All!* As I wrote in that first column: "To the **Hyde Park Herald** itself, (now more than 100 years old), Hyde Park is a challenge, a great source of pride, a sometimes worrisome thing, but above all a community that is synonymous with durability. The physical, social and psychological facets of the people of Hyde Park are our special concern.

"Without its unique amalgam of all sorts of people with all sorts of cultural backgrounds, Hyde Park Village migh never have emerged from its 'sleepy hollow' rusticity."

hp the herald, wednesday, february 15, 1984 page 31

Epilogue

ECB: What is your statement or message to the world and how do you think your work represents that?

SL: It's been a very gratifying lifetime. I've done many exciting things. I've met many fascinating people. I have fulfilled myself through my family—my wife, my children, my grandchildren—and the many friends who think kindly of me. After so many years of writing for the Chicago Daily News, I picked it up again at the Hyde Park Herald, and many people remember me fondly from my days at the Daily News. That's my legend, my history, that people remember me.

[Editors' note: Sam wrote his final article and turned it in to the Hyde Park Herald on December 19, 1990. He died that night. That article was published on December 26th, the day of his funeral.]

HYDE PARKERS, ALL!

SAM LESNER

Here's to a saner, healthier new year

page 20 the herald, wednesday, dec. 26, 1990

THAT LIVE CHRISTMAS TREE in the living room, or family room, looked fantastic Christmas morning, with sparkling lights highlighting the beautifully wrapped gifts under the tree.

But the drying evergreen in a week or two can become a hazard. You start thinking about disposing it. But not in the alley as we have done for many years.

The city of Chicago's Department of Streets and Sanitation has initiated a City-wide Drop-Box Recycling Program that not only takes care of recycling newspapers, glass, plastics, aluminum, steel and tin cans. It also has set up a network of fifteen different locations where your Christmas tree will be turned into mulch you can take home. The tree recycling will begin early in January.

The drop-box centers already are in operation and for Hyde Parkers the 4th Ward Center is located at 4415 South Cottage Grove Ave. and the 5th Ward's Center is located at 1619 East 73rd St.

Toasting the new year with a resolution to make it a happier new year for all is as lasting as the champagne bubbles in your glass.

But a resolution to get more involved in recycling can pay big dividends in health and cleanliness for all.

Some of Hyde Park's streets and parkways look like up-turned garbage cans. Recycling at the private drop-off or buy-back centers won't do the whole job.

The long-overdue cleanup must involve every one of us—young and old.

Look at the I.C. embankment along Lake Park Avenue. It's a garbage dump! Look at Harper Ave. between 53rd and 54th Streets. It's disgusting.

Look at 53rd Street between Lake Park and Woodlawn Avenues. There are ample trash containers. But the trick is to get the trash into the cans, and not around the trash cans and not into the grates that protect the young trees. Just cleaning out the grates would be a giant step for civilized living in Hyde Park.

For more information about the city's recycling programs or to receive a directory of the city's many recycling businesses, write: Recycling Coordinator, City Hall, Room 700, 121 N. La Salle St., Chicago, Il. 60602.

* * *

THE ENERGY EXPENDED in the holiday season—shopping, trimming the tree, hanging the outdoor Christmas decorations, over-indulging in the rich repast and alcoholic beverages—may have left you aching in hands, legs, knees, hips, shoulders and neck when you crawled out of bed this morning.

"Chances are you are either overdid your chores and recreational activities or you have a touch of arthritis," wrote Dr. Alan Xenalsis in the November-December 1990 issue of Self Care Journal which is printed on recycled paper.

"Blaming age for 'morning stiffness' isn't very accurate or fulfilling. Forty-five million Americans have arthritis and half are under the age of fifty.

"Don't get depressed or defensive about the possibility of arthritis in your life. Few living creatures are immune from the problem.

"Ancient Egyptians, pre-historic dinosaurs and even the superstar athletes of today are included in the long list of those affected," added Dr. Xenalsis.

Dr. Xenalsis lowers the boom on all "gadgets, widgets and expensive clutter touted as arthritis cures."

Instead, he says the "most widely effective non-medication formula for arthritis relief includes the following ingredients: watercise (exercising in water), stretching and good eating habits.

"Water acts as a terrific therapeutic regimen with its soothing, fluid resistance and gentle buoyancy.

"As regularly as possible, replace you bath-time routine with a bath. Fill the tub with eighteen to twenty-four inches of water and spend fifteen to twenty minutes per day floating away the pain.

"Initially, use simple limb movements, like waving and flexing. Later, visit your local pool. If time, cost and convenience permit, enroll in a regular swimming program.

"Do your body a real favor when you go to bed at night and when you get up in the morning.

"Set aside ten minutes for stretching exercises. Your joints will benefit from improved circulation and from diminished muscle and tendon stress," says Dr. Xenalsis.

My arthritis gets worse as I age. A few minutes of heavy exercise leaves me almost crippled for the next 48 hours.

From Reader's Digest: "The past 20 years have been less a fitness boom than a battle. Many fitness efforts fail, not because we don't try, but because we try too hard. The solution is a moderate approach. Infiltrate your life with light energizing and productive activity rather than besiege it with exhausting, useless workouts."

And that's a fitting resolution for the new year. Happy New Year to all.

Hyde Parkers, All! We would like to hear from you about your own business backgrounds, ventures and happenings in the Hyde Park community. Write to Sam Lesner, c/o Hyde Park Herald, 5240 S. Harper Ave. 60615.

The *Hyde Park Herald* published a "Farewell to Sam From All" on January 2, 1991.]

HYDE PARKERS, ALL!

Farewell to Sam from all.

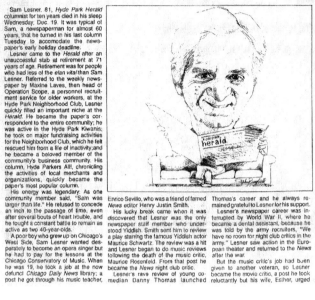

Sam Lesner, 81, *Hyde Park Herald* columnist for ten years died in his sleep Wednesday, Dec. 19. It was typical of Sam, a newspaperman for almost 60 years, that he turned in his last column Tuesday to accommodate the newspaper's early holiday deadline.

Lesner came to the *Herald* after an unsuccessful stab at retirement at 71 years of age. Retirement was for people who had less of the *elan vital* than Sam Lesner. Referred to the weekly newspaper by Maxine Laves, then head of Operation Scope, a personnel recruitment service for older workers, at the Hyde Park Neighborhood Club, Lesner quickly filled an important niche at the *Herald*. He became the paper's correspondent to the entire community; he was active in the Hyde Park Kiwanis; he took on major fundraising activities for the Neighborhood Club, which he felt rescued him from a life of inactivity; and he became a beloved member of the community's business community. His column, Hyde Parkers All!, chronicling the activities of local merchants and organizations, quickly became the paper's most popular column.

His energy was legendary. As one community member said, "Sam was larger than life." He refused to concede an inch to the passage of time, even after several bouts of heart trouble, and he fought a constant battle to remain as active as two 40-year-olds.

A poor boy who grew up on Chicago's West Side, Sam Lesner wanted desperately to become an opera singer but he had to pay for the lessons at the Chicago Conservatory of Music. When he was 19, he took a job at the now defunct *Chicago Daily News* library; a poet he got through his music teacher, Enrico Sevillo, who was a friend of famed *News* editor Henry Justin Smith.

His lucky break came when it was discovered that Lesner was the only newspaper staff member who understood Yiddish. Smith sent him to review a play starring the famous Yiddish actor Maurice Schwartz. The review was a hit and Lesner began to do music reviews following the death of the music critic, Maurice Rosenfeld. From that post he became the *News* night club critic.

Lesner's rave review of young comedian Danny Thomas launched Thomas's career and he always remained grateful to Lesner for his support.

Lesner's newspaper career was interrupted by World War II, where he became a dental assistant, because he was told by the army recruiters, "We have no room for night club critics in the army." Lesner saw action in the European theater and returned to the *News* after the war.

But the music critic's job had been given to another veteran, so Lesner became the movie critic, a post he took reluctantly but his wife, Esther, urged him to do so. For twenty years, Lesner visited movie sets, interviewed stars and even appeared in a cameo role in a film with Doris Day and Clark Gable.

He received the Critic's Award from the Directors Guild of America in 1966 for outstanding motion picture criticism. The walls of his *Herald* office were lined with photos of Lesner and Hollywood notables including Clint Eastwood, Jack Benny and Lucille Ball.

Lesner's enormous energy led him to write a television column for the paper, in addition to his movie reviews, and he had a radio talk show from the penthouse of the Allerton Hotel in the late 1940s and early '50s. At the same time, he was teaching music classes at the YMCA.

Lesner spent 49 years and 11 months at the *News* but the paper folded in 1978, leaving a bored and frustrated Lesner. He was rescued by Scope, and often wrote in his Hyde Parkers, All! column of the story of his coming to the *Hyde Park Herald*, where he quickly moved from a classified advertising staff member to the writer of the popular weekly column.

Lesner's wife died in 1987 after 46 years of marriage, and he had open heart surgery in 1986, followed by two heart attacks in 1990. But he continued to write his highly personal column, even describing in detail some of his medical experiences. His zest for life endeared him to the younger members of the *Herald* staff and he would often take them to plays and concerts around the city.

Survivors include his two daughters, Roberta Bernstein and Judith Holstein; five grandchildren; a sister, Mayme Salkind; and a grieving *Herald* staff.

50 years on job—he asks for more

Chicago Tribune, Sunday, November 8, 1981

"THE NEWSPAPER business — I love it," Sam Lesner said. "It's a way of life."

It's a way of life he's known almost all his life. Lesner, 72, started working for the Chicago Daily News on April 9, 1928, and stayed with the paper until it folded on March 9, 1978.

In the course of that half century he played many roles. Originally an aspiring singer, he got a job in the paper's library to earn cash for his singing lessons. An alert editor picked up on his musical background and sent him out to cover recitals.

LATER, HE landed a permanent spot in the features department, writing about entertainment. In 1941, he became the nightlife reviewer and four years later made his debut as movie critic, a post he held for 25 years.

"I loved what I was doing," Lesner said. "I was always rushing around but I never counted the hours."

Even advancing age didn't slow him down. He recalled: "When I hit 65, they said, 'How about it?' I said, 'How about what?'" Lesner had no thoughts of retiring, and his byline continued to appear in the Daily News until its last issue.

When the paper ceased publication, he finally took a break. "I have a beautiful garden and for a year I gardened like mad," Lesner said. "But I was starting to get terribly bored."

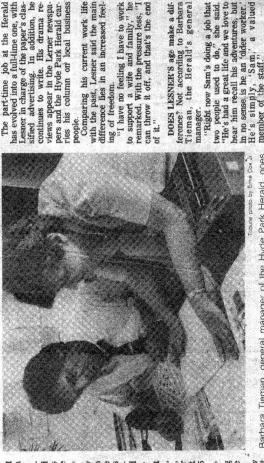

Tribune photo by Ernie Cox Jr.

Barbara Tieman, general manager of the Hyde Park Herald, goes over ads with Sam Lesner. "I'd had 50 years of glory," the former Chicago Daily News reporter says. "I just wanted to be busy."

One evening while watching television, Lesner, a South Sider, learned about Operation Scope, a Hyde Park agency that helps older people find jobs. Through Scope, he found a part-time clerical job at the Hyde Park Herald, a weekly community newspaper.

THE MAN who had once mingled with movie stars and directors found himself typing labels and stuffing envelopes, but he didn't mind. I'd had 50 years of glory," Lesner said.

"I didn't need any more glamor. I just wanted to be busy."

The part-time job at the Herald has evolved into a full-time one, with Lesner in charge of the paper's classified advertising. In addition, he continues to write. His drama reviews appear in the Lerner newspapers and the Hyde Park Herald carries his column on local business people.

Comparing his current work life with the past, Lesner said the main difference lies in an increased feeling of freedom.

"I have no feeling I have to work to support a wife and family," he remarked. "With the pressure less, I can throw it off, and that's the end of it."

DOES LESNER'S age make a difference? Not according to Barbara Tieman, the Herald's general manager.

"Right now Sam's doing a job that two people used to do," she said. "He's had a great life and we love to hear him recall his adventures, but in no sense is he an 'older worker.' He's simply, 'Sam,' a valued member of the staff."

"I never allow myself to lord it over anyone at the paper because I'm the oldest person there," Lesner said. "They don't 'Mr. Lesner' me and I've never got the feeling they think, 'We have to be gentle with him; he's an old man.' If there were ever even a hint of that, I'd just say, 'Come on, I can outrun any of you.'"

Susan Blum

HYDE PARKERS, ALL!

"Our mom, the banker!"

By Sam Lesner

After 40 years of dedicated service in the same job—banking in this instance—Annetta K. Purka understandably could call it a day and settle back for a steady round of library visits and in season, boating with her husband, Joseph, also a retired banker, at Cedar Lake where they have a summer home.

But Annetta Purka, senior vice president and a director of the University National Bank, 1354 E. 55th Street, called it "a new beginning," Tuesday when the bank's officers, many of her long-time customers and invited guests, celebrated her 40th year at the bank, with a late afternoon party in the bank's main banking quarters. (The bank has a second facility at 55th & Lake Park which was opened in 1973 for the added convenience of Hyde Parkers.)

In May of this year University National Bank will have completed 63 years of continuous service to the Hyde Park community.

But this is Annetta K. Purka's story as a banker who has been honored numerous times as much for her "human relations" as for her banking skills.

Tuesday she recalled that one of the proudest days of her life was when she received a Citation of Merit, July 19, 1972.

"I was selected 'Woman of the Day' by radio station WAIT. It was in recognition of her 'outstanding contribution to her community in the field of human relations.' She recalls that she was honored twice during the day in the station's broadcasts.

Mrs. Purka, however, has adjusted easily to the vast changes in both society and the banking business in the past 40 years.

"When one looks ahead, 40 years seems an eternity. However, when one looks back its just a flash in time—one event, one time space, to be followed quickly by other events, in the creativity of which Hyde Parkers will be instrumental."

"Many Hyde Parkers of years ago have had to leave the community for a variety of reasons. But these good business people continue to remain loyal customers of the University National Bank and it is this continuity that has made my 40 years the keystone of my career at the bank."

Mrs. Purka says that her only daughter and her two grandchildren, now young adults, are not given to teasing her about being "my grandma the banker." But she chuckles when she recalls that they say they expect her to keep going to the bank until she's "99 and clicking a cane along the pavement."

Annetta K. Purka should make her 50th year at University National easily. I had forgotten some papers I had placed on her desk during the interview. I was almost half a block away when I heard her calling me back. She hadn't even bothered to put on a coat.

She regrets that the young people going into banking jobs today appear to be "humorless creatures stamped out by a machine."

"They seem to lack warmth, personality, real interest in the people they serve. After all, service is what we really sell. But I guess that's progress and you learn to accept these changes that apparently are dictated by the increasing computerization of society."

Annetta wasn't thinking seriously about a steady job, either, when she graduated from high school. She was living in Hyde Park with her family and travelling to the loop every day to work at two jobs—one in the Chicago Public Library and the other "in a printing concern."

Her father saw an ad in the newspaper advertising a job at the Hyde Park Bank.

"It was a weekend. I had had a Saturday night date and I was in no mood to think about a new job. But my dad (Jack Armstrong) insisted that I sit down right then and there and write a letter of application to the bank.

"In those days the mail was delivered promptly. It seemed like the very next day I got a reply telling me to come in. I was hired."

Annetta, however, did leave the banking business for a few years before March. 17, 1942, when she joined the University State Bank as a collection teller.

In May, 1943, University State Bank became University National and through the years Annetta served as assistant cashier, assistant vice president, vice president and in 1972, she was elevated to senior vice president. In 1978, she was elected to the bank's Board of Directors.

She has a graduate certificate from the American Institute of Banking and currently is a member of the Chicago Association for Bank Women and the National Association of Bank Women. Her husband still gives one day a month as advisor to the board of the Eastside Bank & Trust Company while Annetta gives two days a week to her bank job.

She didn't get a wristwatch Tuesday. She got that on the occasion of her 35th year. But University National Bank's Vice President, Kenneth Stecken, and the bank's public relations director, Susan Westfall, did give Annetta K. Purka "one grand party" for her 40th.

PEOPLE PLUS:

It's always open season on Gilbert & Sullivan and Hyde Park has its G.&S. tradition, too. Since Hyde Park itself drew its very name from London's famous Hyde Park, its appropriate that our local Savoyadians should excel in the beloved ear-catching, tongue-tripping, tunes and lyrics of Gilbert & Sullivan's "The Gondoliers" which was presented last week at Mandel Hall by the Gilbert & Sullivan Opera Company of Hyde Park.

A Hyde Parker known for his Savoyardian skill in this G. & S. company is Ray Lubway who this year created one of his favorite roles, that of the Duke of Plaza Toro, in "The Gondoliers."

Lubway, with the company since its inception, also teaches at the Lab School where he has introduced G. & S. into his classroom. Other Hyde Parkers active in the Hyde Park G. & S. Company are Roland and Helen Baily, Robert Ashenhurst and Rafaello La Manita.

NOTES:

There still is time to learn how to cook Chinese from an expert, Ruth Law who will be conducting her final cooking classes, Tuesday and Wednesday, March 23, 24, at Mr. G's Finer Foods, 1226 E. 53rd St. These last two sessions are devoted to shrimp stuffed black mushrooms, barbecued pork buns and other Chinese delicacies. The fee is $18, plus a $3 lab fee. But what a reason you'll be after Ruth Law's instruction. For more information call 966-1595.

ONE GOOD TURN DESERVES ANOTHER: Helen Wong Jean, who recently kindly supplied me with the information that the new Chinese New Year (Year of the Dog) is 4680, expressed her pleasure at being given credit for that information in a recent column of *Hyde Parkers, All!* Helen Wong Jean who belongs to the Chinese American Civic Council of Chicago, says she is Director of the Oak Leaf Singers, an integrated group of 12 residents of Dearborn Park.

"They are all senior citizens who love to sing at the drop of a hat and would love to sing for any organization in Hyde Park for a fee of only $25, to cover transportation," wrote Helen Wong Jean whose address is 820 S. Park Terrace, No. 508, The Oaks, Dearborn Park, Chicago, IL 60605. Tel. 663-9037.

After reading this column, which I hope you enjoy, don't throw the Hyde Park Herald into the refuse box. It can help beautify your garden. Shred the paper into half inch strips and place on the compost pile. The paper will turn into a mulch that will conserve moisture, shelter young seedlings from the damaging effects of sun, wind and rain on exposed soil. The paper gradually decomposes into soil-enriching humus by the end of the season.

Hyde Parkers, All! We would like to hear from you about your own business, backgrounds, ventures and happenings in the Hyde Park Herald, 5240 S. Harper, 60615

Feature of the Hyde Park Herald Advertising Department.

HYDE PARKERS, ALL!

By Sam Lesner

Three score and fifteen years ago tomorrow, I was born "in humble circumstances," as the novelists like to say. But I have no memory of lying in the buggy in front of my parent's neighborhood grocery store, nor of friendly neighbors and customers shooing the summer flies off of me while I suffered from various infant rashes and fevers.

I learned that much later. The earliest childhood memory I can still vividly recall was being frightened by the prairie weeds which were taller than I and which abscured my view as I waited in an overgrown yard for my parents to negotiate a lease on a far northwest side country store and house where I grew to boyhood before we moved back to the city "to become civilized," my father explained.

I remember also that at the age of six or seven, having been taken to the Lincoln Park Zoo by a friendly neighbor, upon returning home I excitedly exclaimed: "elephants lay eggs in trees!" Everybody laughed, of course, and after my humiliation subsided I figured out that they were ostrich eggs that were laid in elevated nests in the elephant compound so that the pachyderms wouldn't stomp on them, I guess.

Adult relatives visiting us for a day in the country, began to call him "Der Alter Kopf" (the wise old head) because I was always eavesdropping on adult conversations in order to become wise.

The only other traumatic childhood experience I can recall was smoking 16 corn silk, toilet paper—wrapped cigarettes after being peppered by a farmer's buck shot gun for pulling the silk tassles from the still maturing corn.

More pleasantly "fearful" experiences were involved with riding the streetcar up that looping ramp to the upper level of Municipal Pier, now called Navy Pier, where on a warm summer's day the whole "mishpocha" (family) gathered to claim big wooden reclining chairs in invasion—secure locations on the boardwalk, all according to various social organization, largely dictated by the European shtetls from which our respective elders came.

To this day, nobody believes me. But the highlight of those Sunday's at Municipal Pier came at nightfall when a man in fisherman's oil skins dived from a tower on the pier. When he emerged from the water he would predict the weather for the following day. The steel tower, I believe, is still there.

Another "fearful" joy, at age 13, was riding the swift elevated train to the loop, (for the first time) to get off at Congress and Wabash for a visit to the top gallery of the Auditorium Theater to hear my first grand opera. I remember, it was the stupendous "Aida," (with elephants) and with Charles Marshall and Eve Turner singing the leading roles. Now why would I remember that? Were these childhood experiences preparation for the half-century of newspapering at the **Chicago Daily News**, followed by this happy desire to be a newspaper columnist. Yet I have a record of columnizing in my high school newspaper. It was called S-Ays." How about that for journalistic corn? I really wanted to be an opera singer.

And in the U.S. Army (1944-45) lo and behold, in basic training camp (South Carolina and North Carolina) I was "drafted" to write a column in the camp's mimeographed paper, called "Hot Corn-Press." And on the troopship S.S. Lamy returning home from France (August, 1945) again I was drafted to write a column in the daily mimeographed ship's paper and on one sunny unforgettable day at sea, I had to re-do the day's edition to report the dropping of the atomic bomb on Hiroshima, as reported over the ship's wireless.

Incidentally, in the army, the classification officer, after my completion of basic training, snootily informed me that "the army doesn't need a nightclub columnist, so what else can you do?" Just as snootily, what did I have to lose, I was only a basic trainee?) I told him he could put me in the army dental clinic because I had married the daughter of a veteran Chicago dentist. (The late Dr. Louis Malkin)

Incidentally, in my barracks bag was a fine letter of recommendation from the late Col. Frank Knox who was then publisher of the **Chicago Daily News** and Secretary of the Navy in the Roosevelt war cabinet.

But the army, in its wisdom, had assigned me to a medical outfit, the 130th General Hospital, which service eventually earned me two Overseas Service Bars, European, African, Middle Eastern Theater Ribbons with three Bronze Battle Stars, the Good Conduct Medal and the World War II Victory Medal, all for being a conscientious "bed commando," as the heroes referred to us while they were still full of battlefield braggadgio.

But when we hauled them in, shell-shocked and bleeding, and restored them to sanity, they said we were fine fellows, and in my case, voted me "Medico Numero Uno" of the 130th.

When I returned to the **Chicago Daily News** in December, 1945, the managing editor said: "How would you like to be our movie critic?". A new war of words, lasting 25 years, had begun for me. As a civilian movie and nightlife critic, I revisited Europe and Asia too, numerous times in the cause of world wide cinema production with many side-trips to Las Vegas—for the shows, not the gambling casinos.

Incidentally, I was 16 years old before I discovered my true birth date, February 16. My parents and some aged relatives "remembered" that it was warm when I was born, possibly in September because they recalled a religious holiday, probably, Rosh Hashanah.

So all through grade school I observed September 15, as my birthday, but strangely, I never was comfortable with that date. At 16, I visited the Bureau of Vital Statistics in the County Building, and starting with 1909, I soon found my registered birth as February 16. My parents never disputed it. Ma said she was awfully busy the day I was born, "virtually behind the grocery counter," and nobody else thought to record it in the family Bible, as were the birth dates of the other three children born to Jacob and Syma Lesner. May they rest in enternal peace. I forgave them.

Ironically my first child, Roberta, was born on September 15, 1943, and since a wartime provision extended the income tax deadline from April 15, to September 15, my tax form, already completed for mailing that day, was torn up and made over. It gave me an extra $500 deduction. How can you forget that birth date?

The three years since I began this column, *Hyde Parkers, All*," in the **Hyde Park Herald**, (March 3, 1981) have been some of the happiest years of my journalistic life.

I have given you a few "insides" into my personal life and I would enjoy sharing some of yours with readers of *Hyde Parkers, All!* As I wrote in that first column. "To the **Hyde Park Herald** itself, (now more than 100 years old), Hyde Park is a challenge, a great source of pride, a sometimes worrisome thing, but above all a community that is synonymous with durability. The physical, social and psychological facets of the people of Hyde Park are our special concern.

"Without its unique amalgam of all sorts of people with all sorts of cultural backgrounds, Hyde Park Village might never have emerged from its sleepy hollow rusticity."

How old is "old"?

hp the herald, wednesday, february 15, 1984 page 31

HYDE PARKERS, ALL!

SAM LESNER

Here's to a saner, healthier new year

THAT LIVE CHRISTMAS TREE in the living room, or family room, looked fantastic Christmas morning, with sparkling lights highlighting the beautifully wrapped gifts under the tree.

But the drying evergreen in a week or two can become a hazard.

You start thinking about disposing it. But not in the alley as we have done for many years.

The city of Chicago's Department of Streets and Sanitation has initiated a City-wide Drop-Box Recycling Program that not only takes care of recycling newspapers, glass, plastics, aluminum, steel and tin cans. It also has set up a network of fifteen different locations where your Christmas tree will be turned into mulch you can take home. The tree recycling will begin early in January.

The drop-box centers already are in operation and for Hyde Parkers the 4th Ward Center is located at 4415 South Cottage Grove Ave. and the 5th Ward's Center is located at 1619 East 73rd St.

Toasting the new year with a resolution to make it a happier new year for all is as lasting as the champagne bubbles in your glass.

But a resolution to get more involved in recycling can pay big dividends in health and cleanliness for all.

Some of Hyde Park's streets and parkways look like up-turned garbage cans. Recycling at the private drop-off or buy-back centers won't do the whole job.

The long-overdue cleanup must involve every one of us-young and old.

Look at the I.C. embankment along Lake Park Avenue. It's a garbage dump! Look at Harper Ave. between 53rd and 54th Streets. It's disgusting.

Look at 53rd Street between Lake Park and Woodlawn Avenues. There are ample trash containers. But the trick is to get the trash into the cans, and not around the trash cans and not into the grates that protect the young trees. Just cleaning out the grates would be a giant step for civilized living in Hyde Park.

For more information about the city's recycling programs or to receive a directory of the city's many recycling businesses, write: Recycling Coordinator, City Hall, Room 700, 121 N. La Salle St., Chicago, Il. 60602.

* * *

THE ENERGY EXPENDED in the holiday season—shopping, trimming the tree, hanging the outdoor Christmas decorations, over-indulging in the rich repast and alcoholic beverages—may have left you aching in hands, legs, knees, hips, shoulders and neck when you crawled out of bed this morning.

"Chances are you either overdid your chores and recreational activities or you have a touch of arthritis," wrote Dr. Alan Xenalsis in the November-December 1990 issue of *Self Care Journal* which is printed on recycled paper.

"Blaming age for 'morning stiffness' isn't very accurate or fulfilling. Forty-five million Americans have arthritis and half are under the age of fifty.

"Don't get depressed or defensive about the possibility of arthritis in your life. Few living creatures are immune from the problem.

"Ancient Egyptians, pre-historic dinosaurs and even the superstar athletes of today are included in the long list of those affected," added Dr. Xenalsis.

Dr. Xenalsis lowers the boom on all "gadgets, widgets and expensive clutter touted as arthritis cures."

Instead, he says the "most widely effective non-medication formula for arthritis relief includes the following ingredients: watercise (exercising in water), stretching and good eating habits.

"Water acts as a terrific therapeutic regimen with its soothing, fluid resistance and gentle buoyancy.

"As regularly as possible, replace you shower routine with a bath. Fill the tub with eighteen to twenty-four inches of water and spend fifteen to twenty minutes per day floating away the pain.

"Initially, use simple limb movements, like waving and flexing. Later, visit your local pool. If time, cost and convenience permit, enroll in a regular swimming program.

"Do your body a real favor when you go to bed at night and when you get up in the morning.

"Set aside ten minutes for stretching exercises. Your joints will benefit from improved circulation and from diminished muscle and tendon stress," says Dr. Xenalsis.

My arthritis gets worse as I age. A few minutes of heavy exercise leaves me almost crippled for the next 48 hours.

From *Reader's Digest*: "The past 20 years have been less a fitness boom than a battle. Many fitness efforts fail, not because we don't try, but because we try too hard. The solution is a moderate approach. Infiltrate your life with light energizing and productive activity rather than besiege it with exhausting, useless workouts."

And that's a fitting resolution for the new year. **Happy New Year to all.**

Hyde Parkers, All! We would like to hear from you about your own business backgrounds, ventures and happenings in the Hyde Park community. Write to Sam Lesner, c/o Hyde Park Herald, 5240 S. Harper Ave. 60615.

HYDE PARKERS, ALL!

Farewell to Sam from all.

Sam Lesner, 81, *Hyde Park Herald* columnist for ten years died in his sleep Wednesday, Dec. 19. It was typical of Sam, a newspaperman for almost 60 years, that he turned in his last column Tuesday to accommodate the newspaper's early holiday deadline.

Lesner came to the *Herald* after an unsuccessful stab at retirement at 71 years of age. Retirement was for people who had less of the *élan vital* than Sam Lesner. Referred to the weekly newspaper by Maxine Laves, then head of Operation Scope, a personnel recruitment service for older workers, at the Hyde Park Neighborhood Club, Lesner quickly filled an important niche at the *Herald*. He became the paper's correspondent to the entire community; he was active in the Hyde Park Kiwanis; he took on major fundraising activities for the Neighborhood Club, which he felt rescued him from a life of inactivity; and he became a beloved member of the community's business community. His column, Hyde Parkers All!, chronicling the activities of local merchants and organizations, quickly became the paper's most popular column.

His energy was legendary. As one community member said, "Sam was larger than life." He refused to concede an inch to the passage of time, even after several bouts of heart trouble, and he fought a constant battle to remain as active as two 40-year-olds.

A poor boy who grew up on Chicago's West Side, Sam Lesner wanted desperately to become an opera singer but he had to pay for the lessons at the Chicago Conservatory of Music. When he was 19, he took a job at the now defunct *Chicago Daily News* library; a post he got through his music teacher,

Enrico Sevillo, who was a friend of famed *News* editor Henry Justin Smith.

His lucky break came when it was discovered that Lesner was the only newspaper staff member who understood Yiddish. Smith sent him to review a play starring the famous Yiddish actor Maurice Schwartz. The review was a hit and Lesner began to do music reviews following the death of the music critic, Maurice Rosenfeld. From that post he became the *News* night club critic.

Lesner's rave review of young comedian Danny Thomas launched Thomas's career and he always remained grateful to Lesner for his support.

Lesner's newspaper career was interrupted by World War II, where he became a dental assistant, because he was told by the army recruiters, "We have no room for night club critics in the army." Lesner saw action in the European theater and returned to the *News* after the war.

But the music critic's job had been given to another veteran, so Lesner became the movie critic, a post he took reluctantly but his wife, Esther, urged him to do so. For twenty years, Lesner visited movie sets, interviewed stars and even appeared in a cameo role in a film with Doris Day and Clark Gable.

He received the Critic's Award from the Directors Guild of America in 1966 for outstanding motion picture criticism. The walls of his *Herald* office were lined with photos of Lesner and Hollywood notables including Clint Eastwood, Jack Benny and Lucille Ball.

Lesner's enormous energy led him to write a television column for the paper, in addition to his movie reviews, and he had a radio talk show from the penthouse of the Allerton Hotel in the late 1940s and early '50s. At the same time, he was teaching music classes at the YMCA.

Lesner spent 49 years and 11 months at the *News* but the paper folded in 1978, leaving a bored and frustrated Lesner. He was rescued by Scope, and often wrote in his Hyde Parkers, All! column of the story of his coming to the *Hyde Park Herald*, where he quickly moved from a classified advertising staff member to the writer of the popular weekly column.

Lesner's wife died in 1987 after 46 years of marriage, and he had open heart surgery in 1986, followed by two heart attacks in 1990. But he continued to write his highly personal column, even describing in detail some of his medical experiences. His zest for life endeared him to the younger members of the *Herald* staff and he would often take them to plays and concerts around the city.

Survivors include his two daughters, Roberta Bernstein and Judith Holstein; five grandchildren; a sister, Mayme Salkind; and a grieving *Herald* staff.

Bibliography

Brokaw, Tom. *The Greatest Generation*. New York: Random House, 1998, 2004. Excerpts from *The Greatest Generation* are copyright © 1998, 2004 by Tom Brokaw. Used by permission of Random House, an imprint and division of Penguin Random House LLC. All rights reserved.

Browning, Christopher R., Richard S. Hollander, and Nechama Tec, eds. *Every Day Lasts a Year: A Jewish Family's Correspondence from Poland*. New York: Cambridge University Press, 2007. Excerpts from *Every Day Lasts a Year: A Jewish Family's Correspondence from Poland* are used with permission of Cambridge University Press. Copyright © 2007.

Moore, Deborah Dash. *GI Jews: How World War II Changed a Generation*. Cambridge, MA: Harvard University Press, 2005. Excerpts from *GI Jews: How World War II Changed a Generation* are copyright © 2004 by the President and Fellows of Harvard College.

Ray, John. *The Illustrated History of WWII*. London: Weidenfeld and Nicholson, 2003.

Sharpe, George, MD. *Brothers Beyond Blood: A Battalion Surgeon in the South Pacific*. Austin, TX: Diamond Books, an Imprint of Eakin Publications, 1989.

Online resources

"Skylighters—The Web Site of the 225th AAA Searchlight Battalion." Available at https://www.skylighters.org/special/cigcamps/cigintro.htm. Larry M. Belmont, webmaster.

WWII Then and Now Photos. Available at http://www.wwiithenandnow.com. Blog about Carentan, France, prepared by Erwin Jacobs (Netherlands). Jacobs provides pictures of and describes Carentan following the D-Day invasion of WWII and the present-day town.

Index

Part I

American Press, 165, 285
Amsterdam, 289
Antwerp, 173, 269, 286, 287, 288, 289, 290, 291, 294, 295, 296, 302, 304
S.S. Aquitania, 308
Asheville Biltmore Hotel, 31, 33, 35
Asheville Jewish community, 22, 426, 44, 69
Asheville Monte Vista Inn, 54, 56, 57
Associated Press, 165

Battle of the Bulge, 173, 199, 211, 224, 251, 260, 261, 263, 264, 268, 277
Belgians, 180, 185, 186, 217, 222, 229, 271, 294
Belmont, Larry M., xv, 298
Berkowitz, Meyer, 22
Bernstein, Charles B., x, 240, 273
Bernstein, Rabbi Edward C., xiii, xiv, 1, 74, 89, 104, 121, 156, 158, 181, 184, 187, 206, 260, 263, 272, 298, 308, 310
Bland, Madame, and son Jean Pierre, 172, 180, 184, 205, 208, 220, 261
Blumenthal, Bill, 105, 107, 304
Boyer, Chaplain, 44
Brokaw, Tom, x, xi, xiv, 89, 309
Bronze Star, 271, 287
Brussels, 218, 255, 267, 268, 269, 271, 272, 273, 276, 278, 280, 281, 282, 283, 285, 287, 288, 289, 290, 294
Buchenwald, 257
Bulliet, C. J., 9, 100, 220, 223, 251

Camp Newspaper (*Hot Compress*), 15, 16, 24, 32, 63, 65, 67, 117, 208

Cantor, Sidney, 54
Carentan, 89, 90, 91-93, 104, 111
CBI/Pacific Theatre, 257, 258, 274, 280
Chanania Family, 271, 271, 273, 278, 281, 283, 287, 289, 290, 295
Channon Family, 272, 273, 281, 285, 289, 295
Cherbourg, 87, 104, 111, 173
Chez Paree, 271
Chicago Daily News, xviii, xix, 1, 3, 9, 13, 19, 21, 53, 80, 99, 108, 138, 139, 152, 165, 167, 190, 196, 197, 221, 223, 277, 283, 310, 311, 312
Ciney, 121, 261, 262, 263, 264, 269, 270, 290, 292, 294, 300, 305
Crowe, Charlie, 18
Curtwright, Lt., 28
Cytrynbaum, Bryna, x

D-Day, 86, 89, 275
Dash, Cpl., 107
Degas: "The Dancers," 213
de Wein Family, 289, 281
Dinant, 275, 276
Dunkirk, 173
Dunninger, Joseph, 79
Durant, Will and Ariel, 183, 184, 189, 196, 229

Empire Room, 41, 223
ETO, 100, 146, 237, 264, 292, 301, 305

Fiorvanti, Capt., 41
Folke-Wolfe airplane, 269
Fort Sheridan, 3, 6, 10, 16, 65, 221
Friemark, George, 139

Garber, Emil, 3, 15
Garber, Jack, 3, 22, 36, 44, 62, 77, 106, 117, 309
Geneva Agreement, 29, 173
German POWs, 152, 153, 189, 192, 206, 207, 212, 215, 236, 243, 248, 259, 263, 264, 278, 286, 301
Ghent, 287
Goldhammer, Leonard, 150, 177, 180, 184, 191, 199, 203, 263
Grandchildren of Sam Lesner, xv, 240

Halperin, Herzl, 228
Hitler, Adolf, 23, 36, 87, 165, 173, 185, 193, 247, 254, 298
Hollander, Craig, x, xiv,
Hollander, Joseph, ix, xi
Hollander, Richard, x, xiv
Holstein, Debbie, viii, x
Holstein, Dr. Robert, x
Hot Compress. See Camp Newspaper
Hutchins, Robert Maynard, 27
Hyde Park Herald, xix, 313-321

Jacobs, Erwin, xiv, 91
James, Pence, 100
Japanese Surrender, 305, 306, 307
Jenkins, Dr. Albert, 198
Jenning, Capt., 14
Jewish shoemaker/cobbler, 185, 186, 220

Katz, Sgt. Dr., 21, 39
King Leopold of Belgium, 276
Knox, Col. Frank, 1, 277
Knox, Lucky, 32, 42
Kreiser, Jeanette Sharpe, ix, xiii

Launton, Sgt,., 266
Lesher, Lt. Col., 15, 24, 26, 40, 49
Lesner, David, xvii, 187, 225
Lesner, Jacob and Syma, xvii
Lesner, Roy, xvii, 47, 79, 80, 83, 84, 85, 124, 143, 148, 162, 163, 166, 177-8, 187, 214, 215, 216, 235
Levin, Manny, 16, 18, 58, 59, 76, 80, 85, 99, 109, 134, 145, 149, 151, 175, 182, 199, 212, 216, 217, 245, 276, 297, 304
Lewis, Lloyd, 100, 138
Liberated Jewish Prisoners, 257
Liege, 248, 249, 253, 254, 277
Lind Brothers, 105
Luxembourg, 277, 290

Malkin, Hattie (Maga), 5, 149, 154, 169, 210
Malkin, Dr. Louis, 208, 211
Marshall Field's, 5
Mayfair Room, 223
Medical Corps, 3, 10,17, 18, 21, 29, 37, 45
Mering, Major, 33, 36, 41, 42
Meaford Hall, England, 268
Meritorious Serv. Award, 267
Milner, Isadore and Leo, 295
Moore General Hospital, 15, 34
Moore, Deborah Dash, viii, xiii, 74, 103, 104, 106, 237
Music News/Hans Rosenthal, 8, 10, 34, 277
Mussolini, 254

Namur, 173, 261, 262, 263, 270, 271
Nazis, Nazism, 153, 186,193, 194, 207, 227, 231, 244, 249, 250, 252, 253, 254, 257, 260, 272, 286, 289, 295, 296
Max Neiburg, 185, 191, 196, 199, 216, 217, 219, 222, 226, 228, 232, 234, 235, 2326, 238, 239, 242, 246, 249, 251, 256, 264, 265, 267, 268, 269, 273, 274, 275, 276, 277, 278, 279, 280, 281, 283, 284, 285, 287, 290, 294, 295, 296, 297, 300, 301, 302, 304, 307

130th Gen. Hospital, 3, 15, 17, 34, 90, 122, 156, 164, 173, 179, 265, 266, 267, 287, 288, 289, 302, 306, 307, 308

Paris, 81, 82, 120, 123, 124, 125, 148, 156, 171, 172, 174, 177, 181, 183, 202, 205, 213, 218, 220, 222, 254, 255, 260, 261, 262, 282, 296, 300, 307

Index 325

Paris Opera, 171, 261
Passover Seder 1945, 236, 237, 242
Presidential Citation, 84, 264
Probstein, Ruth, 30, 33, 53, 62, 66, 166, 169, 180, 183, 185, 218, 221, 263

Ray, John, xv, 86, 121, 173, 262
Red Cross, 16, 34, 89, 101, 107, 111, 112, 151, 166, 271, 285, 301, 305
Roosevelt, Franklin, 1, 245-248, 252, 253, 254
Roosevelt, Theodore, 115
Rosh Hashanah 1944, 103-105
Rouen, 307
Rubin, Sid, 221
Russian Army, 173, 195, 198, 248

Salkind, Mayme, xvii, 9, 98, 148, 202, 221, 235, 249, 263, 267, 270, 280
Seifert, Edith, 296

Sevillo, Enrico, xiii
Sharpe, Dr. George, ix, x, xi, xiii
Sherman House, 43
Smith, Capt., 291, 292
Special Service, 37, 40, 42, 63, 177, 108, 186, 208
Stark General Hospital, 3, 4,
Stars and Stripes, 136, 138, 148, 230, 231, 268, 271, 285, 301
Stevenson, Lt., 197, 199, 216

USO, 5, 109, 232, 276

Variety & Billboard, 221
VE Day, 256, 257

Whitman, Walt, 183
Wysock, Lt., 15

Zitlin, Lt., 46

Part II

PERFORMERS

Abbott and Costello, 7
Ingrid Bergman, 183
Cab Calloway, 111
Gary Cooper, 119, 183
Cecile B. DeMille, 88, 300
Dorothy Donegan, 111
Judy Garland, 107
Greer Garson, 19
Sam Goldwyn, 219
Helen Hayes, 183
Katherine Hepburn, 183
Woody Herman, 111
Bob Hope, 219
Charles Laughton, 138
Ida Lupino and Paul Henreid, 213
Zazu Pitts, 230
Louise Rayner, 183
Mickey Rooney, 107
Maurice Schwartz, xviii
Sophie Tucker, 23, 111, 194, 197, 211, 271, 287
Lana Turner, 152

MOVIES

Arsenic and Old Lace, 113, 115, 214
Best Foot Forward, 223
The Blue Danube, 235
Casanova Brown, 119
The Dough Girls, 252
Going Home, 234
Hail the Conquering Hero, 69
Hollywood Canteen, 234
Hot Love in Sumatra, 98
In Our Time, 213
Laura, 162, 216
Madame Curie, 19
Marriage Is a Private Affair, 152
Miracle of Morgan's Creek, 8
Mrs. Miniver, 213
The Pirates and the Princess, 219
Saratoga Trunk, 183
Sensations of 1945, 111
Story of Dr. Wassell, 61
Wilson, 277

OPERAS, BALLET

Aida (Giuseppe Verdi), 250
Bricoult, Simon (Singer), 292, 294, 304
Carmen (Georges Bizet), 254
The Chocolate Soldier (Oscar Straus), 273
Count of Luxembourg (Franz Lehár), 254
Clairbert, Clair (Singer), 250
Faust (Charles Gounod), 289, 290
Hérodiade (Jules Massenet), 292, 296, 304
Les Sylphides (Frédéric Chopin), 214
Manon (Giacomo Puccini), 180
Paganini (Franz Lehár), 180
Pagliacci (Ruggero Leoncavallo), 292, 294, 304
Othello (Giuseppe Verdi), 171, 261
Rigoletto (Giuseppe Verdi), 248, 249
Schelomo (Ernest Bloch), 164

BOOKS

Caesar and Christ (Will Durant), 184, 229
For Whom the Bell Tolls (Ernest Hemingway) 103, 210
Here Is Your War (Ernie Pyle), 80
Jamaica (Rebecca DuMaurier), 80
The Razor's Edge (W. Somerset Maugham) 111, 284
Rise to Follow (Albert Spaulding), 183
The Robe (Lloyd Douglas), 305
A Trees Grows in Brooklyn (Betty Smith), 183, 184, 187

Made in the USA
Middletown, DE
13 April 2019